A Commentary on Aristophanes' Knights

A Commentary on

Aristophanes' Knights

Carl Arne Anderson and T. Keith Dix

University of Michigan Press
Ann Arbor

For questions or permissions, please contact um.press.perms@umich.edu

Published in the United States of America by the
University of Michigan Press
Printed and bound by CPI Group (UK) Ltd, Croydon, CR0 4YY

A CIP catalog record for this book is available from the British Library.

Library of Congress Cataloging-in-Publication data has been applied for.

First published May 2020
2

ISBN: 978-0-472-07445-7 (Hardcover : alk paper)
ISBN: 978-0-472-05455-9 (Paper : alk paper)

To Nancy Gilcher Anderson,
who made it all possible
  —CAA

To Naomi Norman,
my partner in all things
  —TKD

Acknowledgments

Many thanks go to our editor, Ellen Bauerle, and to our friends Dennis Kehoe of Tulane University, Maryline Parca of the University of Illinois, Naomi Norman of the University of Georgia, our helpmate in countless difficulties, to our proofreaders, Christian Axelgard of the University of Michigan, Suzanne Jurado of the University of Georgia and Marilyn Scott of Ann Arbor; any infelicities that remain are ours alone. We owe a debt of gratitude to Professors Jeffrey Henderson and S. Douglas Olson, who read and commented extensively on the first draft of the commentary; we are responsible for all errors and oversights.

Carl Arne Anderson and T. Keith Dix

It is my great pleasure to acknowledge the hospitality and generosity of colleagues and friends in the Department of Archaeology and Classical Studies at Stockholm University. My time in the department there as a guest researcher provided an ideal setting in which to develop and solidify this collaborative project. I offer special thanks to my longtime friend and coauthor T. Keith Dix, to Professor Ludwig Koenen, who introduced me to Aristophanic studies, and to Netta Berlin whose unfailing interest insured this project's completion. The love of my family has sustained me and continues to give my life direction and purpose.

Carl Arne Anderson

I offer thanks to my friend and coauthor Carl Arne Anderson, who kept working on this commentary during the long span of my illness and recovery; to Nancy Gilcher Anderson and all the Anderson offspring; to all my instructors in Latin, Greek, and classical archaeology at Princeton University, the Intercollegiate Center for Classical Studies in Rome, and the University of Michigan; to my parents, Thomas and Margaret Dix, who encouraged and supported me always; to my parents-in-law, Harold and Dorothy Norman; and last but not least, to my wife, Naomi Norman, and our son and daughter-in-law, William Dix and Emily Andrews, without whom I would not be alive and working still.

T. Keith Dix

Contents

Introduction

Aristophanes: Life and Literary Career

Outside a poetic career that spanned nearly forty years, little is known of the life of Aristophanes (*PA* 2090; *PAA* 175685).[1] We do not know the exact year of his birth, but since he began his career as an apprentice (cf. *Eq.* 512–13) and may have been too young and inexperienced to produce a play on his own in 427 BCE (*Nu.* 530 with Dover ad loc.), he likely was born in the late 450s or early 440s and died only a few years after the production of *Wealth*, which is securely dated to 388 (*Pl.* hypothesis 3).[2] According to the ancient *Life*, he was the son of a certain Philippus (*PA* 14399; *PAA* 93015), whose name, meaning "lover of horses," suggests that he was a knight. A member of the tribe Pandionis, Aristophanes—like Cleon, the major target of comic abuse in *Knights*—belonged to the deme Cydathenaeum, located just north of the Acropolis.[3] Aristophanes had three sons, Ararus (*PA* 1575; *PAA* 160355), Philippus (*PA* 14400; *PAA* 930115, possibly the same as 930110), and Philetaerus (?), all of whom were comic poets.[4] Apparently, Aristophanes' family owned property on

---

1. Much of the testimonia (T) for Aristophanes' life (collected in *PCG* 3a; see also *IG* ii² 2325; MO, 167–68) is inferred or extrapolated from details that appear in his works and that of fourth to second centuries BCE scholars considered reliable. MO, a thorough re-edition of *IG* ii² 2318–2325, presents much of the factual information about the dramatic competitions at the City Dionysia and the Lenaea, and the poets and actors who participated in them from the fifth century to the mid-second century BCE.

2. See glossary, s.v. "hypothesis." For Aristophanes' apprenticeship and early career, see Halliwell 1980, 41–44.

3. For the Attic demes, see Whitehead 1986.

4. Writing plays, like most crafts in ancient Athens, tended to run in families. Hence Aristophanes' sons Ararus and Philippus (the latter named after his paternal grandfather, as was customary at Athens) followed in their father's footsteps. Ararus is supposedly responsible for staging Aristophanes' *Wealth* in 389/88 and is reported to have revived one of his father's plays, probably *Cocalus*, in the following year (cf. *IG* ii² 2318.1004; MO, 55, 188). For what is known of Philippus, cf. *IG* ii² 2325E.35; MO, 188. Philetaerus is known by name only. The Alexandrian critics

Aegina, a large island in the Saronic Gulf; he himself seems to confirm this connection to Aegina (*Ach.* 652–54).[5] The preceding information is essentially the sum total of what we think we know about Aristophanes' life.

Forty-four comedies are attributed to Aristophanes, eleven of which survive.[6] Those eleven plays are the only complete extant examples of Attic Old Comedy, a theatrical genre that satirized virtually every aspect of Athenian life in a period when Athens was at the height of its power and international prestige.[7] The eleven extant comedies, a small sample of Aristophanes' work, are a reminder that not all comic drama of the fifth century was necessarily like that of Aristophanes and that his was not the only voice for "the ways in which the genre developed."[8] Surviving in addition to his complete plays are nearly a thousand fragments (some on papyrus), most of which consist of quotations, phrases, or words cited by ancient authors and scholars (*PCG* 3a).

Aristophanes' surviving plays allow us to infer some details about the poet and his life.[9] For example, the assumption that he was wealthy is based on a number of factors: the time he had available to write, his apparent ownership of property on Aegina, and his seeming familiarity with the intellectual and social elite of Athens (cf. Pl. *Sym.* 189c2–d6, where Aristophanes is included among the dinner guests). We do not know how wealthy Aristophanes was, but his alignment of himself with the upper-class cavalry corps in *Acharnians* (425 BCE) and *Knights* (424 BCE), his promotion of the values and policies of the upper classes, and his consistent assailing of demagogic leadership suggest both social status and considerable wealth. Such status and wealth does not prevent him from supporting and serving the Athenian demos (cf. *Ach.* 515–16, 595). Seemingly conservative or traditional political views expressed in his comedies feature mostly anodyne moralizing and critiques of behavior and style.

Dicaearchus and Apollodorus apparently believed that Aristophanes had a fourth son, Nicostratus (T 3.14–16).

5. The scholia (at *Ach.* 378) report that Cleon tried, but failed, to use the family's connection to Aegina to denounce Aristophanes as foreign-born and without a deme, thus not an Athenian citizen. This defamation (if true), along with Cleon's many other faults, may account for some of Aristophanes' hostility toward him. *Ach.* 652–54 seems to confirm the connection to Aegina.

6. Ancient critics, for unrecorded reasons, judged four of the plays to be spurious: *Poesy, Dionysus Shipwrecked, Islands,* and *Niobus* or *Dramas*; see Koster 1969, 133–36.

7. The canonical dates for Old Comedy are from 486 BCE, when comedy became an official event at the City Dionysia, to the end of the fifth century. Aristotle (*Po.* 1448a33–34) reports that Chionides was one of the earliest Attic comic poets. The probable date for the performance of comedy at the Lenaea festival is the 440s (cf. *IG* ii² 2325E; MO, 178).

8. Rosen 2010, 228. The examples of other fifth-century comic poets, numbering nearly sixty, survive as disembodied fragments (cf. Storey 2011).

9. For the unreliability of biographies of the ancient Greek poets in general, see Lefkowitz 1981, 105–16, 169–72; 1984.

Nowhere in his work does he advocate oligarchic revolution.[10] In addition, that he survived oligarchic and democratic upheavals with no change in his status, never suffered exile, and continued to produce successful comedies across the span of his career suggests that his political views were largely in agreement with those of most Athenians.[11]

Although there are literary references to dozens of plays by Aristophanes, details about them are scarce. Only the following plays can be securely attested (asterisks mark lost plays, and those of uncertain date are omitted from this list):[12]

427 *Banqueters (festival unknown, second prize), produced by Callistratus

427/26 *Babylonians (City Dionysia, first prize), produced by Callistratus[13]

425 Acharnians (Lenaea, first prize), produced by Callistratus

424 Knights (see below)

423 Clouds, first version (City Dionysia, third place or lower)[14]

422 Wasps (Lenaea, second prize), produced by Philonides[15]

421 Peace (City Dionysia, second prize)[16]

414 *Amphiaraos (Lenaea, prize unknown), produced by Philonides

414 Birds (City Dionysia, second prize), produced by Callistratus

411 Lysistrata (perhaps Lenaea, prize unknown), produced by Callistratus

411 Women at the Thesmophoria (perhaps City Dionysia, prize unknown)[17]

---

10. See Henderson 2003a, 160–61.

11. See Dover 1993, 4.

12. We print Dover's list (1993, 1–2). Henderson (1998, 4–6) and Rusten (2011, 281–326) include lists of Aristophanes' lost and undatable comedies and the possible circumstances of their performance. For a victory list of comic poets and the dramatic competitions in which they competed from the early fifth to the second centuries BCE, see MO passim.

13. This play almost certainly took first place at the City Dionysia (cf. IG ii² 2325C.24; MO, 167–80).

14. The remarks of the chorus in the parabasis of Clouds (520–26) show that we have a revised version of the play: "I thought you [the audience] deserved to be the first to savor . . . a play that cost me very hard work. Then I lost the contest, defeated by vulgar men, though I didn't deserve to" (Henderson 1998).

15. An inscription dated to ca. 400 (IG ii² 2343.2) records a Philonides as a member of a religious association located in the poet's deme. If the member of that association and the producer of Wasps and Frogs are one and the same Philonides, it may be that the roots of Aristophanes' enmity toward Cleon were further nourished in a local dispute between Philonides and Cleon as well as in differences on broader political issues.

16. Aristophanes wrote another play of the same name; cf. Olson 1998, xlviii–li.

17. Scholarly consensus holds that Thesmophoriazusae was performed in the early spring of 411 at the City Dionysia and that Lysistrata appeared at the Lenaea earlier that same year (Sommerstein 1977; Westlake 1980; Henderson 1987, xv–xxv).

408 *Wealth* (dramatic venue and prize unknown); not the play of the
same name that survives
405 *Frogs* (Lenaea, first prize), produced by Philonides; performed again
by civic decree, probably in 404 (Lenaea)
392 *Assemblywomen* (dramatic venue and prize unknown); date may be
off by a year
388 *Wealth* (venue unknown, perhaps first prize)
After 388: *Aeolosicon* and *Cocalus*, staged by Aristophanes' son Ararus

From the start of his career, Aristophanes enjoyed success at the major dramatic festivals, the City Dionysia and the Lenaea.[18] *Knights* won first prize at the Lenaea festival of 424, defeating *Satyrs* (Σάτυροι) by Cratinus, a celebrated but fading star and one of Aristophanes' major rivals (*Eq.* 526–36), and *Woodcarrier* (Ὑλοφόρος) by Aristomenes, about whom little is known.[19] The first comedy that Aristophanes officially produced under his own name (*Eq.* 507–19), *Knights* established his reputation as an incomparable poet (*Nu.* 549–62). In it, he claims that "producing comedies is the hardest of all tasks" (*Eq.* 516). *Frogs*, produced in 405, was perhaps the high point of his career, since he was rewarded for it with an olive crown and given the unique honor of having the play produced again in recognition of the political advice (*Ra.* 686–705) he gave in its parabasis.[20]

Aristophanes was his own best advocate. He is the only recorded poet of Old Comedy to boast of the superior quality and intellectual sophistication of his work, on the grounds that it teaches his audience not just valuable intellectual and moral lessons but also gives them serious and useful political advice (e.g., *Ach.* 628–58; *Nu.* 518–62, 575–95; *Ra.* 686–705).[21] His talent and imagination are evident in his linguistic originality, allusions to other poetic genres, energetic critiques of sophism and intellectual fashions, and use of tragedies (especially those of Euripides) for parodic effect and for the

---

18. Aristophanes (T 21) also produced at least one comedy in the deme theater of Eleusis, but we know neither the title of that play nor the circumstances of its production.

19. Five titles and fifteen disembodied fragments of the comedies of Aristomenes (*PA* 1992; *PAA* 173065) survive (*IG* ii² 2325E.5; MO, 187).

20. Hypothesis I, drawing on the authority of Dicaearchus, a pupil of Aristotle and a polymath (floruit ca. 320–300 BCE), says that *Frogs* was produced again (ἀνεδιδάχθη) the following year. We do not know which dramatic festival hosted the reperformance.

21. Boasting of his superiority as a playwright is in keeping with the competitive character of the dramatic competitions and of Athenian society at large. Other comic poets must have done the same for their work. The depth of Aristophanes' disappointment over the showing of *Clouds* in 423, which placed low (perhaps third or even lower) in the competition, so troubled him that he revised the play and circulated this unperformed version among his friends and supporters; see Dover 1968, lxxx–xcviii.

structure of his own comedies.[22] Aristophanes' use and abuse of Euripides' tragedies prompted Cratinus (fr. 342) to conflate the names of the two poets to coin the term εὐριπιδαριστοφανίζων (Euripidaristophanizing), to describe one of Aristophanes' stylistic tendencies.[23] In *Lysistrata*, Aristophanes created Old Comedy's earliest extant example of a female heroine (which the original audience may have regarded as more ridiculous than innovative).

Aristophanes' claims of superior artistic originality and quality are impossible to evaluate, but ancient critics, who had more of the corpus of Old Comedy at hand and who were familiar with the unique context of the genre, nowhere contradict his evaluation of his talent.[24] Alexandrian scholars, beginning with Callimachus, Eratosthenes, and Lycophron, judged Aristophanes to be the premier poet of Old Comedy, and they all, to some extent, studied and wrote about him. The first continuous commentaries on Aristophanic comedy were produced by either Euphronius, the teacher of the scholar Aristophanes of Byzantium (ca. 257–180 BCE), or Callistratus, who was a pupil of that scholar. Other commentaries followed these two.[25] Such works guaranteed Aristophanes' comedies a place in the school curriculum and, hence, their transmission to late antiquity and following generations.[26]

Origin, Form, and Style of Old Comedy

ORIGIN AND FORM

Attributing the origin of Attic Old Comedy (plays staged in fifth-century Athens) to phallic songs sung by men parading in honor of Dionysus, Aristotle (*Po.* 1449a10–4) links the legacy of this original band of revelers to the comic chorus. As Handley observes, "Aristotle's derivation of comedy is a hypothesis which is interesting and possibly correct, but he does not offer, and we cannot

---

22. Examples are his reconfigurings of the Telephus myth in *Acharnians* and of Euripidean tragedies in *Thesmophoriazusae*.

23. Cf. the allusion to Euripides' name κομψευριπικῶς at line 18. For Cratinus' use of his own term to criticize his younger rival, see Biles 2011, 123–24.

24. The careers of some fifty poets of Attic Old Comedy overlapped that of Aristophanes; ancient critics judged his to be the foremost. His fame was already widespread in the fourth century BCE. Plato is reported to have sent copies of Aristophanes' comedies to Dionysius, the tyrant of Syracuse, who was eager to study "the polity of the Athenians" (T 1.42–45); likewise, an ancient epitaph (attributed to Plato) bears witness to the poet's reputation: "The Graces, searching for a shrine that will not fall, / found the soul of Aristophanes" (*Epigr. Gr.* 553–54 Page).

25. For ancient commentaries on Aristophanes' plays, see Dunbar 1995, 35–42; Dickey 2007, 28–31.

26. For the transmission of Greek literature from antiquity to the Byzantine period, see Reynolds and Wilson 1991, 1–78.

adequately supply, the means by which it might be verified."[27] Whatever the origin of Old Comedy, it was officially included in the dramatic competitions of the City Dionysia sometime in the late 490s or 480s (traditionally in 487/86 BCE).[28]

Poets freely innovated within Old Comedy's structure, which was formalized but flexible and, comparably to that of any genre, changed over the eighty years or so in which it flourished. The standard structural elements of Old Comedy are the prologue, parodos, agon, parabasis, and exodos.[29] The fourth century was a transitional period for Old Comedy, during which the agon and parabasis disappeared, the chorus became virtually irrelevant to the dramatic action, and the plots focused generally on conflicts in private and family life rather than on political issues.[30] This trend eventually developed into the genres known as Middle Comedy and, finally, New Comedy.[31]

STYLE

Old Comedy is topical, employs veiled or thinly veiled attacks on real people and critiques of contemporary trends and issues, features action taking place in the present, and uses language that is often colloquial and shockingly uninhibited. As such, it disrupts the conventions of tragedy. Particularly disruptive elements of Old Comedy are its metatheatrical (see glossary) moments, when the play acknowledges that it is a live performance in the theater of Dionysus. In those moments, which can be used to great effect, characters or even the chorus will step out of the immediate dramatic context and speak directly to the audience, refer to their costumes or the stage setting, mention that they are actors and not the characters they play, or otherwise force the audience to look away from the action of the play and remember where the audience and actors actually are.[32] In the commentary in the present book, we call attention to Aristophanes' use of such moments.

The language of Old Comedy—frank, abusive, rough, and obscene—is perhaps its most distinctive and disruptive element. Scatological and sexual language permeates the genre, as does slang. Along with misogyny, critiques

---

27. Handley 1985, 111, 365.

28. *IG* ii² 2325C; MO, 156.

29. For these structural terms, see glossary, s.vv.

30. For topicality, politics, and economic reality in Aristophanes' fourth-century plays—*Assemblywomen* (393/92), *Wealth* (388), and the lost *Aeolosicon* and *Cocalus*—see Rothwell 1990, 1–7.

31. Arnott 2010 focuses on the transition from Old Comedy to Middle Comedy; Storey 2010 provides an overview of the transition from Old Comedy to Middle Comedy to New Comedy.

32. Lionel Abel, who coined the term metatheater in 1963, also used it to describe the moments when an audience could simultaneously laugh at and emphathize with the protagonist.

of sexual orientation, and xenophobia, such language may disturb a modern reader, but the Athenian audience expected and welcomed it, just as they welcomed and expected fantasies of irresponsibility and unlimited indulgence in food, drink, sleep, and sex, as well as comic heroes and heroines who were unscrupulous connivers in getting what they wanted.[33] Comic poets who omitted these elements were unlikely to win audience favor. Fifth-century Athenian culture was strange and different from our own.

Theatrical Contexts for Comedy

THE LENAEA AND CITY DIONYSIA FESTIVALS

The Athenian demos organized and administered production of two major dramatic festivals, the Lenaea and the City Dionysia, which, certainly in the case of the City Dionysia, brought together more of the Athenian populace at one time and in one place than any other public event.[34] These events featured intertribal competitions in choral song and dance (dithyrambs; see glossary) and performances of tragedy, satyr drama, and comedy. In Athens, the Lenaea was celebrated in the month of Gamelion (late January / early February), the City Dionysia in the month of Elaphebolion (late March / early April).[35] At both festivals, dramatic competitions were (likely) held in the theater of Dionysus, on the south slope of the Acropolis.[36]

Traditionally, five comic poets presented their work at each festival, though that number may have been reduced temporarily to three during the Peloponnesian War.[37] Poets wanting to enter their plays in the competition

---

33. Sausage-seller in *Knights* is a prime example of such a hero. Presumably the portrayal of comic heroes and heroines in the comedies of Aristophanes' rivals did not differ significantly.

34. Festivals like the Panathenaea assembled more people than did the City Dionysia, but during the Panathenaea participants and spectators alike stretched along the length of the city from the Dipylon Gate to the Acropolis and were not collected in one structure or one location. A good comparison for the size of the audience at the City Dionysia is the number of citizens (five to six thousand) said to meet at the Pnyx, the site of the popular assemblies, at Th. 8.72.1; but Hornblower (2008, ad loc.) argues that number "cannot be true," since Thucydides comments that the number was what the Athenian envoys were told to say.

35. In other parts of Greece, the month Gamelion was called Lenaeon, a name that already occurs in Hesiod (μῆνα Ληναιῶνα, *Op.* 504 with West 1978, ad loc.). The Athenian calendar comprised twelve lunar months. The names of these months are known, but correlating them to the modern calendar is contested (R. Osborne 1987, 165–92).

36. The Lenaean plays might have been performed in a makeshift theater (N. W. Slater 1986, 258–63), but availability and seating capacity make the theater of Dionysus the much more likely performance venue for both festivals.

37. Although *Peace* (hypothesis 3) lists only three comedies by their rank (first place, Eupolis' *Spongers* [frr. 156–90]; second, Aristophanes' *Peace*; and third, Leuko's *Phratry-Members* [frr. 1–5]),

"requested a chorus" (cf. *Eq.* 513, χορὸν αἰτοίη) from the archon in charge of each festival—the archon basileus for the Lenaea,[38] the eponymous archon for the City Dionysia.[39] The archons chose the poets, but the criteria they used to select them are unknown.[40] The ten men who judged the plays were chosen by lot from a list of names submitted by each of the ten Athenian tribes. Of their ten votes, only five were counted, or perhaps counting stopped as soon as one competitor had five votes. Although we cannot be sure, the reaction of the audience probably played some role in the decision (cf. *Ec.* 1154–62), since a decision contrary to the general preferences of the audience may have affected the reputation and standing of the judges.[41]

THE THEATER

The theater of Dionysus that occupies the south slope of the Acropolis today is not the theater of Aristophanes' time.[42] Almost everything we now see there dates to the Hellenistic or Roman periods. The few traces left of the fifth-century theater, comparanda from other Greek theaters, the remarks of ancient commentators, and a few passages from the plays of Aristophanes allow us to piece together a general picture of how that theater looked. The audience sat (or stood) on the slope of the Acropolis, looking down on the orchestra, where the chorus sang and danced.[43] Behind the orchestra, to the south, stood a makeshift building, called a skene, with a low stage. The skene was constructed of wood sections that could be reconfigured to accommodate different scene settings

---

it is possible that only the top three of five competitors were awarded prizes and/or had their names inscribed on stones (cf. Körte 1905, 427–28).

38. Arist. *Ath.* 57.1. The religious duties of the archon basileus have their origin in the hereditary Athenian kings, a fact that indicates how old the Lenaea celebration was.

39. Whether a poet could offer the same play for both festivals is uncertain, but a papyrus fragment (*P. Oxy.* XXXV 2737) suggests that the comic poet Plato, having applied and failed to get a chorus because of the poor finish of his *Rhabdouchoi* (fourth place) at the City Dionysia, applied for and was granted a chorus at the Lenaea. Rosen (1989, 226) notes that "what happened to Plato . . . would have happened to many comic poets each year, as they subjected themselves to the caprice of the archon in charge of poet-selection."

40. It is unlikely that the archons read complete scripts (assuming complete ones were even available) or had special expertise for judging plays. They probably favored those poets already known to them and to other Athenians.

41. For the reaction of the audience to the performance and to the judges' verdict, cf. *Eq.* 546–50; *Av.* 445–46; Wallace 1997, 101–6.

42. A permanent stone theater of Dionysus did not appear in Athens until ca. 330 BCE, under the direction of the Athenian statesman Lycurgus (Wycherley 1978, 210–13).

43. Based on linear traces of the surviving seats in the front row of the theater, the early orchestra appears to have been rectilinear rather than circular in shape. In early Greek theaters, orchestras took on different shapes, but the circular orchestra eventually became the norm (cf. Frederiksen, Gebhard, and Sokolicek 2015).

for different plays.[44] There was always a door or an opening of some sort in the center of the skene, and, sometimes, a door to either side of the central one.[45] The skene could also feature an upper story with a window and perhaps a slightly inclined roof.[46]

By convention, "interior scenes" referred to in the plays most often took place in front of the skene. Simple theatrical devices were used, including an eccyclema (see glossary) and a crane or swerving device (μηχανή or κράδη), for epiphanies (divine or heroic) or flying scenes in tragedy.[47] Aristophanes often used these devices for parodic effect to introduce new scenarios or to dispatch various characters or props.[48] There were no stage curtains, so the audience would watch as items needed for the opening scene were brought in and as characters portrayed in certain states, such as sleeping (see, e.g., *Nu.* 1–36), took up their positions. The Athenian audience did not share the modern theatergoers' expectation of "realism," as all performances were in daylight and in the open air. If the poet wanted to portray action in the dark or to indicate nighttime, for example, the actors' speeches would have to make the situation clear (see, e.g., *V.* 216; *Ec.* 20).

PRODUCTION OF THE PLAY: CHOREGOS, POET, CHORUS, AND ACTORS

The archons designated wealthy Athenian citizens (choregoi) to manage and finance production expenses for the dithyrambic competitions and dramatic performances. If the choregos sponsored the play that won first prize, he was awarded a commemorative bronze tripod and, more important, given public favor and prestige. To secure that prestige for future generations, the choregos would often display his tripod on a monument built, at his own expense, near the theater.[49] The major choregic responsibilities were recruiting and training the

---

44. Xenophon (*Cyr.* 6.1.54) compares the thickness of the supporting timbers of the scene building to that of the timbers in a defense tower.

45. Eup. fr. 48 is sometimes cited as evidence for a third flanking door, but the passage is ambiguous (see Reverman 2006, 207–9).

46. For the window, see *V.* 316–402; *Ec.* 884–975. For the roof, see *Ach.* 262; *Nu.* 1502–3; *V.* 68, 143–49; *Lys.* 395, 829–84.

47. Examples are the intervention of Heracles in Sophocles' *Philoctetes* and Medea's escape from the palace rooftop in Euripides' *Medea*.

48. Examples are the dispatch of Paphlagon at *Eq.* 1249, the entrance of Euripides at *Ach.* 407–11, and the preparation of a feast at *Ach.* 1003; cf. the entrance of Socrates at *Nu.* 218–38 and the flight of Trygaeus at *Pax* 80–81.

49. The Lysicrates Monument, commemorating a first-place victory in 335/34 BCE, is the only choregic monument to survive intact (Travlos 1971, 348–51). The inscription on the monument proclaims that Lysicrates (*PA* 9461; *PAA* 615380), the son of Lysitheides, received the prize, but it records neither the name of the play nor that of the winning poet. The monument lined a nearby street that Pausanias (1.20.1) calls the Street of the Tripods because of the large number of choregic monuments located there.

choruses and musicians, paying for the costumes and staging miscellanea, and employing an additional actor and silent supernumeraries beyond the standard three funded by the demos. Apparently, he was also expected to entertain the chorus and others at a celebratory banquet that followed the competition.[50] A choregos could add much to his public standing and reputation by being extravagantly generous in paying for the winning play in the competition.[51]

The poet was normally the producer, or διδάσκαλος (teacher), but Aristophanes entrusted the production of his three earliest works—*Banqueters*, *Babylonians*, and *Acharnians*—to a certain Callistratus.[52] This partnership established Aristophanes as a successful comic poet, and he continued to entrust his comedies to him on occasion. With Callistratus at his side, Aristophanes would have avoided the burden of producing plays but would not have received any formal public recognition.[53]

The comic chorus had twenty-four members.[54] In some of Aristophanes' plays, the chorus could be divided temporarily into antagonistic semichoruses, as perhaps in *Acharnians* (557–77), or into two separate choruses of men and "women" who are physically separated for most of the play, as in *Lysistrata*.[55] Each chorus had a leader (coryphaeus), who served as a kind of in-house conductor of song and dance during the performance, often had a substantial speaking part, usually gave advice to the audience, and encouraged the audience to favor the poet.

The canonical number of principal actors per comedy was three, but if the playwright wished, the choregos was free to use a fourth actor as a kind of "extra," and many of Aristophanes' plays require a fourth actor at some point.[56] Children could also have small roles (see, e.g., *V.* 248–57; *Pax* 114–48), but children, silent characters, and characters with only a few lines did not count

---

50. On the celebratory banquet, cf. *Nu.* 338–39 with Dover ad loc. On the kinds and costs of the various expenses assumed by the choregos, see *DFA* 87–90.

51. The extravagant spending of the Athenian general Nicias as choregos is said to have won him popularity and perhaps to have influenced the successful outcome of performances that he financed (Plut. *Nic.* 3.2–3).

52. These three plays, although produced under the aegis of Callistratus (*PA* 8127; *PAA* 561075), were widely known to have been written by Aristophanes (cf. *Nu.* 528–33). Callistratus also produced *Birds, Lysistrata*, and probably others. Nothing otherwise is known about him.

53. For Aristophanes' relation to Callistratus as his producer, see Hubbard 1991, 227–30.

54. Only Athenian citizens—thus men—could be members of a chorus, although it is possible that metics may have participated as chorus members at the Lenaea (schol. at *Pl.* 953).

55. Olson casts doubt on whether the chorus of *Acharnians* divided abruptly at *Ach.* 557–77; he suggests that one member of the chorus (probably the coryphaeus) denounces Dicaeopolis and that another chorus member defends him.

56. E.g., the opening scene of *Lysistrata* requires four speaking actors: one Spartan (Lampito) and three Athenians (Lysistrata, Kalonike, and Myrrhine). For the motivation behind the "three-actor rule" and for attempts to define its purpose (primarily in connection with tragedy), cf. *DFA* 94; Starkey 2018.

toward the quota of three or four.[57] The actors were professional, and at the Lenaea (but apparently not at the City Dionysia in the classical period), a separate prize was awarded to the best leading comic actor (protagonist), who was not necessarily the lead in the winning play.[58]

THE AUDIENCE

The seating capacity for spectators at the theater of Dionysus is estimated to have been about fourteen to seventeen thousand, and to judge from the demand for seats, attendance must have been high.[59] That wealthy citizens claimed a high proportion of the seats is apparent because, under Pericles, Athens created the Theoric Fund to cover the cost of a seat for poorer citizens.[60] Citizens sat by tribe.[61] Presumably, a block of seats was allotted to noncitizens, who paid for themselves. The demos reserved a section of front-row seats (prohedria) for major religious, military, and political officials, as well as for honoring distinguished citizens and guests. The ten judges must also have claimed front-row seats.

We know little about those who attended the plays and even less about the roles they might have played at the performances, but their collective behavior could sometimes become unruly.[62] Athenian citizens, subject allies, and foreign residents (metics) attended the City Dionysia, though the allies were apparently absent from the Lenaea festival.[63] We know that children and

---

57. There were also many silent parts for children, slaves, girls, and women, some of whom played personified abstractions such as Peace and Reconciliation. Starkey (2018, 295) suggests that in comedy, "the poet might even offer a cameo role to an amateur friend or family member, possibly as a volunteer, with no real risk to the integrity of the production."

58. *DFA* 93–95. Whether second-place and third-place prizes were also awarded to protagonists is unknown.

59. The size of the audience in any particular period cannot be precisely determined. The estimate of fourteen to seventeen thousand spectators is based on the size of the fourth-century stone theater built in the time of Lycurgus (*DFA* 263).

60. Since the distribution of the Theoric Fund was based on the deme roll, "money was distributed according to the same socio-political divisions of the state" (Goldhill 1994, 364–65). The only explicit source for the price of a ticket is Demosthenes (18.28), who implies that two obols (a skilled worker's daily wage) was the regular admission price in 346 BCE. Presumably, the price was the same or perhaps less in Pericles' day.

61. Lead tokens from the fourth century BCE (or later) and inscribed with tribal names are the best evidence for seating spectators by tribe (see *DFA* 270–72).

62. Evidence for the audience becoming restless and unruly, especially while watching comedy, is collected in *DFA* 272–73. Aristotle notes that spectators would often start snacking in the middle of a performance, especially if the acting was poor (*Nic. Eth.* 10.1175b.12–13). For comic actors throwing snacks to the audience, see *Pax* 961–62 with Olson 1998, ad loc.

63. The stage character Dicaeopolis (*Ach.* 503–6), speaking momentarily as if he were the poet himself, refers to the absence of Athens' subject allies (ξένοι) in the audience at the Lenaea. Metics were present at both festivals; for the former see *Ach.* 502–3, for the latter, 507–8, with Olson 2002, ad loc.

slaves attended the performances, but whether women were also present is controversial (and probably always will be), as the evidence is inconsistent.[64] If women were admitted to the theater, they would have been seated far from the skene, along with children, slaves, and foreigners. The arrangement of the spectators—from the front-row seats to the seating at the top rows—reflected the social stratification of Athens. Whether the audience represented all classes of the community is debatable, but these festivals were an institution of the democracy and served, at least in theory, as a communal outlet for the "discontinuity between the political and the larger society" and "the wider world beyond Athens."[65]

Background and Athenian Politics

THE PELOPONNESIAN WAR

Knights is a highly political comedy that unfolds against the backdrop of a particular historical moment during the Peloponnesian War (431–404 BCE).[66] That war between Athens and its allies, on the one hand, and Sparta and its allies, on the other, differed from previous wars in several significant ways. Past conflicts between states usually featured short-lived seasonal campaigns that culminated in a decisive battle. For example, during the Persian Wars, the celebrated Greek victory over invading Persian forces at Marathon in 490 BCE was decided in a single infantry battle, as was the defeat of the Persian forces at Plataea in 479 BCE, which forced their withdrawal from the Greek mainland, never to return. These international conflicts set in motion events that ended with the emergence of Athens and Sparta as the two major powers in the Greek world and, ultimately, ignited the Peloponnesian War. The first six to seven years of that conflict directly bear on Aristophanes' *Knights*.

The protracted length of the war was rooted in the naval strategy of the Athenian leader Pericles. In an unparalleled move, he evacuated citizens from the Attic countryside to live inside the defensive walls of the city during seasonal

64. For children (boys) in the audience as spectators, see *Nu.* 539; *Pax* 50–53, 765–66; Eup. fr. 261.3; Pl. *Grg.* 502d; *Lg.* 817c. For the presence of an attendant slave, see Thphr. *Char.* 9.5, 30.6. Conventionally, Old Comedy regarded its audience as all male (see, e.g., *Pax* 50–53; *Th.* 786–813; *Ec.* 1146). But for possible evidence that women attended theatrical performances in Athens, see *Pax* 966–67; *Lys.* 1050 (cf. Henderson 1991b, 138–47); Pl. *Grg.* 502b–d; *Lg.* 658a–d, 817c. For arguments against the presence of women in the theatrical audience, see Goldhill 1994, 360–69.

65. Henderson 1998, 10.

66. The war is traditionally divided into two parts: (1) the first ten years of conflict, which resulted in the Peace of Nicias, followed by an unstable armistice lasting nearly seven years (Th. 5.25.1), and (2) the last eleven years of conflict, beginning with the Athenian expedition to Sicily (415 BCE) and ending with the blockade of Athens and its surrender to Sparta (404 BCE).

Spartan invasions.[67] In this way, the Athenians simultaneously avoided major confrontations with seasoned Spartan soldiers in the field (confrontations they surely would have lost) and used their superior naval power to control the seas, import goods, and collect tribute payments from the subject states of their empire (Th. 1.141.2–1.143.2). Pericles calculated that waging a war of attrition against the land-based Spartans would eventually persuade them to give up on winning and to accede to terms of peace that were advantageous to Athens. He was wrong.[68]

The political effects of the prolonged war with Sparta transformed the lives of most Athenians and significantly destabilized the social order. Pericles' strategy effectively diminished the strategic importance of the heavy infantry (the hoplites) and the cavalry (the knights), who were drawn from the landowning and wealthier classes, in favor of sea power, which depended on oarsmen, who had neither wealth nor social standing. The process began in the aftermath of the Persian Wars, as the Athenian navy first safeguarded the Aegean and eventually secured the empire. The Peloponnesian War raised the stakes even higher and helped create a state that was increasingly dependent on its navy and the men who rowed its ships.

As these rowers gained prominence, a new kind of politician emerged to represent (and exploit) popular interests and concerns—the very kind of politician who was the target of "demagogue comedy." The traditional criteria for a successful political career—landed aristocratic birth, formal education, and a family record of public service—were replaced both by a politician's ability to persuade the Assembly and law courts to adopt certain policies and actions and by the sheer force of his individual personality.[69] Indeed, politicians had their strongest influence not as holders of high public office, but as speakers in the political and judicial arenas.[70] The foremost example of this "new breed" of politician was Cleon, an owner of tanneries, member of the "commercial

---

67. The Spartan practice was to invade the Attic countryside, expecting to engage those living there in traditional military combat. When the Spartans discovered that most of the residents had abandoned their land and taken shelter inside the city, they focused on the destruction of dwellings and crops, especially olive groves, and then marched back home. This was an untenable strategy, and fighting eventually moved to places throughout the Aegean and Asia Minor.

68. By the end of the war, Sparta had, paradoxically, developed its own navy and, taking a cue from the Athenian playbook, was in control of the sea. This allowed Sparta to blockade Athens and starve it into complete submission.

69. On Cleon's oratorical ability and political style, Thucydides (3.36.6) comments, Κλέων . . . βιαιότατος τῶν πολιτῶν τῷ τε δήμῳ παρὰ πολὺ ἐν τῷ τότε πιθανώτατος, "Cleon most violent of the citizens and at that time by far the most persuasive with the people." The historian offers a similar critique (at 2.65.10–12) of the other "radical" politicians who rose to prominence after the death of Pericles (cf. Connor 1971, 94–98; Ober 1989, 91–93).

70. Cf. Ostwald 1986, 202.

elite," clever orator, and unscrupulous manipulator of public opinion.[71] Cleon dominated Athenian politics from the death of Pericles—after whom he styled himself (cf., in the present book's commentary, 1–5n, at νεώνητον)—until his own death in 422 BCE.[72]

The evacuation of the Attic countryside was especially difficult for the rural population. When the Spartan general Archidamus invaded Attica for the first time in 431 BCE, he ravaged the rural deme of Acharnae (Th. 2.19.2), which could be seen from the city's walls and where a large number of rural citizens lived. His goal was to provoke the Acharnians to abandon Pericles' defensive stance and to confront his army. Aristophanes' *Acharnians*, produced in 425 BCE in response to this particular situation, has a single Attic farmer make his own private peace treaty with Sparta and persuade his fellow demesmen to follow his example. The play begins with that farmer seated alone on the Pnyx waiting for the Assembly to come to order, dreaming of his village and longing for peace (28–33, 37–39).

> I am always the very first one to come to the Assembly
> and take my seat. Then, when I'm alone,
> I sigh, I yawn, I stretch, I fart,
> I fiddle, scribble in the dirt, pluck my beard, do sums,
> gazing off to the countryside and longing for peace,
> loathing the town and yearning for my own deme . . .
> So now I come here, absolutely prepared
> to shout, interrupt, revile the speakers,
> if anyone speaks of anything except peace.[73]

Thucydides' description of the distress caused by the displacement is more serious but no less emotional (2.16.1–2).

> Most of the Athenians of early times and . . . down to the time of this war . . . continued to reside with their households, in the country where they had been born; and so they did not find it easy to move away. . . . They were dejected and aggrieved at having to leave their homes . . . and at the prospect of changing their

---

71. Cleon (along with the Athenian general Nicias) can be called a member of the commercial elite because of his wealth and family alliances, as distinct from men, like Pericles and Alcibiades, who belonged to the traditional landholding military elite. But Saldatti (2014) reminds us that the political and social claims of Cleon's family had much more in common with the interests of the landed elite than Thucydides or Aristophanes acknowledge.

72. For a critique of this new breed of politicians in fifth-century Athens, see Connor 1971.

73. Translation slightly adapted from Henderson 1998.

mode of life, and facing what was nothing less for each of them than forsaking his own town [πόλιν τὴν αὑτοῦ ἀπολείπων ἕκαστος].[74]

This social and emotional upheaval was exploited by demagogues like Cleon, whose political maneuvering lengthened the war and squandered the resources of the city and, ultimately, the lives of its men, in the ill-conceived Sicilian expedition. The figure of Cleon in *Knights* is Aristophanes' response to this exploitation.

PYLOS, SPHACTERIA, AND THE RISE OF CLEON

In 425 BCE, Athenian forces, led by Demosthenes and Nicias, unexpectedly trapped a Spartan garrison on the small island of Sphacteria, located off the coast of Pylos in the southwestern Peloponnese.[75] Spartan leaders were so deeply alarmed by this unexpected misfortune that they sent delegates to Athens to propose an end to the war and a joint alliance in exchange for the release of their troops trapped there. Largely because of the influence of Cleon over the people (demos), the Athenians rejected the Spartan offer, and the fighting resumed at Pylos. Over the course of that winter, the Athenians grew impatient with the slow progress of the siege operations.

As pressure built for the defeat of the Spartans, Cleon, his political influence waning, announced publicly that he could have easily subdued the enemy had he been in command. Nicias, who happened to be in Athens at that time, called his bluff and promptly offered to retire in Cleon's favor. Unable to refuse Nicias' offer, Cleon promised that within twenty days, he would bring back the Spartans alive or kill them on the spot (Th. 4.28). At the moment, that seemed like a laughable claim, but Cleon made good on his promise and returned to Athens with 292 hostages, including around 120 members of the Spartan ruling class, called "Spartiates" (cf. Th. 4.38.4–5). For Spartan soldiers to be taken alive was unthinkable.[76] The surrender of the Spartans was a major victory for Athens, allowing the Athenians to leverage the hostages against further Spartan invasions of Attica. It was a personal coup for Cleon, who became a national hero and was honored with the grant of lifetime meals (σίτησις) at state expense in the Prytaneum and a front-row seat (προεδρία) in the theater of Dionysus at state festivals.[77] Emboldened by this success, the Athenians rejected, without

---

74. Translation from Smith 1928.

75. The historical context is known chiefly from Thucydides 4.2–41.

76. Plutarch (*Moralia* 241) reports that Spartan mothers told their sons who were heading into combat to "come back with your shield—or on it."

77. *Eq.* 280–81, 702–4, 763–68. Cf. *Eq.* 575–66; *IG* i³ 131, Prytaneum Decree, with Mattingly 1990, 114–15.

deliberation, all Spartan proposals for peace.[78] The Spartans' reputation of invincibility was shattered, and Cleon's success both altered the immediate course of the war and ultimately had devastating consequences for Athens.[79]

ARISTOPHANES AND CLEON

The relationship between Aristophanes and Cleon is inferred exclusively from the poet's comedies, which certainly suggest but offer no conclusive proof of personal animus between them.[80] However, independent accounts support Aristophanes' portrait of Cleon's fundamentally violent and aggressive style of leadership (e.g., Th. 3.36.6; Arist. *Ath.* 28.3), and despite comic exaggeration and distortion in those accounts, scholars concur that there was genuine hostility and resentment between the two men. If so, Cleon's success at Pylos surely would have rankled not only his political enemies but also Aristophanes, who had recently attacked Cleon in *Acharnians* (377–82). In that play, Aristophanes reminds his audience that Cleon had hauled Aristophanes before the Council for slandering him and the city in an earlier play, *Babylonians*.[81] Cleon was not above taking legal retaliation against those who publicly embarrassed him. Thus Sommerstein suggests that Aristophanes may have used the allegorical mode of attack in *Knights* as protection against possible retaliation, as the play does not explicitly identify any stage character with the actual Cleon.[82] Given his success at Pylos and the popularity that arose from it, however, Cleon may have felt secure enough simply to ignore these kinds of comic attack. Perhaps he even relished them.[83]

Acharnians also presents a chorus of angry farmers—often thought to represent the voice of the poet—who declare a hatred for Cleon and threaten to cut him up as "shoe leather for the knights" (Κλέωνος, . . . ὃν ἐ- / γὼ τεμῶ τοῖσιν ἱππεῦσι καττύματα, 300–1). This violent threat cleverly calls to mind both tanneries, the source of Cleon's wealth, and the charge of bribery against Cleon that is apparently alluded to in the prologue of the play (5–6).[84] For Aristophanes,

78. See, in the present book's commentary, 794–96n.

79. For example, instead of accepting Spartan overtures for peace, the Athenian Assembly pursued an aggressive policy.

80. See, n. 5 above.

81. Cf. Olson 2002, xl–lii; Orth, *FrC* 2017, 364–65, 385–86, 396–99.

82. The chorus mentions Cleon's father, Cleanetus (*Eq.* 573–77), in connection with a state subsidy and Paphlagon-Cleon's boast of receiving the honor of προεδρία as a public subsidy for the victory at Pylos.

83. After Pylos, Cleon was elected general in his own right and given command of the Amphipolis campaign, where he was killed in battle (422 BCE). Thucydides (5.10.9 with Hornblower 1996, ad loc.) reports that Cleon died fleeing a foreign peltast (light-armed soldier), probably a detail meant to slander him rather than a historical fact.

84. For a possible legal dispute between Cleon and leading knights regarding official misconduct, see, in the present book's commentary, 225–29n.

in whose mind the plot of *Knights* was already taking shape, the threat to cut Cleon into leather scraps would soon be realized on the comic stage.

The Play

So far as we know, *Knights* was the first comedy to be devoted almost entirely to the vilification of a single individual, Cleon.[85] As such, it belongs to a style of comedy often referred to as "demagogue comedy."[86] Both he and Athenian audiences would have been very familiar with this style of comedy, from the plays of Cratinus (450s BCE), Hermippus (430s BCE), and especially Aristophanes' rival Eupolis.[87] Although Aristophanes apparently never wrote another "demagogue comedy," neither prominent figures or groups in Athenian politics and society nor contemporary fashions and manifestations of cultural change escaped his comic ridicule.

THE PLOT

Aristophanes dramatizes the play's main subject, the salvation of the city from demagoguery, through an extended domestic allegory. A newly purchased slave from Paphlagonia, a tanner (like Cleon), has taken over the house of Demos, an old Attic farmer and stand-in for the Athenian demos. The Paphlagonian slave is never given a proper name and is only ever referred to in the play as Paphlagon.[88] Having endeared himself to his master through flattery and deceit, he terrorizes and intimidates his fellow household slaves (i.e., his political rivals) with impunity. Two of these slaves (A and B, labeled ΔΗΜΟΣΘΕΝΗΣ and ΝΙΚΙΑΣ in the Greek text) decide to steal Paphlagon's collection of oracles that predict he will be overthrown by a young sausage seller. When a clueless Athenian seller of sausages (called Sausage-seller here) happens by, the two slaves and the chorus of knights recruit him to be their champion. A series of contests—rhetorical, oracular, and culinary—follow. In accordance with the

---

85. Concerning Aristophanes' personal feud with Cleon, Rosen (1988, 81–12) argues, "Aristophanes' attacks against Cleon are an elaborate literary conceit with direct antecedents in iambic ψόγος [i.e., blame poetry], and the invective against Cleon in *Equites* in particular must be seen, to a great degree, as conventional." Nonetheless, it is hard to view the poet's unrelenting hostility toward Cleon as free from personal animus.

86. For "demagogue comedy" as a subgenre of Old Comedy, see Sommerstein 2000.

87. Eupolis, Cratinus, and Aristophanes were considered the canonical poets of Old Comedy (cf. Hor. *S.* 1.4, 1–2). For the chronology and literary career of Eupolis, see Storey 2011, 2:26–28; Olson, *FrC* 2017, 13–21.

88. At this time, an Athenian's official name was comprised of his proper name plus his deme name (e.g., Dicaeopolis of Acharnae). Naming the slave simply Paphlagon heightens the audience's awareness of his servile status and ethnicity.

oracles, Sausage-seller outdoes Paphlagon, his rival in trickery, and succeeds him as the steward of the house of Demos, a position that allows him to conduct business on his master's behalf. At the end of the comedy, Demos, miraculously rejuvenated to the glory days of Athenian power and idealized rectitude as exemplified by Athenian victories at Marathon and Salamis, acknowledges his former errors, thereby showing that stupidity and selfishness are not his true character traits. Moreover, he promises Sausage-seller (newly honest and renamed Agoracritus) that he will pay closer attention to his true interests and not repeat recent mistakes. Demos anticipates returning to his farm, where he will enjoy the pleasures of peace and prosperity, though, in reality, the war continues. Paphlagon is banished to the gates of the city, to take up Sausage-seller's old job of hawking sausages, now made from the meat of dogs and asses. As a reward for good service, Demos invites the comic hero Agoracritus to take the seat of honor that Paphlagon had previously held at the Prytaneum.[89]

THE CHORUS OF KNIGHTS AND PAPHLAGON-CLEON

Aristophanes' decision to present a chorus of knights and to name the comedy after them is grounded in their identification as a social and political class and in their relationship with hoplites and rowers. In Athens, originally the word *hippeis* (knights) seems to have designated the wealthiest of aristocratic young men, those who could afford to own and keep horses and who formed the Athenian cavalry.[90] At the time of Aristophanes' play, the knights served primarily as a home guard and could be effective on open ground against invading Spartan forces. They were never the decisive force in the long conflict, and there must have been tensions between them and the hoplites over prestige and claims to military importance, as well as between the oarsmen and everyone else.[91]

Given this historical background, a chorus of knights seems entirely

89. Hubbard (1991, 67) notes that "the dramatic role of the Sausage-seller hero, who orchestrates the linguistic and rhetorical assault on the Paphlagon, figures the political role of the dramatist, who perceives his own verbal activity (= the play) as the means for ridding the city of Cleon."

90. In epic, the term *hippeis* seems to have been used to refer to a real or an imaginary time when heroes rode chariots into battle, as they do in Homeric epic, where they are clearly differentiated from infantry (cf., e.g., *Il.* 2.810; 11.151; 12.66; 15.270; 23.130–33, 262). Aristotle (*Ath.* 7.3–4) uses *hippeis* to refer to the second wealthiest of the four propertied classes in the Solonian "constitution." For the history of the Athenian cavalry, which seems not to have existed as a military force until after the Persian Wars, see Spence 1993, 9–19; Bugh 1998, 3–38.

91. At the outbreak of the war, according to Thucydides (2.13.6–8), Athens could muster around thirteen thousand troops that included mounted archers, hoplites, and approximately twelve hundred knights. Hoplite equipment—helmet, shield, corselet, greaves, thrusting spear, and sword—was expensive, but how expensive is unknown. *Peace* (1224–25 with Olson 1998, ad loc.) refers to a corselet costing ten minas (= a thousand drachmas), a gross comic exaggeration. Hoplites ranked just below the knights in wealth in the Solonian system.

appropriate. First, if the evidence of Aristophanes' plays can be trusted, the knights were openly hostile to Cleon. We catch a glimpse of that hostility in the bribery charge, mentioned in *Acharnians*, that some leading knights brought against him. The charge apparently forced Cleon, perhaps a former knight himself who lost his standing,[92] to return five talents (an enormous amount of money) that he was alleged to have demanded of certain allies in exchange for a reduction in their tribute payment (*Ach.* 6–8, 299–301).[93] The same loathing of Cleon is apparent in *Knights* when Slave A declares that the chorus of knights detests him (225–26). In the eyes of the knights, Cleon is a pernicious and divisive politician, who manipulates his public position for selfish gain, without regard for the well-being of the polis as a whole.

Aristophanes' choice is also apt because the knights had cultic associations with Poseidon, the patron god of horses and the sea.[94] That dual affiliation, horses and seamanship, underlines themes that unite the knights, Sausage-seller, and the comic poet himself. The knights' horses are praised for their heroism in recent marine operations (*Eq.* 595–610), Sausage-seller's struggle against Paphlagon is characterized as a sea battle (761–62), and the profession of the comic poet is described in nautical terms (541–44). Moreover, the interests of Poseidon as patron god of horses complement the interests of Athena, herself a patron goddess of horses (ἱππία), as well as the interests of the poet (581–85), Sausage-seller (1203), and the entire city.[95]

In light of the general anti-Cleon stance of the comedy, it is striking that Cleon is called by name only once in the play (976). That a slave from Paphlagonia located on the fringes of the Greek world represents Cleon is also striking.[96] Aristophanes is obviously punning on the Greek word παφλάζειν, "to boil over, to bluster"—a verb that perfectly captures Cleon's bombastic and blustering oratorical style; indeed παφλάζειν became an epithet for Cleon in Old Comedy.[97] Looking beyond this immediate pun, scholars cite certain

---

92. The only evidence for Cleon as a member of the knights is a scholion (at *Eq.* 225); see also Connor 1971, 152n2. The scholiast claims (at *Eq.* 627) that the knights had disciplinary powers over their members.

93. Carawan (1990, 137–47), elaborating on the allegation mentioned in *Acharnians*, suggests that the charge of accepting bribes from a subject ally was dropped when Cleon returned the money (cf. schol. at *Ach.* 6, citing Theopomp. Hist., *FGrH* 115 F 94).

94. In the parabatic ode (*Eq.* 551–64), Poseidon is praised as ἵππι' ἄναξ, "lord of horses," and invoked as the patron of both the chorus and the navy.

95. At Colonus, the precinct of Poseidon ἵππιος shared an altar with Athena ἱππία (Paus. 1.30.4; cf. S., scholia at *OC* 71; see Siewert 1979, 280–89); for Athena's patronage of horses at Athens and elsewhere in Greece, see Yalouris 1950, 19–101. Hubbard (1991 78–83) discusses Poseidon's interest in the success of the navy and, hence, his support of the city as a whole in the play.

96. Paphlagonia is a region on the coast of the Black Sea, in what is now Turkey.

97. Cf. *Eq.* 919; *Pax* 313–15; Eup. fr. 192.135–36: Κλέων παφλ[/ παφλάζειν[, "Cleon is called Paphlagon, from the verb 'to splutter' [paphlazein]"; Taillardat §352.

individuals who deepen the insult: first and foremost, a notorious Paphlagonian eunuch and kingmaker;[98] second, Pylaimenes, the Paphlagonian leader and hero of the Trojan War.[99]

Aristophanes regarded his attacks on Cleon in *Knights* as a milestone in his career. In the parabasis of *Clouds*, produced in 423 BCE, the chorus of clouds, speaking on behalf of the poet, expresses great pride in and admiration for the success of *Knights* and in the poet's personal courage in attacking Cleon, who was then at the height of his popularity.[100] Aristophanes was not yet finished with Cleon: the barbs and insults appeared in his next two plays, *Wasps* (422 BCE) and *Peace* (421 BCE), even though the latter was performed a year after Cleon's death.[101]

Note to the Reader

Despite a steady stream of books and articles on Aristophanes, the last full commentary of *Knights* in English, by R. Neil, was published in 1901.[102] It is time for a fresh look. The target audience for the commentary in the present book is advanced undergraduates and graduate students of ancient Greek, although we believe that motivated intermediate-level, fourth-semester undergraduates can use it as well.[103] The commentary cites secondary sources and references in the modern languages and addresses a broad range of issues, from grammar, syntax, language, formal structure, festivals, staging, prosopography, and meter, to historical, topical, and literary references and allusions. Its notes on these issues will help guide students to a mature appreciation of the comedy's humor and artistry.

---

98. Pointing to a passage in Ctesias' *History of Persia*, D. M. Lewis (1977, 20–21) speculates that Aristophanes' choice "may owe something to knowledge of the greatest Paphlagonian of the day," the kingmaker and eunuch Artoxares. For Artoxares, see Llewellyn-Jones and Robson 2010, 195; Stronk 2010, 350.

99. A. M. Bowie (1993, 58–62) notes the euphony between the first element of Pylaimenes' name, *pulai*, and the name Pylos. In addition, Pylaimenes' name may well evoke the practice of certain Anatolian slaves and noncitizen residents of Athens to include heroic pedigrees on their epitaphs, particularly descent from Trojan heroes (e.g., in *CEG* 2.572, from the mid-fourth century BCE, Atotas, a Paphlagonian miner, claims descent "from the race of great-hearted Pylaimenes").

100. See, e.g., *Nu.* 549: ὃς μέγιστον ὄντα Κλέων' ἔπαισ' εἰς τὴν γαστέρα.

101. Cf. *V.* 1029–37, 1284–91; *Pax* 751–60 (a nearly verbatim echo of *V.* 1029–37).

102. Sommerstein's translation and commentary, which appeared in 1981, is aimed at an interested audience that may not know ancient Greek.

103. At Michigan State University, Anderson successfully taught several of Aristophanes' comedies to students of fourth-semester Greek, using Dover's edition of *Clouds*, Olson's edition of *Acharnians*, and Austin and Olson's *Thesmophoriazusae*. The enthusiasm and curiosity of those students, which inspired Anderson's note on the gecko scene in *Clouds* (1998), suggest that intermediate-level Greek students can read and enjoy *Knights* as well.

Essential to our project are the series of commentaries on Aristophanes' complete plays by Sommerstein (1981–2001) and the individual commentaries and editions by Austin and Olson (*Thesmophoriazusae*, 2004), Biles and Olson (*Wasps*, 2015), Dover (*Clouds*, 1968; *Frogs*, 1993), Dunbar (*Birds*, 1995), Henderson (*Lysistrata*, 1987), and Olson (*Peace*, 1998; *Acharnians*, 2002). We are also indebted to Kassel and Austin's edition of the fragments of Greek comic poetry (*PCG*), to Storey's 2011 edition of the fragments of Old Comedy, and, most recently, to the ongoing commentaries and translations of Kassel and Austin's edition, by Olson (2017), Olson and Seaberg (2018), Orth (2017), and Papachrysostomou (2016). Sommerstein has written a clear and concise history of the text of Aristophanes (2010).

Iambic Trimeter (Comic)

	I		II		III	
foot	1	2	3	4	5	6
iamb	˘–	˘–	˘|–	˘|–	˘–	˘–
spondee	- -		-|-		- -	
tribrach	˘˘˘	˘˘˘	˘|˘˘	˘|˘˘	˘˘˘	
dactyl	-˘˘		-|˘˘		-˘˘	
anapest	˘˘–	˘˘–	˘˘|-	˘|˘-	˘˘–	

Caesura (indicated by |) occurs in the second metron in either the third or fourth foot.

Example from *Knights* 40–45:

```
 ˘  –  ˘  – –|  –  ˘  – ˘  –  ˘–
λέγοιμ’ ἂν ἤδη. νῷν γάρ ἐστι δεσπότης
 ˘  –  ˘  –  – |  ˘˘  ˘  ˘ – ˘ – ˘ –
ἄγροικος ὀργήν, κυαμοτρώξ, ἀκράχολος,
 –  –  ˘  – –|  –  ˘  –  ˘  – ˘–
Δῆμος Πυκνίτης, δύσκολον γερόντιον
 ˘  ˘˘ –  ˘  –  – | –   ˘  ˘ – –  – ˘ –
ὑπόκωφον. οὗτος τῇ προτέρᾳ νουμηνίᾳ
 ˘  ˘˘ –  ˘  – |  –   ˘ ˘ –  – – ˘ ˘–
ἐπρίατο δοῦλον, βυρσοδέψην Παφλαγόνα
 ˘  –  ˘˘ –  –|  ˘˘ ˘ – ˘  –  ˘–
πανουργότατον καὶ διαβολώτατόν τινα.
```

22

Abbreviations

Abbreviations of the names and works of Greek authors are as in LSJ.

ABV   Beazley, J. D. 1956. *Attic Black-Figure Vase Painters*. Oxford.

AGPS   Cooper, G. L., III, after K. W. Krüger. 1998–2002. *Attic Greek Prose Syntax*. Vols. 1–2. *Greek Syntax: Early Greek Poetic and Herodotean Syntax*. Vols. 3–4. Ann Arbor, MI.

ARV²   Beazley, J. D. 1963. *Attic Red-Figure Vase Painters*. 2nd ed. Oxford.

CEG   Hansen, P. A., ed. 1983–89. *Carmina Epigraphica Graeca*. Vols. 1–2. Berlin.

DFA   Pickard-Cambridge, A. 1988. *The Dramatic Festivals of Athens*. 2nd ed., revised by J. Gould and D. M. Lewis. Oxford.

DK   Diels, H. 1952. *Die Fragmente der Vorsokratiker*. 6th ed., revised with additions and index by W. Kranz. Berlin.

FGrH   Jacoby, F. 1923–. *Die Fragmente der griechischen Historiker*. Leiden.

FrC   *Fragmenta Comica*. Heidelberg.

    Bagordo, A. 2016. Vol. 10.9, *Aristophanes Frr. 590–674: Übersetzung und Kommentar*.

    Olson, S. D. 2017. Vol. 8.1, *Eupolis, Testimonia and "Aiges"–"Demoi" Frr. 1–146: Introduction, Translation, Commentary*.

    Olson, S. D., and R. Seaberg. 2018. Vol. 3.6, *Kratinus Frr. 299–514: Translation and Commentary*.

    Orth, C. 2017. Vol. 10.3, *Aristophanes "Aiolosikon-Babylonioi" Frr. 1–100: Übersetzung und Kommentar*.

    Papachrysostomou, A. 2016. Vol. 20, *Amphis: Translation and Commentary*.

GP   Denniston, J. D. 1954. *The Greek Particles*. 2nd ed., revised by K. J. Dover. Oxford.

KB   Kühner, R., and F. Blass. 1978. *Ausführliche Grammatik der griechischen Sprach*. Vol. 1, *Elementar- und Formenlehre*. Hannover.

KG   Kühner, R., and B. Gerth. 1978. *Ausführliche Grammatik der griechischen Sprach*. Vol. 2, *Satzlehre*. Hannover.

LGPN Osborne, M. J., and S. G. Byrne. 1994. *Lexicon of Greek Personal Names: Attica.* Vol. 2. Oxford.

LIMC Boardman, J., et al. 1981–99, 8 vols. *Lexicon Iconographicum Mythologiae Classicae.* Zurich.

LSJ Liddell, H. G., and R. Scott. 1996. *A Greek–English Lexicon.* 9th ed., revised by H. S. Jones and R. McKenzie, with revised supplement by P. G. W. Glare. Oxford.

MO Millis, B. W., and S. D. Olson. 2012. *Inscriptional Records for the Dramatic Festivals in Athens: IG II² 2318–2325 and Related Texts.* Leiden.

MT Goodwin, W. W. 1896. *Syntax of the Moods and Tenses of the Greek Verb.* 3rd ed. London. Reprint, Philadelphia, 1992.

MW Merkelbach, R., and M. W. West. 1967. *Fragmenta Hesiodea.* Oxford.

OCD Hornblower S., S. Spawforth, and E. Eidinow. 2012. *The Oxford Classical Dictionary.* 4th ed. Oxford.

PA Kirchner, J. E., ed. 1981. *Prosopographia Attica.* 2 vols. Chicago.

PAA Traill, J. 1994–2016. *Persons of Ancient Athens.* Toronto.

PCG Kassel, R., and C. Austin, eds. 1983–. *Poetae Comici Graeci.* Berlin.

PMG Page, D. 1962. *Poetae Melici Graeci.* Oxford.

PMGF Davies, M. 1991. *Poetarum Melicorum Graecorum Fragmenta.* Oxford.

POxy Grenell, B. P., and A. S. Hunt, eds. 1899. *Oxyrhynchus Papyri, 2.* London.

schol. Koster, W. J., et al. 1969. *Scholia in Aristophanem.* Groningen.

Smyth Smyth, H. W. 1956. *Greek Grammar.* Revised by G. Messing. Cambridge, MA.

T testimonia

TrGF Snell, B., R. Kannicht, and S. Radt, eds. 1971–2004. *Tragicorum Graecorum Fragmenta.* Göttingen.

W *West, M. L. 1971. Iambi et Elegi Graeci.* 2nd ed. Oxford.

ΤΑ ΤΟΥ ΔΡΑΜΑΤΟΣ ΠΡΟΣΩΠΑ
Characters of the Play

ΟΙΚΕΣΤΗΣ Α ΔΗΜΟΥ	SLAVE A of DEMOS, labeled ΔΗΜΟΣΘΕΝΗΣ (Δη.) in the Greek text
ΟΙΚΕΣΤΗΣ Β ΔΗΜΟΥ	SLAVE B of DEMOS, labeled ΝΙΚΙΑΣ (Νι.) in the Greek text
ΑΛΛΑΝΤΟΠΩΛΗΣ (ΑΓΟΡΑΚΡΙΤΟΣ)	SAUSAGE-SELLER (later named AGORACRITUS)
ΠΑΦΛΑΓΩΝ, ΤΑΜΙΑΣ ΔΗΜΟΥ	PAPHLAGON, STEWARD OF DEMOS
ΔΗΜΟΣ ΠΥΚΝΙΤΗΣ	DEMOS of the PNYX
ΧΟΡΟΣ ΙΠΠΕΩΝ	CHORUS of ATHENIAN KNIGHTS (CAVALRYMEN)

ΤΑ ΤΟΥ ΔΡΑΜΑΤΟΣ ΠΡΟΣΩΠΑ

Characters of the Play

Text

Ι Π Π Η Σ

ΔΗΜΟΣΘΕΝΗΣ
    Ἰατταταιὰξ τῶν κακῶν, ἰατταταί.   1
    κακῶς Παφλαγόνα τὸν νεώνητον κακὸν
    αὐταῖσι βουλαῖς ἀπολέσειαν οἱ θεοί.
    ἐξ οὗ γὰρ εἰσήρρησεν εἰς τὴν οἰκίαν
    πληγὰς ἀεὶ προστρίβεται τοῖς οἰκέταις.   5

ΝΙΚΙΑΣ
    κάκιστα δῆθ᾽ οὗτός γε πρῶτος Παφλαγόνων
    αὐταῖς διαβολαῖς.
Δη.   ὦ κακόδαιμον, πῶς ἔχεις;
Νι.   κακῶς, καθάπερ σύ.
Δη.   δεῦρό νυν πρόσελθ᾽, ἵνα
    ξυναυλίαν κλαύσωμεν Οὐλύμπου νόμον.
Δη. καὶ Νι.
    μυμῦ μυμῦ μυμῦ μυμῦ μυμῦ μυμῦ.   10
Δη. τί κινυρόμεθ᾽ ἄλλως; οὐκ ἐχρῆν ζητεῖν τινα
    σωτηρίαν νῷν, ἀλλὰ μὴ κλάειν ἔτι;
Νι. τίς οὖν γένοιτ᾽ ἄν;
Δη.   λέγε σύ.
Νι.   σὺ μὲν οὖν μοι λέγε,
    ἵνα μὴ μάχωμαι.
Δη.   μὰ τὸν Ἀπόλλω ᾽γὼ μὲν οὔ.
    ἀλλ᾽ εἰπὲ θαρρῶν, εἶτα κἀγώ σοι φράσω.   15
Νι. ἀλλ᾽ οὐκ ἔνι μοι τὸ θρέττε. πῶς ἂν οὖν ποτε 17
    εἴποιμ᾽ ἂν αὐτὸ δῆτα κομψευριπικῶς;   18
    "πῶς ἂν σύ μοι λέξειας ἁμὲ χρὴ λέγειν;"   16
Δη. μὴ ᾽μοιγε, μὴ ᾽μοί, μὴ διασκανδίκισῃς·   19
    ἀλλ᾽ εὑρέ τιν᾽ ἀπόκινον ἀπὸ τοῦ δεσπότου. 20
Νι. λέγε δὴ "μο‒λω‒μεν" ξυνεχὲς ὡδὶ ξυλλαβών.
Δη. καὶ δὴ λέγω "μο‒λω‒μεν."

Νι.   ἐξόπισθε νῦν
"αὐ–το" φάθι τοῦ "μο–λω–μεν."
Δη.   "αὐ–το."
Νι.   πάνυ καλῶς.
ὥσπερ δεφόμενος νῦν ἀτρέμα πρῶτον λέγε
τὸ "μο–λω–μεν", εἶτα δ᾽ "αὐ–το", κᾆτ᾽ ἐπάγων πυκνόν.   25
Δη.   μο–λω—μεν αὐ–το μο–λω–μεν αὐτομολῶμεν.
Νι.   ἤν,
οὐχ ἡδύ;
Δη.   νὴ Δία· πλήν γε περὶ τῷ δέρματι
δέδοικα τουτονὶ τὸν οἰωνόν.
Νι.   τί δαί;
Δη.   ὁτιὴ τὸ δέρμα δεφομένων ἀπέρχεται.
Νι.   κράτιστα τοίνυν τῶν παρόντων ἐστὶ νῷν,   30
θεῶν ἰόντε προσπεσεῖν του πρὸς βρέτας.
Δη.   ποῖον βρετέτετας; ἐτεὸν ἡγεῖ γὰρ θεούς;
Νι.   ἔγωγε.
Δη.   ποίῳ χρώμενος τεκμηρίῳ;
Νι.   ὁτιὴ θεοῖσιν ἐχθρός εἰμ᾽. οὐκ εἰκότως;
Δη.   εὖ προσβιβάζεις μ᾽. ἀλλ᾽ ἑτέρᾳ πη σκεπτέον.   35
βούλει τὸ πρᾶγμα τοῖς θεαταῖσιν φράσω;
Νι.   οὐ χεῖρον· ἓν δ᾽ αὐτοὺς παραιτησώμεθα,
ἐπίδηλον ἡμῖν τοῖς προσώποισιν ποιεῖν,
ἢν τοῖς ἔπεσι χαίρωσι καὶ τοῖς πράγμασιν.
Δη.   λέγοιμ᾽ ἂν ἤδη. νῷν γάρ ἐστι δεσπότης   40
ἄγροικος ὀργήν, κυαμοτρώξ, ἀκράχολος,
Δῆμος Πυκνίτης, δύσκολον γερόντιον
ὑπόκωφον. οὗτος τῇ προτέρᾳ νουμηνίᾳ
ἐπρίατο δοῦλον, βυρσοδέψην Παφλαγόνα,
πανουργότατον καὶ διαβολώτατόν τινα.   45
οὗτος καταγνοὺς τοῦ γέροντος τοὺς τρόπους,
ὁ βυρσοπαφλαγών, ὑποπεσὼν τὸν δεσπότην
ἤκαλλ᾽, ἐθώπευ᾽, ἐκολάκευ᾽, ἐξηπάτα
κοσκυλματίοις ἄκροισι, τοιαυτὶ λέγων·
"ὦ Δῆμε, λοῦσαι πρῶτον ἐκδικάσας μίαν,   50
ἔνθοῦ, ῥόφησον, ἔντραγ᾽, ἔχε τριώβολον.
βούλει παραθῶ σοι δόρπον;" εἶτ᾽ ἀναρπάσας
ὅ τι ἄν τις ἡμῶν σκευάσῃ, τῷ δεσπότῃ
Παφλαγὼν κεχάρισται τοῦτο. καὶ πρώην γ᾽ ἐμοῦ
μᾶζαν μεμαχότος ἐν Πύλῳ Λακωνικήν,   55
πανουργότατά πως περιδραμὼν ὑφαρπάσας

αὐτὸς παρέθηκε τὴν ὑπ' ἐμοῦ μεμαγμένην.
ἡμᾶς δ' ἀπελαύνει κοὐκ ἐᾷ τὸν δεσπότην
ἄλλον θεραπεύειν, ἀλλὰ βυρσίνην ἔχων
δειπνοῦντος ἑστὼς ἀποσοβεῖ τοὺς ῥήτορας.   60
ᾄδει δὲ χρησμούς· ὁ δὲ γέρων σιβυλλιᾷ.
εἶτ' αὐτὸν ὡς ὁρᾷ μεμακκοακότα,
τέχνην πεπόηται· τοὺς γὰρ ἔνδον ἄντικρυς
ψευδῆ διαβάλλει· κᾆτα μαστιγούμεθα
ἡμεῖς· Παφλαγὼν δὲ περιθέων τοὺς οἰκέτας   65
αἰτεῖ, ταράττει, δωροδοκεῖ, λέγων τάδε·
"ὁρᾶτε τὸν Ὕλαν δι' ἐμὲ μαστιγούμενον;
εἰ μή μ' ἀναπείσετ', ἀποθανεῖσθε τήμερον."
ἡμεῖς δὲ δίδομεν· εἰ δὲ μή, πατούμενοι
ὑπὸ τοῦ γέροντος ὀκταπλάσιον χέζομεν.   70
νῦν οὖν ἀνύσαντε φροντίσωμεν, ὦγαθέ,
ποίαν ὁδὸν νὼ τρεπτέον καὶ πρὸς τίνα.
Νι. κράτιστ' ἐκείνην τὴν "μόλωμεν", ὦγαθέ.
Δη. ἀλλ' οὐχ οἷόν τε τὸν Παφλαγόν' οὐδὲν λαθεῖν·
ἐφορᾷ γὰρ αὐτὸς πάντ'. ἔχει γὰρ τὸ σκέλος   75
τὸ μὲν ἐν Πύλῳ, τὸ δ' ἕτερον ἐν τἠκκλησίᾳ.
τοσόνδε δ' αὐτοῦ βῆμα διαβεβηκότος
ὁ πρωκτός ἐστιν αὐτόχρημ' ἐν Χάοσιν,
τὼ χεῖρ' ἐν Αἰτωλοῖς, ὁ νοῦς δ' ἐν Κλωπιδῶν.
Νι. κράτιστον οὖν νῷν ἀποθανεῖν.
Δη.   ἀλλὰ σκόπει,   80
ὅπως ἂν ἀποθάνωμεν ἀνδρικώτατα.
Νι. πῶς δῆτα, πῶς γένοιτ' ἂν ἀνδρικώτατα;
βέλτιστον ἡμῖν αἷμα ταύρειον πιεῖν·
ὁ Θεμιστοκλέους γὰρ θάνατος αἱρετώτερος.
Δη. μὰ Δί', ἀλλ' ἄκρατον οἶνον ἀγαθοῦ δαίμονος.   85
ἴσως γὰρ ἂν χρηστόν τι βουλευσαίμεθα.
Νι. ἰδού γ' ἄκρατον. περὶ πότου γοῦν ἐστί σοι.
πῶς δ' ἂν μεθύων χρηστόν τι βουλεύσαιτ' ἀνήρ;
Δη. ἄληθες, οὗτος; κρουνοχυτρολήραιόν εἶ.
οἶνον σὺ τολμᾷς εἰς ἐπίνοιαν λοιδορεῖν;   90
οἴνου γὰρ εὕροις ἄν τι πρακτικώτερον;
ὁρᾷς, ὅταν πίνωσιν ἄνθρωποι, τότε
πλουτοῦσι, διαπράττουσι, νικῶσιν δίκας,
εὐδαιμονοῦσιν, ὠφελοῦσι τοὺς φίλους.
ἀλλ' ἐξένεγκέ μοι ταχέως οἴνου χοᾶ,   95
τὸν νοῦν ἵν' ἄρδω καὶ λέγω τι δεξιόν.

Νι. οἴμοι, τί ποθ᾿ ἡμᾶς ἐργάσει τῷ σῷ πότῳ;
Δη. ἀγάθ᾿· ἀλλ᾿ ἔνεγκ᾿· ἐγὼ δὲ κατακλινήσομαι.
    ἢν γὰρ μεθυσθῶ, πάντα ταυτὶ καταπάσω
    βουλευματίων καὶ γνωμιδίων καὶ νοιδίων.   100
Νι. ὡς εὐτυχῶς ὅτι οὐκ ἐλήφθην ἔνδοθεν
    κλέπτων τὸν οἶνον.
Δη.   εἰπέ μοι, Παφλαγὼν τί δρᾷ;
Νι. ἐπίπαστα λείξας δημιόπραθ᾿ ὁ βάσκανος   103
    ῥέγκει μεθύων ἐν ταῖσι βύρσαις ὕπτιος.
Δη. ἴθι νυν, ἄκρατον ἐγκάναξόν μοι πολὺν   105
    σπονδήν.
Νι.   λαβὲ δὴ καὶ σπεῖσον ἀγαθοῦ δαίμονος.
Δη. ἕλχ᾿ ἕλκε τὴν τοῦ δαίμονος τοῦ Πραμνίου.
    ὦ δαῖμον ἀγαθέ, σὸν τὸ βούλευμ᾿, οὐκ ἐμόν.
Νι. εἴπ᾿, ἀντιβολῶ, τί ἐστι;
Δη.   τοὺς χρησμοὺς ταχὺ
    κλέψας ἔνεγκε τοῦ Παφλαγόνος ἔνδοθεν,   110
    ἕως καθεύδει.
Νι.   ταῦτ᾿. ἀτὰρ τοῦ δαίμονος
    δέδοιχ᾿ ὅπως μὴ τεύξομαι κακοδαίμονος.
Δη. φέρε νυν ἐγὼ ᾿μαυτῷ προσαγάγω τὸν χοᾶ,
    τὸν νοῦν ἵν᾿ ἄρδω καὶ λέγω τι δεξιόν.
Νι. ὡς μεγάλ᾿ ὁ Παφλαγὼν πέρδεται καὶ ῥέγκεται,   115
    ὥστ᾿ ἔλαθον αὐτὸν τὸν ἱερὸν χρησμὸν λαβών,
    ὅνπερ μάλιστ᾿ ἐφύλαττεν.
Δη.   ὦ σοφώτατε,
    φέρ᾿ αὐτόν, ἵν᾿ ἀναγνῶ· σὺ δ᾿ ἔγχεον πιεῖν
    ἀνύσας τι. φέρ᾿ ἴδω, τί ἄρ᾿ ἔνεστιν αὐτόθι;
    ὦ λόγια. δός μοι, δὸς τὸ ποτήριον ταχύ.   120
Νι. ἰδού. τί φησ᾿ ὁ χρησμός;
Δη.   ἑτέραν ἔγχεον.
Νι. ἐν τοῖς λογίοις ἔνεστιν "ἑτέραν ἔγχεον";
Δη. ὦ Βάκι.
Νι.   τί ἐστι;
Δη.   δὸς τὸ ποτήριον ταχύ.
Νι. πολλῷ γ᾿ ὁ Βάκις ἐχρῆτο τῷ ποτηρίῳ.
Δη. ὦ μιαρὲ Παφλαγών, ταῦτ᾿ ἄρ᾿ ἐφυλάττου πάλαι,   125
    τὸν περὶ σεαυτοῦ χρησμὸν ὀρρωδῶν.
Νι.   τιή;
Δη. ἐνταῦθ᾿ ἔνεστιν, αὐτὸς ὡς ἀπόλλυται.
Νι. καὶ πῶς;

Δη.   ὅπως; ὁ χρησμὸς ἄντικρυς λέγει
        ὡς πρῶτα μὲν στυππειοπώλης γίγνεται,   129
        ὃς πρῶτος ἕξει τῆς πόλεως τὰ πράγματα.   130
Νι.   εἷς οὑτοσὶ πώλης. τί τοὐντεῦθεν; λέγε.
Δη.   μετὰ τοῦτον αὖθις προβατοπώλης δεύτερος.
Νι.   δύο τώδε πώλα. καὶ τί τόνδε χρὴ παθεῖν;
Δη.   κρατεῖν, ἕως ἕτερος ἀνὴρ βδελυρώτερος
        αὐτοῦ γένοιτο· μετὰ δὲ ταῦτ᾽ ἀπόλλυται.   135
        ἐπιγίγνεται γὰρ βυρσοπώλης ὁ Παφλαγών,
        ἅρπαξ, κεκράκτης, Κυκλοβόρου φωνὴν ἔχων.
Νι.   τὸν προβατοπώλην ἦν ἄρ᾽ ἀπολέσθαι χρεὼν
        ὑπὸ βυρσοπώλου;
Δη.   νὴ Δί᾽.
Νι.   οἴμοι δείλαιος.
        πόθεν οὖν ἂν ἔτι γένοιτο πώλης εἷς μόνος;   140
Δη.   ἔτ᾽ ἔστιν εἷς, ὑπερφυᾶ τέχνην ἔχων.
Νι.   εἴπ᾽, ἀντιβολῶ, τίς ἐστιν;
Δη.   εἴπω;
Νι.   νὴ Δία.
Δη.   ἀλλαντοπώλης ἔσθ᾽ ὁ τοῦτον ἐξελῶν.
Νι.   ἀλλαντοπώλης; ὦ Πόσειδον, τῆς τέχνης.
        φέρε, ποῦ τὸν ἄνδρα τοῦτον ἐξευρήσομεν;   145
Δη.   ζητῶμεν αὐτόν. ἀλλ᾽ ὁδὶ προσέρχεται
        ὥσπερ κατὰ θεὸν εἰς ἀγοράν. ὦ μακάριε
        ἀλλαντοπῶλα, δεῦρο δεῦρ᾽, ὦ φίλτατε,
        ἀνάβαινε, σωτὴρ τῇ πόλει καὶ νῷν φανείς.

ΑΛΛΑΝΤΟΠΩΛΗΣ
        τί ἐστι; τί με καλεῖτε;
Δη.   δεῦρ᾽ ἔλθ᾽, ἵνα πύθῃ   150
        ὡς εὐτυχὴς εἶ καὶ μεγάλως εὐδαιμονεῖς.   151
Νι.   ἴθι δή, κάθελ᾽ αὐτοῦ τοὐλεὸν καὶ τοῦ θεοῦ
        τὸν χρησμὸν ἀναδίδαξον αὐτὸν ὡς ἔχει·
        ἐγὼ δ᾽ ἰὼν προσκέψομαι τὸν Παφλαγόνα.
Δη.   ἄγε δὴ σὺ κατάθου πρῶτα τὰ σκεύη χαμαί·   155
        ἔπειτα τὴν γῆν πρόσκυσον καὶ τοὺς θεούς.
Αλ.   ἰδού· τί ἐστιν;
Δη.   ὦ μακάρι᾽, ὦ πλούσιε,
        ὦ νῦν μὲν οὐδείς, αὔριον δ᾽ ὑπέρμεγας,
        ὦ τῶν Ἀθηνῶν ταγὲ τῶν εὐδαιμόνων.

Αλ. τί μ᾽, ὦγάθ᾽, οὐ πλύνειν ἐᾷς τὰς κοιλίας   160
     πωλεῖν τε τοὺς ἀλλᾶντας, ἀλλὰ καταγελᾷς;
Δη. ὦ μῶρε, ποίας κοιλίας; δευρὶ βλέπε.
     τὰς στίχας ὁρᾷς τὰς τῶνδε τῶν λαῶν;
Αλ.   ὁρῶ.
Δη. τούτων ἁπάντων αὐτὸς ἀρχέλας ἔσει,
     καὶ τῆς ἀγορᾶς καὶ τῶν λιμένων καὶ τῆς Πυκνός   165
     βουλὴν πατήσεις καὶ στρατηγοὺς κλαστάσεις,
     δήσεις, φυλάξεις, ἐν πρυτανείῳ λαικάσει.
Αλ. ἐγώ;
Δη.   σὺ μέντοι· κοὐδέπω γε πάνθ᾽ ὁρᾷς.
     ἀλλ᾽ ἐπανάβηθι κἀπὶ τοὐλεὸν τοδὶ
     καὶ κάτιδε τὰς νήσους ἁπάσας ἐν κύκλῳ.   170
Αλ. καθορῶ.
Δη.   τί δαί; τἀμπόρια καὶ τὰς ὁλκάδας;
Αλ. ἔγωγε.
Δη.   πῶς οὖν οὐ μεγάλως εὐδαιμονεῖς;
     ἔτι νῦν τὸν ὀφθαλμὸν παράβαλ᾽ εἰς Καρίαν
     τὸν δεξιόν, τὸν δ᾽ ἕτερον εἰς Καρχηδόνα.
Αλ. εὐδαιμονήσω γ᾽ εἰ διαστραφήσομαι.   175
Δη. οὔκ, ἀλλὰ διὰ σοῦ ταῦτα πάντα πέρναται.
     γίγνει γάρ, ὡς ὁ χρησμὸς οὑτοσὶ λέγει,
     ἀνὴρ μέγιστος.
Αλ.   εἰπέ μοι, καὶ πῶς ἐγὼ
     ἀλλαντοπώλης ὢν ἀνὴρ γενήσομαι;
Δη. δι᾽ αὐτὸ γάρ τοι τοῦτο καὶ γίγνει μέγας,   180
     ὁτιὴ πονηρὸς κἀξ ἀγορᾶς εἶ καὶ θρασύς.
Αλ. οὐκ ἀξιῶ ᾽γὼ ᾽μαυτὸν ἰσχύειν μέγα.
Δη. οἴμοι, τί ποτ᾽ ἔσθ᾽ ὅτι σαυτὸν οὐ φὴς ἄξιον;
     ξυνειδέναι τί μοι δοκεῖς σαυτῷ καλόν.
     μῶν ἐκ καλῶν εἶ κἀγαθῶν;
Αλ.   μὰ τοὺς θεούς,   185
     εἰ μὴ ᾽κ πονηρῶν γ᾽.
Δη.   ὦ μακάριε τῆς τύχης,
     ὅσον πέπονθας ἀγαθὸν εἰς τὰ πράγματα.
Αλ. ἀλλ᾽, ὦγάθ᾽, οὐδὲ μουσικὴν ἐπίσταμαι
     πλὴν γραμμάτων, καὶ ταῦτα μέντοι κακὰ κακῶς.
Δη. τουτί σε μόνον ἔβλαψεν, ὅτι καὶ κακὰ κακῶς.   190
     ἡ δημαγωγία γὰρ οὐ πρὸς μουσικοῦ
     ἔτ᾽ ἐστὶν ἀνδρὸς οὐδὲ χρηστοῦ τοὺς τρόπους,
     ἀλλ᾽ εἰς ἀμαθῆ καὶ βδελυρόν. † ἀλλὰ μὴ παρῇς
     ἅ σοι διδόασ᾽ ἐν τοῖς λογίοισιν οἱ θεοί.

Αλ. πῶς δῆτά φησ' ὁ χρησμός;
Δη.   εὖ νὴ τοὺς θεούς,   195
καὶ ποικίλως πως καὶ σοφῶς ἠνιγμένος·
"ἀλλ' ὁπόταν μάρψῃ βυρσαίετος ἀγκυλοχήλης
γαμφηλῇσι δράκοντα κοάλεμον αἱματοπώτην,
δὴ τότε Παφλαγόνων μὲν ἀπόλλυται ἡ σκοροδάλμη,
κοιλιοπώλῃσιν δὲ θεὸς μέγα κῦδος ὀπάζει,   200
αἴ κεν μὴ πωλεῖν ἀλλᾶντας μᾶλλον ἕλωνται."
Αλ. πῶς οὖν πρὸς ἐμὲ ταῦτ' ἐστίν; ἀναδίδασκέ με.
Δη. βυρσαίετος μὲν ὁ Παφλαγών ἐσθ' οὑτοσί.
Αλ. τί δ' ἀγκυλοχήλης ἐστίν;
Δη.   αὐτό που λέγει,
ὅτι ἀγκύλαις ταῖς χερσὶν ἁρπάζων φέρει.   205
Αλ. ὁ δράκων δὲ πρὸς τί;
Δη.   τοῦτο περιφανέστατον.
ὁ δράκων γάρ ἐστι μακρὸν ὅ τ' ἀλλᾶς αὖ μακρόν·
εἶθ' αἱματοπώτης ἔσθ' ὅ τ' ἀλλᾶς χὠ δράκων.
τὸν οὖν δράκοντά φησι τὸν βυρσαίετον
ἤδη κρατήσειν, αἴ κε μὴ θαλφθῇ λόγοις.   210
Αλ. τὰ μὲν λόγι' αἰκάλλει με· θαυμάζω δ' ὅπως
τὸν δῆμον οἷός τ' ἐπιτροπεύειν εἴμ' ἐγώ.
Δη. φαυλότατον ἔργον· ταῦθ' ἅπερ ποιεῖς ποίει·
τάραττε καὶ χόρδευ' ὁμοῦ τὰ πράγματα
ἅπαντα, καὶ τὸν δῆμον ἀεὶ προσποιοῦ   215
ὑπογλυκαίνων ῥηματίοις μαγειρικοῖς.
τὰ δ' ἄλλα σοι πρόσεστι δημαγωγικά,
φωνὴ μιαρά, γέγονας κακῶς, ἀγόραιος εἶ·
ἔχεις ἅπαντα πρὸς πολιτείαν ἃ δεῖ·
χρησμοί τε συμβαίνουσι καὶ τὸ Πυθικόν.   220
ἀλλὰ στεφανοῦ καὶ σπένδε τῷ Κοαλέμῳ·
χὤπως ἀμυνεῖ τὸν ἄνδρα.
Αλ.   καὶ τίς ξύμμαχος
γενήσεταί μοι; καὶ γὰρ οἵ τε πλούσιοι
δεδίασιν αὐτὸν ὅ τε πένης βδύλλει λεώς.
Δη. ἀλλ' εἰσὶν ἱππῆς ἄνδρες ἀγαθοὶ χίλιοι   225
μισοῦντες αὐτόν, οἳ βοηθήσουσί σοι,
καὶ τῶν πολιτῶν οἱ καλοί τε κἀγαθοί.
καὶ τῶν θεατῶν ὅστις ἐστὶ δεξιός,
κἀγὼ μετ' αὐτῶν, χὠ θεὸς ξυλλήψεται.
καὶ μὴ δέδιθ'· οὐ γάρ ἐστιν ἐξῃκασμένος,   230
ὑπὸ τοῦ δέους γὰρ αὐτὸν οὐδεὶς ἤθελεν

τῶν σκευοποιῶν εἰκάσαι. πάντως γε μὴν
γνωσθήσεται· τὸ γὰρ θέατρον δεξιόν.
Νι. οἴμοι κακοδαίμων, ὁ Παφλαγὼν ἐξέρχεται.

ΠΑΦΛΑΓΩΝ
οὗτοι μὰ τοὺς δώδεκα θεοὺς χαιρήσετον,   235
ὁτιὴ 'πὶ τῷ δήμῳ ξυνόμνυτον πάλαι.
τουτὶ τί δρᾷ τὸ Χαλκιδικὸν ποτήριον;
οὐκ ἔσθ' ὅπως οὐ Χαλκιδέας ἀφίστατον.
ἀπολεῖσθον, ἀποθανεῖσθον, ὦ μιαρωτάτω.
Δη. οὗτος, τί φεύγεις; οὐ μενεῖς; ὦ γεννάδα   240
ἀλλαντοπῶλα, μὴ προδῷς τὰ πράγματα.
ἄνδρες ἱππῆς, παραγένεσθε· νῦν ὁ καιρός. ὦ Σίμων,
ὦ Παναίτι', οὐκ ἐλᾶτε πρὸς τὸ δεξιὸν κέρας;
ἄνδρες ἐγγύς. ἀλλ' ἀμύνου κἀπαναστρέφου πάλιν.
ὁ κονιορτὸς δῆλος αὐτῶν ὡς ὁμοῦ προσκειμένων.   245
ἀλλ' ἀμύνου καὶ δίωκε καὶ τροπὴν αὐτοῦ ποιοῦ.

ΧΟΡΟΣ
παῖε παῖε τὸν πανοῦργον καὶ ταραξιππόστρατον
καὶ τελώνην καὶ φάραγγα καὶ Χάρυβδιν ἁρπαγῆς,
καὶ πανοῦργον καὶ πανοῦργον· πολλάκις γὰρ αὔτ' ἐρῶ·
καὶ γὰρ οὗτος ἦν πανοῦργος πολλάκις τῆς ἡμέρας.   250
ἀλλὰ παῖε καὶ δίωκε καὶ τάραττε καὶ κύκα
καὶ βδελύττου, καὶ γὰρ ἡμεῖς, κἀπικείμενος βόα·
εὐλαβοῦ δὲ μὴ 'κφύγῃ σε· καὶ γὰρ οἶδε τὰς ὁδούς,
ἅσπερ Εὐκράτης ἔφευγεν εὐθὺ τῶν κυρηβίων.
Πα. ὦ γέροντες ἡλιασταί, φράτερες τριωβόλου,   255
οὓς ἐγὼ βόσκω κεκραγὼς καὶ δίκαια κἄδικα,
παραβοηθεῖθ', ὡς ὑπ' ἀνδρῶν τύπτομαι ξυνωμοτῶν.
Δη. ἐν δίκῃ γ', ἐπεὶ τὰ κοινὰ πρὶν λαχεῖν κατεσθίεις,
κἀποσυκάζεις πιέζων τοὺς ὑπευθύνους, σκοπῶν
ὅστις αὐτῶν ὠμός ἐστιν ἢ πέπων ἢ †μὴ πέπων.   260
καὶ σκοπεῖς γε τῶν πολιτῶν ὅστις ἐστὶν ἀμνοκῶν,   264
πλούσιος καὶ μὴ πονηρὸς καὶ τρέμων τὰ πράγματα.   265
κἄν τιν' αὐτῶν γνῷς ἀπράγμον' ὄντα καὶ κεχηνότα,   261
καταγαγὼν ἐκ Χερρονήσου, διαβαλών, ἀγκυρίσας,
εἶτ' ἀποστρέψας τὸν ὦμον αὐτὸν ἐνεκολήβασας.
Πα. ξυνεπίκεισθ' ὑμεῖς; ἐγὼ δ', ἄνδρες, δι' ὑμᾶς τύπτομαι,   266
ὅτε λέγειν γνώμην ἔμελλον ὡς δίκαιον ἐν πόλει
ἱστάναι μνημεῖον ὑμῶν ἐστιν ἀνδρείας χάριν;

Χο. ὡς δ' ἀλαζών, ὡς δὲ μάσθλης· εἶδες οἷ' ὑπέρχεται
ὡσπερεὶ γέροντας ἡμᾶς κἀκκοβαλικεύεται.   270
ἀλλ' ἐὰν ταύτῃ γ' ἐνιῇ, ταυτῃὶ πεπλήξεται·
ἢν δ' ὑπεκκλίνῃ γε δευρί, πρὸς σκέλος κυρηβάσει.
Πα. ὦ πόλις καὶ δῆμ', ὑφ' οἵων θηρίων γαστρίζομαι.
Δη. καὶ κέκραγας, ὥσπερ ἀεὶ τὴν πόλιν καταστρέφεις;
Πα. ἀλλ' ἐγώ σε τῇ βοῇ ταύτῃ γε πρῶτα τρέψομαι.   275
Χο. ἀλλ' ἐὰν μὲν τόνδε νικᾷς τῇ βοῇ, τήνελλος εἶ·
ἢν δ' ἀναιδείᾳ παρέλθῃ σ', ἡμέτερος ὁ πυραμοῦς.
Πα. τουτονὶ τὸν ἄνδρ' ἐγὼ 'νδείκνυμι, καὶ φήμ' ἐξάγειν
ταῖσι Πελοποννησίων τριήρεσι ζωμεύματα.
Αλ. ναὶ μὰ Δία κἄγωγε τοῦτον, ὅτι κενῇ τῇ κοιλίᾳ   280
εἰσδραμὼν εἰς τὸ πρυτανεῖον, εἶτα πάλιν ἐκθεῖ πλέα.
Δη. νὴ Δί', ἐξάγων γε τἀπόρρηθ', ἅμ' ἄρτον καὶ κρέας
καὶ τέμαχος, οὗ Περικλέης οὐκ ἠξιώθη πώποτε.
Πα. ἀποθανεῖσθον αὐτίκα μάλα.
Αλ. τριπλάσιον κεκράξομαί σου.   285
Πα. καταβοήσομαι βοῶν σε.
Αλ. κατακεκράξομαί σε κράζων.
Πα. διαβαλῶ σ' ἐὰν στρατηγῇς.
Αλ. κυνοκοπήσω σου τὸ νῶτον.
Πα. περιελῶ σ' ἀλαζονείαις.   290
Αλ. ὑποτεμοῦμαι τὰς ὁδούς σου.
Πα. βλέψον εἴς μ' ἀσκαρδάμυκτον.
Αλ. ἐν ἀγορᾷ κἀγὼ τέθραμμαι.
Πα. διαφορήσω σ' εἴ τι γρύξει.
Αλ. κοπροφορήσω σ' εἰ λακήσει.   295
Πα. ὁμολογῶ κλέπτειν· σὺ δ' οὐχί.
Αλ. νὴ τὸν Ἑρμῆν τὸν ἀγοραῖον,
κἀπιορκῶ γε βλεπόντων.
Πα. ἀλλότρια τοίνυν σοφίζει.
καί σε φαίνω τοῖς πρυτάνεσιν   300
ἀδεκατεύτους τῶν θεῶν ἱερὰς ἔχοντα κοιλίας.

Χο. ὦ μιαρὲ καὶ βδελυρὲ κρᾶκτα, τοῦ σοῦ θράσους   [στρ. α
πᾶσα μὲν γῆ πλέα, πᾶσα δ' ἐκκλησία,   305
καὶ τέλη καὶ γραφαὶ καὶ δικαστήρι', ὦ
βορβοροτάραξι καὶ τὴν πόλιν ἄπασαν ἡ-
μῶν ἀνατετυρβακώς,   310
ὅστις ἡμῖν τὰς Ἀθήνας ἐκκεκώφωκας βοῶν
κἀπὸ τῶν πετρῶν ἄνωθεν τοὺς φόρους θυννοσκοπῶν.

Πα. οἶδ᾽ ἐγὼ τὸ πρᾶγμα τοῦθ᾽ ὅθεν πάλαι καττύεται.

Αλ. εἰ δὲ μὴ σύ γ᾽ οἶσθα κάττυμ᾽, οὐδ᾽ ἐγὼ χορδεύματα,   315
ὅστις ὑποτέμνων ἐπώλεις δέρμα μοχθηροῦ βοὸς
τοῖς ἀγροίκοισιν πανούργως, ὥστε φαίνεσθαι παχύ,
καὶ πρὶν ἡμέραν φορῆσαι, μεῖζον ἦν δυοῖν δοχμαῖν.

Δη. νὴ Δία κἀμὲ τοῦτ᾽ ἔδρασε ταὐτόν, ὥστε κατάγελων
πάμπολυν τοῖς δημόταισι καὶ φίλοις παρασχεθεῖν.   320
πρὶν γὰρ εἶναι Περγασῆσιν, ἔνεον ἐν ταῖς ἐμβάσιν.

Χο. ἆρα δῆτ᾽ οὐκ ἀπ᾽ ἀρχῆς ἐδήλους ἀναίδειαν, ἥπερ μόνη   [στρ. β
προστατεῖ ῥητόρων;   325
ἢ σὺ πιστεύων ἀμέργεις τῶν ξένων τοὺς καρπίμους,
πρῶτος ὤν· ὁ δ᾽ Ἱπποδάμου λείβεται θεώμενος.
ἀλλ᾽ ἐφάνη γὰρ ἀνὴρ ἕτερος πολὺ
σοῦ μιαρώτερος, ὥστε με χαίρειν,
ὅς σε παύσει καὶ πάρεισι, δῆλός ἐστιν αὐτόθεν,   330
πανουργίᾳ τε καὶ θράσει
καὶ κοβαλικεύμασιν.
ἀλλ᾽, ὦ τραφεὶς ὅθενπέρ εἰσιν ἄνδρες οἵπερ εἰσίν,
νῦν δεῖξον ὡς οὐδὲν λέγει τὸ σωφρόνως τραφῆναι.

Αλ. καὶ μὴν ἀκούσαθ᾽ οἷός ἐστιν οὑτοσὶ πολίτης.   335
Πα. οὐκ αὖ μ᾽ ἐάσεις;
Αλ.   μὰ Δί᾽, ἐπεὶ κἀγὼ πονηρός εἰμι.
Δη. ἐὰν δὲ μὴ ταύτῃ γ᾽ ὑπείκῃ, λέγ᾽ ὅτι κἀκ πονηρῶν.
Πα. οὐκ αὖ μ᾽ ἐάσεις;
Αλ.   μὰ Δία.
Πα.   ναὶ μὰ Δία.
Αλ.   μὰ τὸν Ποσειδῶ.
ἀλλ᾽ αὐτὸ περὶ τοῦ πρότερος εἰπεῖν πρῶτα διαμαχοῦμαι.
Πα. οἴμοι, διαρραγήσομαι.
Αλ.   καὶ μὴν ἐγὼ οὐ παρήσω.   340
Δη. πάρες πάρες πρὸς τῶν θεῶν αὐτῷ διαρραγῆναι.
Πα. τῷ καὶ πεποιθὼς ἀξιοῖς ἐμοῦ λέγειν ἔναντα;
Αλ. ὁτιὴ λέγειν οἷός τε κἀγὼ καὶ καρυκοποιεῖν.
Πα. ἰδοὺ λέγειν. καλῶς γ᾽ ἂν οὖν σὺ πρᾶγμα προσπεσόν σοι
ὠμοσπάρακτον παραλαβὼν μεταχειρίσαιο χρηστῶς.   345
ἀλλ᾽ οἶσθ᾽ ὅ μοι πεπονθέναι δοκεῖς; ὅπερ τὸ πλῆθος.
εἴ που δικίδιον εἶπας εὖ κατὰ ξένου μετοίκου,
τὴν νύκτα θρυλῶν καὶ λαλῶν ἐν ταῖς ὁδοῖς σεαυτῷ,

Knights 39

ὕδωρ τε πίνων κἀπιδεικνὺς τοὺς φίλους τ’ ἀνιῶν,
ᾧου δυνατὸς εἶναι λέγειν. ὦ μῶρε, τῆς ἀνοίας. 350
Αλ. τί δαὶ σὺ πίνων τὴν πόλιν πεποίηκας ὥστε νυνὶ
ὑπὸ σοῦ μονωτάτου κατεγλωττισμένην σιωπᾶν;
Πα. ἐμοὶ γὰρ ἀντέθηκας ἀνθρώπων τιν’; ὅστις εὐθὺς
θύννεια θερμὰ καταφαγών, κᾆτ’ ἐπιπιὼν ἀκράτου
οἴνου χοᾶ κασαλβάσω τοὺς ἐν Πύλῳ στρατηγούς. 355
Αλ. ἐγὼ δέ γ’ ἤνυστρον βοὸς καὶ κοιλίαν ὑείαν
καταβροχθίσας, κᾆτ’ ἐκπιὼν τὸν ζωμὸν ἀναπόνιπτος
λαρυγγιῶ τοὺς ῥήτορας καὶ Νικίαν λαπάξω.
Δη. τὰ μὲν ἄλλα μ’ ἤρεσας λέγων· ἓν δ’ οὐ προσίεταί με,
τῶν πραγμάτων ὁτιὴ μόνος τὸν ζωμὸν ἐκροφήσει. 360
Πα. ἀλλ’ οὐ λάβρακας καταφαγὼν Μιλησίους κλονήσεις.
Αλ. ἀλλὰ σχελίδας ἐδηδοκὼς ὠνήσομαι μέταλλα.
Πα. ἐγὼ δ’ ἐπεισπηδῶν γε τὴν βουλὴν βίᾳ κυκήσω.
Αλ. ἐγὼ δὲ βυνήσω γέ σοι τὸν πρωκτὸν ἀντὶ φύσκης.
Πα. ἐγὼ δέ γ’ ἐξέλξω σε τῆς πυγῆς θύραζε κύβδα. 365
Δη. νὴ τὸν Ποσειδῶ κἀμέ γ’ ἄρ’, ἤνπερ γε τοῦτον ἕλκῃς.
Πα. οἷόν σε δήσω <’ν> τῷ ξύλῳ.
Αλ. διώξομαί σε δειλίας.
Πα. ἡ βύρσα σου θρανεύσεται.
Αλ. δερῶ σε θύλακον κλοπῆς. 370
Πα. διαπατταλευθήσει χαμαί.
Αλ. περικόμματ’ ἔκ σου σκευάσω.
Πα. τὰς βλεφαρίδας σου παρατιλῶ.
Αλ. τὸν πρηγορεῶνά σούκτεμῶ.
Δη. καὶ νὴ Δί’ ἐμβαλόντες αὐ- 375
τῷ πάτταλον μαγειρικῶς
εἰς τὸ στόμ’, εἶτα δ’ ἔνδοθεν
τὴν γλῶτταν ἐξείραντες αὐτοῦ σκεψόμεσθ’ εὖ κἀνδρικῶς
κεχηνότος 380
τὸν πρωκτόν, εἰ χαλαζᾷ.
Χο. ἦν ἄρα πυρός θ’ ἕτερα θερμότερα καὶ λόγων [ἀντ. α
ἐν πόλει τῶν ἀναιδῶν ἀναιδέστεροι· 385
καὶ τὸ πρᾶγμ’ ἦν ἄρ’ οὐ φαῦλον ὧδ’ <‒ ᴗ ᴗᴗ>.
ἀλλ’ ἔπιθι καὶ στρόβει, μηδὲν ὀλίγον ποίει·
νῦν γὰρ ἔχεται μέσος·
ὡς ἐὰν νυνὶ μαλάξῃς αὐτὸν ἐν τῇ προσβολῇ,
δειλὸν εὑρήσεις· ἐγὼ γὰρ τοὺς τρόπους ἐπίσταμαι. 390

Αλ. ἀλλ᾽ ὅμως οὗτος τοιοῦτος ὢν ἅπαντα τὸν βίον,
κᾆτ᾽ ἀνὴρ ἔδοξεν εἶναι, τἀλλότριον ἀμῶν θέρος.
νῦν δὲ τοὺς στάχυς ἐκείνους, οὓς ἐκεῖθεν ἤγαγεν,
ἐν ξύλῳ δήσας ἀφανεῖ κἀποδόσθαι βούλεται.

Πα. οὐ δέδοιχ᾽ ὑμᾶς, ἕως ἂν ζῇ τὸ βουλευτήριον   395
καὶ τὸ τοῦ Δήμου πρόσωπον μακκοᾷ καθήμενον.

Χο. ὡς δὲ πρὸς πᾶν ἀναιδεύεται κοὐ μεθίησι τοῦ χρώματος   [ἀντ. β
τοῦ παρεστηκότος.
εἴ σε μὴ μισῶ, γενοίμην ἐν Κρατίνου κῴδιον   400
καὶ διδασκοίμην προσᾴδειν Μορσίμου τραγῳδίᾳ.
ὦ περὶ πάντ᾽ ἐπὶ πᾶσί τε πράγμασι
δωροδόκοισιν ἐπ᾽ ἄνθεσιν ἵζων,
εἴθε φαύλως, ὥσπερ ηὗρες, ἐκβάλοις τὴν ἔνθεσιν.
ᾄσαιμι γὰρ τότ᾽ ἂν μόνον·   405
"πῖνε πῖν᾽ ἐπὶ συμφοραῖς."
τὸν Οὔλιόν τ᾽ ἂν οἴομαι γέροντα πυροπίπην,
ἡσθέντ᾽ ἰηπαιωνίσαι καὶ βακχέβακχον ᾆσαι.

Πα. οὗτοί μ᾽ ὑπερβαλεῖσθ᾽ ἀναιδείᾳ μὰ τὸν Ποσειδῶ,
ἢ μήποτ᾽ ἀγοραίου Διὸς σπλάγχνοισι παραγενοίμην.   410

Αλ. ἔγωγε νὴ τοὺς κονδύλους, οὓς πολλὰ δὴ 'πὶ πολλοῖς
ἠνεσχόμην ἐκ παιδίου, μαχαιρίδων τε πληγάς,
ὑπερβαλεῖσθαί σ᾽ οἴομαι τούτοισιν, ἢ μάτην γ᾽ ἂν
ἀπομαγδαλιὰς σιτούμενος τοσοῦτος ἐκτραφεὶς ἦ.

Δη. ἀπομαγδαλιὰς ὥσπερ κύων· ὦ παμπόνηρε, πῶς οὖν   415
κυνὸς βορὰν σιτούμενος μαχεῖ σὺ κυνοκεφάλλῳ;

Αλ. καὶ νὴ Δί᾽ ἄλλα γ᾽ ἐστί μου κόβαλα παιδὸς ὄντος.
ἐξηπάτων γὰρ τοὺς μαγείρους ἂν λέγων τοιαυτί·
"σκέψασθε, παῖδες· οὐχ ὁρᾶθ᾽; ὥρα νέα, χελιδών."
οἱ δ᾽ ἔβλεπον, κἀγὼ 'ν τοσούτῳ τῶν κρεῶν ἔκλεπτον.   420

Δη. ὦ δεξιώτατον κρέας, σοφῶς γε προὐνοήσω·
ὥσπερ ἀκαλήφας ἐσθίων πρὸ χελιδόνων ἔκλεπτες.

Αλ. καὶ ταῦτα δρῶν ἐλάνθανόν γ᾽. εἰ δ᾽ οὖν ἴδοι τις αὐτῶν,
ἀποκρυπτόμενος εἰς τὰ κοχώνα τοὺς θεοὺς ἀπώμνυν·
ὥστ᾽ εἶπ᾽ ἀνὴρ τῶν ῥητόρων ἰδών με τοῦτο δρῶντα·   425
"οὐκ ἔσθ᾽ ὅπως ὁ παῖς ὅδ᾽ οὐ τὸν δῆμον ἐπιτροπεύσει."

Δη. εὖ γε ξυνέβαλεν αὔτ᾽· ἀτὰρ δῆλόν γ᾽ ἀφ᾽ οὗ ξυνέγνω·
ὁτιὴ 'πιώρκεις θ᾽ ἡρπακὼς καὶ κρέας ὁ πρωκτὸς εἶχεν.

Πα. ἐγώ σε παύσω τοῦ θράσους, οἶμαι δὲ μᾶλλον ἄμφω.
ἔξειμι γάρ σοι λαμπρὸς ἤδη καὶ μέγας καθιείς,   430
ὁμοῦ ταράττων τήν τε γῆν καὶ τὴν θάλατταν εἰκῇ.

Αλ.   ἐγὼ δὲ συστείλας γε τοὺς ἀλλᾶντας εἶτ᾽ ἀφήσω
κατὰ κῦμ᾽ ἐμαυτὸν οὔριον, κλάειν σε μακρὰ κελεύων.
Δη.   κἄγωγ᾽, ἐάν τι παραχαλᾷ, τὴν ἀντλίαν φυλάξω.
Πα.   οὗτοι μὰ τὴν Δήμητρα καταπροίξει τάλαντα πολλὰ   435
κλέψας Ἀθηναίων.
Δη.   ἄθρει καὶ τοῦ ποδὸς παρίει·
ὡς οὗτος ἤδη καικίας καὶ συκοφαντίας πνεῖ.
Αλ.   σὲ δ᾽ ἐκ Ποτειδαίας ἔχοντ᾽ εὖ οἶδα δέκα τάλαντα.
Πα.   τί δῆτα; βούλει τῶν ταλάντων ἓν λαβὼν σιωπᾶν;
Δη.   ἀνὴρ ἂν ἡδέως λάβοι. τοὺς τερθρίους παρίει·   440
τὸ πνεῦμ᾽ ἔλαττον γίγνεται.
Πα.   φεύξει γραφὰς <δωροδοκίας>
ἑκατονταλάντους τέτταρας.
Αλ.   σὺ δ᾽ ἀστρατείας γ᾽ εἴκοσιν,
κλοπῆς δὲ πλεῖν ἢ χιλίας.
Πα.   ἐκ τῶν ἀλιτηρίων σέ φη-   445
μι γεγονέναι τῶν τῆς θεοῦ.
Αλ.   τὸν πάππον εἶναί φημί σου
τῶν δορυφόρων—
Πα.   ποίων; φράσον.
Αλ.   τῶν Βυρσίνης τῆς Ἱππίου.
Πα.   κόβαλος εἶ.
Αλ.   πανοῦργος εἶ.   450
Δη.   παῖ᾽ ἀνδρικῶς.
Πα.   ἰοὺ ἰού,
τύπτουσί μ᾽ οἱ ξυνωμόται.
Δη.   παῖ᾽ αὐτὸν ἀνδρειότατα, καὶ
γάστριζε καὶ τοῖς ἐντέροις
καὶ τοῖς κόλοις,   455
χὤπως κολᾷ τὸν ἄνδρα.
Χο.   ὦ γεννικώτατον κρέας ψυχήν τ᾽ ἄριστε πάντων,
καὶ τῇ πόλει σωτὴρ φανεὶς ἡμῖν τε τοῖς πολίταις,
ὡς εὖ τὸν ἄνδρα ποικίλως τ᾽ ἐπῆλθες ἐν λόγοισιν.
πῶς ἄν σ᾽ ἐπαινέσαιμεν οὕτως ὥσπερ ἡδόμεσθα;   460
Πα.   ταυτὶ μὰ τὴν Δήμητρά μ᾽ οὐκ ἐλάνθανεν
τεκταινόμενα τὰ πράγματ᾽, ἀλλ᾽ ἠπιστάμην
γομφούμεν᾽ αὐτὰ πάντα καὶ κολλώμενα.
Αλ.   οὔκουν μ᾽ ἐν Ἄργει γ᾽ οἷα πράττεις λανθάνει.
πρόφασιν μὲν Ἀργείους φίλους ἡμῖν ποιεῖ,   465
ἰδίᾳ δ᾽ ἐκεῖ Λακεδαιμονίοις ξυγγίγνεται.
Δη.   οἴμοι, σὺ δ᾽ οὐδὲν ἐξ ἁμαξουργοῦ λέγεις;   464

Αλ. καὶ ταῦτ' ἐφ' οἷσίν ἐστι συμφυσώμενα 468
ἐγᾦδ'· ἐπὶ γὰρ τοῖς δεδεμένοις χαλκεύεται.
Δη. εὖ γ' εὖ γε, χάλκευ' ἀντὶ τῶν κολλωμένων. 470
Αλ. καὶ ξυγκροτοῦσιν ἄνδρες αὔτ' ἐκεῖθεν αὖ.
καὶ ταῦτά μ' οὔτ' ἀργύριον οὔτε χρυσίον
διδοὺς ἀναπείσεις, οὐδὲ προσπέμπων φίλους,
ὅπως ἐγὼ ταῦτ' οὐκ Ἀθηναίοις φράσω.
Πα. ἐγὼ μὲν οὖν αὐτίκα μάλ' εἰς βουλὴν ἰὼν 475
ὑμῶν ἁπάντων τὰς ξυνωμοσίας ἐρῶ,
καὶ τὰς ξυνόδους τὰς νυκτερινὰς ἐπὶ τῇ πόλει,
καὶ πάνθ' ἃ Μήδοις καὶ βασιλεῖ ξυνόμνυτε,
καὶ τἀκ Βοιωτῶν ταῦτα συντυρούμενα.
Δη. πῶς οὖν ὁ τυρὸς ἐν Βοιωτοῖς ὤνιος; 480
Πα. ἐγώ σε νὴ τὸν Ἡρακλέα καταστορῶ.
Δη. ἄγε δὴ σύ, τίνα νοῦν ἢ τίνα ψυχὴν ἔχεις,
νυνὶ διδάξεις, εἴπερ ἀπεκρύψω τότε
εἰς τὰ κοχώνα τὸ κρέας, ὡς αὐτὸς λέγεις·
θεύσει γὰρ ἄξας εἰς τὸ βουλευτήριον, 485
ὡς οὗτος εἰσπεσὼν ἐκεῖσε διαβαλεῖ
ἡμᾶς ἅπαντας καὶ κράγον κεκράξεται.
Αλ. ἀλλ' εἶμι· πρῶτον δ' ὡς ἔχω τὰς κοιλίας
καὶ τὰς μαχαίρας ἐνθαδὶ καταθήσομαι.
Δη. ἔχε νυν, ἄλειψον τὸν τράχηλον τουτῳί, 490
ἵν' ἐξολισθάνειν δύνῃ τὰς διαβολάς.
Αλ. ἀλλ' εὖ λέγεις καὶ παιδοτριβικῶς ταυταγί.
Δη. ἔχε νυν, ἐπέγκαψον λαβὼν ταδί.
Αλ. τί δαί;
Δη. ἵν' ἄμεινον, ὦ τᾶν, ἐσκοροδισμένος μάχῃ.
καὶ σπεῦδε ταχέως.
Αλ. ταῦτα δρῶ.
Δη. μέμνησό νυν 495
δάκνειν, διαβάλλειν, τοὺς λόφους κατεσθίειν,
χὤπως τὰ κάλλαι' ἀποφαγὼν ἥξεις πάλιν.

Χο. ἀλλ' ἴθι χαίρων, καὶ πράξειας
κατὰ νοῦν τὸν ἐμόν, καί σε φυλάττοι
Ζεὺς ἀγοραῖος· καὶ νικήσας 500
αὖθις ἐκεῖθεν πάλιν ὡς ἡμᾶς
ἔλθοις στεφάνοις κατάπαστος.
ὑμεῖς δ' ἡμῖν προσέχετε τὸν νοῦν
τοῖς ἀναπαίστοις,

ὦ παντοίας ἤδη Μούσης 505
πειραθέντες καθ᾽ ἑαυτούς.

εἰ μέν τις ἀνὴρ τῶν ἀρχαίων κωμῳδοδιδάσκαλος ἡμᾶς
ἠνάγκαζεν λέξοντας ἔπη πρὸς τὸ θέατρον παραβῆναι,
οὐκ ἂν φαύλως ἔτυχεν τούτου· νῦν δ᾽ ἄξιός ἐσθ᾽ ὁ ποιητής,
ὅτι τοὺς αὐτοὺς ἡμῖν μισεῖ τολμᾷ τε λέγειν τὰ δίκαια, 510
καὶ γενναίως πρὸς τὸν Τυφῶ χωρεῖ καὶ τὴν ἐριώλην.
ἃ δὲ θαυμάζειν ὑμῶν φησιν πολλοὺς αὐτῷ προσιόντας
καὶ βασανίζειν, ὡς οὐχὶ πάλαι χορὸν αἰτοίη καθ᾽ ἑαυτόν,
ἡμᾶς ὑμῖν ἐκέλευε φράσαι περὶ τούτου. φησὶ γὰρ ἀνὴρ
οὐχ ὑπ᾽ ἀνοίας τοῦτο πεπονθὼς διατρίβειν, ἀλλὰ νομίζων 515
κωμῳδοδιδασκαλίαν εἶναι χαλεπώτατον ἔργον ἁπάντων·
πολλῶν γὰρ δὴ πειρασάντων αὐτὴν ὀλίγοις χαρίσασθαι·
ὑμᾶς τε πάλαι διαγιγνώσκων ἐπετείους τὴν φύσιν ὄντας
καὶ τοὺς προτέρους τῶν ποιητῶν ἅμα τῷ γήρᾳ προδιδόντας·
τοῦτο μὲν εἰδὼς ἄπαθε Μάγνης ἅμα ταῖς πολιαῖς κατιούσαις, 520
ὃς πλεῖστα χορῶν τῶν ἀντιπάλων νίκης ἔστησε τροπαῖα·
πάσας δ᾽ ὑμῖν φωνὰς ἱεὶς καὶ ψάλλων καὶ πτερυγίζων
καὶ λυδίζων καὶ ψηνίζων καὶ βαπτόμενος βατραχείοις
οὐκ ἐξήρκεσεν, ἀλλὰ τελευτῶν ἐπὶ γήρως, οὐ γὰρ ἐφ᾽ ἥβης,
ἐξεβλήθη πρεσβύτης ὤν, ὅτι τοῦ σκώπτειν ἀπελείφθη· 525
εἶτα Κρατίνου μεμνημένος, ὃς πολλῷ ῥεύσας ποτ᾽ ἐπαίνῳ
διὰ τῶν ἀφελῶν πεδίων ἔρρει, καὶ τῆς στάσεως παρασύρων
ἐφόρει τὰς δρῦς καὶ τὰς πλατάνους καὶ τοὺς ἐχθροὺς προθελύμνους·
ᾆσαι δ᾽ οὐκ ἦν ἐν συμποσίῳ πλὴν "Δωροῖ συκοπέδιλε,"
καὶ "τέκτονες εὐπαλάμων ὕμνων·" οὕτως ἤνθησεν ἐκεῖνος. 530
νυνὶ δ᾽ ὑμεῖς αὐτὸν ὁρῶντες παραληροῦντ᾽ οὐκ ἐλεεῖτε,
ἐκπιπτουσῶν τῶν ἠλέκτρων καὶ τοῦ τόνου οὐκέτ᾽ ἐνόντος
τῶν θ᾽ ἁρμονιῶν διαχασκουσῶν· ἀλλὰ γέρων ὢν περιέρρει,
ὥσπερ Κοννᾶς, "στέφανον μὲν ἔχων αὖον, δίψῃ δ᾽ ἀπολωλώς",
ὃν χρῆν διὰ τὰς προτέρας νίκας πίνειν ἐν τῷ πρυτανείῳ, 535
καὶ μὴ ληρεῖν, ἀλλὰ θεᾶσθαι λιπαρὸν παρὰ τῷ Διονύσῳ.
οἵας δὲ Κράτης ὀργὰς ὑμῶν ἠνέσχετο καὶ στυφελιγμούς,
ὃς ἀπὸ σμικρᾶς δαπάνης ὑμᾶς ἀριστίζων ἀπέπεμπεν,
ἀπὸ κραμβοτάτου στόματος μάττων ἀστειοτάτας ἐπινοίας·
χοὗτος μέντοι μόλις ἀντήρκει, τοτὲ μὲν πίπτων, τοτὲ δ᾽ οὐχί. 540
ταῦτ᾽ ὀρρωδῶν διέτριβεν ἀεί, καὶ πρὸς τούτοισιν ἔφασκεν
ἐρέτην χρῆναι πρῶτα γενέσθαι πρὶν πηδαλίοις ἐπιχειρεῖν,
κᾆτ᾽ ἐντεῦθεν πρῳρατεῦσαι καὶ τοὺς ἀνέμους διαθρῆσαι,
κᾆτα κυβερνᾶν αὐτὸν ἑαυτῷ. τούτων οὖν οὕνεκα πάντων,

ὅτι σωφρονικῶς οὐκ ἀνοήτως εἰσπηδήσας ἐφλυάρει,   545
αἴρεσθ᾽ αὐτῷ πολὺ τὸ ῥόθιον, παραπέμψατ᾽ ἐφ᾽ ἕνδεκα κώπαις,
θόρυβον χρηστὸν Ληναΐτην,
ἵν᾽ ὁ ποιητὴς ἀπίῃ χαίρων
κατὰ νοῦν πράξας,
φαιδρὸς λάμποντι μετώπῳ.   550
ἵππι᾽ ἄναξ Πόσειδον, ᾧ   [*στρ.*
χαλκοκρότων ἵππων κτύπος
καὶ χρεμετισμὸς ἁνδάνει
καὶ κυανέμβολοι θοαὶ
μισθοφόροι τριήρεις,   555
μειρακίων θ᾽ ἅμιλλα λαμ-
πρυνομένων ἐν ἅρμασιν
καὶ βαρυδαιμονούντων,
δεῦρ᾽ ἔλθ᾽ εἰς χορόν, ὦ χρυσοτρίαιν᾽, ὦ
δελφίνων μεδέων Σουνιάρατε,   560
ὦ Γεραίστιε παῖ Κρόνου,
Φορμίωνί τε φίλτατ᾽ ἐκ
τῶν ἄλλων τε θεῶν Ἀθη-
ναίοις πρὸς τὸ παρεστός.

εὐλογῆσαι βουλόμεσθα τοὺς πατέρας ἡμῶν, ὅτι   565
ἄνδρες ἦσαν τῆσδε τῆς γῆς ἄξιοι καὶ τοῦ πέπλου,
οἵτινες πεζαῖς μάχαισιν ἔν τε ναυφάρκτῳ στρατῷ
πανταχοῦ νικῶντες ἀεὶ τήνδ᾽ ἐκόσμησαν πόλιν·
οὐ γὰρ οὐδεὶς πώποτ᾽ αὐτῶν τοὺς ἐναντίους ἰδὼν
ἠρίθμησεν, ἀλλ᾽ ὁ θυμὸς εὐθὺς ἦν ἀμυνίας·   570
εἰ δέ που πέσοιεν εἰς τὸν ὦμον ἐν μάχῃ τινί,
τοῦτ᾽ ἀπεψήσαντ᾽ ἄν, εἶτ᾽ ἠρνοῦντο μὴ πεπτωκέναι,
ἀλλὰ διεπάλαιον αὖθις. καὶ στρατηγὸς οὐδ᾽ ἂν εἷς
τῶν πρὸ τοῦ σίτησιν ᾔτησ᾽ ἐρόμενος Κλεαίνετον·
νῦν δ᾽ ἐὰν μὴ προεδρίαν φέρωσι καὶ τὰ σιτία,   575
οὐ μαχεῖσθαί φασιν. ἡμεῖς δ᾽ ἀξιοῦμεν τῇ πόλει
προῖκα γενναίως ἀμύνειν καὶ θεοῖς ἐγχωρίοις.
καὶ πρὸς οὐκ αἰτοῦμεν οὐδὲν πλὴν τοσουτονὶ μόνον·
ἤν ποτ᾽ εἰρήνη γένηται καὶ πόνων παυσώμεθα,
μὴ φθονεῖθ᾽ ἡμῖν κομῶσι μηδ᾽ ἀνεστλεγγισμένοις.   580

Ὦ πολιοῦχε Παλλάς, ὦ   [*ἀντ.*
τῆς ἱερωτάτης ἁπα-
σῶν πολέμῳ τε καὶ ποιη-

ταῖς δυνάμει θ᾽ ὑπερφερού-
σης μεδέουσα χώρας,   585
δεῦρ᾽ ἀφικοῦ λαβοῦσα τὴν
ἐν στρατιαῖς τε καὶ μάχαις
ἡμετέραν ξυνεργὸν
Νίκην, ἢ Χαρίτων ἐστὶν ἑταίρα
τοῖς τ᾽ ἐχθροῖσι μεθ᾽ ἡμῶν στασιάζει.   590
νῦν οὖν δεῦρο φάνηθι· δεῖ
γὰρ τοῖς ἀνδράσι τοῖσδε πά-
σῃ τέχνῃ πορίσαι σε νί-
κην, εἴπερ ποτέ, καὶ νῦν.

ἃ ξύνισμεν τοῖσιν ἵπποις, βουλόμεσθ᾽ ἐπαινέσαι.   595
ἄξιοι δ᾽ εἴσ᾽ εὐλογεῖσθαι· πολλὰ γὰρ δὴ πράγματα
ξυνδιήνεγκαν μεθ᾽ ἡμῶν, εἰσβολάς τε καὶ μάχας.
ἀλλὰ τἀν τῇ γῇ μὲν αὐτῶν οὐκ ἄγαν θαυμάζομεν,
ὡς <δ᾽> ὅτ᾽ εἰς τὰς ἱππαγωγοὺς εἰσεπήδων ἀνδρικῶς,
πριάμενοι κώθωνας, οἱ δὲ καὶ σκόροδα καὶ κρόμμυα,   600
εἶτα τὰς κώπας λαβόντες ὥσπερ ἡμεῖς οἱ βροτοὶ
ἐμβαλόντες ἂν ἐφρυάξανθ᾽, "ἱππαπαῖ, τίς ἐμβαλεῖ;
ληπτέον μᾶλλον. τί δρῶμεν; οὐκ ἐλᾷς, ὦ σαμφόρα;"
ἐξεπήδων τ᾽ εἰς Κόρινθον· εἶτα δ᾽ οἱ νεώτατοι
ταῖς ὁπλαῖς ὤρυττον εὐνὰς καὶ μετῇσαν βρώματα·   605
ἤσθιον δὲ τοὺς παγούρους ἀντὶ ποίας Μηδικῆς,
εἴ τις ἐξέρποι θύραζε, κἀκ βυθοῦ θηρώμενοι·
ὥστ᾽ ἔφη Θέωρος εἰπεῖν καρκίνον Κορίνθιον,
"δεινά γ᾽, ὦ Πόσειδον, εἰ μηδ᾽ ἐν βυθῷ δυνήσομαι
μήτε γῇ μήτ᾽ ἐν θαλάττῃ διαφυγεῖν τοὺς ἱππέας."   610

Χο. ὦ φίλτατ᾽ ἀνδρῶν καὶ νεανικώτατε,
     ὅσην ἀπὼν παρέσχες ἡμῖν φροντίδα·
     καὶ νῦν ἐπειδὴ σῶς ἐλήλυθας πάλιν,
     ἄγγειλον ἡμῖν πῶς τὸ πρᾶγμ᾽ ἠγωνίσω.
Αλ. τί δ᾽ ἄλλο γ᾽ εἰ μὴ Νικόβουλος ἐγενόμην;   615
Χο. νῦν ἄρ᾽ ἄξιόν γε πᾶσίν ἐστιν ἐπολολύξαι.   [στρ.
     ὦ καλὰ λέγων, πολὺ δ᾽ ἄμεινον ἔτι τῶν λόγων
     ἐργασάμεν᾽, εἴθ᾽ ἐπέλθοις ἅπαντά μοι σαφῶς·
     ὡς ἐγώ μοι δοκῶ   620
     κἂν μακρὰν ὁδὸν διελθεῖν ὥστ᾽ ἀκοῦσαι. πρὸς τάδ᾽, ὦ βέλ-
     τιστε, θαρρήσας λέγ᾽, ὡς ἅπαντες ἡδόμεσθά σοι.

Αλ. καὶ μὴν ἀκοῦσαί γ' ἄξιον τῶν πραγμάτων.
     εὐθὺς γὰρ αὐτοῦ κατόπιν ἐνθένδ' ἱέμην·   625
     ὁ δ' ἄρ' ἔνδον ἐλασίβροντ' ἀναρρηγνὺς ἔπη
     τερατευόμενος ἤρειδε κατὰ τῶν ἱππέων,
     κρημνοὺς ἐρείπων καὶ ξυνωμότας λέγων
     πιθανώταθ'· ἡ βουλὴ δ' ἅπασ' ἀκροωμένη
     ἐγένεθ' ὑπ' αὐτοῦ ψευδατραφάξυος πλέα,   630
     κἄβλεψε νᾶπυ καὶ τὰ μέτωπ' ἀνέσπασεν.
     κἄγωγ' ὅτε δὴ 'γνων ἐνδεχομένην τοὺς λόγους
     καὶ τοῖς φενακισμοῖσιν ἐξαπατωμένην,
     "ἄγε δὴ Σκίταλοι καὶ Φένακες", ἦν δ' ἐγώ,
     "Βερέσχεθοί τε καὶ Κόβαλοι καὶ Μόθων,   635
     ἀγορά τ' ἐν ᾗ παῖς ὢν ἐπαιδεύθην ἐγώ,
     νῦν μοι θράσος καὶ γλῶσσαν εὔπορον δότε
     φωνήν τ' ἀναιδῆ." ταῦτα φροντίζοντί μοι
     ἐκ δεξιᾶς ἐπέπαρδε καταπύγων ἀνήρ.
     κἀγὼ προσέκυσα· κᾆτα τῷ πρωκτῷ θενὼν   640
     τὴν κιγκλίδ' ἐξήραξα κἀναχανὼν μέγα
     ἀνέκραγον· "ὦ βουλή, λόγους ἀγαθοὺς φέρων
     εὐαγγελίσασθαι πρῶτον ὑμῖν βούλομαι·
     ἐξ οὗ γὰρ ἡμῖν ὁ πόλεμος κατερράγη,
     οὐπώποτ' ἀφύας εἶδον ἀξιωτέρας."   645
     οἱ δ' εὐθέως τὰ πρόσωπα διεγαλήνισαν·
     εἶτ' ἐστεφάνουν μ' εὐαγγέλια· κἀγὼ 'φρασα
     αὐτοῖς, ἀπόρρητον ποιησάμενος, ταχύ,
     ἵνα τὰς ἀφύας ὠνοῖντο πολλὰς τοὐβολοῦ,
     τῶν δημιουργῶν ξυλλαβεῖν τὰ τρύβλια.   650
     οἱ δ' ἀνεκρότησαν καὶ πρὸς ἔμ' ἐκεχήνεσαν.
     ὁ δ' ἐπινοήσας, ὁ Παφλαγών, εἰδὼς ἄρα
     οἷς ἤδεθ' ἡ βουλὴ μάλιστα ῥήμασιν,
     γνώμην ἔλεξεν· "ἄνδρες, ἤδη μοι δοκεῖ
     ἐπὶ συμφοραῖς ἀγαθαῖσιν εἰσηγγελμέναις   655
     εὐαγγέλια θύειν ἑκατὸν βοῦς τῇ θεῷ."
     ἐπένευσεν εἰς ἐκεῖνον ἡ βουλὴ πάλιν.
     κἄγωγ' ὅτε δὴ 'γνων τοῖς βολίτοις ἡττώμενος,
     διηκοσίῃσι βουσὶν ὑπερηκόντισα,
     τῇ δ' Ἀγροτέρᾳ κατὰ χιλίων παρήνεσα   660
     εὐχὴν ποιήσασθαι χιμάρων εἰς αὔριον,
     αἱ τριχίδες εἰ γενοίαθ' ἑκατὸν τοὐβολοῦ.
     ἐκαραδόκησεν εἰς ἔμ' ἡ βουλὴ πάλιν.
     ὁ δὲ ταῦτ' ἀκούσας ἐκπλαγεὶς ἐφληνάφα.

κᾇθ' εἷλκον αὐτὸν οἱ πρυτάνεις χοἰ τοξόται,　　　665
οἱ δ' ἐθορύβουν περὶ τῶν ἀφύων ἑστηκότες·
ὁ δ' ἠντεβόλει γ' αὐτοὺς ὀλίγον μεῖναι χρόνον,
"ἵν' ἄτθ' ὁ κῆρυξ οὐκ Λακεδαίμονος λέγει
πύθησθ'· ἀφῖκται γὰρ περὶ σπονδῶν" λέγων.
οἱ δ' ἐξ ἑνὸς στόματος ἅπαντες ἀνέκραγον·　　　670
"νυνὶ περὶ σπονδῶν; ἐπειδή γ', ὦ μέλε,
ᾔσθοντο τὰς ἀφύας παρ' ἡμῖν ἀξίας.
οὐ δεόμεθα σπονδῶν· ὁ πόλεμος ἑρπέτω."
ἐκεκράγεσάν τε τοὺς πρυτάνεις ἀφιέναι·
εἶθ' ὑπερεπήδων τοὺς δρυφάκτους πανταχῇ.　　　675
ἐγὼ δὲ τὰ κορίανν' ἐπριάμην ὑποδραμὼν
ἅπαντα τά τε γήτει' ὅσ' ἦν ἐν τἀγορᾷ·
ἔπειτα ταῖς ἀφύαις ἐδίδουν ἡδύσματα
ἀποροῦσιν αὐτοῖς προῖκα κἀχαριζόμην.
οἱ δ' ὑπερεπήνουν ὑπερεπύππαζόν τέ με　　　680
ἅπαντες οὕτως ὥστε τὴν βουλὴν ὅλην
ὀβολοῦ κοριάννοις ἀναλαβὼν ἐλήλυθα.

Χο.　πάντα τοι πέπραγας οἷα χρὴ τὸν εὐτυχοῦντα·　　　[ἀντ.
ηὗρε δ' ὁ πανοῦργος ἕτερον πολὺ πανουργίαις
μείζοσι κεκασμένον καὶ δόλοισι ποικίλοις　　　685
ῥήμασίν θ' αἱμύλοις.
ἀλλ' ὅπως ἀγωνιεῖ φρόντιζε τἀπίλοιπ' ἄριστα·
συμμάχους δ' ἡμᾶς ἔχων εὔνους ἐπίστασαι πάλαι.　　　690

Αλ.　καὶ μὴν ὁ Παφλαγὼν οὑτοσὶ προσέρχεται,
ὠθῶν κολόκυμα καὶ ταράττων καὶ κυκῶν,
ὡς δὴ καταπιόμενός με. μορμώ, τοῦ θράσους.
Πα.　εἰ μή σ' ἀπολέσαιμ', εἴ τι τῶν αὐτῶν ἐμοὶ
ψευδῶν ἐνείη, διαπέσοιμι πανταχῇ.　　　695
Αλ.　ἥσθην ἀπειλαῖς, ἐγέλασα ψολοκομπίαις,
ἀπεπυδάρισα μόθωνα, περιεκόκκασα.
Πα.　οὔτοι μὰ τὴν Δήμητρά γ', εἰ μή σ' ἐκφάγω
ἐκ τῆσδε τῆς γῆς, οὐδέποτε βιώσομαι.
Αλ.　εἰ μὴ 'κφάγῃς; ἐγὼ δέ γ', εἰ μή σ' ἐκπίω,　　　700
κᾆν ἐκροφήσας αὐτὸς ἐπιδιαρραγῶ.
Πα.　ἀπολῶ σε νὴ τὴν προεδρίαν τὴν ἐκ Πύλου.
Αλ.　ἰδοὺ προεδρίαν· οἷον ὄψομαί σ' ἐγὼ
ἐκ τῆς προεδρίας ἔσχατον θεώμενον.
Πα.　ἐν τῷ ξύλῳ δήσω σε, νὴ τὸν οὐρανόν.　　　705

Αλ. ὡς ὀξύθυμος. φέρε, τί σοι δῶ καταφαγεῖν;
 ἐπὶ τῷ φάγοις ἥδιστ' ἄν; ἐπὶ βαλλαντίῳ;
Πα. ἐξαρπάσομαί σου τοῖς ὄνυξι τἄντερα.
Αλ. ἀπονυχιῶ σου τἀν πρυτανείῳ σιτία.
Πα. ἕλξω σε πρὸς τὸν δῆμον, ἵνα δῷς μοι δίκην. 710
Αλ. κἀγώ σέ γ' ἕλξω διαβαλῶ τε πλείονα.
Πα. ἀλλ', ὦ πόνηρε, σοὶ μὲν οὐδὲν πείσεται·
 ἐγὼ δ' ἐκείνου καταγελῶ γ' ὅσον θέλω.
Αλ. ὡς σφόδρα σὺ τὸν δῆμον σεαυτοῦ νενόμικας.
Πα. ἐπίσταμαι γὰρ αὐτὸν οἷς ψωμίζεται. 715
Αλ. κᾆθ' ὥσπερ αἱ τίτθαι γε σιτίζεις κακῶς.
 μασώμενος γὰρ τῷ μὲν ὀλίγον ἐντίθης,
 αὐτὸς δ' ἐκείνου τριπλάσιον κατέσπακας.
Πα. καὶ νὴ Δί' ὑπό γε δεξιότητος τῆς ἐμῆς
 δύναμαι ποιεῖν τὸν δῆμον εὐρὺν καὶ στενόν. 720
Αλ. χὡ πρωκτὸς οὑμὸς τουτογὶ σοφίζεται.
Πα. οὐκ, ὦγάθ', ἐν βουλῇ με δόξεις καθυβρίσαι.
 ἴωμεν εἰς τὸν δῆμον.
Αλ.   οὐδὲν κωλύει.
 ἰδού. βάδιζε· μηδὲν ἡμᾶς ἰσχέτω.
Πα. ὦ Δῆμε, δεῦρ' ἔξελθε.
Αλ.   νὴ Δί', ὦ πάτερ, 725
 ἔξελθε δῆτ'.
Πα.   ὦ Δημίδιον <ὦ> φίλτατον,
 ἔξελθ', ἵν' εἰδῇς οἷα περιυβρίζομαι.

ΔΗΜΟΣ
 τίνες οἱ βοῶντες; οὐκ ἄπιτ' ἀπὸ τῆς θύρας;
 τὴν εἰρεσιώνην μου κατεσπαράξατε.
 τίς, ὦ Παφλαγών, ἀδικεῖ σε;
Πα.   διὰ σὲ τύπτομαι 730
 ὑπὸ τουτουὶ καὶ τῶν νεανίσκων.
Δημ.   τιή;
Πα. ὁτιὴ φιλῶ σ', ὦ Δῆμ', ἐραστής τ' εἰμὶ σός.
Δημ. σὺ δ' εἶ τίς ἐτεόν;
Αλ.   ἀντεραστὴς τουτουί,
 ἐρῶν πάλαι σου βουλόμενός τέ σ' εὖ ποιεῖν,
 ἄλλοι τε πολλοὶ καὶ καλοί τε κἀγαθοί. 735
 ἀλλ' οὐχ οἷοί τ' ἐσμὲν διὰ τουτονί. σὺ γὰρ
 ὅμοιος εἶ τοῖς παισὶ τοῖς ἐρωμένοις·
 τοὺς μὲν καλούς τε κἀγαθοὺς οὐ προσδέχει,

σαυτὸν δὲ λυχνοπώλαισι καὶ νευρορράφοις
καὶ σκυτοτόμοις καὶ βυρσοπώλαισιν δίδως. 740
Πα. εὖ γὰρ ποιῶ τὸν δῆμον.
Αλ. εἰπέ μοι, τί δρῶν;
Πα. ὅ τι; τοὺς στρατηγοὺς ὑποδραμὼν τοὺς ἐν Πύλῳ,
πλεύσας ἐκεῖσε, τοὺς Λάκωνας ἤγαγον.
Αλ. ἐγὼ δὲ περιπατῶν γ᾽ ἀπ᾽ ἐργαστηρίου
ἕψοντος ἑτέρου τὴν χύτραν ὑφειλόμην. 745
Πα. καὶ μὴν ποιήσας αὐτίκα μάλ᾽ ἐκκλησίαν,
ὦ Δῆμ᾽, ἵν᾽ εἰδῇς ὁπότερος νῷν ἐστί σοι
εὐνούστερος, διάκρινον, ἵνα τοῦτον φιλῇς.
Αλ. ναὶ ναί, διάκρινον δῆτα, πλὴν μὴ ᾽ν τῇ Πυκνί.
Δημ. οὐκ ἂν καθιζοίμην ἐν ἄλλῳ χωρίῳ. 750
ἀλλ᾽ εἰς τὸ πρόσθε. χρὴ παρεῖν᾽ εἰς τὴν Πύκνα.
Αλ. οἴμοι κακοδαίμων, ὡς ἀπόλωλ᾽. ὁ γὰρ γέρων
οἴκοι μὲν ἀνδρῶν ἐστι δεξιώτατος,
ὅταν δ᾽ ἐπὶ ταυτησὶ καθῆται τῆς πέτρας,
κέχηνεν ὥσπερ ἐμποδίζων ἰσχάδας. 755

Χο. νῦν δή σε πάντα δεῖ κάλων ἐξιέναι σεαυτοῦ, [στρ.
καὶ λῆμα θούριον φορεῖν καὶ λόγους ἀφύκτους,
ὅτοισι τόνδ᾽ ὑπερβαλεῖ. ποικίλος γὰρ ἀνὴρ
κἀκ τῶν ἀμηχάνων πόρους εὐμήχανος πορίζειν.
πρὸς ταῦθ᾽ ὅπως ἕξει πολὺς καὶ λαμπρὸς εἰς τὸν ἄνδρα. 760

ἀλλὰ φυλάττου, καὶ πρὶν ἐκεῖνον προσκεῖσθαί σοι πρότερος σὺ
τοὺς δελφῖνας μετεωρίζου καὶ τὴν ἄκατον παραβάλλου.
Πα. τῇ μὲν δεσποίνῃ Ἀθηναίᾳ, τῇ τῆς πόλεως μεδεούσῃ
εὔχομαι, εἰ μὲν περὶ τὸν δῆμον τὸν Ἀθηναίων γεγένημαι
βέλτιστος ἀνὴρ μετὰ Λυσικλέα καὶ Κύνναν καὶ Σαλαβακχώ, 765
ὥσπερ νυνὶ μηδὲν δράσας δειπνεῖν ἐν τῷ πρυτανείῳ·
εἰ δέ σε μισῶ καὶ μὴ περί σου μάχομαι μόνος ἀντιβεβηκώς,
ἀπολοίμην καὶ διαπρισθείην κατατμηθείην τε λέπαδνα.
Αλ. κἄγωγ᾽, ὦ Δῆμ᾽, εἰ μή σε φιλῶ καὶ μὴ στέργω, κατατμηθεὶς
ἑψοίμην ἐν περικομματίοις· κεἰ μὴ τούτοισι πέποιθας, 770
ἐπὶ ταυτησὶ κατακνησθείην ἐν μυττωτῷ μετὰ τυροῦ
καὶ τῇ κρεάγρᾳ τῶν ὀρχιπέδων ἑλκοίμην εἰς Κεραμεικόν.
Πα. καὶ πῶς ἂν ἐμοῦ μᾶλλόν σε φιλῶν, ὦ Δῆμε, γένοιτο πολίτης;
ὃς πρῶτα μὲν ἡνίκ᾽ ἐβούλευόν σοι χρήματα πλεῖστ᾽ ἀπέδειξα
ἐν τῷ κοινῷ, τοὺς μὲν στρεβλῶν, τοὺς δ᾽ ἄγχων, τοὺς δὲ μεταιτῶν, 775
οὐ φροντίζων τῶν ἰδιωτῶν οὐδενός, εἰ σοὶ χαριοίμην.

Αλ. τοῦτο μέν, ὦ Δῆμ', οὐδὲν σεμνόν· κἀγὼ γὰρ τοῦτό σε δράσω.
     ἁρπάζων γὰρ τοὺς ἄρτους σοι τοὺς ἀλλοτρίους παραθήσω.
     ὡς δ' οὐχὶ φιλεῖ σ' οὐδ' ἔστ' εὔνους, τοῦτ' αὐτό σε πρῶτα διδάξω,
     ἀλλ' ἢ διὰ τοῦτ' αὖθ' ὁτιή σου τῆς ἀνθρακιᾶς ἀπολαύει.   780
     σὲ γάρ, ὃς Μήδοισι διεξιφίσω περὶ τῆς χώρας Μαραθῶνι,
     καὶ νικήσας ἡμῖν μεγάλως ἐγγλωττοτυπεῖν παρέδωκας,
     ἐπὶ ταῖσι πέτραις οὐ φροντίζει σκληρῶς σε καθήμενον οὕτως,
     οὐχ ὥσπερ ἐγὼ ῥαψάμενός σοι τουτὶ φέρω. ἀλλ' ἐπαναίρου,
     κᾆτα καθίζου μαλακῶς, ἵνα μὴ τρίβῃς τὴν ἐν Σαλαμῖνι.   785
Δημ. ἄνθρωπε, τίς εἶ; μῶν ἔκγονος εἶ τῶν Ἁρμοδίου τις ἐκείνων;
     τοῦτό γέ τοί σου τοὔργον ἀληθῶς γενναῖον καὶ φιλόδημον.
Πα. ὡς ἀπὸ μικρῶν εὔνους αὐτῷ θωπευματίων γεγένησαι.
Αλ. καὶ σὺ γὰρ αὐτὸν πολὺ μικροτέροις τούτων δελεάσμασιν εἷλες.
Πα. καὶ μὴν εἴ πού τις ἀνὴρ ἐφάνη τῷ δήμῳ μᾶλλον ἀμύνων   790
     ἢ μᾶλλον ἐμοῦ σε φιλῶν, ἐθέλω περὶ τῆς κεφαλῆς περιδόσθαι.
Αλ. καὶ πῶς σὺ φιλεῖς, ὃς τοῦτον ὁρῶν οἰκοῦντ' ἐν ταῖς φιδάκναισι
     καὶ γυπαρίοις καὶ πυργιδίοις ἔτος ὄγδοον οὐκ ἐλεαίρεις,
     ἀλλὰ καθείρξας αὐτὸν βλίττεις; Ἀρχεπτολέμου δὲ φέροντος
     τὴν εἰρήνην ἐξεσκέδασας, τὰς πρεσβείας τ' ἀπελαύνεις   795
     ἐκ τῆς πόλεως ῥαθαπυγίζων, αἳ τὰς σπονδὰς προκαλοῦνται.
Πα. ἵνα γ' Ἑλλήνων ἄρξῃ πάντων. ἔστι γὰρ ἐν τοῖς λογίοισιν
     ὡς τοῦτον δεῖ ποτ' ἐν Ἀρκαδίᾳ πεντωβόλου ἡλιάσασθαι,
     ἢν ἀναμείνῃ· πάντως δ' αὐτὸν θρέψω 'γὼ καὶ θεραπεύσω,
     ἐξευρίσκων εὖ καὶ μιαρῶς ὁπόθεν τὸ τριώβολον ἕξει.   800
Αλ. οὐχ ἵνα γ' ἄρξῃ μὰ Δί' Ἀρκαδίας προνοούμενος, ἀλλ' ἵνα μᾶλλον
     σὺ μὲν ἁρπάζῃς καὶ δωροδοκῇς παρὰ τῶν πόλεων, ὁ δὲ δῆμος
     ὑπὸ τοῦ πολέμου καὶ τῆς ὁμίχλης ἃ πανουργεῖς μὴ καθορᾷ σου,
     ἀλλ' ὑπ' ἀνάγκης ἅμα καὶ χρείας καὶ μισθοῦ πρός σε κεχήνῃ.
     εἰ δέ ποτ' εἰς ἀγρὸν οὗτος ἀπελθὼν εἰρηναῖος διατρίψῃ,   805
     καὶ χῖδρα φαγὼν ἀναθαρρήσῃ καὶ στεμφύλῳ εἰς λόγον ἔλθῃ,
     γνώσεται οἵων ἀγαθῶν αὐτὸν τῇ μισθοφορᾷ παρεκόπτου·
     εἶθ' ἥξει σοι δριμὺς ἄγροικος, κατὰ σοῦ τὴν ψῆφον ἰχνεύων.
     ἃ σὺ γιγνώσκων τόνδ' ἐξαπατᾷς καὶ ὀνειροπολεῖς περὶ αὑτοῦ.
Πα. οὔκουν δεινὸν ταυτί σε λέγειν δῆτ' ἔστ' ἐμὲ καὶ διαβάλλειν   810
     πρὸς Ἀθηναίους καὶ τὸν δῆμον, πεποιηκότα πλείονα χρηστὰ
     νὴ τὴν Δήμητρα Θεμιστοκλέους πολλῷ περὶ τὴν πόλιν ἤδη;
Αλ. ὦ πόλις Ἄργους, κλύεθ' οἷα λέγει; σὺ Θεμιστοκλεῖ ἀντιφερίζεις;
     ὃς ἐποίησεν τὴν πόλιν ἡμῶν μεστὴν εὑρὼν ἐπιχειλῆ,
     καὶ πρὸς τούτοις ἀριστώσῃ τὸν Πειραιᾶ προσέμαξεν,   815
     ἀφελών τ' οὐδὲν τῶν ἀρχαίων ἰχθῦς καινοὺς παρέθηκεν·
     σὺ δ' Ἀθηναίους ἐζήτησας μικροπολίτας ἀποφῆναι

διατειχίζων καὶ χρησμῳδῶν, ὁ Θεμιστοκλεῖ ἀντιφερίζων.
κἀκεῖνος μὲν φεύγει τὴν γῆν, σὺ δ᾽ Ἀχιλλείων ἀπομάττει.
Πα. οὔκουν ταυτὶ δεινὸν ἀκούειν, ὦ Δῆμ᾽, ἐστίν μ᾽ ὑπὸ τούτου,   820
ὁτιή σε φιλῶ;
Δημ. παῦ παῦ᾽, οὗτος, καὶ μὴ σκέρβολλε πονηρά.
πολλοῦ δὲ πολύν με χρόνον καὶ νῦν ἐλελήθεις ἐγκρυφιάζων.
Αλ. μιαρώτατος, ὦ Δημακίδιον, καὶ πλεῖστα πανοῦργα δεδρακώς·
ὁπόταν χασμᾷ, καὶ τοὺς καυλοὺς
τῶν εὐθυνῶν ἐκκαυλίζων   825
καταβροχθίζει, κἀμφοῖν χειροῖν
μυστιλᾶται τῶν δημοσίων.
Πα. οὐ χαιρήσεις, ἀλλά σε κλέπτονθ᾽
αἱρήσω ᾽γὼ τρεῖς μυριάδας.
Αλ. τί θαλαττοκοπεῖς καὶ πλατυγίζεις,   830
μιαρώτατος ὢν περὶ τὸν δῆμον
τὸν Ἀθηναίων; καί σ᾽ ἐπιδείξω
νὴ τὴν Δήμητρ᾽, ἢ μὴ ζῴην,
δωροδοκήσαντ᾽ ἐκ Μυτιλήνης
πλεῖν ἢ μνᾶς τετταράκοντα.   835

Χο. ὦ πᾶσιν ἀνθρώποις φανεὶς μέγιστον ὠφέλημα,   [ἀντ.
ζηλῶ σε τῆς εὐγλωττίας. εἰ γὰρ ὧδ᾽ ἐποίσει,
μέγιστος Ἑλλήνων ἔσει, καὶ μόνος καθέξεις
τἀν τῇ πόλει, τῶν ξυμμάχων τ᾽ ἄρξεις ἔχων τρίαιναν,
ᾗ πολλὰ χρήματ᾽ ἐργάσει σείων τε καὶ ταράττων.   840

καὶ μὴ μεθῇς τὸν ἄνδρ᾽, ἐπειδή σοι λαβὴν δέδωκεν·
κατεργάσει γὰρ ῥᾳδίως πλευρὰς ἔχων τοιαύτας.
Πα. οὔκ, ὠγαθοί, ταῦτ᾽ ἐστί πω ταύτῃ μὰ τὸν Ποσειδῶ.
ἐμοὶ γὰρ ἔστ᾽ εἰργασμένον τοιοῦτον ἔργον ὥστε
ἁπαξάπαντας τοὺς ἐμοὺς ἐχθροὺς ἐπιστομίζειν,   845
ἕως ἂν ᾖ τῶν ἀσπίδων τῶν ἐκ Πύλου τι λοιπόν.
Αλ. ἐπίσχες ἐν ταῖς ἀσπίσιν· λαβὴν γὰρ ἐνδέδωκας.
οὐ γάρ σ᾽ ἐχρῆν, εἴπερ φιλεῖς τὸν δῆμον, ἐκ προνοίας
ταύτας ἐᾶν αὐτοῖσι τοῖς πόρπαξιν ἀνατεθῆναι.
ἀλλ᾽ ἐστὶ τοῦτ᾽, ὦ Δῆμε, μηχάνημ᾽, ἵν᾽, ἢν σὺ βούλῃ   850
τὸν ἄνδρα κολάσαι τουτονί, σοι τοῦτο μὴ ᾽γένηται.
ὁρᾷς γὰρ αὐτῷ στῖφος οἷόν ἐστι βυρσοπωλῶν
νεανιῶν· τούτους δὲ περιοικοῦσι μελιτοπῶλαι
καὶ τυροπῶλαι· τοῦτο δ᾽ εἰς ἕν ἐστι συγκεκυφός,
ὥστ᾽ εἰ σὺ βριμήσαιο καὶ βλέψειας ὀστρακίνδα,   855

  νύκτωρ καθαρπάσαντες ἂν τὰς ἀσπίδας θέοντες
  τὰς εἰσβολὰς τῶν ἀλφίτων ἂν καταλάβοιεν ἡμῶν.
Δημ. οἴμοι τάλας· ἔχουσι γὰρ πόρπακας; ὦ πονηρέ,
  ὅσον με παρεκόπτου χρόνον τοιαῦτα κρουσιδημῶν.
Πα. ὦ δαιμόνιε, μὴ τοῦ λέγοντος ἴσθι, μηδ' οἰηθῇς 860
  ἐμοῦ ποθ' εὑρήσειν φίλον βελτίον', ὅστις εἷς ὢν
  ἔπαυσα τοὺς ξυνωμότας· καί μ' οὐ λέληθεν οὐδὲν
  ἐν τῇ πόλει ξυνιστάμενον, ἀλλ' εὐθέως κέκραγα.
Αλ. ὅπερ γὰρ οἱ τὰς ἐγχέλεις θηρώμενοι πέπονθας.
  ὅταν μὲν ἡ λίμνη καταστῇ, λαμβάνουσιν οὐδέν· 865
  ἐὰν δ' ἄνω τε καὶ κάτω τὸν βόρβορον κυκῶσιν,
  αἱροῦσι· καὶ σὺ λαμβάνεις, ἢν τὴν πόλιν ταράττῃς.
  ἓν δ' εἰπέ μοι τοσουτονί· σκύτη τοσαῦτα πωλῶν
  ἔδωκας ἤδη τουτῳὶ κάττυμα παρὰ σεαυτοῦ
  ταῖς ἐμβάσιν, φάσκων φιλεῖν;
Δημ.   οὐ δῆτα μὰ τὸν Ἀπόλλω. 870
Αλ. ἔγνωκας οὖν δῆτ' αὐτὸν οἷός ἐστιν; ἀλλ' ἐγώ σοι
  ζεῦγος πριάμενος ἐμβάδων τουτὶ φορεῖν δίδωμι.
Δημ. κρίνω σ' ὅσων ἐγᾦδα περὶ τὸν δῆμον ἄνδρ' ἄριστον
  εὐνούστατόν τε τῇ πόλει καὶ τοῖσι δακτύλοισιν.
Πα. οὐ δεινὸν οὖν δῆτ' ἐμβάδας τοσουτονὶ δύνασθαι, 875
  ἐμοῦ δὲ μὴ μνείαν ἔχειν ὅσων πέπονθας; ὅστις
  ἔπαυσα τοὺς βινουμένους, τὸν Γρῦπον ἐξαλείψας.
Αλ. οὔκουν σε ταῦτα δῆτα δεινόν ἐστι πρωκτοτηρεῖν
  παῦσαί τε τοὺς βινουμένους; κοὐκ ἔσθ' ὅπως ἐκείνους
  οὐχὶ φθονῶν ἔπαυσας, ἵνα μὴ ῥήτορες γένωνται. 880
  τονδὶ δ' ὁρῶν ἄνευ χιτῶνος ὄντα τηλικοῦτον,
  οὐπώποτ' ἀμφιμασχάλου τὸν Δῆμον ἠξίωσας
  χειμῶνος ὄντος· ἀλλ' ἐγώ σοι τουτονὶ δίδωμι.
Δημ. τοιουτονὶ Θεμιστοκλῆς οὐπώποτ' ἐπενόησεν.
  καίτοι σοφὸν κἀκεῖν' ὁ Πειραιεύς· ἔμοιγε μέντοι 885
  οὐ μεῖζον εἶναι φαίνετ' ἐξεύρημα τοῦ χιτῶνος.
Πα. οἴμοι τάλας, οἵοις πιθηκισμοῖς με περιελαύνεις.
Αλ. οὔκ, ἀλλ' ὅπερ πίνων ἀνὴρ πέπονθ' ὅταν χεσείη,
  τοῖσιν τρόποις τοῖς σοῖσιν ὥσπερ βλαυτίοισι χρῶμαι.
Πα. ἀλλ' οὐχ ὑπερβαλεῖ με θωπείαις· ἐγὼ γὰρ αὐτὸν 890
  προσαμφιῶ τοδί· σὺ δ' οἴμωζ', ὦ πονήρ'.
Δημ.   ἰαιβοῖ.
  οὐκ ἐς κόρακας ἀποφθερεῖ, βύρσης κάκιστον ὄζον;
Αλ. καὶ τοῦτό <γ'> ἐπίτηδές σε περιήμπεσχ', ἵνα σ' ἀποπνίξῃ·
  καὶ πρότερον ἐπεβούλευσέ σοι. τὸν καυλὸν οἶσθ' ἐκεῖνον
  τοῦ σιλφίου τὸν ἄξιον γενόμενον;

Δημ.	οἶδα μέντοι.	895
Αλ.	ἐπίτηδες οὗτος αὐτὸν ἔσπευσ᾽ ἄξιον γενέσθαι,	
	ἵν᾽ ἐσθίοιτ᾽ ὠνούμενοι, κἄπειτ᾽ ἐν ἡλιαίᾳ	
	βδέοντες ἀλλήλους ἀποκτείνειαν οἱ δικασταί.	
Δημ.	νὴ τὸν Ποσειδῶ καὶ πρὸς ἐμὲ τοῦτ᾽ εἶπ᾽ ἀνὴρ Κόπρειος.	
Αλ.	οὐ γὰρ τόθ᾽ ὑμεῖς βδεόμενοι δήπου ᾽γένεσθε πυρροί;	900
Δημ.	καὶ νὴ Δί᾽ ἦν γε τοῦτο Πυρράνδρου τὸ μηχάνημα.	
Πα.	οἴοισί μ᾽, ὦ πανοῦργε, βωμολοχεύμασιν ταράττεις.	
Αλ.	ἡ γὰρ θεός μ᾽ ἐκέλευε νικῆσαί σ᾽ ἀλαζονείαις.	
Πα.	ἀλλ᾽ οὐχὶ νικήσεις. ἐγὼ γάρ φημί σοι παρέξειν,	
	ὦ Δῆμε, μηδὲν δρῶντι μισθοῦ τρύβλιον ῥοφῆσαι.	905
Αλ.	ἐγὼ δὲ κυλίχνιόν γέ σοι καὶ φάρμακον δίδωμι	
	τἀν τοῖσιν ἀντικνημίοις ἑλκύδρια περιαλείφειν.	
Πα.	ἐγὼ δὲ τὰς πολιάς γέ σοὐκλέγων νέον ποιήσω.	
Αλ.	ἰδού, δέχου κέρκον λαγῶ τὠφθαλμιδίω περιψῆν.	
Πα.	ἀπομυξάμενος, ὦ Δῆμέ, μου πρὸς τὴν κεφαλὴν ἀποψῶ.	910
Αλ.	ἐμοῦ μὲν οὖν.	
Πα.	ἐμοῦ μὲν οὖν.	
	ἐγώ σε ποιήσω τριη-	
	ραρχεῖν, ἀναλίσκοντα τῶν	
	σαυτοῦ, παλαιὰν ναῦν ἔχοντ᾽,	
	εἰς ἣν ἀναλῶν οὐκ ἐφέ-	915
	ξεις οὐδὲ ναυπηγούμενος·	
	διαμηχανήσομαί θ᾽ ὅπως	
	ἂν ἱστίον σαπρὸν λάβῃς.	
Αλ.	ἀνὴρ παφλάζει—παῦε παῦ᾽—	
	ὑπερζέων· ὑφελκτέον	920
	τῶν δαλίων ἀπαρυστέον	
	τε τῶν ἀπειλῶν ταυτηί.	
Πα.	δώσεις ἐμοὶ καλὴν δίκην,	
	ἱπούμενος ταῖς εἰσφοραῖς.	
	ἐγὼ γὰρ εἰς τοὺς πλουσίους	925
	σπεύσω σ᾽ ὅπως ἂν ἐγγραφῇς.	
Αλ.	ἐγὼ δ᾽ ἀπειλήσω μὲν οὐ-	
	δέν, εὔχομαι δέ σοι ταδί·	
	τὸ μὲν τάγηνον τευθίδων	
	ἐφεστάναι σίζον, σὲ δὲ	930
	γνώμην ἐρεῖν μέλλοντα περὶ	
	Μιλησίων καὶ κερδανεῖν	
	τάλαντον, ἢν κατεργάσῃ,	
	σπεύδειν ὅπως τῶν τευθίδων	

      ἐμπλήμενος φθαίης ἔτ᾽ εἰς   935
      ἐκκλησίαν ἐλθών· ἔπει-
      τα πρὶν φαγεῖν ἀνὴρ μεθή-
      κοι, καὶ σὺ τὸ τάλαντον λαβεῖν
      βουλόμενος ἐ-
      σθίων ἐπαποπνιγείης.   940
Χο.   εὖ γε νὴ τὸν Δία καὶ τὸν Ἀπόλλω καὶ τὴν Δήμητρα.
Δημ. κἀμοὶ δοκεῖ, καὶ τἆλλα γ᾽ εἶναι καταφανῶς
      ἀγαθὸς πολίτης, οἷος οὐδείς πω χρόνου
      ἀνὴρ γεγένηται τοῖσι πολλοῖς τοὐβολοῦ.   945
      σὺ δ᾽, ὦ Παφλαγών, φάσκων φιλεῖν μ᾽ ἐσκορόδισας.
      καὶ νῦν ἀπόδος τὸν δακτύλιον, ὡς οὐκέτι
      ἐμοὶ ταμιεύσεις.
Πα.   ἔχε· τοσοῦτον δ᾽ ἴσθ᾽ ὅτι,
      εἰ μή μ᾽ ἐάσεις ἐπιτροπεύειν, ἕτερος αὖ
      ἐμοῦ πανουργότερός τις ἀναφανήσεται.   950
Δημ. οὐκ ἔσθ᾽ ὅπως ὁ δακτύλιός ἐσθ᾽ οὑτοσὶ
      οὑμός· τὸ γοῦν σημεῖον ἕτερον φαίνεται.
      ἀλλ᾽ ἦ οὐ καθορῶ;
Αλ.   φέρ᾽ ἴδω, τί σοι σημεῖον ἦν;
Δημ. δημοῦ βοείου θρῖον ἐξωπτημένον.
Αλ.   οὐ τοῦτ᾽ ἔνεστιν.
Δημ.   οὐ τὸ θρῖον; ἀλλὰ τί;   955
Αλ.   λάρος κεχηνὼς ἐπὶ πέτρας δημηγορῶν.
Δημ. αἰβοῖ τάλας.
Αλ.   τί ἐστιν;
Δημ.   ἀπόφερ᾽ ἐκποδών.
      οὐ τὸν ἐμὸν εἶχεν, ἀλλὰ τὸν Κλεωνύμου.
      παρ᾽ ἐμοῦ δὲ τουτονὶ λαβὼν ταμίευέ μοι.
Πα.   μὴ δῆτά πώ γ᾽, ὦ δέσποτ᾽, ἀντιβολῶ σ᾽ ἐγώ,   960
      πρὶν ἄν γε τῶν χρησμῶν ἀκούσῃς τῶν ἐμῶν.
Αλ.   καὶ τῶν ἐμῶν νυν.
Πα.   ἀλλ᾽ ἐὰν τούτῳ πίθῃ,
      μολγὸν γενέσθαι δεῖ σε.
Αλ.   κἄν γε τουτῳί,
      ψωλὸν γενέσθαι δεῖ σε μέχρι τοῦ μυρρίνου.
Πα.   ἀλλ᾽ οἵ γ᾽ ἐμοὶ λέγουσιν ὡς ἄρξαι σε δεῖ   965
      χώρας ἁπάσης ἐστεφανωμένον ῥόδοις.
Αλ.   οὑμοὶ δέ γ᾽ αὖ λέγουσιν ὡς ἁλουργίδα
      ἔχων κατάπαστον καὶ στεφάνην ἐφ᾽ ἅρματος
      χρυσοῦ διώξεις Σμικύθην καὶ κύριον.

Δημ. καὶ μὴν ἔνεγκ᾽ αὐτοὺς ἰών, ἵν᾽ οὑτοσὶ   970
     αὐτῶν ἀκούσῃ.
Αλ.   πάνυ γε.
Δημ.   καὶ σύ νυν φέρε.
Πα. ἰδού.
Αλ.   ἰδοὺ νὴ τὸν Δί᾽· οὐδὲν κωλύει.
Χο. ἥδιστον φάος ἡμέρας   [στρ.
     ἔσται τοῖσι παροῦσι καὶ
     τοῖσιν εἰσαφικνουμένοις,   975
     ἢν Κλέων ἀπόληται.
     καίτοι πρεσβυτέρων τινῶν
     οἵων ἀργαλεωτάτων
     ἐν τῷ δείγματι τῶν δικῶν
     ἤκουσ᾽ ἀντιλεγόντων,   980
     ὡς εἰ μὴ ᾽γένεθ᾽ οὗτος ἐν
     τῇ πόλει μέγας, οὐκ ἂν ἤ-
     στην σκεύει δύο χρησίμω,
     δοῖδυξ οὐδὲ τορύνη.

     ἀλλὰ καὶ τόδ᾽ ἔγωγε θαυ-   [ἀντ.
     μάζω τῆς ὑομουσίας   986
     αὐτοῦ· φασὶ γὰρ αὐτὸν οἱ
     παῖδες οἳ ξυνεφοίτων,
     τὴν Δωριστὶ μόνην ἂν ἁρ-
     μόττεσθαι θαμὰ τὴν λύραν,   990
     ἄλλην δ᾽ οὐκ ἐθέλειν μαθεῖν·
     κᾆτα τὸν κιθαριστὴν
     ὀργισθέντ᾽ ἀπάγειν κελεύ-
     ειν, "ὡς ἁρμονίαν ὁ παῖς
     οὗτος οὐ δύναται μαθεῖν   995
     ἢν μὴ Δωροδοκιστί."

Πα. ἰδού, θέασαι· κοὐχ ἅπαντας ἐκφέρω.
Αλ. οἴμ᾽ ὡς χεσείω· κοὐχ ἅπαντας ἐκφέρω.
Δημ. ταυτὶ τί ἐστι;
Πα.   λόγια.
Δημ.   πάντ᾽;
Πα.   ἐθαύμασας;
     καὶ νὴ Δί᾽ ἔτι γέ μοῦστι κιβωτὸς πλέα.   1000
Αλ. ἐμοὶ δ᾽ ὑπερῷον καὶ ξυνοικία δύο.
Δημ. φέρ᾽ ἴδω, τίνος γάρ εἰσιν οἱ χρησμοί ποτε;

Πα. οὑμοὶ μέν εἰσι Βάκιδος.
Δημ.   οἱ δὲ σοὶ τίνος;
Αλ. Γλάνιδος, ἀδελφοῦ τοῦ Βάκιδος γεραιτέρου.
Δημ. εἰσὶν δὲ περὶ τοῦ;
Πα.   περὶ Ἀθηνῶν, περὶ Πύλου,   1005
       περὶ σοῦ, περὶ ἐμοῦ, περὶ ἁπάντων πραγμάτων.
Δημ. οἱ σοὶ δὲ περὶ τοῦ;
Αλ.   περὶ Ἀθηνῶν, περὶ φακῆς,
       περὶ Λακεδαιμονίων, περὶ σκόμβρων νέων,
       περὶ τῶν μετρούντων τἄλφιτ᾽ ἐν ἀγορᾷ κακῶς,
       περὶ σοῦ, περὶ ἐμοῦ. τὸ πέος οὑτοσὶ δάκοι.   1010
Δημ. ἄγε νυν ὅπως αὐτοὺς ἀναγνώσεσθέ μοι,
       καὶ τὸν περὶ ἐμοῦ ᾽κεῖνον ᾧπερ ἥδομαι,
       ὡς ἐν νεφέλησιν αἰετὸς γενήσομαι.
Πα. ἄκουε δή νυν καὶ πρόσεχε τὸν νοῦν ἐμοί.
       "φράζευ, Ἐρεχθεΐδη, λογίων ὁδόν, ἥν σοι Ἀπόλλων   1015
       ἴαχεν ἐξ ἀδύτοιο διὰ τριπόδων ἐριτίμων.
       σῴζεσθαί σ᾽ ἐκέλευ᾽ ἱερὸν κύνα καρχαρόδοντα,
       ὃς πρὸ σέθεν χάσκων καὶ ὑπὲρ σοῦ δεινὰ κεκραγὼς
       σοὶ μισθὸν ποριεῖ· κἂν μὴ δρᾷ ταῦτ᾽, ἀπολεῖται.
       πολλοὶ γὰρ μίσει σφε κατακρώζουσι κολοιοί."   1020
Δημ. ταυτὶ μὰ τὴν Δήμητρ᾽ ἐγὼ οὐκ οἶδ᾽ ὅ τι λέγει.
       τί γάρ ἐστ᾽ Ἐρεχθεῖ καὶ κολοιοῖς καὶ κυνί;
Πα. ἐγὼ μέν εἰμ᾽ ὁ κύων· πρὸ σοῦ γὰρ ἀπύω·
       σοὶ δ᾽ εἶπε σῴζεσθαί μ᾽ ὁ Φοῖβος τὸν κύνα.
Αλ. οὐ τοῦτό φησ᾽ ὁ χρησμός, ἀλλ᾽ ὁ κύων ὁδὶ   1025
       ὥσπερ θύρας σου τῶν λογίων παρεσθίει.
       ἐμοὶ γάρ ἐστ᾽ ὀρθῶς περὶ τούτου τοῦ κυνός.
Δημ. λέγε νυν· ἐγὼ δὲ πρῶτα λήψομαι λίθον,
       ἵνα μή μ᾽ ὁ χρησμὸς ὁ περὶ τοῦ κυνὸς δάκῃ.
Αλ. "φράζευ, Ἐρεχθεΐδη, κύνα Κέρβερον ἀνδραποδιστήν,   1030
       ὃς κέρκῳ σαίνων σ᾽, ὁπόταν δειπνῇς, ἐπιτηρῶν
       ἐξέδεταί σου τοὔψον, ὅταν σύ ποι ἄλλοσε χάσκῃς·
       εἰσφοιτῶν τ᾽ εἰς τοὐπτάνιον λήσει σε κυνηδὸν
       νύκτωρ τὰς λοπάδας καὶ τὰς νήσους διαλείχων."
Δημ. νὴ τὸν Ποσειδῶ πολύ γ᾽ ἄμεινον, ὦ Γλάνι.   1035
Πα. ὦ τᾶν, ἄκουσον, εἶτα διάκρινον τόδε·
       "ἔστι γυνή, τέξει δὲ λέονθ᾽ ἱεραῖς ἐν Ἀθήναις,
       ὃς περὶ τοῦ δήμου πολλοῖς κώνωψι μαχεῖται
       ὥς τε περὶ σκύμνοισι βεβηκώς· τὸν σὺ φύλαξαι,
       τεῖχος ποιήσας ξύλινον πύργους τε σιδηροῦς."   1040
       ταῦτ᾽ οἶσθ᾽ ὅ τι λέγει;

Δημ.　　　　　μὰ τὸν Ἀπόλλω ’γὼ μὲν οὔ.
Πα.　ἔφραζεν ὁ θεός σοι σαφῶς σῴζειν ἐμέ·
　　　ἐγὼ γὰρ ἀντὶ τοῦ λέοντός εἰμί σοι.
Δημ.　καὶ πῶς μ’ ἐλελήθεις Ἀντιλέων γεγενημένος;
Αλ.　ἐν οὐκ ἀναδιδάσκει σε τῶν λογίων ἑκών,　　　　　1045
　　　ὃ μόνον σιδήρου τεῖχός ἐστι καὶ ξύλων,
　　　ἐν ᾧ σε σῴζειν τόνδ’ ἐκέλευ’ ὁ Λοξίας.
Δημ.　πῶς δῆτα τοῦτ’ ἔφραζεν ὁ θεός;
Αλ.　　　　　τουτονὶ
　　　δῆσαί σ’ ἐκέλευ’ ἐν πεντεσυρίγγῳ ξύλῳ.
Δημ.　ταυτὶ τελεῖσθαι τὰ λόγι’ ἤδη μοι δοκεῖ.　　　　　1050
Πα.　μὴ πείθου· φθονεραὶ γὰρ ἐπικρώζουσι κορῶναι.
　　　“ἀλλ’ ἱέρακα φίλει μεμνημένος ἐν φρεσίν, ὅς σοι
　　　ἤγαγε συνδήσας Λακεδαιμονίων κορακίνους.”
Αλ.　τοῦτό γέ τοι Παφλαγὼν παρεκινδύνευσε μεθυσθείς.
　　　“Κεκροπίδη κακόβουλε, τί τοῦθ’ ἡγεῖ μέγα τοὔργον;　　　1055
　　　καί κε γυνὴ φέροι ἄχθος, ἐπεί κεν ἀνὴρ ἀναθείη·
　　　ἀλλ’ οὐκ ἂν μαχέσαιτο· χέσαιτο γάρ, εἰ μαχέσαιτο.”
Πα.　ἀλλὰ τόδε φράσσαι, πρὸ Πύλου Πύλον ἥν σοι ἔφραζεν.
　　　“ἔστι Πύλος πρὸ Πύλοιο—”
Δημ.　　　　　τί τοῦτο λέγει, “πρὸ Πύλοιο”;
Αλ.　τὰς πυέλους φησὶν καταλήψεσθ’ ἐν βαλανείῳ.　　　　　1060
Δημ.　ἐγὼ δ’ ἄλουτος τήμερον γενήσομαι;
Αλ.　οὗτος γὰρ ἡμῶν τὰς πυέλους ὑφαρπάσει.
　　　ἀλλ’ οὑτοσὶ γάρ ἐστι περὶ τοῦ ναυτικοῦ
　　　ὁ χρησμός, ᾧ σε δεῖ προσέχειν τὸν νοῦν πάνυ.
Δημ.　προσέχω· σὺ δ’ ἀναγίγνωσκε, τοῖς ναύταισί μου　　　1065
　　　ὅπως ὁ μισθὸς πρῶτον ἀποδοθήσεται.
Αλ.　“Αἰγεΐδη, φράσσαι κυναλώπεκα, μή σε δολώσῃ,
　　　λαίθαργον, ταχύπουν, δολίαν κερδώ, πολύιδριν.”
　　　οἶσθ’ ὅ τι ἐστὶν τοῦτο;
Δημ.　　　　　Φιλόστρατος ἡ κυναλώπηξ.
Αλ.　οὐ τοῦτό φησιν, ἀλλὰ ναῦς ἑκάστοθ’ ἃς　　　　　1070
　　　αἰτεῖ ταχείας ἀργυρολόγους οὑτοσί,
　　　ταύτας ἀπαυδᾷ μὴ διδόναι σ’ ὁ Λοξίας.
Δημ.　πῶς δὴ τριήρης ἐστὶ κυναλώπηξ;
Αλ.　　　　　ὅπως;
　　　ὅτι ἡ τριήρης ἐστὶ χὠ κύων ταχύ.
Δημ.　πῶς οὖν ἀλώπηξ προσετέθη πρὸς τῷ κυνί;　　　　　1075
Αλ.　ἀλωπεκίοισι τοὺς στρατιώτας ἤκασεν,
　　　ὅτιὴ βότρυς τρώγουσιν ἐν τοῖς χωρίοις.

Δημ. εἶέν.
τούτοις ὁ μισθὸς τοῖς ἀλωπεκίοισι ποῦ;
Αλ. ἐγὼ ποριῶ, καὶ τοῦτον ἡμερῶν τριῶν.
"ἀλλ' ἔτι τόνδ' ἐπάκουσον, ὃν εἶπέ σοι ἐξαλέασθαι   1080
χρησμὸν Λητοΐδης Κυλλήνην, μή σε δολώσῃ."
Δημ. ποίαν Κυλλήνην;
Αλ.   τὴν τούτου χεῖρ' ἐποίησεν
Κυλλήνην ὀρθῶς, ὁτιή φησ' "ἔμβαλε κυλλῇ."
Πα. οὐκ ὀρθῶς φράζει· τὴν Κυλλήνην γὰρ ὁ Φοῖβος
εἰς τὴν χεῖρ' ὀρθῶς ᾐνίξατο τὴν Διοπείθους.   1085
ἀλλὰ γάρ ἐστιν ἐμοὶ χρησμὸς περὶ σοῦ πτερυγωτός,
αἰετὸς ὡς γίγνει καὶ πάσης γῆς βασιλεύεις.
Αλ. καὶ γὰρ ἐμοί· καὶ γῆς καὶ τῆς Ἐρυθρᾶς γε θαλάσσης,
χὥτι γ' ἐν Ἐκβατάνοις δικάσεις, λείχων ἐπίπαστα.
Πα. ἀλλ' ἐγὼ εἶδον ὄναρ, καί μοὐδόκει ἡ θεὸς αὐτὴ   1090
τοῦ δήμου καταχεῖν ἀρυταίνῃ πλουθυγίειαν.
Αλ. νὴ Δία καὶ γὰρ ἐγώ· καί μοὐδόκει ἡ θεὸς αὐτὴ
ἐκ πόλεως ἐλθεῖν καὶ γλαῦξ αὐτῇ 'πικαθῆσθαι·
εἶτα κατασπένδειν κατὰ τῆς κεφαλῆς ἀρυβάλλῳ
ἀμβροσίαν κατὰ σοῦ, κατὰ τούτου δὲ σκοροδάλμην.   1095
Δημ. ἰοὺ ἰού.
οὐκ ἦν ἄρ' οὐδεὶς τοῦ Γλάνιδος σοφώτερος.
καὶ νῦν ἐμαυτὸν ἐπιτρέπω σοι τουτονὶ
γεροντἀγωγεῖν κἀναπαιδεύειν πάλιν.
Πα. μήπω γ', ἱκετεύω σ', ἀλλ' ἀνάμεινον, ὡς ἐγὼ   1100
κριθὰς ποριῶ σοι καὶ βίον καθ' ἡμέραν.
Δημ. οὐκ ἀνέχομαι κριθῶν ἀκούων· πολλάκις
ἐξηπατήθην ὑπό τε σοῦ καὶ Θουφάνους.
Πα. ἀλλ' ἄλφιτ' ἤδη σοι ποριῶ 'σκευασμένα.
Αλ. ἐγὼ δὲ μαζίσκας γε διαμεμαγμένας   1105
καὶ τοὔψον ὀπτόν· μηδὲν ἄλλ' εἰ μὴ 'σθιε.
Δημ. ἀνύσατέ νυν ὅ τι περ ποιήσεθ'· ὡς ἐγώ,
ὁπότερος ἂν σφῷν εὖ με μᾶλλον ἂν ποιῇ,
τούτῳ παραδώσω τῆς Πυκνὸς τὰς ἡνίας.
Πα. τρέχοιμ' ἂν εἴσω πρότερος.
Αλ.   οὐ δῆτ', ἀλλ' ἐγώ.   1110

Χο. ὦ Δῆμε, καλήν γ' ἔχεις   [στρ.
ἀρχήν, ὅτε πάντες ἄν-
θρωποι δεδίασί σ' ὥσ-
περ ἄνδρα τύραννον.
ἀλλ' εὐπαράγωγος εἶ,   1115

θωπευόμενός τε χαί-
ρεις κἀξαπατώμενος,
πρὸς τόν τε λέγοντ᾽ ἀεὶ
κέχηνας· ὁ νοῦς δέ σου
παρὼν ἀποδημεῖ. 1120
Δημ. νοῦς οὐκ ἔνι ταῖς κόμαις
ὑμῶν, ὅτε μ᾽ οὐ φρονεῖν
νομίζετ᾽· ἐγὼ δ᾽ ἑκὼν
ταῦτ᾽ ἠλιθιάζω.
αὐτός τε γὰρ ἥδομαι 1125
βρύλλων τὸ καθ᾽ ἡμέραν,
κλέπτοντά τε βούλομαι
τρέφειν ἕνα προστάτην·
τοῦτον δ᾽, ὅταν ᾖ πλέως,
ἄρας ἐπάταξα. 1130

Χο. οὕτω μὲν ἄρ᾽ εὖ ποιεῖς, [ἀντ.
καί σοι πυκνότης ἔνεστ᾽
ἐν τῷ τρόπῳ, ὡς λέγεις,
τούτῳ πάνυ πολλή,
εἰ τούσδ᾽ ἐπίτηδες ὥσ- 1135
περ δημοσίους τρέφεις
ἐν τῇ Πυκνί, κᾆθ᾽ ὅταν
μή σοι τύχῃ ὄψον ὄν,
τούτων ὅς ἂν ᾖ παχύς,
θύσας ἐπιδειπνεῖς. 1140
Δημ. σκέψασθε δέ μ᾽, εἰ σοφῶς
αὐτοὺς περιέρχομαι,
τοὺς οἰομένους φρονεῖν
κἄμ᾽ ἐξαπατύλλειν.
τηρῶ γὰρ ἑκάστοτ᾽ αὐ- 1145
τούς, οὐδὲ δοκῶν ὁρᾶν,
κλέπτοντας· ἔπειτ᾽ ἀναγ-
κάζω πάλιν ἐξεμεῖν
ἅττ᾽ ἂν κεκλόφωσί μου,
κημὸν καταμηλῶν. 1150

Πα. ἄπαγ᾽ ἐς μακαρίαν ἐκποδών.
Αλ. σύ γ᾽, ὦ φθόρε.
Πα. ὦ Δῆμ᾽, ἐγὼ μέντοι παρεσκευασμένος
τρίπαλαι κάθημαι βουλόμενός σ᾽ εὐεργετεῖν.

Αλ. ἐγὼ δὲ δεκάπαλαί γε καὶ δωδεκάπαλαι
     καὶ χιλιόπαλαι καὶ προπαλαιπαλαίπαλαι.   1155
Δημ. ἐγὼ δὲ προσδοκῶν γε τρισμυριόπαλαι
     βδελύττομαί σφω καὶ προπαλαιπαλαίπαλαι.
Αλ. οἶσθ' οὖν ὃ δρᾶσον;
Δημ.   εἰ δὲ μή, φράσεις γε σύ.
Αλ. ἄφες ἀπὸ βαλβίδων ἐμέ τε καὶ τουτονί,
     ἵνα σ' εὖ ποιῶμεν ἐξ ἴσου.
Δημ.   δρᾶν ταῦτα χρή.   1160
     ἄπιτον.
Πα. καὶ Αλ. ἰδού.
Δημ.   θέοιτ' ἄν.
Αλ.   ὑποθεῖν οὐκ ἐῶ.
Δημ. ἀλλ' ἦ μεγάλως εὐδαιμονήσω τήμερον.
     ὑπὸ τῶν ἐραστῶν; νὴ Δί' ἦ 'γὼ θρύψομαι.
Πα. ὁρᾷς; ἐγώ σοι πρότερος ἐκφέρω δίφρον.
Αλ. ἀλλ' οὐ τράπεζαν, ἀλλ' ἐγὼ προτεραίτερος.   1165
Πα. ἰδού, φέρω σοι τήνδε μαζίσκην ἐγὼ
     ἐκ τῶν ὀλῶν τῶν ἐκ Πύλου μεμαγμένην.
Αλ. ἐγὼ δὲ μυστίλας μεμυστιλημένας
     ὑπὸ τῆς θεοῦ τῇ χειρὶ τηλεφαντίνῃ.
Δημ. ὡς μέγαν ἄρ' εἶχες, ὦ πότνια, τὸν δάκτυλον.   1170
Πα. ἐγὼ δ' ἔτνος γε πίσινον εὔχρων καὶ καλόν·
     ἐτόρυνε δ' αὔθ' ἡ Παλλὰς ἡ Πυλαιμάχος.
Αλ. ὦ Δῆμ', ἐναργῶς ἡ θεός σ' ἐπισκοπεῖ,
     καὶ νῦν ὑπερέχει σου χύτραν ζωμοῦ πλέαν.
Δημ. οἴει γὰρ οἰκεῖσθ' ἂν ἔτι τήνδε τὴν πόλιν,   1175
     εἰ μὴ φανερῶς ἡμῶν ὑπερεῖχε τὴν χύτραν;
Πα. τουτὶ τέμαχός σοὔδωκεν ἡ Φοβεσιστράτη.
Αλ. ἡ δ' Ὀβριμοπάτρα γ' ἐφθὸν ἐκ ζωμοῦ κρέας
     καὶ χόλικος ἠνύστρου τε καὶ γαστρὸς τόμον.
Δημ. καλῶς γ' ἐποίησε τοῦ πέπλου μεμνημένη.   1180
Πα. ἡ Γοργολόφα σ' ἐκέλευε τουτουὶ φαγεῖν
     ἐλατῆρος, ἵνα τὰς ναῦς ἐλαύνωμεν καλῶς.
Αλ. λαβὲ καὶ ταδί νυν.
Δημ.   καὶ τί τούτοις χρήσομαι
     τοῖς ἐντέροις;
Αλ.   ἐπίτηδες αὕτ' ἔπεμψέ σοι
     εἰς τὰς τριήρεις ἐντερόνειαν ἡ θεός·   1185
     ἐπισκοπεῖ γὰρ περιφανῶς τὸ ναυτικόν.
     ἔχε καὶ πιεῖν κεκραμένον τρία καὶ δύο.

Δημ. ὡς ἡδύς, ὦ Ζεῦ, καὶ τὰ τρία φέρων καλῶς.
Αλ. ἡ Τριτογενὴς γὰρ αὐτὸν ἐνετριτώνισεν.
Πα. λαβέ νυν πλακοῦντος πίονος παρ' ἐμοῦ τόμον.   1190
Αλ. παρ' ἐμοῦ δ' ὅλον γε τὸν πλακοῦντα τουτονί.
Πα. ἀλλ' οὐ λαγῷ' ἕξεις ὁπόθεν δῷς, ἀλλ' ἐγώ.
Αλ. οἴμοι, πόθεν λαγῷά μοι γενήσεται;
   ὦ θυμέ, νυνὶ βωμολόχον ἔξευρέ τι.
Πα. ὁρᾷς τάδ', ὦ κακόδαιμον;
Αλ.   ὀλίγον μοι μέλει·   1195
   ἐκεινοιὶ γὰρ ὡς ἔμ' ἔρχονταί τινες
   πρέσβεις ἔχοντες ἀργυρίου βαλλάντια.
Πα. ποῦ ποῦ;
Αλ.   τί δὲ σοὶ τοῦτ'; οὐκ ἐάσεις τοὺς ξένους;
   ὦ Δημίδιον, ὁρᾷς τὰ λαγῷ' ἅ σοι φέρω;
Πα. οἴμοι τάλας, ἀδίκως γε τἄμ' ὑφήρπασας.   1200
Αλ. νὴ τὸν Ποσειδῶ, καὶ σὺ γὰρ τοὺς ἐκ Πύλου.
Δημ. εἴπ', ἀντιβολῶ, πῶς ἐπενόησας ἁρπάσαι;
Αλ. τὸ μὲν νόημα τῆς θεοῦ, τὸ δὲ κλέμμ' ἐμόν.
Πα. ἐγὼ δ' ἐκινδύνευσ', ἐγὼ δ' ὤπτησά γε.
Δημ. ἄπιθ'· οὐ γὰρ ἀλλὰ τοῦ παραθέντος ἡ χάρις.   1205
Πα. οἴμοι κακοδαίμων, ὑπεραναιδευθήσομαι.
Αλ. τί οὐ διακρίνεις, Δῆμ', ὁπότερός ἐστι νῷν
   ἀνὴρ ἀμείνων περὶ σὲ καὶ τὴν γαστέρα;
Δημ. τῷ δῆτ' ἂν ὑμᾶς χρησάμενος τεκμηρίῳ
   δόξαιμι κρίνειν τοῖς θεαταῖσιν σοφῶς;   1210
Αλ. ἐγὼ φράσω σοι. τὴν ἐμὴν κίστην ἰὼν
   ξύλλαβε σιωπῇ καὶ βασάνισον ἅττ' ἔνι,
   καὶ τὴν Παφλαγόνος· κἀμέλει κρινεῖς καλῶς.
Δημ. φέρ' ἴδω, τί οὖν ἔνεστιν;
Αλ.   οὐχ ὁρᾷς κενήν,
   ὦ παππίδιον; ἅπαντα γάρ σοι παρεφόρουν.   1215
Δημ. αὕτη μὲν ἡ κίστη τὰ τοῦ δήμου φρονεῖ.
Αλ. βάδιζέ νυν καὶ δεῦρο πρὸς τὴν Παφλαγόνος.
   ὁρᾷς <τάδ';>
Δημ.   οἴμοι, τῶν ἀγαθῶν ὅσων πλέα.
   ὅσον τὸ χρῆμα τοῦ πλακοῦντος ἀπέθετο·
   ἐμοὶ δ' ἔδωκεν ἀποτεμὼν τυννουτονί.   1220
Αλ. τοιαῦτα μέντοι καὶ πρότερόν σ' ἠργάζετο·
   σοὶ μὲν προσεδίδου μικρὸν ὧν ἐλάμβανεν,
   αὐτὸς δ' ἑαυτῷ παρετίθει τὰ μείζονα.

Δημ. ὦ μιαρέ, κλέπτων δή με ταῦτ' ἐξηπάτας;
ἐγὼ δέ τυ ἐστεφάνιξα κἠδωρησάμαν.   1225
Πα. ἐγὼ δ' ἔκλεπτον ἐπ' ἀγαθῷ γε τῇ πόλει.
Δημ. κατάθου ταχέως τὸν στέφανον, ἵν' ἐγὼ τουτῳὶ
αὐτὸν περιθῶ.
Αλ.   κατάθου ταχέως, μαστιγία.
Πα. οὐ δῆτ', ἐπεί μοι χρησμός ἐστι Πυθικὸς
φράζων ὑφ' οὗ δεῖ μ' ἀνδρὸς ἡττᾶσθαι μόνου.   1230
Αλ. τοὐμόν γε φράζων ὄνομα καὶ λίαν σαφῶς.
Πα. καὶ μήν σ' ἐλέγξαι βούλομαι τεκμηρίῳ,
εἴ τι ξυνοίσεις τοῦ θεοῦ τοῖς θεσφάτοις.
καί σου τοσοῦτο πρῶτον ἐκπειράσομαι·
παῖς ὢν ἐφοίτας εἰς τίνος διδασκάλου;   1235
Αλ. ἐν ταῖσιν εὔστραις κονδύλοις ἡρμοττόμην.
Πα. πῶς εἶπας; ὥς μού χρησμὸς ἅπτεται φρενῶν.
εἶέν.
ἐν παιδοτρίβου δὲ τίνα πάλην ἐμάνθανες;
Αλ. κλέπτων ἐπιορκεῖν καὶ βλέπειν ἐναντία·
Πα. ὦ Φοῖβ' Ἄπολλον Λύκιε, τί ποτέ μ' ἐργάσει;   1240
τέχνην δὲ τίνα ποτ' εἶχες ἐξανδρούμενος;
Αλ. ἠλλαντοπώλουν καί τι καὶ βινεσκόμην.
Πα. οἴμοι κακοδαίμων· οὐκέτ' οὐδέν εἰμ' ἐγώ.
λεπτή τις ἐλπίς ἐστ' ἐφ' ἧς ὀχούμεθα.
καί μοι τοσοῦτον εἰπέ· πότερον ἐν ἀγορᾷ   1245
ἠλλαντοπώλεις ἐτεὸν ἢ 'πὶ ταῖς πύλαις;
Αλ. ἐπὶ ταῖς πύλαισιν, οὗ τὸ τάριχος ὤνιον.
Πα. οἴμοι, πέπρακται τοῦ θεοῦ τὸ θέσφατον.
κυλίνδετ' εἴσω τόνδε τὸν δυσδαίμονα.
ὦ στέφανε, χαίρων ἄπιθι· καί σ' ἄκων ἐγὼ   1250
λείπω· σὲ δ' ἄλλος τις λαβὼν κεκτήσεται,
κλέπτης μὲν οὐκ ἂν μᾶλλον, εὐτυχὴς δ' ἴσως.
Αλ. Ἑλλάνιε Ζεῦ, σὸν τὸ νικητήριον.
Δη. ὦ χαῖρε, καλλίνικε, καὶ μέμνησ' ὅτι
ἀνὴρ γεγένησαι δι' ἐμέ· καί σ' αἰτῶ βραχύ,   1255
ὅπως ἔσομαί σοι Φᾶνος, ὑπογραφεὺς δικῶν.
Δημ. ἐμοὶ δέ γ' ὅ τι σοι τοὔνομ' εἴπ'.
Αλ.   Ἀγοράκριτος·
ἐν τἀγορᾷ γὰρ κρινόμενος ἐβοσκόμην.
Δημ. Ἀγορακρίτῳ τοίνυν ἐμαυτὸν ἐπιτρέπω
καὶ τὸν Παφλαγόνα παραδίδωμι τουτονί.   1260

Αλ.	καὶ μὴν ἐγώ σ᾽, ὦ Δῆμε, θεραπεύσω καλῶς,
	ὥσθ᾽ ὁμολογεῖν σε μηδέν᾽ ἀνθρώπων ἐμοῦ
	ἰδεῖν ἀμείνω τῇ Κεχηναίων πόλει.

Χο.	τί κάλλιον ἀρχομένοισιν ἢ καταπαυομένοισιν	[στρ.
	ἢ θοᾶν ἵππων ἐλατῆρας ἀείδειν	1266
	μηδὲν εἰς Λυσίστρατον,
	μηδὲ Θούμαντιν τὸν ἀνέστιον αὖ
	λυπεῖν ἑκούσῃ καρδίᾳ;
	καὶ γὰρ οὗτος, ὦ φίλ᾽ Ἄπολλον, <ἀεὶ>	1270
	πεινῇ, θαλεροῖς δακρύοις
	σᾶς ἁπτόμενος φαρέτρας
	Πυθῶνι δίᾳ μὴ κακῶς πένεσθαι.

	λοιδορῆσαι τοὺς πονηροὺς οὐδέν ἐστ᾽ ἐπίφθονον,
	ἀλλὰ τιμὴ τοῖσι χρηστοῖς, ὅστις εὖ λογίζεται.	1275
	εἰ μὲν οὖν ἄνθρωπος, ὃν δεῖ πόλλ᾽ ἀκοῦσαι καὶ κακά,
	αὐτὸς ἦν ἔνδηλος, οὐκ ἂν ἀνδρὸς ἐμνήσθην φίλου.
	νῦν δ᾽ Ἀρίγνωτον γὰρ οὐδεὶς ὅστις οὐκ ἐπίσταται,
	ὅστις ἢ τὸ λευκὸν οἶδεν ἢ τὸν ὄρθιον νόμον.
	ἔστιν οὖν ἀδελφὸς αὐτῷ τοὺς τρόπους οὐ συγγενής,	1280
	Ἀριφράδης πονηρός. ἀλλὰ τοῦτο μὲν καὶ βούλεται·
	ἔστι δ᾽ οὐ μόνον πονηρός, οὐ γὰρ οὐδ᾽ ἂν ᾐσθόμην,
	οὐδὲ παμπόνηρος, ἀλλὰ καὶ προσεξηύρηκέ τι.
	τὴν γὰρ αὑτοῦ γλῶτταν αἰσχραῖς ἡδοναῖς λυμαίνεται,
	ἐν κασωρείοισι λείχων τὴν ἀπόπτυστον δρόσον,	1285
	καὶ μολύνων τὴν ὑπήνην καὶ κυκῶν τὰς ἐσχάρας,
	καὶ Πολυμνήστεια ποιῶν καὶ ξυνῶν Οἰωνίχῳ.
	ὅστις οὖν τοιοῦτον ἄνδρα μὴ σφόδρα βδελύττεται,
	οὔποτ᾽ ἐκ ταὐτοῦ μεθ᾽ ἡμῶν πίεται ποτηρίου.	1289

	ἦ πολλάκις ἐννυχίαισι φροντίσι συγγεγένημαι,	[ἀντ.
	καὶ διεζήτηχ᾽ ὁπόθεν ποτὲ φαύλως
	ἐσθίει Κλεώνυμος.
	φασὶ γάρ <ποτ᾽> αὐτὸν ἐρεπτόμενον
	τὰ τῶν ἐχόντων ἀνέρων	1295
	οὐκ ἂν ἐξελθεῖν ἀπὸ τῆς σιπύης·
	τοὺς δ᾽ ἀντιβολεῖν ἂν ὁμῶς·
	"ἴθ᾽, ὦ ἄνα, πρὸς γονάτων,
	ἔξελθε καὶ σύγγνωθι τῇ τραπέζῃ."

φασὶν ἀλλήλαις ξυνελθεῖν τὰς τριήρεις εἰς λόγον,   1300
καὶ μίαν λέξαι τιν᾿ αὐτῶν, ἥτις ἦν γεραιτέρα·
"οὐδὲ πυνθάνεσθε ταῦτ᾿, ὦ παρθένοι, τὰν τῇ πόλει;
φασὶν αἰτεῖσθαί τιν᾿ ἡμῶν ἑκατὸν εἰς Καρχηδόνα,
ἄνδρα μοχθηρὸν πολίτην, ὀξίνην Ὑπέρβολον·"
ταῖς δὲ δόξαι δεινὸν εἶναι τοῦτο κοὐκ ἀνασχετόν,   1305
καί τιν᾿ εἰπεῖν, ἥτις ἀνδρῶν ἆσσον οὐκ ἐληλύθει·
"ἀποτρόπαι᾿, οὐ δῆτ᾿ ἐμοῦ γ᾿ ἄρξει ποτ᾿, ἀλλ᾿ ἐάν με χρῇ,
ὑπὸ τερηδόνων σαπεῖσ᾿ ἐνταῦθα καταγηράσομαι."—
"οὐδὲ Ναυφάντης γε τῆς Ναύσωνος, οὐ δῆτ᾿, ὦ θεοί,
εἴπερ ἐκ πεύκης γε κἀγὼ καὶ ξύλων ἐπηγνύμην.   1310
ἢν δ᾿ ἀρέσκῃ ταῦτ᾿ Ἀθηναίοις, καθῆσθαί μοι δοκῶ
εἰς τὸ Θησεῖον πλεούσας ἢ ᾿πὶ τῶν Σεμνῶν θεῶν.
οὐ γὰρ ἡμῶν γε στρατηγῶν ἐγχανεῖται τῇ πόλει·
ἀλλὰ πλείτω χωρὶς αὐτὸς ἐς κόρακας, εἰ βούλεται,
τὰς σκάφας, ἐν αἷς ἐπώλει τοὺς λύχνους, καθελκύσας."   1315

Αλ. εὐφημεῖν χρὴ καὶ στόμα κλῇειν καὶ μαρτυριῶν ἀπέχεσθαι,
     καὶ τὰ δικαστήρια συγκλῄειν, οἷς ἡ πόλις ἥδε γέγηθεν,
     ἐπὶ καιναῖσιν δ᾿ εὐτυχίαισιν παιωνίζειν τὸ θέατρον.
Χο. ὦ ταῖς ἱεραῖς φέγγος Ἀθήναις καὶ ταῖς νήσοις ἐπίκουρε,
     τίν᾿ ἔχων φήμην ἀγαθὴν ἥκεις, ἐφ᾿ ὅτῳ κνισῶμεν ἀγυιάς;   1320
Αλ. τὸν Δῆμον ἀφεψήσας ὑμῖν καλὸν ἐξ αἰσχροῦ πεποίηκα.
Χο. καὶ ποῦ ᾿στιν νῦν, ὦ θαυμαστὰς ἐξευρίσκων ἐπινοίας;
Αλ. ἐν ταῖσιν ἰοστεφάνοις οἰκεῖ ταῖς ἀρχαίαισιν Ἀθήναις.
Χο. πῶς ἂν ἴδοιμεν; ποίαν <τιν᾿> ἔχει σκευήν; ποῖος γεγένηται;
Αλ. οἷός περ Ἀριστείδῃ πρότερον καὶ Μιλτιάδῃ ξυνεσίτει.   1325
     ὄψεσθε δέ· καὶ γὰρ ἀνοιγνυμένων ψόφος ἤδη τῶν προπυλαίων.
     ἀλλ᾿ ὀλολύξατε φαινομέναισιν ταῖς ἀρχαίαισιν Ἀθήναις
     ταῖς θαυμασταῖς καὶ πολυύμνοις, ἵν᾿ ὁ κλεινὸς Δῆμος ἐνοικεῖ.
Χο. ὦ ταὶ λιπαραὶ καὶ ἰοστέφανοι καὶ ἀριζήλωτοι Ἀθῆναι,
     δείξατε τὸν τῆς Ἑλλάδος ἡμῖν καὶ τῆς γῆς τῆσδε μόναρχον.   1330
Αλ. ὅδ᾿ ἐκεῖνος ὁρᾶν τεττιγοφόρας, ἀρχαίῳ σχήματι λαμπρός,
     οὐ χοιρινῶν ὄζων ἀλλὰ σπονδῶν, σμύρνῃ κατάλειπτος.
Χο. χαῖρ᾿, ὦ βασιλεῦ τῶν Ἑλλήνων· καί σοι ξυγχαίρομεν ἡμεῖς.
     τῆς γὰρ πόλεως ἄξια πράττεις καὶ τοῦ ᾿ν Μαραθῶνι τροπαίου.

Δημ. ὦ φίλτατ᾿ ἀνδρῶν, ἐλθὲ δεῦρ᾿, Ἀγοράκριτε.   1335
     ὅσα με δέδρακας ἀγάθ᾿ ἀφεψήσας.
Αλ.   ἐγώ;
     ἀλλ᾿, ὦ μέλ᾿, οὐκ οἶσθ᾿ οἷος ἦσθ᾿ αὐτὸς πάρος,
     οὐδ᾿ οἷ᾿ ἔδρας· ἐμὲ γὰρ νομίζοις ἂν θεόν.

Δημ. τί δ' ἔδρων πρὸ τοῦ, κάτειπε, καὶ ποῖός τις ἦ;
Αλ. πρῶτον μέν, ὁπότ' εἴποι τις ἐν τἠκκλησίᾳ,   1340
 "ὦ Δῆμ', ἐραστής εἰμι σὸς φιλῶ τέ σε
 καὶ κήδομαί σου καὶ προβουλεύω μόνος,"
 τούτοις ὁπότε χρήσαιτό τις προοιμίοις,
 ἀνωρτάλιζες κἀκερουτίας.
Δημ.   ἐγώ;
Αλ. εἶτ' ἐξαπατήσας σ' ἀντὶ τούτων ᾤχετο.   1345
Δημ. τί φής;
 ταυτί μ' ἔδρων, ἐγὼ δὲ τοῦτ' οὐκ ᾐσθόμην;
Αλ. τὰ δ' ὦτά γ' ἄν σου νὴ Δί' ἐξεπετάννυτο
 ὥσπερ σκιάδειον καὶ πάλιν ξυνήγετο.
Δημ. οὕτως ἀνόητος ἐγεγενήμην καὶ γέρων;
Αλ. καὶ νὴ Δί' εἴ γε δύο λεγοίτην ῥήτορε,   1350
 ὁ μὲν ποιεῖσθαι ναῦς μακράς, ὁ δ' ἕτερος αὖ
 καταμισθοφορῆσαι τοῦθ', ὁ τὸν μισθὸν λέγων
 τὸν τὰς τριήρεις παραδραμὼν ἂν ᾤχετο.
 οὗτος, τί κύπτεις; οὐχὶ κατὰ χώραν μενεῖς;
Δημ. αἰσχύνομαί τοι ταῖς πρότερον ἁμαρτίαις.   1355
Αλ. ἀλλ' οὐ σὺ τούτων αἴτιος, μὴ φροντίσῃς,
 ἀλλ' οἵ σε ταῦτ' ἐξηπάτων. νυνδὶ φράσον·
 ἐάν τις εἴπῃ βωμολόχος ξυνήγορος,
 "οὐκ ἔστιν ὑμῖν τοῖς δικασταῖς ἄλφιτα,
 εἰ μὴ καταγνώσεσθε ταύτην τὴν δίκην,"   1360
 τοῦτον τί δράσεις, εἰπέ, τὸν ξυνήγορον;
Δημ. ἄρας μετέωρον εἰς τὸ βάραθρον ἐμβαλῶ,
 ἐκ τοῦ λάρυγγος ἐκκρεμάσας Ὑπέρβολον.
Αλ. τουτὶ μὲν ὀρθῶς καὶ φρονίμως ἤδη λέγεις·
 τὰ δ' ἄλλα, φέρ' ἴδω, πῶς πολιτεύσει; φράσον.   1365
Δημ. πρῶτον μὲν ὁπόσοι ναῦς ἐλαύνουσιν μακράς,
 καταγομένοις τὸν μισθὸν ἀποδώσω 'ντελῆ.
Αλ. πολλοῖς γ' ὑπολίσφοις πυγιδίοισιν ἐχαρίσω.
Δημ. ἔπειθ' ὁπλίτης ἐντεθεὶς ἐν καταλόγῳ
 οὐδεὶς κατὰ σπουδὰς μετεγγραφήσεται,   1370
 ἀλλ' οὗπερ ἦν τὸ πρῶτον ἐγγεγράψεται.
Αλ. τοῦτ' ἔδακε τὸν πόρπακα τὸν Κλεωνύμου.
Δημ. οὐδ' ἀγοράσει γ' ἀγένειος οὐδεὶς ἐν ἀγορᾷ.
Αλ. ποῦ δῆτα Κλεισθένης ἀγοράσει καὶ Στράτων;
Δημ. τὰ μειράκια ταυτὶ λέγω τἀν τῷ μύρῳ,   1375
 ἃ τοιαδὶ στωμύλλεται καθήμενα,
 "σοφός γ' ὁ Φαίαξ, δεξιῶς τ' οὐκ ἀπέθανεν.
 συνερτικὸς γάρ ἐστι καὶ περαντικός,

καὶ γνωμοτυπικὸς καὶ σαφὴς καὶ κρουστικός,
καταληπτικός τ᾽ ἄριστα τοῦ θορυβητικοῦ." 1380
Αλ. οὔκουν καταδακτυλικὸς σὺ τοῦ λαλητικοῦ;
Δημ. μὰ Δί᾽, ἀλλ᾽ ἀναγκάσω κυνηγετεῖν ἐγὼ
τούτους ἅπαντας, παυσαμένους ψηφισμάτων.
Αλ. ἔχε νυν ἐπὶ τούτοις τουτονὶ τὸν ὀκλαδίαν
καὶ παῖδ᾽ ἐνόρχην, ὃς περιοίσει τόνδε σοι· 1385
κἂν που δοκῇ σοι, τοῦτον ὀκλαδίαν ποίει.
Δημ. μακάριος εἰς τἀρχαῖα δὴ καθίσταμαι.
Αλ. φήσεις γ᾽, ἐπειδὰν τὰς τριακοντούτιδας
σπονδὰς παραδῶ σοι. δεῦρ᾽ ἴθ᾽, αἱ Σπονδαί, ταχύ.
Δημ. ὦ Ζεῦ πολυτίμηθ᾽, ὡς καλαί· πρὸς τῶν θεῶν, 1390
ἔξεστιν αὐτῶν κατατριακοντουτίσαι;
πῶς ἔλαβες αὐτὰς ἐτεόν;
Αλ.   οὐ γὰρ ὁ Παφλαγὼν
ἀπέκρυπτε ταύτας ἔνδον, ἵνα σὺ μὴ λάβῃς;
νῦν οὖν ἐγώ σοι παραδίδωμ᾽ εἰς τοὺς ἀγροὺς
αὐτὰς ἰέναι λαβόντα.
Δημ.   τὸν δὲ Παφλαγόνα, 1395
ὃς ταῦτ᾽ ἔδρασεν, εἴφ᾽ ὅ τι ποιήσεις κακόν.
Αλ. οὐδὲν μέγ᾽ ἀλλ᾽ ἢ τὴν ἐμὴν ἕξει τέχνην·
ἐπὶ ταῖς πύλαις ἀλλαντοπωλήσει μόνος,
τὰ κύνεια μιγνὺς τοῖς ὀνείοις τρώγμασιν,
μεθύων τε ταῖς πόρναισι λοιδορήσεται, 1400
κἀκ τῶν βαλανείων πίεται τὸ λούτριον.
Δημ. εὖ γ᾽ ἐπενόησας οὗπέρ ἐστιν ἄξιος,
πόρναισι καὶ βαλανεῦσι διακεκραγέναι,
καί σ᾽ ἀντὶ τούτων εἰς τὸ πρυτανεῖον καλῶ
εἰς τὴν ἕδραν θ᾽, ἵν᾽ ἐκεῖνος ἦσθ᾽ ὁ φαρμακός. 1405
ἕπου δὲ ταυτηνὶ λαβὼν τὴν βατραχίδα·
κἀκεῖνον ἐκφερέτω τις ὡς ἐπὶ τὴν τέχνην,
ἵν᾽ ἴδωσιν αὐτόν, οἷς ἐλωβᾶθ᾽, οἱ ξένοι.

Commentary

We use the Oxford text of Wilson (2007a), indicating by asterisk where our reading differs from his. Where we do differ, we follow, unless otherwise stated, the readings in the paradoses (see glossary). A semicolon following a lemma indicates a question in the text; we mark questions only when relevant to the comment. When referring to fragments in *PCG*, we use only the number of the fragment and omit individual *PCG* volume numbers. Concerning elision and crasis, we do not mark instances that are easily recognized, such as σ᾽ for σε; we do mark those instances that students may have more difficulty understanding, and then usually only the first time they occur in this commentary.

Stage setting: Two household slaves of Demos, an old Attic farmer whose name is the usual word for the Athenian people, enter from the central door of their master's house. They are dressed in conventional comic slave costumes: beard, large gaping mouth, bulbous nose, exaggerated comic padding of the belly and rump, and a leather phallus (see Stone 1981, 19–42). A large rock representing the Pnyx, the regular meeting place of the Athenian Assembly, sits off to the side of the stage. Throughout the commentary, stage directions appear in italics.

1–241. Prologue (see glossary). Meter: iambic trimeter (see "Iambic Trimeter" in the present book), except for the dactylic hexameter oracles of 197–201. The comedy opens with a characteristic cry of distress (cf. the opening of *Clouds*, *Thesmophoriazusae*, and *Wealth*). Having just suffered a beating instigated by a newly purchased Paphlagonian slave (a thin disguise for the politician Cleon [*PA* 8674; *PAA* 579130]), an unnamed slave (Slave A) rushes wailing from the house of Demos. He is accompanied by a fellow slave (Slave B) who has likewise suffered a beating. The two slaves, desperate to get rid of Paphlagon, conspire to steal oracles in his possession that prophesy the coming of a savior, a lowly sausage-seller, to champion and rescue them and their master, Demos, from an intolerable situation. We do not follow Wilson's designation of the slaves as Demosthenes and Nicias and instead refer to them as Slave A and B respectively.

1–5. Ἰατταταιὰξ . . . ἰατταταί: "Yeowowow . . . yeowowow." The suffix άξ intensifies the expression of the physical pain that seems to linger in his body (see Nordgren 2015, 109). ἰατταταί (ἀτταταῖ: see *Ach.* 1190, 1198; *Nu.* 707; *Th.* 223, ἀτταταῖ ἰατταταῖ; S. *Ph.* 743, 790) is one of several all-purpose interjections used to express pain, vexation, grief, horror, sorrow, surprise, etc. (see López Eire 1996, 89; Labriano Ilundain 2000, 97–103, 276–86). For the shift in accent from oxytone (ἰατταταί) to perispomenon (ἰατταταῖ, ἀτταταῖ), see KB 2.252.2.   **τῶν κακῶν**: "what pains!" The exclamatory genitive is often signaled by an interjection (e.g., *Ach.* 67; *Nu.* 153; *V.* 161; *Pax* 238; see Poultney 1936, 125; Stevens 1976, 61–62; López Eire 1996, 75–76). The construction is colloquial, comprised of vocabulary, phrases, constructions, etc. that are mostly absent in elevated poetry and contemporary prose but are common in daily conversation.   **κακῶς Παφλαγόνα τὸν . . . κακὸν / . . . ἀπολέσειαν οἱ θεοί**: "god-damn low-grade Paphlagon . . . may the gods destroy him." κακῶς is used idiomatically as a curse with forms of the verb ὄλλυμι (see López Eire 1996, 76; Collard 2018, 49). The adjective κακόν carries the sense of morally "wicked" as well as the sense of socially "inferior"—i.e., "descended from the inferior strata of Athenian society" (Storey 2008, 128). Slaves in comedy and tragedy nearly always utter their wishes, including curses, in the optative rather than in a carefully formulated prayer, which suggests that the curse against Paphlagon reflects how a slave actually would have made such a wish or request to the gods (see Pulleyn 1997, 171–72).   **νεώνητον**: "newly bought Paphlagon"; cf. 43n. The denigration of "newcomer" politicians (i.e., demagogues) as loathsome slaves and foreigners is a trope of fifth-century Attic comedy (e.g., *Ra.* 680–82, Cleophon as a foreigner; Eup. fr. 192, Hyperbolus as a barbarian slave; Pl. Com. frr. 182.4–7, 185, 203, Hyperbolus as a slave or foreigner by birth). The portrayal of Cleon as the exemplary demagogue in Aristophanes and Thucydides exaggerates his parvenu status, since there was considerable continuity in the public policies of Cleon and Pericles; see Henderson 2017, 613–15.   **αὐταῖσι βουλαῖς**: "along with his plans." With dative of accompaniment, αὐτός is idiomatic (Stevens 1976, 52–53) and especially associated with the destruction of the person or the thing mentioned (e.g., *V.* 119–20; *Pax* 1288; *Av.* 1257; see KG 1.433–34; Smyth §1525).   **ἐξ οὗ**: "ever since." The phrase "designates the time at which an action begins and *from which* it continues" (Poultney 1936, 163); cf. 412.   **εἰσήρρησεν**: "got inside." This is the paradosis (see glossary). In comedy, the verb ἔρρω and its compounds often suggest hostility and contempt (e.g., *V.* 1329; *Lys.* 1240; *Pax* 500), here reinforced by the curse (see Stevens 1976, 12–13; Dover 2002, 86). A scholion reports a variant, εἰσέφρησεν ("slipped in"), which Wilson (2007b, ad loc.) explains as an "unlikely gloss" given the verb's rarity; if the variant is correct, the paradosis is a gloss.   **πληγὰς ἀεὶ προστρίβεται**: "He's always inflicting on [us] slaves beatings." The middle voice stresses that "the action is carried out at the command or behest of the subject" (*AGPS* 52.11.0).

6–7. *Slave B, who has been on stage to hear what the other slave said, echoes his companion's complaint.* **κάκιστα:** Sc., ἀπόλοιτο (1–3). **δῆθ':** = δῆτα, example of elision with preceding aspirate, "yes"; an emphatic endorsement (*GP* 276), indicating that the speaker has been on stage from the beginning. **γε:** as often in comic dialogue, seems to be otiose, as the demonstrative pronoun "apparently requires no stress, or at most a secondary stress" (*GP* 122). **αὐταῖς διαβολαῖς:** Slander is a hallmark of Paphlagon's political style (e.g., 45, 63–64, 261–62, 288, 486–87, 490–91; *Ach.* 377–80, 502 [which mention Cleon explicitly]). Cf. also *V.* 950, where the character Philocleon ("Cleon lover") slanders the dog. *Slave A now speaks.* **κακόδαιμον:** "you pathetic wretch"; a mild and presumably colloquial insult (attested only once in tragedy, at E. *Hipp.* 1362) generally used contemptuously in Aristophanes (see Stevens 1976, 14–15). **πῶς ἔχεις;** "how you doing?"; a colloquialism with the same meaning as πῶς πράττεις (see Collard 2018, 95).

8–12. Kraus (1985, 119), following van Leeuwen (ad loc.), argues that the speakers' assignments in this passage should be reversed on the grounds that Slave A should not call for wailing (8–9) and then reject wailing (11–12). But there is no reason that the speaker cannot have a change of heart (see Sommerstein 2001, 239; Wilson 2001b, ad loc.).

9. ξυναυλίαν κλαύσωμεν Οὐλύμπου νόμου: "Let's wail a wind duet of Olympus." The (Phrygian?) aulos was an oboe-like instrument that provided accompaniment in poetry and various musical performances (West 1992, 91–92). The term ξυναυλία seems to denote a nonvocal performance, which is further suggested by the inarticulate noises of line 10. Olympus was a quasi-legendary figure believed to have come from Phrygia (E. *IA* 576–77, Φρυγίων / αὐλῶν Οὐλύμπου; Ps-Plu. *De mus.* 1133d, Οὐλύμπον, αὐλητὴν ὄντα τῶν ἐκ Φρυγίας) and to have introduced purely instrumental music into Greece; see Campbell (2014, 272, "Olympus" T). The rhythm (unresolved iambic trimeter) appears to be paratragic (see Rau 1967, 187).

10. μυμῦ μυμῦ μυμῦ μυμῦ μυμῦ μυμῦ: Imitating the sound of the aulos, the slaves intone a mournful duet (cf. schol. ad loc., ὡς θρηνητικόν; López Eire 1996, 91–92; Labiano Ilundain 2000, 245–46). Ordinarily, the aulos player wore an elaborately embroidered costume (for a pictorial representation, see Getty vase 82.AE.83; Greene 1994, 30; *ARV*² 1336, Pronomos vase). The sight of two shabbily dressed slave "singers" adds to the comic incongruity.

11–12. τί κινυρόμεθ' ἄλλως; "But why do we just whine [about it]?" The verb, found only here in comedy, is attested once in tragedy (A. *Th.* 123).

ἄλλως, "just, merely," is colloquial (*Ach.* 114; *Nu.* 1203; fr. 592.18; Pl. *Cri.* 46d; see Stevens 1976, 52).   **οὐκ ἐχρῆν ζητεῖν;** "shouldn't we be looking for . . . ?" The imperfect ἐχρῆν (treated as a present tense) expresses unfulfilled obligation (cf. *Th.* 74; E. *Hipp.* 467 with Barrett 1964; see KG 1.204–5).   **τινα / σωτηρίαν:** "some means of safety"; a major theme of the play (cf. 147–49n).   **ἀλλὰ μὴ:** "rather than" (e.g., Pl. *R.* 1.347c2; Smyth §2776a).   **κλάειν:** Sc., ἐχρῆν.

13–14. The effect of this exchange shows that neither of the slave characters has a clue about how to proceed or is willing to admit that (Dover 1959, 197).   **μὲν οὖν:** "No"; emphatically adversative and corrective in dialogue (e.g., Pherecr. fr. 76.2; Eup. fr. 84.2; cf. *GP* 475).   **ἵνα μὴ μάχωμαι:** "so I don't fight [about it]"; an expression often used in dialogue to mean "I won't debate/argue over" (e.g., Pl. *Cra.* 430d, ἵνα τοίνυν μὴ μαχώμεθα ἐν τοῖς λόγοις; cf. also Pl. *R.* 1.342d, ἐπεχείρει δὲ περὶ αὐτὰ μάχεσθαι). Critics who want to identify the speaker with Nicias (*PA* 10808; *PAA* 712520) see an allusion to the latter's reputation for excessive public and individual caution and timidity; see Sommerstein 1980, 46–47.   **μὰ τὸν Ἀπόλλω 'γὼ μὲν οὔ:** "By Apollo, absolutely not"; a standard oath formula of emphatic denial (*GP* 275). The phrase is repeated verbatim at 1041 and variously adapted; for examples, see Olson at *Ach.* 59–60.

17–18. ἔνι: For ἔνεστι.   **τὸ θρέττε:** The scholia (see glossary) explain the word, found only here in extant Greek literature, as a barbarism derived from θαρρεῖν, "to have courage." The term is apparently an onomatopoetic imitation of the sound of a lyre or kithara, θρεττανελο, unaccented (*Pl.* 290, 296); cf. φλαττοθραττοφλαττοθρατ, used of a musical phrase, at *Ra.* 1285–96. See López Eire 1996, 95; Labiano Ilundain 2000, 178–88.   **πῶς ἄν . . . ποτε / εἴποιμ(ι) ἄν . . . ;** "How could I ever say?" πῶς ἄν + the optative is highly emotional and expresses a hopeless wish framed as a question (e.g., 16, 140; *Ach.* 991–92; *Th.* 22–23); see KG 1.235; Gildersleeve 1900, §446. The repetition of ἄν with optatives in main clauses is probably colloquial (cf. 856–57). See KG 1.246–47; Slings 1992, 102–5.   **οὖν . . . δῆτα;** Adds a tone of surprise or indignation to a question (cf. 810, 871; *GP* 272).   **κομψευριπικῶς:** Syncopated form of κομψευριπιδικῶς; an allusion to Euripides' name and a parody of his reputation for theatrical and verbal ingenuity (κομψός = "witty," "clever"). Adjectives (and presumably adverbs) in -ικός were a characteristic of the language of philosophers, orators, sophists, and their acolytes (cf. 545–46, 1378–80); see Willi 2003, 139–45. By the late fifth century, such usage had become characteristic of the languages of technology and administration (Peppler 1910; Dover 1987, 229).

16. "πῶς ἂν σύ μοι λέξειας ἁμὲ χρὴ λέγειν"; "How could you say for me what I need to say?" A parody of Phaedra's words to her Nurse (E. *Hipp.* 345). The transposition of v. 16 after v. 18 was proposed by K. F. Hermann. Although we cannot be certain how the scene was acted, each actor may have suggested through gesture and body language his reluctance to be the first to admit the solution (i.e., flight).

19–20. μὴ 'μοιγε, μὴ 'μοί . . . : "No, no, don't . . ." **διασκανδικίσῃς:** "chervil me over." The herb σκάνδιξ, "chervil," is a member of the parsley family and associated with the diet of rural people (And. fr. 4). Here, the word alludes to Aristophanes' frequent slander that Euripides' mother was a vegetable seller (e.g., *Ach.* 475–78; *Th.* 387, 456; *Ra.* 840; see Hubbard 1991, 165n13); it is thus a retort to κομψευριπικῶς (16). In fact, Euripides was descended from a noble family (Philoch., *FGrH* 328 F 218, τῶν σφόδρα εὐγενῶν). The origin of this kind of (false) slander against Euripides' mother is unknown, but similar slanders against mothers of prominent Athenians are fairly common in Old Comedy (e.g., *Nu.* 552, of Hyperbolus; Hermipp. fr. 9, unnamed target; Eup. fr. 262, unnamed target; cf. also D. 18.129, 57.35). **ἀπόκινον:** From κινέω; a lewd comic dance (Lawler 1964, 73). In this scene, the slaves presumably swing their buttocks (cf. fr. 287) as if swaying away from the house of Demos (i.e., escaping). **δεσπότου:** A slave's standard epithet for his or her master (40, 53, 58, 960; *V.* 142; *Pax* 875).

21. λέγε δὴ: "Now say." δή intensifies the imperative (*GP* 216). **"μο-λω-μεν":** "Let's go." The dash (–) is used by Wilson to suggest a chant or incantation.

22–23. καὶ δὴ: "Okay"; indicates completion of the action commanded (*GP* 251–52). **πάνυ καλῶς:** "very good," "excellent." For the use of πάνυ as an intensifier in comedy, see Dover 1987, 53–57.

24. δεφόμενος: "Jerking off" (cf. *Pax* 290; *Ec.* 709; Eub. fr. 118.5).

26–28. αὐτομολῶμεν: "Let's desert," "run away." **ἤν, / οὐχ ἡδύ;** "See, wasn't that sweet?" ἤν is an interjection (*Pax* 327; *Ra.* 1390; *Pl.* 75). See López Eire 1996, 111; Nordgren 2015, 172, 224. **νὴ Δία:** "by Zeus"; i.e., "indeed." The oath affirms the previous statement. For oaths as a mark of colloquial Attic, see Dover 1997, 62–63. **τῷ δέρματι:** The retracted foreskin, or prepuce. **τουτονὶ τὸν οἰωνόν:** The deictic affix -ι is colloquial (see Dover 1997, 63–64; Willi 2003, 244–45). It may, as here, refer to something or point to what has just been said (492, 820) or to what follows (578, 928); see Wilson

2007b, ad loc. οἰωνός is a regular word for "omen."   **τί δαί;** "How so?" This colloquial particle, which always follows an interrogative, makes the question more emphatic (*GP* 262–63; Stevens 1976, 45; López Eire 1996, 122).

29. ὁτιὴ: "Because"; a strengthened form of ὅτι that is found only in Attic comedy (*GP* 287) and satyr plays. Presumably, it is a "short-lived colloquialism" (Olson's note at *Ach.* 1062).   **τὸ δέρμα . . . ἀπέρχεται:** As at 27, but also an allusion to a flayed back from a whipping; see Sommerstein 1981, ad loc.; Henderson 1991, 115.

30–31. τοίνυν: "Well then;" a lively conversational particle marking a transition when, as here, a speaker moves on to a new point in his or her own argument (*GP* 568–77).   **νῷν:** Dual dative.   **βρέτας:** A wooden cult image (cf. *Lys.* 261, of Athena; A. *Th.* 95–96, of ancestral gods; *Eu.* 79–80, of Athena).

32–33. βρετέτετας; The stammering stresses the slave's anxiety and fear. Cf. αὐ-το-μο-λῶ-μεν, "let's run off."   **ἐτεὸν;** "really . . . ?" The adverb adds a note of surprise and bewilderment to the question (1246, 1392; *Nu.* 35).   **γὰρ:** For the postponement of γάρ, which normally comes second in its clause, see *GP* 96.   **ἔγωγε:** "I certainly do" (i.e., "Absolutely"); a terse affirmative answer (see KG 2.539–40; Collard 2018, 143).   **ποίῳ χρώμενος τεκμηρίῳ;** "Based on what proof?" τεκμήρια are inferences drawn from known facts. The terms τεκμήριον, εἰκότως (34) along with substantive εἰκός (*Nu.* 393), and σκεπτέον (35) echo the kind of rhetorical language used by politicians to win support in the assemblies and law courts and by historians and natural philosophers to support speculation on past history and science (cf., for τεκμήριον, Hdt. 2.13.1; Th. 1.1.3; Pl. *Tht.* 158b; for εἰκότως, Th. 1.37.1; Antiph 1.6; for εἰκός, Th. 1.121.2; Pl. *Tht.* 162e; for σκεπτέον, Lys. 26.8; D. 20.10). For the connection between τεκμήρια and public speaking, see Dunbar at *Av.* 482.

34. θεοῖσιν ἐχθρός εἰμ(ι): "I'm godforsaken." The phrase θεοῖσιν ἐχθρός can be understood both colloquially, as "godforsaken" (without religious connotation), and literally, as "hateful to the gods" (θεοισεχθρία).   **οὐκ εἰκότως;** "not unreasonably."

35–36. εὖ προσβιβάζεις μ(ε): "You're winning me over"; cf. *Av.* 425, προσβιβᾷ λέγων, "he'll win [you] over by saying."   **ἑτέρα:** I.e., other options since he is godforsaken.   **σκεπτέον:** Suggests that a serious intellectual investigation is in order (e.g., Th. 1.1.3, 1.72; Pl. *Tht.* 188c; X.

Smp. 8.39).   **βούλει:** When used paratactically with the subjunctive (here φράσω) is colloquial and idiomatic (cf. 52–53; *Lys.* 938, *Av.* 813; Pl. Com. fr. 19; Stevens 1976, 60).   **πρᾶγμα:** "dramatic situation," "plot." Cf. *Pax* 43–44, τόδε πρᾶγμα τί; "what's the situation?"; *Ra.* 1122, ἐν τῇ φράσει τῶν πραγμάτων, "in the expression of his plots."

36–39. The actors introduce a metatheatrical moment to explain the dramatic situation and to solicit audience approval and support of their plot to escape Paphlagon's oppression (see Littlefield 1968, 6–7; Revermann 2006, 161). For metatheater, a distinct feature of Old Comedy, see the present book's introduction and glossary.

37–39. οὐ χεῖρον: "Not worse" (i.e., "good idea"); an example of litotes, a rhetorical understatement used to intensify a negative to the contrary (Smyth §3032).   **ἕν δ᾽ αὐτοὺς παραιτησώμεθα:** "but let's ask them [i.e., spectators] for one favor."   **ἐπίδηλον . . . ποιεῖν:** Sc., αὐτούς (subject).   **τοῖς προσώποισιν:** "in their [facial] expressions."   **τοῖς πράγμασιν:** "in our actions."

40–70. Slave A elaborates for the audience the political and topical circumstances of the drama. The master of the house, Demos of the Pnyx, an ill-tempered and decrepit countryman, is under the control of a Paphlagonian slave, who, like Cleon, is a tanner. In less than a month (cf. 43n), Paphlagon has come to hold Demos in the palm of his hand, and the slave manages to keep his master there through feigned servility, deceit, flattery, and the recitation of self-serving oracles. The situation of the household slaves has become intolerable because of Paphlagon's tyranny. Shakedowns, bribes, and threats of whippings are the order of the day. Slave characters in two other comedies by Aristophanes likewise similarly explain their situation (*V.* 54–135; *Pax* 50–59, 64–67); whereas they simply focus on the madness of their respective masters, the slaves in *Knights* characterize their master, Demos, as clueless and ill-tempered; see Newiger 1957, 11–12.

40–42. νῷν: Cf. 30.   **γάρ:** "Well then," introducing the facts of the situation (cf. Neil ad loc.).   **δεσπότης:** Cf. 19–20n.   **κυαμοτρώξ:** Often, when performing tedious work, the Athenians stayed awake by chewing beans (cf. *Lys.* 537, 689–90, with schol.). Cf. *Suda* κ 2578, κρινεῖ δὲ τούτους οὐ κυαμοτρὼξ Ἀττικός, "a bean chewer from Attica will not judge them." The primarily unresolved iambs of lines 41–42 are perhaps paratragic.   **Δῆμος Πυκνίτης:** "Demos of the Pnyx." The demotic Πυκνίτης, "of the Pnyx," is a comic invention; the Pnyx hill was located just inside the city walls, to

the west of the Acropolis and Aeropagus. Aristophanes may be hinting at
a contemporary Athenian named Demos (*PA* 3573; *PAA* 317910), a son
of Pyrilampes, friend of Pericles, and well-known keeper of peacocks (cf.
Eup. fr. 41 with Olson, *FrC* 2017, 170), who was presumably well known to
members of the audience.   δύσκολον γερόντιον: "cranky little geezer";
carries a tone of contempt (cf. *Nu.* 790, σκαιότατον γερόντιον; *Com. adesp.*
fr. 162, νύσταλον γερόντιον; Petersen 1910, 121–22). The characterization
of elderly men as ill-tempered, unfriendly, and difficult (δύσκολος) is a comic
trope (e.g., *Pax* 349, of Athenian jurors; *V.* 882–84, 942, 1066–70, 1104–6, of
Philocleon and his cohort; Men. *Dys.*, of Cnemon).

43. τῇ προτέρᾳ νουμηνίᾳ: The *noumenia* (first day of the lunar month) was
the main market day for purchasing and selling slaves and livestock (*V.* 169–
71; Luc. *Merc. Cond.* 23; see Mikalson 1972, 292–93).

44–45. βυρσοδέψην Παφλαγόνα: This detail confirms the association
of the Paphlagonian tanner and slave with Cleon, who was a
tanner.   πανουργότατον: "utter rogue," "villain"; a term favored by
Aristophanes for describing Cleon and his actions (247–50, 450, 684; cf. 56,
317; *V.* 1227; *Pax* 652). The term is also attested in tragedy (e.g., A. *Th.* 603; S.
El. 1387; E. *Med.* 583).   διαβολώτατόν τινα: Aristophanes characterizes
Paphlagon as habitually slandering, intimidating, and denouncing his
enemies for political and personal gain (cf. 6–7n). For comic portrayals of
the tendency of Cleon (and demagogues in general) to use the law courts
(dikasteria), Council (Boule), and Assembly (Ekklesia) to slander and attack
political rivals, see Ostwald 1986, 202–3.

46. καταγνοὺς τοῦ γέροντος τοὺς τρόπους: "Having figured out the old
man's ways." The prefix κατα- often carries a pejorative sense, "find fault with,
criticize" (LSJ s.v. I), but the sense here seems more like "size up, figure out."

48–49. ᾖκαλλ': "He was wagging his tail"; a rare verb, found only once in
tragedy (E. *Andr.* 630) and properly used of a dog fawning over someone
(schol. at 211; *Th.* 869; Pl. Com. fr. 248; Taillardat §695). The canine
metaphor plays on Paphlagon's claim to be a "watchdog of the people"
(1017–18, 1023, 1030–31; *V.* 895, 970, 1031; *Pax* 313).   ἐθώπευ': "he
was wheedling."   ἐκολάκευ': "he was flattering."   ἐξηπάτα: "he was
swindling." Accumulating items in lists is a stylistic feature of Old Comedy
(cf. *Pax* 571–79, 999–1003; Pherecr. fr. 113.3–33; Hermipp. fr. 63.3–23); see
Silk 2000, 131–36.   κοσκυλματίοις: "with scraps of leather," i.e., "scraps of
flattery." The scraps symbolize the paltry amount of money Paphlagon needs

to win popular favor; cf. Bdelycleon's complaint of the excesses of politicians, who scatter crumbs to placate ordinary citizens (*V.* 664–85). **τοιαυτὶ:** "what follows"; cf. 26–28n.

50–51. ὦ Δῆμε: Cf. 905, 910, 1152 (all uttered by Paphlagon). **λοῦσαι:** For the imperatival infinitive (aorist middle), cf. Smyth §2013. Bathing, presumably in warm water, is often mentioned in connection with seductions, weddings, symposia, and festivals (e.g., *Pax* 1139; *Av.* 132; *Lys.* 377–78, 1065–67; Pl. *Smp.* 174a). The suggestion here is that the bathing anticipates symposiastic dining and perhaps also foreshadows Paphlagon's many declarations of love for Demos (cf. 1166–67n with Anderson 1995, 23–24). **πρῶτον:** "first," "as soon as." **μίαν:** Sc., δίκην (cf. *V.* 595 for the ellipsis). **ἐνθοῦ:** ἐντίθημι is the term used of a nurse putting food in an infant's mouth (cf. 717). **ἔχε:** "here [take it]" (literally, "have," as at 493, 948). **τριώβολον:** Pay for jurors was introduced around 450 BCE at a rate of two obols daily and had been recently increased to three obols (= half a drachma) per day in 425 or 424, probably at Cleon's urging (cf. *V.* 300–302; *Av.* 1541 with Dunbar ad loc.).

52–53. βούλει παραθῶ: Cf. 35–36n for the construction. παρατίθημι is the *vox propria* for serving food, especially the main course in a meal (e.g., 1223; *Ach.* 85; *Pax* 27; Antiph. fr. 61.1; Archestra. fr. 13.4 with Olson and Sens ad loc.). **δόρπον:** Epic term for the evening meal (*Il.* 19.208; *Od.* 4.429, 12.439); seems to refer to a snack or after-dinner treat here (see Neil ad loc.). The mention of food anticipates the food-serving contest (1151–1252). **ἀναρπάσας:** Paphlagon is characterized as a thief (e.g., 296), extortionist (e.g., 802), and robber (e.g., 137) throughout the play.

54–57. πρῴην γ' ἐμοῦ / μᾶζαν μεμαχότος ἐν Πύλῳ Λακωνικήν: "Although I [emphatic] was first to have kneaded Laconian cake at Pylos." μεμαχότος is a pun on the verb μαχέσθαι, "to fight." Pylos is referred to a total of ten times in the play: seven times by Paphlagon (355, 702, 742, 846, 1005, 1058–59, 1167), twice in the prologue by Slave A (55, 76), and once, for the final time, by the triumphant Sausage-seller (1201). At first glance this comment seems to identify Slave A with the Athenian general Demosthenes (*PA* 3585; *PAA* 318425), whose troops had occupied the promontory of Pylos before the arrival of Cleon (Th. 4.2–3) and whom Thucydides and Cleon's other critics regarded as truly responsible for the Athenian victory at Sphachteria (Th. 4.29–30). Granted that this accusation perhaps reminds the audience of Demosthenes and, thus, of the general Nicias (*PAA* 712520), who played a role in the defeat of the Spartans at Pylos (Th. 4.27–28) and might here be identified with Slave B, the allusions are incidental to the overall characterization of both slaves, who, as Henderson notes (1998, 222) seem more generally to represent a class of "political outs" rather than specific individuals. For a contrary view, see Wilson 2007b, 39.

πανουργότατα: Adverbial; cf. the adjective at 45.   **ὑφαρπάσας:** "snatched, filched" (cf. 1200); "is attested in the classical period only in comedy . . . and must be colloquial" (Austin and Olson at *Th.* 204–5).   **παρέθηκε:** Cf. 52–53n.   **τὴν ὑπ' ἐμοῦ μεμαγμένην:** Cf. 1166–67n.

59–60. βυρσίνην: "Leather fan/swatter"; a surprise substitute for μυρσίνην, "myrtle branch" (cf. schol. ad loc.).   **τοὺς ῥήτορας:** "the politicians." For the metaphor of batting away "flies" (i.e., politicians), cf. 1038; *V.* 597; Taillardat §694. Myrtle branches were commonly used as flyswatters in antiquity (cf. Mart. 3.82.12, *fugatque muscas myrtea puer virga*, "the boy drives away the flies with a myrtle branch").

61. ᾄδει δὲ χρησμούς: Like a professional expounder of oracles, a χρησμῳδός (cf. 818), Paphlagon chants his prophecies from written texts, which he claims come from the legendary seer Bacis (1003) and which he may or may not be able to read (cf. 118–54n). For the popularity of consulting oracles in Athens in the sixth and earlier fifth centuries, especially during the Peloponnesian War, see Th. 2.8.2, 2.21.3, 8.1.1; Pritchett 1979, 319–21; Shapiro 1990, 345.   **δέ:** Amounts, here, to an explanatory γάρ with γέρων (*GP* 169–70).   **σιβυλλιᾷ:** Verbs in -ιάω often denote a physical illness or a crazed mental state (see Willi 2003, 85n86). The Sibyl, a legendary female soothsayer first mentioned in a fragment of Heraclitus (22 B92), is a source of concocted oracles at *Pax* 1090–95; see also Amips. fr. 10 for "making up oracles" (ποιοῦντες χρησμούς). As many cities claimed to be the Sibyl's birthplace, her name eventually became a generic term for prophetess.

62–63. μεμακκοακότα: "Moron." The scholia (ad loc.) derive this word from a legendarily dim-witted woman named Μακκώ (cf. 396, μακκοᾷ).   ***τέχνην πεπόηται:** Read instead τέχνην πεποίηται. Implies a technique or method to Paphlagon's manipulation of Demos. Wilson's πεπόηται is a misprint.

64–66. ψευδῆ διαβάλλει: Cf. 6–7n.   **κᾆτα:** "and then"; suggests a tone of outrage and indigence (KG 2.254; *GP* 308; see Stevens 1976, 46–47).   **μαστιγούμεθα / ἡμεῖς:** "we get whipped." The enjambment intensifies the tone of indignation. Whipping was also a regular punishment for runaway slaves (cf. *Pax* 451–52 with Olson ad loc.). ταράττει: "he agitates." ταράττειν, which often occurs in combination with κυκᾶν (stir up), is a common metaphor for stirring up or causing political confusion. Aristophanes uses the verbs to characterize Paphlagon-Cleon's politics throughout the play (363, 431, 692, 840, 865–67, 984); the chorus dubs him ταραξιππόστρατον (247) and βορβοροτάραξις (309). When applied to Sausage-seller, the verb ταράττειν equates him with his rival (214, 358, 840); cf. the command of the coryphaeus (see glossary, s.v. epirrhema) to the chorus to employ Paphlagon's same methods (251). For the use of this verb and its synonyms in *Knights*, see Newiger 1957, 27–30; Edmunds 1987a, 233–53. For the metaphor, see Taillardat §597.

67–68. Ὕλαν: In myth, Hylas is a handsome Adonis-like figure who accompanies Heracles on the Argo adventure and is the hero's lover (*eromenos*). The name could be given to a slave in Athens (cf. the Athenian casualty list of 465/64, *IG* i³ 1144, 10) and could be used as a comic nickname for a comely household slave (as here) or notorious figure. Examples of Athenian nicknames drawn from myth include Orestes (*Ach.* 1166; *Av.* 712); Atreus, Phrixus, and Jason (Anaxandr. fr. 35.10–11; cf. *IG* ii² 2325E.37; MO, 188); and Capaneus and Telamon (Aristopho fr. 5; cf. *IG* ii² 2325E.46; MO, 189). εἰ μή μ᾽ ἀναπείσετ᾽, ἀποθανεῖσθε: An emotional future condition (future indicative in both the protasis and the apodosis); "the protasis commonly expresses something undesired, or feared, or intended independently of the speaker's will [cf. 175]; the apodosis commonly expresses a threat or warning [see 949–50], or an earnest appeal to the feelings" (Smyth §2328). τήμερον: "adds vividness by suggesting the imminence of pain, suffering, or the like" (Biles and Olson at *V.* 643).

69–72. ἡμεῖς δὲ δίδομεν: I.e., "we give [him money]." εἰ δὲ μή: "other-wise" (e.g., *Nu.* 1433; *Pax* 262; E. *And.* 254); see *MT* §478. ὀκταπλάσιον: "eight times over." For a similar scatological exaggeration, cf. *Ec.* 351, where Blepyrus' fecal production is likened to the length of a rope used to draw a bucket from a well. χέζομεν: "we shit." Evacuation of the bowels is often linked to a serious beating (cf. *Lys.* 440; *Th.* 570); see Henderson 1991a, 190. νῦν οὖν: "so now"; colloquial, marking a transition to the speaker's main point (cf. 1393; *Ach* 37, 383; *Nu.* 75) ἀνύσαντε: Dual aorist vocative participle used adverbially, "quickly" (cf. 119, 1107; *Nu.* 181, 506, 635, 1253; *V.* 30; *Lys.* 438; KG 2.81). ὠγαθέ: = ὦ (ἀ)γαθέ "my good man"; presumably a colloquial address with no especially friendly or hostile connotations, although it sometimes, but not always, "seems to indicate the speaker's superiority" and can suggest sarcasm (Dickey 1996, 119, 139). νώ: Dual accusative of agent in place of the usual dative of agent governed by the verbal adjective τρεπτέον (see *Av.* 1237, οἷς θυτέον αὐτούς, with Dunbar ad loc.).

73. κράτιστ᾽ ἐκείνην τὴν "μόλωμεν": "[I say] that 'we run away' is best"; his original suggestion with a pun on αὐτομολεῖν (23–26).

74–79. The litany of complaints about Paphlagon's corrupt political style and his all-consuming ambition for domestic and international domination (cf. 797–800; Th. 3.86.3–4, 4.2.2, 6.15.2) reflects common comedic accusations against demagogues (cf. the personified triremes' critique of Hyperbolus' plan for a military expedition to Carthage at 1300–1315 with Anderson 2003; in general, see Henderson 2017, 614). For Paphlagon's body as an imagined colossus whose limbs straddle geographic boundaries, see Newiger 1957, 17–20.

74–76. οὐχ οἷόν τε τὸν Παφλαγόν᾽ οὐδὲν λαθεῖν: Sc., ἐστίν; cf. Paphlagon's boast at 862–63: μ᾽ οὐ λέληθεν οὐδέν / ἐν τῇ πόλει.   **ἐφορᾷ γὰρ αὐτὸς πάντ᾽:** Paphlagon is represented as an all-seeing, omnipresent deity who, like the sun, "sees and hears all things" (cf. Ἥλιός θ᾽, ὃς πάντ᾽ ἐφορᾷς καὶ πάντ᾽ ἐπακούεις, *Il.* 3. 277; *Od.* 11.109, 12.323). The verb ἐφορᾶν is used of gods and of human beings (see Willi 2003, 28n81). Eupolis (fr. 316.1) likewise substitutes Cleon's name for that of the sun: ὦ καλλίστη πόλι πασῶν ὅσας Κλέων ἐφορᾶι, "Oh fairest city of all those Cleon oversees."   **ἐν Πύλῳ:** See 54–57n.

77–79. τοσόνδε . . . διαβεβηκότος: "Spread his gait so far [apart]"; cf. *Av.* 486, διαβάσκει (of the cock's majestic strutting). The interlocking word order (accusative, genitive, accusative, genitive) highlights the actors' step-like forward motion (i.e., διαβαίνειν can refer to forward as well as to back-and-forth motion; see MacQueen 1984, 456).   **ὁ πρωκτός:** "asshole." In comedy, the term πρωκτός is used only of the male anatomy (Henderson 1991a, 201). A running joke in Aristophanes and other poets of Old Comedy is that successful politicians habitually submit to anal penetration to advance their careers (878–80; cf. *Nu.* 1093–94; *Ec.* 110–14; Pl. Com. fr. 202; Pl. *Smp.* 192a, Aristophanes' speech). For comic attitudes toward pathic homosexuality, see Dover 1978, 135–53; Henderson 1991a, 209–13.   **ἐν Χάοσιν:** A geographical pun on χάος, "gaping hole." The Chaonians, a barbarian tribe living in Epirus (southern Albania) fought with Sparta's allies against the Acarnanians, allies of the Athenians, in 429 (Th. 2.80–82). In 425/24, the Athenians apparently hoped to win the Chaonians over to their side (cf. *Ach.* 604 with Sommerstein 1981, ad loc.).   ἐν Αἰτωλοῖς: "among the Aetolians," with a pun on αἰτεῖν, "to demand." The memory of the Aetolian victory over the Athenian expedition commanded by Demosthenes in 426 would be fresh in Athenian minds; Thucydides (3.98.4) notes that in addition to the loss of many allies in that expedition, 120 Athenian hoplites perished, "all in the prime of life and the best men in the city."   ἐν Κλωπιδῶν: "in the [company] of thieves." For the dative ellipsis (colloquial), see Poultney 1936, 6; Stevens 1976, 27–28. Note the pun on κλώψ (thief) and the comic distortion of the Attic deme named Cropidae (schol. ad loc.); there was also a small community in northeast Attica named Clopidae and associated with the deme Aphidna (Traill 1975, 90–91). Cf. the geographical pun on Γαληψός and λαμβάνειν in Eup. fr. 439, which implies that Cleon personally profited when he captured Galepsos in his campaign against Amphipolis (Th. 5.6.1). For wordplay involving deme names in Old Comedy, see Whitehead 1986, 334–36.

80–81. οὖν: "Well then"; a connective particle marking a new point or new stage in events (*GP* 426).   νῷν: Cf. 30.   ὅπως ἄν: + the subjunctive in object clauses is colloquial. Cf. 926; KG 2.375; *MT* §348.

82–84. πῶς δῆτα; "How then . . . ?" As an intensifier, δῆτα frequently follows the interrogative pronoun or pronominal adverb (*GP* 270).   βέλτιστον ἡμῖν αἷμα ταύρειον πιεῖν: "The best thing for us is to drink bull's blood." The scholiast (at 84) says that this line parodies Sophocles' *Return of Helen* (*TrGF* fr. 178), where the heroine says, ἐμοὶ δὲ λῷστον αἷμα ταύρειον πιεῖν / καὶ μὴ 'πὶ πλεῖον τῶνδ' ἔχειν δυσφημίας, "for me it's better to drink bull's blood and no more endure their slanders" (see Rau 1967, 187).   ὁ Θεμιστοκλέους . . . θάνατος: "the death of Themistocles." That the Athenian general Themistocles (*PA* 6669; *PAA* 502610) committed suicide by drinking bull's blood is oral tradition (cf. the account of the suicide of Midas at Str. 1.3.21; Marr 1995, 164–66). Herodotus does not mention the story. Thucydides (1.138.4) qualifies his account of Themistocles' death with the phrase "some say" (λέγουσι δέ τινες). Later writers accept and embellish the story (Plu. *Themis.* 31.5; Diodorus 11.58.3).

85–100. The mention of drinking moves Slave A to order his fellow slave to bring wine from the house, as wine will help inspire a foolproof plan of action (90–94). That the two slaves have such easy access to wine and can indulge themselves with impunity underscores Demos' lack of attention to the doings in his own household.

85–86. μὰ Δί᾽: "No, by Zeus"; i.e., "Absolutely not." The oath, which strengthens the preceding statement, is commonplace, colloquial, and strongly affirmative (cf. 280, 336, 1382; Nordgren 2015, 230).   **ἀλλ᾽:** "Instead"; signals an alternative suggestion (*GP* 9).   **ἄκρατον:** Cf. the joke on the proportions of wine (more) mixed with water (less) and Athena's title τριτογενής at 1187–89 and the paraprosdokeion joke (see glossary) at *V.* 525, where Philocleon substitutes "unmixed jury pay" for "unmixed wine" as he toasts the Agathos Daimon.   **ἀγαθοῦ δαίμονος:** "for the Good Deity"; an objective genitive (see KG 1.376; Poultney 1936, 44). It was customary to end a symposiastic meal by toasting the Agathos Daimon with a libation of "unmixed" wine (cf. fr. 651 with Bagordo, *FrC* 2016, 205–6; for libation rituals in general, see R. Parker 1996, 231).   **ἴσως γάρ:** "Perhaps then." The particle "gives the motive for saying what has just been said" (*GP* 60–61).

87. ἰδού γ᾽: "Indeed!" (sc., "unmixed"). ἰδού (colloquial) marks dismissal of another's words, quoted with contempt (344, 703; *Pax* 198 with Olson ad loc.). See Collard 2018, 35; Dover 1987, 20–21; López Eire 1996, 101–3. The particle γε is an intensifier (*GP* 129). For the accent of ἰδού as a proclitic variation of ἴδου, see Probert 2003, 42, §83.   **γοῦν:** "of course!"; probably sarcastic (cf. *GP* 455).

89–90. ἄληθες; "Really, is that so?" (accented thus in contrast to the attributive ἀληθές); expresses ironic indignation or surprise (e.g., *Ach.* 557; *Nu.* 841; *V.* 1223, 1412; *Av.* 174—all at line opening). See Stevens 1976, 23.   **κρουνοχυτρολήραιον:** "a gushing-water/wine pot-of-nonsense"; an Aristophanic coinage taken by some scholars as support for the identification of Slave B with the Athenian general Nicias, who purportedly had a reputation for being abstemious (see Plu. *Nic.* 5.1; Sommerstein 1980, 46–47). But there is no independent evidence that Nicias was abstemious about wine drinking. For the metaphor, see Taillardat §482, §893.   **εἰς ἐπίνοιαν . . . ;** The phrase εἰς τι regularly occurs with verbs of praise or abuse (Neil ad loc.). ἐπίνοια and its cognates imply creative thinking (cf. 1203, 1403).   **λοιδορεῖν:** "to insult, revile aggressively" (cf. 1274, 1400; *Pax* 56–57). On the attribution of creative ideas and inspirations to an outside authority, see 107–8n.

91–94: For jokes on the positive effects of wine on making sound decisions, see *Lys.* 1228–30; W. J. Slater 1976, 165. Neil (ad loc.) notes that the rhythm here (mostly unresolved iambs) "is mock-serious."

92. ὁρᾷς: "You see"; colloquial, pointing at a proof or illustration of something that the speaker has been saying or expecting (cf. 1164, 1214). See Stevens 1976, 36–37; López Eire 1996, 107–8.

94. ὠφελοῦσι τοὺς φίλους: Cf. the Greek heroic ethos "Help one's friends and harm one's enemies" (Dover 1994, 180–84).

95–96. χοᾶ: A liquid measure equal to slightly more than three liters, a little less than a gallon (Young 1939, 278–80). The slave, here drinking alone, presumably quaffs the drink down in one gulp, as if he were a competitor in the speed-drinking contest at the Choes, part of the Anthesteria festival. For the festival, which is treated extensively in *Acharnians*, see Habash 1995, 567–74.   **τὸν νοῦν . . . ἄρδω:** "I can water my wit," i.e., "get drunk." ἄρδω = ποτίσω (schol. at 114; see Taillardat §161).   **τι δεξιόν:** "something clever," "sophisticated."

96–108. As if a symposiast, Slave A praises the quality of the (stolen) wine and reclines to enjoy his drink, while Slave B plays the role of servant, bringing a garland and sweet cakes and refilling Slave A's cup; see Pütz 2003, 136.

97. οἴμοι: "Horrors, oh no"; a stock colloquial interjection with a wide scope of uses, ranging from annoyance to impatience, alarm, despair, surprise, and the like. See Stevens 1976, 17; López Eire 1996, 90–91; Labiano Ilundain 2000, 251.   **τί ποθ᾽ ἡμᾶς ἐργάσει . . . ;** The question, repeated at 1240, although it appears to be generic may echo Eur. fr. 700: ὦ Φοῖβ᾽ Ἄπολλον Λύκιε, τί ποτέ μ᾽ ἐργάσῃ (cf. schol. at *Eq.* 1240).

98. ἀγάθ᾽: Direct object of the verb (97): "I'm going to do good things." The verbal ellipsis is colloquial (Stevens 1976, 27).   **ἔνεγκ᾽:** Equivalent to ἐξένεγκε (cf. 95); the second time a compound verb occurs, the prefix is often omitted (see Smyth §3018e). *Slave B goes inside.*   **κατακλινήσομαι:** Slave A reclines on the ground in symposiastic anticipation (cf. *V.* 1208–9, δευρὶ κατακλινεῖς).

99–100. *Slave A addresses himself (and the audience).*   **πάντα ταυτὶ:** "all these things here" (i.e., items on the stage); cf. *Pax* 319 with Olson ad loc.   **καταπάσω:** With genitive of the thing being sprinkled and accusative of the thing besprinkled (KG 1.357). Note the accumulation of diminutives (βουλευματίων καὶ γνωμιδίων καὶ νοιδίων; cf. 792–93). Neil (ad loc.) writes, "The want of caesura [at 100] is probably intentional, to be emphasized by the delivery of the line (cf. 165)"; i.e., a slight pause for stress was perhaps given after each metron.

101. *Slave B returns from the house with wine, a jug, and a garland.*   **ὅτι οὐκ:** An allowable hiatus before a long vowel in comedy (e.g., *Ach.* 516; *Lys.* 611); cf. KB 1.197.

103–4. ἐπίπαστα: Canapés sprinkled with a rich sauce (schol. ad loc.); cf. λείχων ἐπίπαστα (1089) and Pherecr. fr. 137.3, λιπαροῖς ἐπιπάστοις, in a catalog of the good life.   **λείξας:** The charge that Paphlagon (standing in for Cleon and politicians in general) greedily consumes public revenues appears regularly in the comedy (cf. also 258, 706–7, 826–27, 1030–34; *V.* 554; *Th.* 811–12).   **δημιόπραθ':** = δημιόπρατα. "Confiscated goods" sold by public authority were an ongoing source of revenue (*V.* 659).   **ὁ βάσκανος:** A common term of abuse, often associated with sycophancy and slander (cf. fr. 921; D. 18.242), but also linked to malignant magic (*Pl.* 571) and the evil eye. Cf. the proverb "Ill-natured and envious, it is the eye of your neighbor" (Alciphr. 1.15). For the etymology, see Frisk 1960–72, s.v.   **ἐν ταῖσι βύρσαις:** "on his hides."   **ὕπτιος:** "supine." Paphlagon, overcome by wine and snoring on his back (ὕπτιος), recalls the image of the drunken, supine Cyclops Polyphemus (ὕπτιος, *Od.* 9.371).

105. ἴθι νυν: "Come on now"; a formulaic and mainly colloquial phrase at line openings (*GP* 214–18; López Eire 1996, 97–100).   **ἄκρατον ἐγκάναξον:** "pour it unmixed" (i.e., don't water it down"; cf. 1183–87n). The scholiast (ad loc.) comments that the verb is onomatopoeic: ἐγκάναξον, δὲ ἐπὶ θορύβου τάττουσι τοῦτο παρὰ τὴν χαναχήν, ἥγουν μετὰ ψόφου ἔγχεον). Cf. E. *Cyc.* 152, φέρ' ἐγκάναξον: Silenus bids Odysseus to offer the wine unmixed into his cup.

106. σπεῖσον: Sc., σπονδήν.   **ἀγαθοῦ δαίμονος:** Cf. 85–86n.

107–8. ἔλχ' ἕλκε: "Quaff, quaff [sc., "cup" or the like]." Cf. E. *Cyc.* 417, where the Cyclops takes the unmixed wine of Odysseus and downs it in one draught (ἐδέξατ' ἔσπασέν <τ'> ἄμυστιν ἑλκύσας).   **τὴν:** Sc., σπονδήν.   **τοῦ δαίμονος τοῦ Πραμνίου:** A paraprosdokeion joke for τοῦ ἀγαθοῦ δαίμονος. Pramnian wine was a potent dry red wine (cf. fr. 688; *Il.* 11.639; *Od.* 10.235; cf. also Phryn. Com. fr. 68, on the poetic style of Sophocles, οὐ γλύξις . . . ἀλλὰ Πράμνιος). The vintage was produced across the eastern Aegean, but the Lesbos variety was most prized (cf. Ephipp. fr. 28; see Dalby 2000, 402).   **σὸν τὸ βούλευμ', οὐκ ἐμόν:** The attribution of original ideas and inspirations to an outside source (cf. 1203) suggests paratragedy (e.g., [A.] *Pr.* 619, βούλευμα μὲν τὸ Δῖον, Ἡφαίστου δὲ χεὶρ ἐφορᾷ; E. *Ph.* 1646, Ἐτεοκλέους βουλεύματ', οὐχ ἡμῶν, τάδε; E. *Cyc.* 285, θεοῦ τὸ πρᾶγμα· μηδέν' αἰτιῶ βροτῶν).

109–10. ἀντιβολῶ: "Please"; colloquial (cf. 142, 960, 1202; López Eire 1996, 58–59, 64–65). **κλέψας . . . Παφλαγόνος:** κλέπτειν with the genitive carries the notion of separation as well as possession (e.g., 436, 1149; Poultney 1936, 121).

111–12. ταῦτ': Sc., δράσω: "Okay, I'll do it." *Slave B goes into the house.* In response to a command or request, ταῦτα in ellipsis is colloquial (*Ach.* 815; *Pax* 275; *V.* 142, 851, 1008; cf. Stevens 1976, 30; López Eire 1996, 182). **ἀτὰρ:** "But"; an adversative particle mainly expressing a sudden change in topic (*GP* 52); has a colloquial feel (see Stevens 1976, 44–45; López Eire 1996, 131). **δέδοιχ' ὅπως μὴ τεύξομαι:** + future indicative; the equivalent of μή with the subjunctive in a fearing clause (cf. S. *OT.* 1074–75; E. *Hipp.* 518; KG 2.396). The construction reflects semantic confusion between caution and purpose (*MT* §370).

113–14. φέρε: "Here"; a colloquial interjection (cf. 706, *Th.* 788; *Ra.* 120, 1399; Stevens 1976, 42; López Eire 1996, 27). **τὸν νοῦν . . . τι δεξιόν:** Cf. 95–96n.

115–17. *Slave B returns with a scroll.* **μεγάλ':** "loudly." **πέρδεται:** Crepitation jokes are stock-in-trade in Old Comedy (Henderson 1991a, 195–99) and can often imply laziness and self-satisfaction (e.g., Pheidippides farting and snoring away without a care in the world at *Nu.* 9–11). **ῥέγκεται:** A scholiast (ad loc.) claims that the middle voice (the proper Attic form is active; cf. 104, ῥέγκει) is used here to balance πέρδεται (115). But linguistic consistency is not a comic virtue. Indeed, an unexpected joke on the confusion of active and middle voice by the same slave character may account for this use of the middle voice. The confusion of active and middle voice by barbarian speakers is referred to as *datismos*; cf. the recitation at *Pax* 291 of the song of Datis, where χαίρομαι appears in place of proper Attic χαίρω; see Colvin 1999, 291–92. Datis was either a name for one of the Persian commanders who led the Persian expedition against Athens in 490 (Hdt. 6.94.2) or the name (or nickname) of a tragedian, a son of the Athenian Carcinus; see Olson at *Pax* 289–91. **χρησμὸν . . . , / ὅνπερ μάλιστ' ἐφύλαττεν:** Closely guarding his "holy" (ἱερόν) oracle is reminiscent of tyrants guarding and controlling secret collections of oracles to maintain power; cf. 1011–13n.

118–54. Much of the humor of this scene rests on claims of the characters' literacy that cannot be verified. When Slave B, e.g., enters with Paphlagon's prized oracle (116), Slave A first takes the scroll and seems to read it silently; then he announces its contents, which suggests that his fellow slave may be unable to read it for himself. We may imagine that Slave A is no more educated than his fellow slave or, for that matter, than Sausage-seller, who never had a proper education (188–89). The exchange between the two slaves suggests that Slave A does not read the scroll aloud as was the normal contemporary procedure (see Knox 1968, 421–35; Burnyeat 1997, 74–76; see also Thomas 2009, 23–24) but, rather, glances at the scroll and paraphrases its alleged content as he drinks his cup of unmixed wine (see Anderson and Dix 2014, 79–81). In fact, the scroll is probably entirely blank. For a different understanding of literacy and silent reading, see Svenbro 1990, 367–68; Sommerstein 2001, 241.

118–20. ἀναγνῶ: "So I can read it [aloud]." Cf. 118–54n. See Nagy 1990, 171–72, for ἀναγιγνώσκειν (literally, "to know again") coming to mean "Read!" **ἔγχεον πιεῖν:** "pour [wine] to drink." The infinitive expresses purpose (cf. *V.* 616; E. *Cyc.* 520, ὃν πιεῖν ἔδωκά σοι; X. *HG.*7.2.9, τὰς δὲ γυναῖκας πιεῖν τε φερούσας, cf. Smyth §2008). **ἀνύσας:** "hurry up"; adverbial (cf. 69–72n). **φέρ᾽ ἴδω . . . ;** "Here, [let me] see"; a colloquial expression with the first-person subjunctive (e.g., 953, 1002, 1214, 1365) or the imperative (e.g., *Nu.* 1088; *Ra.* 1417; *Ec.* 710). It is often followed by a question (e.g., *Nu.* 21; Pherecr. fr. 6.1; E. *Cyc.* 8; see Stevens 1976, 42; López Eire 1996, 98–99). **ἄρ᾽:** Following the interrogative, ἄρα suggests that the answer will bring enlightenment (*GP* 39–40). **ἔνεστιν:** Cf., all in oracular contexts, 122; *Av.* 974, 976, 980.

120. ὦ λόγια: "What prophecies!" The interjection signals joy (Labiano Ilundain 2000, 320). The accent normally depends on whether the particle marks an exclamation, as here, or a vocative (cf. 123). *Slave A begins to unroll the oracle.* **δός μοι, δός . . . :** Repetition of the imperative stresses his impatience. Cf. *Ach.* 1054–55; *Pax* 1221.

121. ἰδού: "Okay [take it]"; a regular (colloquial) formula of compliance with a request or command (although, in many cases, it can be translated literally; cf. 997–98n).

123. ὦ Βάκι: As there was more than one Sibyl (61n), so there was more than one Bacis. The scholion (ad loc.) lists three of the latter, one from Eleon in Boeotia, one from Athens, and one from Arcadia; cf. schol. at *Pax* 1071 and *Av.* 962 with Dunbar ad loc. Collections of prophecies under his name were widely circulated during the Persian Wars (Hdt. 8.20.2, 8.77, 8.96.2, 9.43). To keep a collection of oracles might smack of tyranny; Bacis was a name assumed, e.g., by the tyrant Pisistratus (*PA* 11793; *PAA* 771760; *Suda* β 47), whose family controlled the city before the establishment of the democracy in 510 BCE.

124. πολλῷ γ᾽: "A lot!" γε is emphatic. At the opening of a sentence and "often when following an adjective or adverb," [the particle] "has a force that may be fairly described as exclamatory" (*GP* 127); cf. 609, 616, 1368.

125-26. μιαρὲ: "You slime" or the like. This vehement colloquial insult is common in Aristophanes (e.g., 304; *Ach.* 557; *Pax* 182–83, 362; *Ra.* 465–66; fr. 26—all in an accumulation of insults). See Dickey 1996, 167; Dover 2002, 95–96. The adjective is used in the same insulting way in satyr drama (e.g., S. *Ichneutae* 197; E. *Cyc.* 677). For the religious basis of the term, as meaning "polluted," see R. Parker 1983, 4–5.   **ἄρ᾽:** "So that's why . . ."; an idiom with the imperfect, to mark a fact that the speaker has only just recognized and that continues to be true (*Ach.* 90, 990; *Nu.* 1271; *Pax* 414–15; *GP* 36–37).   **ἐφυλλάτου:** The middle voice stresses Paphlagon's caution in keeping the oracle to himself; cf. Xerxes' remarks on the caution of the Thessalians in guarding information, ταῦτ᾽ ἄρα πρὸ πολλοῦ ἐφυλάσσοντο (Hdt. 7.130.2).   **ὀρρωδῶν:** "shitting in fear of the oracle" (cf. schol. at 126, ὀρρωδῶν: φοβούμενος, εὐλαβούμενος, ἀπὸ τοῦ τὸν ὄρρον τῶν δειλῶν ἰδίειν).   **τιή:** "Why?"; an emphatic form of τί (731; cf. *V.* 1155; *Pax* 927, 1018; *Th.* 84).

127-43. The oracle parodies succession myths of gods or dynasts whose fall ultimately legitimizes the power of the subsequent ruler (e.g., in Hes. *Th.*, Uranus-Cronus-Zeus). Such myths regularly involve a battle or battles between a hero (or a god), who represents the new order, and a monstrous opponent, representing chaos. In *Knights*, the hero Sausage-seller, roughly the age of young Athenian knights and third in a succession myth of the new order of leaders from the agora (each worse—and thus better—than his predecessor) faces Paphlagon, an older, monster-like opponent (511; *V.* 1029–37; *Pax* 752–60). See A. M. Bowie 1993, 58–66, for the monster motif.

127. αὐτός: "Himself"; i.e., Paphlagon.   **ἀπόλλυται:** The oracular present is used to predict imminent downfall (199; cf. Eup. fr. 195, ἄκουε νῦν Πείσανδρος ὡς ἀπόλλυται, "hear now how Peisander is being destroyed"; Smyth §1882).

128-29. καὶ πῶς; "But how?" Preceding an interrogative, καί often expresses a strong degree of surprise and bewilderment and implies an emotional objection (*GP* 309–10).   **ὅπως;** "How so, [you ask]?" Indirect interrogatives following direct inquiries are frequently conversational (e.g., 1073; *Ach.* 594–95; *Nu.* 689–90). See KG 2.517; Smyth §2670. **ἄντικρυς:** "directly," "explicitly." Cf. *Av.* 962, where the adverb is also used in connection with an oracle. **πρῶτα:** "First off"; adverbial. **στυππειοπώλης:** "hempmonger." The reference seems to be to a certain Eucrates of Melite (*PA* 5759; *PAA* 437755), a contemporary politician (see 254), who may also have sold bran; cf. fr. 716, where he is given the nickname στύππαξ, "Hempster" (cf. also Cratin. fr. 339 with Olson and Seaberg, *FrC* 2018, 112). Eucrates exemplifies the new breed of nonaristocratic politician who rose to prominence after the death of Pericles. Aristophanes also refers to him as Μελιτέα κάπρον, "Boar of Miletus" (fr. 149). Since hemp was needed for caulking, rigging, and the sailcloth of triremes, it would have been a lucrative enterprise for the dealer; see Morrison, Coates, and Rankov 2000, 184–85, 189–90, 204–5. Whether this Eucrates is the same as the Athenian general who was sent to Macedonia in 432/31 (*IG* i³ 365.5 = *PAA* 437450) is unknown.

131. εἰς οὑτοσὶ πώλης: The word πώλης, "monger," normally appears as an element in compounds.

132. προβατοπώλης: "Sheepmonger." The scholiast (at 765) identifies him as the general and demagogue Lysicles (*PA* 9417; *PAA* 614815), who was killed on a military mission in Caria in 428/27 (Th. 3.19.2). Also called a προβατοκάπηλος, "sheep dealer," he is said to have become the lover of Pericles' free Milesian partner Aspasia (*PAA* 222330), after Pericles' death (Plu. *Per.* 24. 4).

133. δύο τώδε πώλα: "[That's] a pair of mongers" (nominative duals). The use of δύο with the dual is pleonastic (e.g., 1350; *Ach.* 527; *Av.* 320; *Ra.* 134).

134–37. κρατεῖν: Sc., χρῆ. **βδελυρώτερος:** "utterly vile, ignorant, disgusting." A common Aristophanic insult (Dickey 1996, 167); the adjective βδελυρός and its cognates are often applied to demagogues (e.g., 193, 252, 303, 1157, βδελύττομαι); see Kanavou 2011, 80–83 on the character name Bdelycleon, "Loathe-Cleon" (as well as Philocleon, "Love-Cleon") in *Wasps*. **γένοιτο:** The optative is used despite the dependence of its clause on a primary tense, because his fate was formed in the past (cf. *V.* 110; *Ra.* 24, 766; *MT* §323; KG 2.382–83). **γὰρ:** Explanatory. **βυρσοπώλης ὁ Παφλαγών:** Cf. 44–45n. **ἅρπαξ:** "robber," "embezzler." **κεκράκτης:** "screecher." The onomatopoetic word and its cognates mimic a harsh, shrill, shrieking voice and is sometimes used by Aristophanes to describe Cleon's

legendarily loud, screaming voice (e.g., 256; 287; *Ach.* 711; *Pax* 314–15).
For Cleon's bellowing, see also Arist. *Ath.* 28.3, Κλέων . . . ὅς . . . πρῶτος ἐπὶ
τοῦ βήματος ἀνέκραγει. Of the thirteen appearances of the word (and its
cognates) in our play, nine refer to Paphlagon (256, 274, 304, 487 bis, 863,
1018, 1403), while four refer to Sausage-seller boasting that he can outshout
his rival (285, 287 bis, 640–44, where he "bellows" [ἀνέκραγον] the good news
of lower sardine prices to the Boule).   **Κυκλοβόρου:** The Cycloborus was
an Athenian stream renowned for its deafening roar in flood stage. For the
metaphor of a raging river sweeping away all that lies in its path, cf. *Il.* 11.492–
97 (of Ajax); 21.233–56 (of the personified Scamander battling Achilles). Cf.
also Hor. *Carm.* 4.2.5–12 (of Pindar's poetic power); Taillardat §504.

138. ἦν ἄρ᾽: Cf. 125–26n.

139. νὴ Δί᾽: Cf. 26–28n.   **οἴμοι δείλαιος:** "Good heavens!" The metrical
shortening of the diphthong -αι- is regular when δείλαιος occurs at line end
(cf. *Nu.* 1473; *V.* 40, 165, 202, 1150; *Av.* 990).

140. πόθεν οὖν ἂν ἔτι γένοιτο πώλης εἷς μόνος; "If only one more [ἔτι]
dealer could come from somewhere!" For the hopeless wish posed as a
question, see 17–18n.

141. ὑπερφυᾶ: "Extraordinary." The word and its cognates are probably
colloquial (cf. *Ach.* 142 with Olson ad loc.). It is tempting to take the verse's
unresolved rhythm as paratragic, but it may just be coincidental.

142. ἀντιβολῶ: Cf. 109–10n.   **νὴ Δία:** "Yes, tell me now!" For the oath, cf.
26–28n. Here, the oath with the imperative implies that Slave B is impatient to
hear the oracle's prediction (for similar impatience, cf. *Av.* 661; *Ra.* 164–65);
see Werres 1936, 25–26, 38–39.

144-45. ἀλλαντοπώλης; ὦ Πόσειδον: "Sausage-seller? O Poseidon!";
an exclamation of shock and surprise, as at 609. See Blaszczak 1932,
27–32.   **τῆς τέχνης:** "what a trade!"; genitive of exclamation (see 1–
5n).   **ἐξευρήσομεν;** The actors would scan the stage and perhaps the
audience for their destined savior (σωτήρ, 149), when Sausage-seller
"miraculously" enters.

147-49. ὥσπερ κατὰ θεόν: "As if by a god"; cf. 1338. *Sausage-seller comes on
stage, carrying a butcher's block and various tools of his trade.*   **φίλτατε:**
"dearest"; almost always an affectionate form of address (e.g., 1335; *Ach.* 885,
Pax 1198). See Dickey 1996, 119.   **δεῦρο δεῦρ᾽:** "over here, over here!"

The adverb with a second-person singular imperative of motion is colloquial (López Eire 1996, 41).   ἀνάβαινε: "step up." Cf. *Ach.* 732, ἄμβατε ποττάν (Megarian dialect); *V.* 1341, ἀνάβαινε δεῦρο (with Biles and Olson ad loc.).   σωτὴρ τῇ πόλει καὶ νῷν φανείς: The address to Sausage-seller as σωτήρ of the city (cf. 458; cf. also, 836, 1319) parodies greetings customarily given to revealed gods (591), heroes, and their messengers; see Kleinknecht 1937, 23, and 79n1; Horn 1970, 46, 51; Landfester 1967, 36–37. For σωτήρ as a political term, see Habicht 1956, 156.

151. μεγάλως εὐδαιμονεῖς: "You're greatly blessed." μεγάλως has a quasi-heroic tone (cf. *Il.* 17. 723; *Od.* 16.432; Hes. *Th.* 429).

152–53. ἴθι δή: "Come now"; cf. 105n.   ἐλεὸν: = τραπέζιον, "small portable table," "butcher's block" (schol. ad loc.); see Sparkes 1975, 132, with plate XVI a–b.   ἀναδίδαξον: "explain," "explicate," as at 1045.

154. *Slave B goes into the house.*   ἰὼν προσκέψομαι: "I'll go and spy on." The use of the main verb + ἰών (in the sense "go and . . .") with verbs of perception and verbs of motion is colloquial (cf. 970; *Ach.* 954; *Pax* 1294); see Renehan 1976, 157–58.

155–56. ἄγε δή: "Now then"; a formulaic interjection at line opening that draws a person's attention or sometimes points to a consideration or action (e.g., 482, 634, 1011; *Ach.* 98; *Pax* 263, 431; *Av.* 434). The entire verse is recycled at *Pax* 886. The formula ἄγε νυν takes its place before a vowel (e.g., 1011; *Nu.* 489); see Collard 2018, 146.   πρόσκυσον: In a Greek setting, προσκυνεῖν signals a kind of salutation in recognition of good fortune (cf., e.g., S. *El.* 1374, of Orestes [with Pylades] greeting the images of the gods in his ancestral home; *Ph.* 533, of Philoctetes bidding farewell to his "home" on Lemnos), rather than the Persian custom of prostrating one's body in obeisance to authority (cf. Hdt. 1.119.1, of Harpagus in honor of Astyages; 8.118.4, of a Persian soldier in honor of Xerxes); see Pulleyn 1997, 191–93.

157–59. μακάρι': "O lucky man."   πλούσιε: "you're rich"; effectively explains the reason for the preceding vocative.   ὦ νῦν μὲν οὐδείς, αὔριον δ' ὑπέρμεγας: "O a nobody today, but a super big shot tomorrow." Here, the pronoun οὐδείς designates a person of no importance (KG 1.61, 2.198); ὑπέρμεγας suggests "exceedingly big" (cf. *Ach.* 971, ὑπέρσοφον, "exceedingly wise").   ὦ τῶν Ἀθηνῶν ταγὲ τῶν εὐδαιμόνων: "O captain of blessed Athens." ταγός (commander, ruler) is a favorite word of the tragedians, particularly Aeschylus (e.g., *Pers.* 23, 324, 480; [A.] *Pr.* 96; cf. also S. *Ant.* 1057;

E. *IA* 269). For traditional praises of Athens, "land of Pallas," see the song of the cloud chorus at *Nu.* 300–1: ἔλθωμεν λιπαρὰν χθόνα Παλλάδος, εὔανδρον γᾶν | Κέκροπος ὀψόμεναι πολυήρατον, "Let us go to the gleaming land of Pallas to see the much loved manly land of Cecrops."

160–61. ὠγάθε: "sir,"; cf. 69–72n. The address here suggests a tone of impatience.   **πλύνειν ... τὰς κοιλίας;** "Wash my entrails." Sausage-seller's expertise lies in washing and stuffing entrails (κοιλίαι) and treating meat with spices and other ingredients (213–16; see Wilkins 2000, 195–96).   **καταγελᾷς:** "you're mocking me." The compound and its derivatives always denote laughter at the expense of someone else (Sommerstein 2009, 107).

162–75. The previous geographical joke on Paphlagon's unbridled imperial ambitions (74–79n) is here applied to Sausage-seller, who is destined to control international and domestic markets, the Council, the Assembly, the courts, and the military; see Neil ad loc.

162–63. ὦ μῶρε: A moderately inoffensive insult; see Dickey 1996, 168.   **ποίας κοιλίας;** "indeed, tripe!" When a word of the previous speaker is repeated, ποῖος (colloquial) implies not a question (about tripe, in this case) but indignation or contempt (cf. 1082; *Ach.* 109, 157; Stevens 1976, 38–39; López Eire 1996, 14).   **δευρὶ βλέπε:** "look there" (i.e., toward the audience). Cf. *Nu.* 91, δεῦρό νυν ἀπόβλεπε, "now look there!" (i.e., toward the stage); Cratin. fr. 315, δεῦρ(ο) ὅρα, "look here!" (with Olson, *FrC* 2018, 57).   **τὰς στίχας;** "the serried ranks," i.e., the audience. The term στίξ gives the question a mock-epic tone. Cf. *Il.* 4.90–91, στίχες ἀσπιστάων / λαῶν; Willi 2003, 242n51.

164–67. ἀρχέλας: "Leader of the people"; a poetic word, contracted from ἀρχέλαος, found elsewhere only at A. *Pers.* 297. It is also a proper name. The vowel contraction (α for αο), which is neither normal Attic nor Homeric, suggests a lyric model (Pi. *N.* 7.28, Μενάλα) and a tragic one (E. *Andr.* 487, Μενάλα).   **τῆς Πυκνός:** Metonymy for the Athenian Assembly. For the absence of caesura, cf. 99–100n.   **δήσεις:** "you'll bind" (by clamping them in wooden stocks as public prisoners). Cf. 367 (οἷόν σε δήσω <(ἐ)ν> τῷ ξύλῳ), 394 (ἐν ξύλῳ δήσας), 705 (ἐν τῷ ξύλῳ δήσω σε), 1049 (δῆσαί σ' ... ἐν πεντεσυρίγγῳ ξύλῳ); see also *Nu.* 592; *Pax* 479 with Olson ad loc.   **ἐν πρυτανείῳ λαικάσει:** "You'll [enjoy] sucking dick in the Prytaneion." The verb form is second-person future middle; for the abusive and degrading tone of the verb, see Jocelyn 1980, 12–16. This is a paraprosdokeion joke for "dining" in the Prytaneion, a lifelong honor of meals at public expense that was bestowed on only the greatest benefactors of the city (cf. *Pax* 1084 with Olson ad loc.). On the categories of people who might receive permanent maintenance (σίτησις) in the Prytaneion, see M. J. Osborne 1981, 158–60. The Prytaneion was located close to the agora, somewhere along the north slope of the Acropolis (Paus. 1.18.3), and housed the sacred hearth of the city (see Travlos 1971, fig. 722; Thompson and Wycherley 1972, 46–47; Hurwit 1999, 100). As a leading politician, Sausage-seller will indulge in the same sexual perversities as other contemporary political leaders (Hubbard 1991, 67–68).

168. ἐγώ; "Who me?" **σὺ μέντοι:** "Yes, you." The particle μέντοι with the second-person pronoun signals confirmation (*GP* 401).

169–70. ἐπανάβηθι κἀπὶ τοὐλεὸν τοδὶ: "Step up onto this here table." **κάτιδε:** Cf. ἐφορᾷ also 74–76n. **τὰς νήσους:** Refers specifically to the subject allies of the Cyclades (ἐν κύκλῳ) and more generally to all subject islands of the Athenian Empire (e.g., 839, ξυμμάχων; 1319; *Pax* 760). Following the imperative of motion, the second imperative here is tantamount to a final (ἵνα) clause. See López Eire 1996, 203–4, for additional examples in Aristophanes.

171. τί δαί; "What else?" The particle following an interrogative is colloquial (*GP* 262–63; Stevens 1976, 45–46; López Eire 1996, 123). **τἀμπόρια καὶ τὰς ὁλκάδας;** τἀμπόρια = τὰ ἐμπόρια and refers to the commercial ports and merchant ships of the empire.

172. πῶς οὖν; The particle following an interrogative signals an impatient question needing clarification (202, 415, 480, 1075; KG 2.161d; Smyth §2962). **μεγάλως:** Cf. 151n.

173–74. The geography of the empire and of Athens' imperial ambitions seems to be suggested in the stage action. From Athens, Caria is nearly due east, Carthage nearly due west; Sausage-seller is facing north, "as in fact the actor is when facing the audience in the Theater of Dionysus" (Sommerstein 1981, ad loc.; cf. also Revermann 2006, 119n27, 200–1). Neither Caria nor Carthage was part of the Athenian Empire, but some politicians, as depicted in comedy, aspired to conquer both; cf. 132n (Lysicles in Caria), 1300–1315 (Hyperbolus and Carthage).

175. εὐδαιμονήσω γ' εἰ διαστραφήσομαι: "I'll be really happy, if I get squint-eyed"; an emotional future condition (cf. 67–68n). The scholiast (ad

Sections 164-67–185-87

loc.) glosses διαστραφήσομαι as στρεβλωθήσομαι τοὺς ὀφθαλμούς, "I'll be cockeyed." Sausage-seller complains that he is being asked to turn his neck to cast his right eye in one direction and then his left eye in the other. In a similar joke in *Birds*, Euelpides twists his neck muscles to look in different directions in order to catch a glimpse of the future that awaits him (175–86 with Dunbar ad loc.).

176–78. πάντα πέρναται: "Everything is bought and sold" (under his supervision). πέρνημι (athematic) is often used of commerce, especially imports and exports (LSJ s.v.).   **λέγει:** "foretells."   **ἀνὴρ μέγιστος:** "a big shot" (cf. 158, ὑπέρμεγας). ἀνήρ often means a "real man," i.e., the "real deal," "a strong and fearless advocate" (e.g., 566, 1255), especially when used in political, historical, and agonistic contexts that involve praise (cf. 514). Paphlagon uses ἀνήρ to describe himself (765, 790).   **καὶ πῶς . . . ;** Cf. 128–29n.

180–81. αὐτὸ γάρ . . . καί: The particle following the demonstrative "denotes that the words following it add something . . . important"; i.e., "καί binds the demonstrative more closely to the following words" (*GP* 307–8).   **τοι:** "brings the point home to the person" (*GP* 548–50, citing this passage).   **ὁτιή:** Cf. 29n.   **πονηρός:** "wicked, useless rogue"; an antonym of χρηστός.   **κἀξ ἀγορᾶς:** To be "of the marketplace" (ἀγοραῖος) implies low social status; cf. 218. The phrase is often used to denote demagogues: see Grossmann 1950, 112–15; Connor 1971, 154–55 with n39.   **θρασύς:** "brash," "daring," "bold." θρασύς is a quality admired in epic heroes but regarded as insolent when directed against fellow citizens; cf. *Lys.* 318 with Henderson ad loc. On the verbal combination, Dover (2002, 90) notes that "the noun θρασύς appears in vituperation, coupled with πονηρός."

182. 'γῶ (ἐ)μαυτὸν: The reflexive strengthens the first-person pronoun.   **ἰσχύειν μέγα:** "to be greatly powerful"; μέγα is adverbial. Cf. *Av.* 1606–7, μεῖζον ὑμεῖς οἱ θεοί / ἰσχύσετ(ε).

184. ξυνειδέναι τί μοι δοκεῖς σαυτῷ καλόν: His concern is whether Sausage-seller is conscious of having something good in his character; see Cairns 1993, 35. The view that success in politics depends on having "nothing good" in one's character (τὸ καλόν) is a comic trope (77–79n, 164–67n).

185–87. μῶν . . . ; = μὴ οὖν: "Surely [you're] not, are you?"   **καλῶν . . . κἀγαθῶν:** A formulaic designation of well-bred, educated, and politically astute citizens, whose claims to leadership rested on genealogy, inherited wealth, and presumed moral excellence; see Dover 1994, 41–45. The phrase here seems to include all upright and patriotic citizens; see Heath 1987, 30.   **μὰ τοὺς θεούς:** "No, by the gods [may I perish]"; sc., ἀπολοίμην or the like. For the ellipsis of the verb of the apodosis, see Neil ad loc.; Werres 1936, 17–18. Boegehold (1999, 72) suggests that "when the Sausage-seller starts his oath, 'No, by the gods,' a gesture can supply the punishment he asks for if he does not fulfill his oath."   **εἰ μὴ . . . γ':** "If I'm not just"; a set phrase. The ellipsis is generated by the preceding question. See Neil ad loc.; *GP* 121.   **μακάριε:** Cf. 157.   **τῆς τύχης:** "what good luck"; genitive of exclamation (see 1–5n).   **τὰ πράγματα:** I.e., "public affairs," "politics." Cf. also 839; E. *IA* 366; *Ion* 599.

188–89. Sausage-seller may have minimum literacy (he can write his name and perhaps recognize some written words and phrases), but he is ill-equipped to read much more than that. For citizen literacy in general, see W. V. Harris 1989, 67–68, 109–10; Thomas 2009, 18–24. For literacy in ancient Greek (and Roman) education in general, see Cribiore 2001, 137–47.   **ὠγάθ':** The address is frequently used, as here, in expostulations (e.g., *Nu.* 675; *Pax* 478, 1238; *V.* 920).   **μουσικήν:** Sausage-seller declares that he lacks the Athenian knights' traditional aristocratic education, which was based on training in *mousike* (music, dance and poetry) and *gymnastike* (athletics), and that he had neither a *didaskalos* (school teacher) nor a *paidotribes* (athletic trainer). Cf. 1234–35, where Paphlagon questions Sausage-seller's education; see also Morgan 1999, 49–54.   **πλὴν γραμμάτων:** "except for letters" (i.e., rudimentary literacy).   **καὶ . . . μέντοι:** The combination is progressive and often introduces a clause (as here) or a sentence (cf. 537); see *GP* 414.   **κακὰ κακῶς:** "bad at those." The pairing of the adjective and adverb is colloquial and emphatic; cf. 1–5n.

190–93. τουτί σε μόνον ἔβλαψεν: "This thing alone hurts you." ἔβλαψεν is a gnomic or empirical aorist for a primary tense (*MT* §157; KG 1.159; Smyth §§1931–32).   **δημαγωγία:** "leadership of the people." The abstract noun and its cognates originally were without pejorative connotations. Rather, δημαγωγία was a judgment-free term associated with participation in public debate (Ostwald 1986, 201–2); cf. 956. This seems to be the earliest attestation of the word.   **μουσικὴν:** An antonym of ἀμαθῆ (193).   **χρηστοῦ τοὺς τρόπους:** "useful," "desirable," "good character." The term χρηστός often connotes the class of established respectable social standing and implies a hereditary privilege to political and intellectual leadership in the city.   **†ἀλλὰ μὴ παρῇς:** "but don't throw away . . ." Although damaged (as indicated by the dagger), the text makes good sense. Wilson (2007b, ad loc.) wonders whether a line has fallen out after βδελυρόν, and some editors unnecessarily tried to insert ἦκεν (Meineke ad loc.) or ἦκει (Herwerden 1862, xii) after βδελυρόν, with ἀλλά then deleted.

195. πῶς δῆτά . . . ; Cf. 82–84n.   **εὖ νὴ τοὺς θεούς:** "By the gods, [the oracle foretells] well."

196. ποικίλως . . . σοφῶς ἠνιγμένος: "[The oracle] riddles intricately and subtly." Riddles are closely associated with oracles (e.g., 1084–85; Pi. P. 8.40; Hdt. 5.56; E. Suppl. 138; Ion 533). The adjectives ποικίλος and σοφός are often associated with oracles and riddles (e.g., Hdt. 7.111.2, οὐδὲν ποικιλώτερον, of a Thracian oracle of Dionysus; S. OT 130, ποικιλῳδός, of the Sphinx; E. Med. 675, σοφώτερα . . . ἔπη, of the Delphic oracle). For enigma terms in oracular language, see Struck 2005, 160–64.

197–201. Dactylic hexameters (- ⌣ ⌣ [dactyl] or - - [spondee]) are characteristic of quasi-epic poetic oracles. The opening words and the mix of epic diction and comic language parody oracular style. Oracles pairing eagles and snakes are common and often portend trouble for the snake (e.g., Il. 12.200–207). Paphlagon is the eagle (203). Cf. V. 15–19, where Aristophanes uses the image of an eagle swooping down into the marketplace to seize a bronze shield; soaring skyward, the eagle is transformed into Cleonymus, and the shield is lost. Cleonymus as a ῥίψασπις is a frequent target of comic abuse; cf. 957–59n.

ἀλλ᾿ ὁπόταν: "But whenever . . ."; a common oracular opening (cf. Hdt. 1.55.2, ἀλλ᾿ ὅταν; Av. 967, ἀλλ᾿ ὅταν; Lys. 770, ἀλλ᾿ ὁπόταν).   **βυρσαίετος ἀγκυλοχήλης:** "hook-clawed rawhide eagle." The title befits Cleon, a rawhide tanner and the prime representative of a grasping, thievish politician in Aristophanes.   **κοάλεμον:** obscure but generally taken to mean "dim-witted" and the like. The scholiast (ad loc.) explains the etymology as κοεῖν, "to perceive" (synonym of νοεῖν), + ἠλεός, "crazed." Κοάλεμος (221) is the personified spirit of "Stupidity," "Foolishness." Cf. μεμακκοακότα at 62–63n.   **δὴ τότε:** "Then indeed." The particle, with or without a temporal adverb, often introduces the apodosis after a temporal or conditional clause (i.e., ὁπόταν, 197; GP 224). Cf. Av. 983–85; Hdt. 3.57.4—both oracles.   **Παφλαγόνων . . . σκοροδάλμη:** "garlic brine of Paphlagons." Garlic and its by-products are associated with fierce and bellicose natures (e.g., 946, Paphlagon; Ec. 292, dicasts; X. Smp. 4.9, gamecocks; Taillardat §378). The play's only other reference to garlic brine occurs in the contest of dream oracles, where Athena is envisioned as ladling garlic brine over

Paphlagon (1090–95); for discussion, see Anderson 1991. The comic poet
Cratinus (see 400–1) mentions that garlic brine was a favorite of the Cyclops
(fr. 150); it may also have been a favorite relish of Paphlagonia (Luc. *Alex.*
39).   **ἀπόλλυται:** Oracular present (127n).   **θεὸς . . . κῦδος ὀπάζει:**
Apollo. The phrasing recalls two Homeric formulae: κῦδος ὀπάζει (of Zeus:
Il. 8.141, 12.255, 17.566, 21.570; *Od.* 19.161; of Poseidon: *Il.* 14.357–58; *Od.*
3.55–57; of Apollo: *Il.* 15.326–27; of Hermes: *Od.* 15.320) and μέγα κῦδος
Ἀχαιῶν (*Il.* 9.673, 10.87, 11.511, 14.42).   **αἴ κεν μὴ:** "Unless." αἴ κεν (epic
and Doric forms) = Attic ἐάν. Cf. αἴ κε μή, 210; αἰ δέ κε μὴ, *Av.* 978; KG
2.463n1; Smyth §§2282–83.

202–3. πῶς οὖν . . . ; Cf. 172n.   **βυρσαίετος . . . οὑτοσί:** "this here
leather-eagle." The actor may point toward Cleon, who was presumably in
the front-row seat (προεδρία) that was awarded to honor his victory at Pylos.
For the use of the deictic suffix -ί to point out a specific individual, cf. *V.* 74,
Ἀμυνίας . . . οὑτοσί; *Pl.* 800, Δεξίνικος . . . οὑτοσί.

204–5. αὐτό που λέγει: "I suppose it means" (cf. *V.* 921, αὐτὸ γὰρ βοᾷ, "It
speaks for itself"). For the sense of που, see *GP* 491.   **ἁρπάζων:** Cf. 52–
53n.   **φέρει:** "carry away," "plunder"; cf. LSJ s.v. VI.2.

206. ὁ δράκων δὲ πρὸς τί; "But to what does the snake [apply]?" In questions,
connective δέ often bears "a note of surprise, impatience, or indignation" (*GP*
173). For the postponement of the interrogative, see Thomson 1939, 147–52.

207–08. ὁ δράκων γάρ ἐστι μακρὸν ὅ τ' ἀλλᾶς αὖ μακρόν: A parody of
literal interpretations of oracles; cf. 1073–74, where Sausage-seller explains
to Demos how a trireme can be like a fox-dog (ὅτι ἡ τριήρης ἐστὶ χὠ κύων
ταχύ).   **γάρ:** "Obviously." The particle "denotes that that question need
never have been put, had not the questioner overlooked an answer rhetorically
presented as obvious" (*GP* 79).   **εἴθ':** = εἴτα.   **αἱματοπώτης:**
"bloodthirsty."   **ἀλλᾶς:** A kind of blood sausage (Sophil. fr. 6.2, χορδήν τιν'
αἱματῖτην). Blood was a thickener; spices and garlic add flavor. See *Od.* 20.25–
27 for a description of roasting sausages stuffed with fat and blood.

210. ἤδη: "Soon"; denoting a result in the immediate future (cf. 1050; KG
2.122–23).   **αἴ κε μὴ:** Cf. 197–201n.   **θαλφθῇ λόγοις:** "he's softened by
[Paphlagon's] words," i.e., "deceived" (LSJ s.v. θάλπω). θάλπειν which suggests
uncomfortable heat (*Av.* 1092 with Dunbar ad loc.) continues the roasting
image.

211–12. αἰκάλλει: The verb is commonly used of a fawning dog (48n). Here, it means "encourages," "stirs up hope" (cf. *Th.* 869 with Austin and Olson ad loc.; Taillardat §696). **ἐπιτροπεύειν:** "to govern," "to steward." The responsibilities of the ἐπίτροπος, "trustee/steward," are like those of the ταμίας, "treasurer" (fr. 305.2). The struggle between Sausage-seller and Paphlagon centers on winning the right to become the ταμίας of Demos (426, 947–49, 1098–99, 1259). **ἐγώ:** Emphatic at line end (cf. 634, 636, 703).

213–16. Sausage-seller's work of "feeding the public" is an "apt metaphor of political leadership and rhetoric" (Hubbard 1991, 69). **φαυλότατον:** "very simple." **τάραττε:** Cf. 64–66n. **χόρδευ(ε):** "make sausage of" (cf. the culinary metaphor at 343). **τὰ πράγματα:** "political affairs"; cf. 185–87n. **τὸν δῆμον ἀεὶ προσποιοῦ:** "always win the demos over" (a mock recipe follows). For the pun on δῆμος = "people" and δημός = "fat," cf. 954; *V.* 40–41. **ὑπογλυκαίνων:** "discretely sweetening." In compounds, ὑπο- often suggests "gradually" (see LSJ s.v. ὑπό F.II; Smyth §1698.4). The term is here used metaphorically for rhetorical persuasion; see also 343, where Sausage-seller says that he can "make a stew of everything." **ῥηματίοις:** "phraselets." Aristophanes uses the diminutive pejoratively to mark deceptive oratory (e.g., *Ach.* 444; for use in culinary metaphors, see *Nu.* 943 and *V.* 668). **μαγειρικοῖς:** "befitting a cook." Providing Demos (i.e., the Athenian demos) with "culinary goodies" as a means of control is a recurring motif in the play (see Anderson 1995, 22–35; Wilkins 2000, 179–201).

217–21. Sausage-seller has even more extreme forms of all the vices that account for Cleon's political success: a loud, repulsive (μιαρά) voice; low birth; and vulgar marketplace values. Cf. 180–81n. **δημαγωγικά:** Cf. 190–93n. **ἀγόραιος:** I.e., a lowlife; cf. 293, 409–10n. **πολιτείαν:** "political career." **χρησμοί τε συμβαίνουσι:** "and the oracles agree." Cf. the use of συμβαίνειν to confirm an oracle's truth at S. *Tr.* 173, 1164, 1174. **τὸ Πυθικόν:** The Delphic oracle. Wilson (2007b, ad loc.) suspects that τὸ Πυθικόν was a marginal comment that entered the text because it "occurred to a learned reader." If the reading τὸ Πυθικόν is correct, Slave A has forgotten that the oracle was ascribed to Bacis (123–40); cf. also 1015–20. **Κοαλέμῳ:** Cf. 197–201n. For similar ad hoc "divine" personifications, cf. Sausage-seller's apostrophe (see glossary) to the "gods" before heading into the Boule (634–35). Κοάλεμος was also a nickname for the grandfather of Cimon (Plu. *Cim.* 4.3). **χὤπως ἀμυνεῖ:** ὅπως with the future indicative (with ellipse of σκόπει or the like) is used colloquially to denote an urgent exhortation or a warning (e.g., 497, 760, 1011; *V.* 1222). See KG 2.376; Smyth §2213 (ellipsis); *MT* §§271–73; Stevens 1976, 29.

222-24: καὶ τίς ξύμμαχος . . . ; "But who [will be] my ally . . . ?" For the force of καί preceding an interrogative, cf. 128-29n.   **γὰρ:** Explanatory (*GP* 59-60).   **πένης βδύλλει λεώς:** "poor people are deathly afraid." πένης is here used adjectively; cf. E. *El.* 372, ἐν πένητι σώματι; 1139, πένητας ἐς δόμους. The poor (like the wealthy πλούσιοι) fear his political power. There may also be a hint here at a scatological joke, since "to be in deadly fear" (βδύλλειν) often affects the bowels of characters in Aristophanes' comedies (e.g., 1057, χέζω, of a woman facing combat; *Nu.* 1133, βδελύττομαι; *V.* 626, ἐγχέζω; *Av.* 65-68, ὑποδέδω . . . ἐπιχέζω; *Lys.* 354, βδύλλω; *Ra.* 479-90, ἐγχέζω; *Pl.* 700, βδελύττομαι). See Henderson 1991a, 195-96; Taillardat §309. The suffix -ύλλω is colloquial; see Peppler 1921, 152-53.

225-29. Slave A answers Sausage-seller's question about his allies which include first and foremost the *Knights* chorus and the knights as a class. For the knights' hatred of Cleon, cf. *Ach.* 299-302. The feeling was mutual. Their hostility seems to have originated in a legal dispute of some kind, perhaps a charge of official misconduct brought against Cleon by leading knights (schol. at *Ach.* 6-8). Carawan (1990, 137-47) argues that the dispute involved an accusation by influential knights that Cleon took bribes from certain subject allies to reduce their tribute (cf. 832-35) and that Cleon was compelled by them to return the money in exchange for having the charges dropped. Fornara (1973, 124) posits that Cleon initiated an attack denouncing the money paid to the cavalry for the provision of their equipment. It seems fairly clear that the dispute between Cleon and the knights was public and almost certainly involved official misconduct. The scholia (ad loc.) report that Cleon was himself once a knight but was treated badly by them, a statement that is "consistent with what we know of him from Plutarch's *Moralia* 806f-807a" (Connor, 1971, 152n32).

ἱππῆς . . . χίλιοι: This number would effectively amount to nearly the total number of Athenian knights who were available at the beginning of the Peloponnesian War (estimated to number twelve hundred at Th. 2.13.8). The expansion of the cavalry from three hundred to one thousand sometime between 445-438 BCE would have resulted in a composite corps of wealthy and less wealthy citizens who had no genuine equestrian traditions; nonetheless, the knights still would have constituted an elite social group. See Spence 1993, 9-10, 186-91.   **καλοί τε κἀγαθοί:** Cf. 185-87n.   **ὧν θεατῶν . . . δεξιός:** "The sophisticated member of the audience." δεξιός is a popular contemporary term that designates (and here flatters) the spectator who is capable, in Aristophanes' opinion, of both appreciating Aristophanes' exceptional artistic expertise—his creative intelligence as a comic poet (cf.

233; *Nu.* 521, 527; *Ra.* 71)—and supporting his goal of toppling Cleon. Indeed, that the knights (and audience supporters) "hate" Cleon confirms their support of Aristophanes; see Dover 1993, 13–14.   χὠ θεὸς ξυλλήψεται: "and the god will assist" (i.e., Apollo). The phrasing is oracular (cf. Th. 1.118.3, 1.123.1, 2.54.4, [θεὸς] αὐτὸς ἔφη ξυλλήψεσθαι). For the parody of oracular phrasing, see Rau 1967, 174–75.

231–33. Portrait masks must have been used to represent well-known contemporaries. Why else would the poet draw attention to the mask here? Dover (1975, 162, 164) suggests that either the mask makers refused to make a realistic likeness, for fear of angering Cleon for contributing to his public ridicule, or Cleon's face was so hideous that no mask maker would have dared to risk looking at such a representation (as if to look at his portrait was to behold the Gorgon Medusa). Cratinus apparently mocked Cleon's ugly eyebrows (fr. 228; cf. Welsh 1979, 214–15). Olson (1999a, 320–21) argues that Aristophanes was probably referring to the terrifying facial expressions (frowns, scowls, sneers, glowering) supposedly typical of Cleon, rather than to his physical appearance. Olson adds that a portrait mask would not have been necessary, as Aristophanes takes plenty of care to ensure that the "smart/ aware" members of the audience (233) would recognize the caricature.

232–33. τῶν σκευοποιῶν: There must have been many mask-making workshops in Athens, given the number of individual masks of actors and choruses needed at the dramatic festivals. E.g., a conservative estimate for the City Dionysia suggests that around 240 masks would be needed for the three tetralogies, plus 170 for the choruses and actors in the five comic performances (perhaps reduced temporarily to three performances during the Peloponnesian War). For these estimates, see Hughes 2012, 174.   μὴν: "in any case"; a strong adversative (*GP* 348).   τὸ γὰρ θέατρον δεξιόν: "for the audience is sophisticated" (cf. 228, 233). θέατρον = audience (cf. 507–11, 1318); for a similar metonymy, cf. τὸ βουλευτήριον = the Boule (395).

234. οἴμοι κακοδαίμων: "Alas, woe is me"; a colloquial expression of alarm and distress (cf. 752, 1206, 1243). See Stevens 1976, 14–15; Labiano Ilundain 2000, 256.

235–46. *Paphlagon, wearing a garland (1227) and steward's ring that Demos later takes back (947–58), storms out of the house of Demos.*   Paphlagon's costume would include exaggerated stomach and buttock padding, a leather phallus (as worn by the two slaves; cf. 24–29), a short chiton, and perhaps other costume features or items to highlight his occupation; see Landfester

1967, 17. In one of the few references to costumes in the play, Demos rejects Paphlagon's offer of a jacket on the grounds that it "utterly stinks of rawhide" (βύρσης κάκιστον ὄζον, 892). On costumes in Aristophanes, see Stone 1981.

235–36. οὗτοι: "Absolutely not." οὗτοι with oaths strengthens the speaker's objection (435, 698; *Nu.* 814).   **μὰ τοὺς δώδεκα θεούς:** The Twelve Gods, probably the twelve Olympians, were conceived as a kind of corporate body (*Av.* 95 with Dunbar ad loc.); their altar in the agora was a place of asylum and refuge (Hdt. 6.108.4; Th. 6.54.6) as well as the symbolic center of Attica from where distances were measured (Hdt. 2.7.1; *IG* i³ 1092, dated to 440–430; *IG* ii² 2640, dated to ca. 400 BCE; Wycherley 1978, 205; Camp 2010, 89–91). The promissory oath stresses Paphlagon's outraged reaction; see Sommerstein and Torrance 2014, 183n11.   **χαιρήσετον:** Future dual; a threat: "You two won't be happy," "you'll come to regret this" (cf. 828). In Aristophanes, the verb in an oath is usually in the future as it is here (*GP* 543–44).   **τῷ δήμῳ ξυνόμνυτον:** "You're both plotting against the demos." Aristophanes portrays Paphlagon-Cleon as habitually accusing political opponents of conspiring to overthrow the democracy (257, 452, 476–79, 628, 862; cf. *V.* 345, 464–65, 482–83, 487–88, 507, 953; *Lys.* 577–78 with Henderson ad loc.). The portrayal reflects the rhetorical practices of the historical Cleon and contemporary politicians like him (e.g., the picture of Cleon in the Mytilenian debate, Th. 3.37.2). On conspiratorial rhetoric in Aristophanes and Thucydides, see Roisman 2006, 66–67.

237. τουτὶ τί δρᾷ τὸ Χαλκιδικὸν ποτήριον: Paphlagon points to the drinking cup (τουτί . . . ποτήριον) that Slave B lifted from the master's cupboard (95–102). The origin of the cup calls to mind the silver vessels made in Chalcis and housed in the treasury of Athena on the Acropolis (cf. *IG* i³ 299–315, 350–58); see D. Harris 1995, III.33–40, IV.55. Chalcis was located at the narrowest part of the channel separating the island of Euboea from the Greek mainland and was strategically and commercially important; hence the Peloponnesians established the colony of Heraclea nearby (426 BCE) in order to threaten supply lines for Athenian grain (Th. 3.92–93). For similar self-serving political accusations, cf. *Ach.* 915–25, where the sycophant Nicarchus claims that a Theban in possession of a lampwick intends to set the Piraeus ship sheds on fire.

238–39. οὐκ ἔσθ᾽ ὅπως οὐ: "There's no way that not"; i.e., "it can only mean." The idiomatic phrase adds strong, undeniable emphasis to a point (KG 2.405 A9; Smyth §2515).   **ἀφίστατον:** "inciting revolution" (dual present).   **ἀπολεῖσθον, ἀποθανεῖσθον:** dual futures.

240–41. οὐ μενεῖς; This idiomatic use of future tense with a negative in a question is equivalent to an imperative (e.g., *Ach.* 165, 564; *Av.* 354, 1055; *Th.* 689; cf. KG 1.176–77).   **ὦ γεννάδα:** A deferential form of address that here functions as tactical praise intended to prevent Sausage-seller from running away in panic. On the use of the term in Aristophanes, see Dover 2002, 89.   **τὰ πράγματα:** "matters of state"; cf. 185–87n.

242-332. Parados (see glossary). The chorus enters, singing and dancing. For a detailed discussion of the role played by the chorus, both specific to this play and in general (from *Babylonians* to *Wasps*), see Henderson 2013. This chorus is made up of twenty-four knights, probably wearing wigs of fashionably long hair (cf. 580, 1121) and perhaps riding "piggy-back" on other men dressed as horses (for a vase depicting young riders mounted on the shoulders of men costumed as horses, see Berlin Staatlichen Museen F 1697 [= *ABV* 297.17] with Rothwell 2007, 37), or wearing "horses" attached at the waist (Rothwell 2007, 142). Right from the start, the chorus supports Sausage-seller as an ally and fellow enemy of Paphlagon-Cleon. Indeed, only the chorus refers to Cleon by name in the play (976 where his ruin is presented as a blessing for the city and its friends), a fact which highlights their hatred of Cleon.

242-302: Meter: trochaic tetrameter catalectics and trochaic dimeters at 284–302. Catalectic meters omit the final beat to signal the end of the verse or sequence of verses (West 1982, 92–93).

242-46. Katakeleusmos (see glossary).

242-43. ἄνδρες ἱππῆς: "Cavalrymen." Substantives that designate occupations of particular individuals can often be treated as adjectives with the word ἀνήρ (cf. 507; KG 1.271; Smyth §986).   **νῦν ὁ καιρός:** "The moment is at hand" (cf. Pl. Com. fr. 189.17).   **Σίμων:** *PA* 12687; *PAA* 822085. He could be the author of a treatise on horsemanship (*PA* 12689; *PAA* 822090; cf. X. *Eq.* 1.1) and/or the leader (*PA* 12702; *PAA* 822460) of a *thiasos* (a religious guild of Heracles) who resided in the same deme (Cydathenaeum) as Aristophanes and Cleon, suggesting that Simon was personally acquainted with both the poet and Cleon; see Lind 1991, 135.   **Παναίτι(ε):** *PA* 11566; *PAA* 763445. Aristophanes compares a Panaetius (*PA* 11567; *PAA* 763450) to a "monkey" (fr. 409) and "son of a cook" (schol. at *Av.* 440); Andocides (1.13) reports a Panaetius (*PA* 11567+; *PAA* 763480) who was denounced for profanation of the mysteries and mutilation of the Herms in 415 BCE. Members of choruses are addressed sometimes by fictional names, sometimes by names of real people (cf. Wilson 2007b, ad loc.; *V.* 230–34 with Biles and Olson ad loc.). We cannot positively identify either Simon or Panaetius, but both could easily have been hipparchs on recent campaigns (see 266–68n).   **οὐκ ἐλᾶτε πρὸς τὸ δεξιὸν κέρας;** The cavalry was regularly positioned on the wings in preparation for battle. The scholiast (ad loc.) notes, ὡς ἐπὶ τάξεως φησίν, "he speaks as if giving battle orders."

244–46. ἄνδρες ἐγγύς: Refers to both the entering chorus of knights and the knights seated in the audience. *Slave A speaks to Sausage-seller.*   **ἀμύνου:** "defend yourself."   **ὁμοῦ:** "Close at hand."   **προσκειμένων:** In military contexts, πρόσκειμαι often describes cavalry charges and pursuits (Hdt. 9.40, 57.3; Th. 7.30.2, 7.78.3).   **τροπὴν αὐτοῦ ποιοῦ:** "rout him." For the military expression τροπὴν ποιεῖν/ποιεῖσθαι, cf. Hdt. 1.30.5; Th. 2.19.2.

247–81. For the attribution of the actors' lines, we follow Wilson (2007b, ad loc.). Coulon and van Daele (1972), Sommerstein (1981), and Henderson (1998) attribute lines 258–65 and 276–77 to the coryphaeus.

247–48. παῖε, παῖε: "Strike, strike him." The repeated imperative both marks the speaker's agitation (cf. 821, 919; *Ach.* 281–82; *V.* 456; *Pax* 1119) and functions as a kind of war cry, suggesting a threatening motion of some sort on the part of the chorus.   **πανοῦργον:** Cf. 45. The speaker runs out of abusive epithets for Paphlagon and returns to his first choice (καὶ πανοῦργον καὶ πανοῦργον, 249).   **ταραξιππόστρατον:** "disturber of the cavalry"; an Aristophanic coinage found only here. It recalls ταράξιππος (frightener of horses), and the application of that term for an evil spirit on the race track (Paus. 6.20.15–19; cf. *Palatine Anthology* 14.4) hints that Cleon is its monstrous human counterpart and a threat to the knights. Cf. also ταραξικάρδιον at *Ach.* 315. For Paphlagon-Cleon's hostility to the knights, cf. 626–29.   **τελώνην:** "tax collector"; i.e., "extortionist," "robber." Contracts to collect taxes for the city were bid on by private collectors, who were stereotypically regarded as extortionists. Sommerstein (1981, ad loc.) observes that this is apparently "the earliest occasion on which this term is used (as it often is in later Greek) to mean 'robber, villain.'"   **Χάρυβδιν ἁρπαγῆς:** "Charybdis of rapacity." Cleon is like the monstrous belching whirlpool that vacuums up everything that comes in its path (cf. *Od.* 12.103–10, 235–43, 430–41). Cf. also the use of the epithet ποντοχάρυβδις, "sea swallowing," for a glutton (Hippon. fr. 128.1 W).

250. καὶ γὰρ οὗτος ἦν: "Because this man was." Here, καί refers to the previous sentence as a whole (*GP* 108–9).

251-52. τάραττε καὶ κύκα: Cf. 64–66n.   **βδελύττου:** Cf. 134–37n.   **καὶ γὰρ ἡμεῖς:** "as we do" (*GP* 108).   **κἀπικείμενος:** "and attacking, pressing hard."   **βόα:** Imperative, here functioning as a kind of war cry.   **καὶ γὰρ:** "For in fact" (*GP* 109).

254. Εὐκράτης: Cf. 128–29n.   **εὐθὺ τῶν κυρηβίων:** A locative adverb with the genitive = "straight toward" (cf. *Av.* 1421, εὐθὺ Πελλήνης; fr. 671, εὐθὺ Σικελίας). The term κυρήβια, "bran shop," refers to Eucrates and alludes to the proverbial saying "like a donkey running off to a bran heap"; cf. *V.* 1306–10 with the note (ad loc.) of Biles and Olson, who refer to the gloss of Photius (ο 353 = *Suda* ο 389), "those who unexpectedly get something good and enjoy it enthusiastically."

255-57. Under attack, Paphlagon appeals to the spectators for support, as if he were addressing members of a jury. Cf. *V.* 197, where Philocleon, "Cleon-lover," calls on his fellow jurors and Cleon for aid (ὦ ξυνδικασταὶ καὶ Κλέων, ἀμύνατε).   **ὦ γέροντες ἡλιασταί:** By comic convention (and presumably in fact), Athenian juries consisted largely of lower-class old men who welcomed the prospect of earning money and socializing with fellow elders (cf. 800, 977–80; *Ach.* 375–76; *V.* 605–6, 689–90).   **φράτερες τριωβόλου:** "brethren of the three obols." The reference is to the three obols that had recently become the daily pay of citizen jurors, thanks to Cleon (cf. 50–51n). "Brethren" (φράτερες) comically suggests that they belong to the same phratry, an ancient kinship group, membership in which had become a basic requirement for citizenship (see Lambert 1993, 25–57, especially 31–43).   **βόσκω:** The word is often used of supporting oneself or dependent members of one's household (e.g., at 1258, of Sausage-seller rearing himself in the agora; at *Lys.* 1203–4, of feeding slaves and children; cf. Taillardat §126). Paphlagon feeds and supports his charges, the jurymen, by providing court cases for prosecution and by securing convictions that produce revenue for the city and for the jurymen's daily pay (50–51, 1019; cf. 897–98, 1316–17, 1356–70; *V.* 242, 596–97).   **κεκραγώς:** Cf. 134–37n.   **καὶ δίκαια κἄδικα:** An idiom meaning "whether right or wrong" (cf. *Ach.* 373; *Nu.* 99).   **παραβοηθεῖτε:** "help"; i.e., "send reinforcements" (Th. 3.22.7; X. *HG* 1.1.6).   **ὑπ' ἀνδρῶν . . . ξυνωμοτῶν:** Neil (ad loc.) explains that "with a word of unfavorable meaning ἀνήρ deepens the dislike implied"; see 235–36n.

258-60. ἐν δίκῃ γ': An idiom meaning "yes, and rightly so" (*Nu.* 1379; *V.* 508). Postpositive γε is often postponed in poetry to add urgency and to affirm the speaker's response (*GP* 146–49).   **τὰ κοινά:** I.e., public funds.   **πρὶν λαχεῖν:** I.e., "before you're allotted public office." In Old

Comedy, public officers are regularly portrayed as embezzlers of public funds (cf. 103–4n). Excluding some military positions (e.g., generals) and civic magistracies (e.g., financial experts), most public offices in the democracy were filled by lot (e.g., the jury courts and the Council).   **κατεσθίεις:** "you devour." For similar culinary metaphors, cf. 103–4n.   **κἀποσυκάζεις:** "[like] a fig picker." For the play on figs (σῦκον) and sycophancy, cf. *V.* 145, 895; *Av.* 1699, *Pl.* 946; Cratin. fr. 70.1; Taillardat §717, §729.   **τοὺς ὑπευθύνους:** All Athenian magistrates leaving office underwent a procedure called εὔθυνα, a public examination of their handling of state finances and their conduct in office; see MacDowell 1978, 170–72. The implication seems to be that Paphlagon is so eager for personal power and gain that he would challenge outgoing public officials even before their formal audit is due (cf. 824–27).   **σκοπῶν:** With an object clause. Cf. 264; Smyth §2210, §2224a.   **ἢ †μὴ πέπων:** "or unripe." Whether this phrase means "unripe" or "ripening" is problematic. Gomme (1958, 1) notes that the phrase ἢ πέπων ἢ μὴ πέπων (either ripe or not ripe) is equivalent to εἴτε πέπων εἴτε μή (cf. KG 2.300n1) and that there is no parallel for μὴ πέπων = "ripening," favored by Neil (ad loc.). Wilson (2007b, ad loc.) questions whether the sense "ripening" can be achieved in Greek without an "adverbial modifier; hence Kock's μηδέπω."

264–65. Transposed after 260 by Brunck.   **καὶ σκοπεῖς:** "and you're looking into . . ."   **γε:** For the particle's postponement, cf. 258–60n.   **τῶν πολιτῶν ὅστις:** "whoever of private citizens," as distinct from city magistrates (259–60). Presumably, Cleon's favorite targets for *euthynai* proceedings were wealthy individuals with low public profiles.   **ἀμνοκῶν:** "lamb-minded"; i.e., "simple-minded," "naïve."   **πονηρὸς:** 180–81n.   **τρέμων:** "dreading"; cf. *Ach.* 494, τρέμει τὸ πρᾶγμ(α).   **τὰ πράγματα:** I.e., litigation.

261–63. ἀπράγμον': "Apolitical" (Th. 2.40.2, 2.63.2–3). See Dover 1994, 188–90; Carter 1986.   **κεχηνότα:** "gaping, open mouthed"; the perfect of χάσκω and a favorite word of Aristophanes in the play (380, 651, 755, 804, 824, 956, 1018, 1032, 1119, 1263).   **Χερρονήσου:** Comic orthography generally prefers the spelling -ρρ- to -ρσ- for non-Attic place-names (Willi 2002, 207–8). The Thracian Chersonese was a peninsula under Athenian control and populated by many Athenian settlers and grain merchants. Presumably, this citizen, who is to be recalled to face trial on trumped-up charges, was either a trader with business dealings in the Chersonese or an Athenian official on assignment there.   **διαβαλών, ἀγκυρίσας:** "having seized, tripped up." Note the pun on διαβαλών as a wrestling term ["seized around the waist"]. On wrestling terminology, see Poliakoff 1987, 33–53. Ignore the reference to

Henderson. **ἐνεκολήβασας:** "step on him"; an apparent ad hoc coinage, which the *Suda* (ε 525, ἐγκολαβήσας, κοληβάζειν) equates with ἐπὶ κόλοις βαίνειν, "sodomize." Henderson (1991a, 155) compares βιβάζειν at Alc. Com. fr. 18 to ὀχεύειν ("copulate"); see also the suggestion by Henderson (200) of a possible pederastic pun on the element κόλον.

266–68. ξυνεπίκεισθ' ὑμεῖς; Paphlagon, realizing that the chorus of knights is also against him, asks indignantly, "You [all] are joining the attack?"   **λέγειν γνώμην:** A procedural phrase: "to propose a motion in the Assembly" (cf. γνώμην ἔλεξεν, 654; γνώμην ἐρεῖν, 931).   **ἔμελλον:** In Aristophanes, ἔμελλον never takes the augment ἠ-, except in anapests (e.g., *Ra.*. 1038; *Ec.* 597; see Willi 2003, 248); for ἔμελλον + an inchoative present infinitive (rather than future infinitive), cf. Neil ad loc.; *Th.* 1177 ; *Ra.* 518.   **ἐν πόλει:** "in the city." The article is often omitted in prepositional phrases (KG 1.603; Smyth §1128).   **μνημεῖον:** The promise to dedicate a monument ostensibly to commemorate the knights' successful expedition of 425 may be an allusion to the captured Spartan shields from Pylos that may have been displayed on the Athena Nike bastion to commemorate the Athenian (i.e., Cleon's) victory at Sphacteria (cf. 843–46n).   **ἀνδρείας χάριν:** Probably a reference to the maritime expedition of 425 in which the Athenian cavalry played a "manfully" (ἀνδρικῶς) decisive role against Corinthian defenders (599–604; *Th.* 4.42–44). If Simon and Panaetius (242–43) were real hipparchs, they may have been the cavalry commanders of the expedition (cf. *Th.* 4.44.1 with Hornblower 2008).

269–302. Proagon (see glossary). The dialogue introduces the nature of the impending conflict. Paphlagon and Sausage-seller engage in mutual threats, insults, and slanders, to prove who is in fact the most shameless. For the agon proper, see 303–460n.

269–70. ὡς δ': δέ adds an indignant tone to the exclamation (cf. 397); see *GP* 175.iii.   **ἀλαζών:** An ἀλαζών, a common term of abuse in Old Comedy and tragedy, is a man who somehow claims a respect he does not deserve (Arist. *EN* 1127a20ff.; see MacDowell 1990).   **μάσθλης:** "leather strap" or "whip"; here used figuratively as a term of abuse (cf. *Nu.* 449 with Dover ad loc.).   **εἶδες:** "Do you see"; colloquial use of the aorist to express a realization that an action is now happening (*MT* §60; Collard 2018, 177). The singular form may be addressed to a fellow chorus member or to Slave A or may simply reflect his overall exasperation.   **ὑπέρχεται:** "flatters, fawns over." Cf. [X.] *Ath.* 2.14; Rutherford 1881, 110.   **ὡσπερεὶ:** "as if."   **κἀκκοβαλικεύεται:** "and bamboozles, plays tricks on"; perhaps an Aristophanic coinage.

271-72. ἐνιῇ: "Charges"; a technical term of cavalry warfare (X. *Cyr.* 7. 1.29; *HG* 2. 4.32). The paradosis, γε νικᾷ, "is victorious," makes little sense, as Paphlagon is contained on all sides; cf. Wilson 2007b, ad loc.   **ταύτῃ:** "in this direction."   **ταυτηὶ:** Sc., τῇ χειρὶ or the like.   **ὑπεκκλίνη . . . δευρί:** "he retreats in that direction."   **πρὸς σκέλος κυρηβάσει:** "he'll butt against a leg," as if Paphlagon were a goat or ram with horns (cf. Cratin. fr. 465 with Olson, *FrC* 2018, 298–99).

273. ὦ πόλις καὶ δῆμ᾽: His apostrophe of woe is probably paratragic (S. *OT* 629; *Ach.* 27, 75; Eup. fr. 219.2); cf. the Latin exclamation *o tempora! o mores!* (Cic. *Cat.* 1.1). For πόλις (city) and δῆμος (people) similarly distinguished, cf. 810–12 with van Leeuwen ad loc.; *Ach.* 631; *Pl.* 508.   **γαστρίζομαι:** "I'm getting punched in the belly" (cf. the exhortation of the chorus at 453–55, παι᾽ αὐτὸν . . . καὶ / γάστριζε καὶ τοῖς ἐντέροις / καὶ τοῖς κόλοις). The Athenians seem also to have used this word to mean "stuff one's belly with food" (cf. *V.* 1528–31 with Biles and Olson ad loc.). In contrast to the treatment of Paphlagon-Cleon here (at the height of his influence and power), the chorus of clouds notes the poet's restraint over such an attack when Cleon was in political eclipse (*Nu.* 549, Κλέων᾽ ἔπαισ᾽ εἰς τὴν γαστέρα).

274. Wilson, following Coulon and van Daele, attributes the line to Slave A; Sommerstein (1981, ad loc.) and Henderson (ad loc.) attribute it to Sausage-seller. In either case, the hostility between the speaker of this line and Paphlagon (275) is palpable.   **καταστρέφεις:** "you're turning [the city] upside down" (cf. 309–12); see Sommerstein 2001, 239.

276-77. ἐὰν μὲν τόνδε νικᾷς: "If on the one hand you defeat this man . . ." Wilson (2007b, ad loc.) follows "Porson's slight change" from the paradosis (μέντοι γε), as it "creates a good antithesis between the two accusative pronouns" (τόνδε and σε).   **τήνελλος:** A traditional triumphal address to victors in games (*Ach.* 1227; *Av.* 1764).   **ἀναιδείᾳ:** Shamelessness is a regular and consistent charge against Paphlagon (324–25, 409–14, 1206).   **ἡμέτερος ὁ πυραμοῦς:** "it's our cake"; i.e., "we win." πυραμοῦς is a honey cake often served at banquets and symposia (schol. ad loc.; cf. Ephipp. frr. 8.3, 13.4).

278-79. τουτονὶ τὸν ἄνδρ᾽ ἐγὼ ᾽νδείκνυμι: "I'm informing against this man here" (cf. 44–45n). Paphlagon threatens Sausage-seller through a procedure known as ἔνδειξις; see Harrison 1971, 228–31. The charge could be brought in wartime, as here, to prosecute persons accused of trading with the enemy

(And. 2.14). Each character refers to the other in the third person, as if opposing litigants presenting a case for deliberation by a jury (here, the audience). **φήμ᾽**: "I denounce"; a technical legal term (Pl. Com. fr. 141), here used to introduce the pun. For the legal procedure known by the verb φαίνειν and by the noun φάσις, see MacDowell 2018. For comic portrayals of Cleon and demagogues using the law courts, the Council (Boule), and the Assembly (Ekklesia) to denounce and attack rivals for personal and political gains, see Ostwald 1986, 202–3. **ταῖσι Πελοποννσίων τριήρεσι ζωμεύματα**: "meaty ribs for the Spartans' triremes"; a pun on ζωμός (meaty soup) and ὑποζώματα (cables or braces used to strengthen a trireme's hull). Cf. the pun on ἔντερα, the inedible sections of an animal's colon, and ἐντερόνεια, a ship's "belly timbers" or "ribs" (1185–86 with Anderson 1995, 32).

281. εἰσδραμὼν εἰς τὸ πρυτανεῖον: The poet frequently says that Paphlagon-Cleon does not deserve such an honor (709, 766, 1404–5; cf. also 573–74); hence the demagogue himself is open to the threat of ἔνδειξις (278–79n). For σίτησις, cf. 164–67n.

282-83. γε: "Yes." The particle often adds a detail to an assent (*GP* 136). **ἐξάγων γε τἀπόρρηθ᾽**: "he exports contraband" (cf. *Ra.* 362–63, τἀπόρρητ᾽ ἀποπέμπει / ἐξ Αἰγίνης, "he ships contraband from Aegina," with Dover ad loc.). Slave A insinuates that Paphlagon is involved in smuggling. **οὐ Περικλέης οὐκ ἠξιώθη πώποτε:** Probably means that Pericles (*PA* 11811; *PAA* 772645) was never awarded the lifetime honor of σίτησις.

284-302. "At 284, the slanging match between the Paphlagonian and the Sausage-seller runs into a rapid-fire exchange of dimeters. At 297–98, the Sausage-seller interjects two dimeters, but the Paphlagonian gets the upper hand with eight trochaic metra to Sausage-seller's four" (L. P. E. Parker 1997, 162).

284. ἀποθανεῖσθον: Future dual.

285. τριπλάσιον: "Thrice"; first attested in *Ach.* 88 and perhaps colloquial (cf. 718). **κεκράξομαι:** Future perfect used for future, like the use of perfect for present (*Ra.* 265; fr. 81; Eup. fr. 1.3; KG 1.148–49; Smyth §1947). Sausage-seller will scream three times as loud as Paphlagon, the acknowledged master of loud and raucous shouting.

286. καταβοήσομαι βοῶν σε: "I'll shout you down in shouting"; cf. *Ach.* 711, καταβοήσε . . . κεκραγώς. Compounds with κατά (down) sometimes take the accusative (KG 1.301).

287. κατακεκράξομαί σε κράζων: "I'll outscream you in screaming." Sausage-seller adopts Paphlagon's methods on the spot: κατα + shouting verb, followed by participle of the same shouting verb. Note also the alliteration of κα-, κε-, κρ-, κρ-.

288. διαβαλῶ: "I'll slander," "discredit." Plutarch (*Pers.* 35.4) says that Cleon was one of the accusers of Pericles for the military failure at Epidaurus in 431/30. For Cleon's propensity to slander and otherwise intimidate political opponents, see Ostwald 1986, 211–12, 222–23.

290. περιελῶ σ' ἀλαζονείαις: "I'll corral you with nonsense"; a metaphor for cavalry tactics (cf. Th. 7.44.8, οἱ ἱππῆς τῶν Συρακοσίων περιελάσαντες). Paphlagon's boast changes to grievance and complaint at 887: πιθηκισμοῖς με περιελαύνεις, "you're corralling me with monkey-business"; cf. also 269–70n, ἀλαζών.

291. ὑποτεμοῦμαι τὰς ὁδούς σου: "I'll cut off your retreats." Paphlagon is familiar with escape routes, οἶδε τὰς ὁδούς (253); for this word used of a cavalry tactic, cf. X. *Cyr.* 1.4.21, [οἱ ἱππεῖς] ὑποτεμοῦνται ἡμᾶς, "the cavalry will cut off [our retreat]."

293. ἐν ἀγορᾷ κἀγὼ τέθραμμαι: "I too have been brought up in the agora." As a well-known place, ἀγορά does not require a definite article (cf. 1373; *Ach.* 21; *Nu.* 1005; *V.* 492).

294. διαφορήσω σ': "I'll tear you in pieces."   **γρύξει:** "you'll mutter, babble"; colloquial (López Eire 1996, 18). The γρύ- element is onomatopoetic. For the force of the condition, see 67–68n. The characterization of Cleon as a self-appointed watchdog of the people (49n) recalls imagery of battlefield mutilation by dogs and birds (cf. Hdt. 7.10.θ3, of Mardonius: ὑπὸ κυνῶν τε καὶ ὀρνίθων διαφορεύμενον), which is consistent with the characterization of Cleon as a dog.

295. κοπροφορήσω σ': "I'll carry you off like shit"; this insult apes Paphlagon's διαφορήσω σε and is perhaps a play on removing night soil from the city. For the collection and removal of dung and other organic materials in Athens by private entrepreneurs (κοπρολόγοι) or their slaves, see *Pax* 9–10

with Olson ad loc.; Owens 1983, 45–48.   λακήσει: Second-person future
middle deponent from λάσκω, "ring, make loud noise," etc. (proposed by
Blaydes). In comedy, λαλεῖν often implies that the chatterer should just shut
up (536; *Nu.* 505; *V.* 1135); see Willi 2003, 169n44.

297–98. νὴ τὸν Ἑρμῆν τὸν ἀγοραῖον: Hermes Agoraios, patron god of
market activities and a god of deceit, trickery, and theft, is, like his devotee
Sausage-seller, a shameless denier of wrongdoings, even under oath (cf. *h.*
Hom. Merc. 384). A bronze statue of the god stood in the agora (Philoch.,
FGrH 328 F 31; Paus. 1.15.1).   κἀπιορκῶ γε βλεπόντων: "I even swear
[my innocence], when people see [me stealing]"; cf. 423–26, 1239.

299–302. τοίνυν: "Well then"; cf. 30–31n. Here, the particle signals
a transition to a new subject.   σοφίζει: "you're inventing . . ." (i.e.,
"plagiarizing"). The verb is used of the poet "inventing fresh ideas" at *Nu.* 547
(καινὰς ἰδέας . . . σοφίζομαι).   σε φαίνω τοῖς πρυτάνεσιν: "I'm denouncing
you to the prytanies." For φάσις, see 278–79n. Procedurally, Paphlagon would
point out the physical evidence to the prytanies, who would then refer the
case to the Boule; should Paphlagon win the case, he would receive a premium
of half the fine assessed by the jury (see Harrison 1971, 18–19; MacDowell
2018, 168–69). The prytanies (members of the Prytanis, a rotating fifty-man
standing executive committee of the five-hundred-man Council, the Boule)
held office for one-tenth of the year (see Rhodes 1972, 16–25). A block of
prominent seats was reserved for them in the theater (*Av.* 794 with Dunbar ad
loc.). For their various responsibilities, including supervision of a police force
of around three hundred Scythian archers to enforce their will (cf. 665), see
Rhodes 1972.   ἀδεκατεύτους τῶν θεῶν: A tithe of the spoils of war was
owed to Athena, with an additional 2 percent going to the other gods (Lys.
20.24; D. 24.120, 128–29). For the vow of a tithe (a pledge to pay a god one-
tenth of income), see R. Parker 2005, 444.   ἱεράς . . . κοιλίας: The adjective
ἱεράς shows that the tripe (κοιλίας) is not only a tithe but also the meat from a
sacrifice (cf. MacDowell 2018, 162–63). Cf. Paphlagon's impiety in connection
with the possession of sacrificial cake from Pylos (cf. 54–57, 1166–67, with
Anderson 1995, 23–24).

303–460. Agon I (see glossary). This is the first epirrhematic agon (see
glossary); the second is at 756–941. Agon I deviates from the traditional
structure in having two choral strophes (α and β) and two metrically
equivalent antistrophes (α and β) instead of one. In the two mesodic
(see glossary) interludes (314–21, 391–96) between the strophes and the
antistrophes, Paphlagon and Sausage-seller exchange threats and accusations
in trochaic tetrameter catalectics. The agon ends with the two of them

withdrawing to the Boule to argue their respective cases in that more formal setting.

303–13. Strophe; the meter of this strophe (see glossary) is identical to that of the antistrophe (see glossary) at lines 382–90. Throughout this commentary, we indicate this metrical balance by writing "strophe = antistrophe, 382–90." Meter: lines 303–11, cretic-paeonic (- ◡ -) and its resolved form (◡ ◡ ◡ - or - ◡ ◡ ◡); lines 312–13, trochaic tetrameter catalectics; (see Zimmermann 1984, 1:118–19; L. P. E. Parker 1997, 160–63). The choral song sums up Paphlagon's worst qualities: he is loud and brazen (304), self-serving, and politically subversive (309–10).

303–13. ὦ μιαρὲ: Cf. 125n.   **τοῦ σοῦ θράσους:** "[full] of your brazenness" (cf. 181–82n).   **τέλη:** "taxes."   **γραφαί:** "[bills of] indictment." The word literally means "writing" and thus indicates a "written indictment" that could be initiated by any person "qualified to plead the charge" (Harrison 1971, 76–77). The term could also be used to designate a type of procedure in which the indictment was followed by the specific charge of wrongdoing, as in γραφή βουλεύσεως (for conspiracy), γραφή δώρων (for bribery), or γραφή κλοπῆς (for theft); see Phillips 2013, 30. For a table of select legal terms in Aristophanes, see Willi 2003, 72–79.   **βορβοροτάραξι:** "muckraker," "churner of filth" (cf. 864–67). Aristophanes routinely associates Paphlagon's rhetoric with filth and excrement (e.g., *Pax* 753, ἀπειλὰς βορβοροθύμους, "filthy-minded threats," with Olson's note).   **ἀνατετυρβακώς:** "stir up," "make a muddle"; expands on Cleon as a βορβοροτάραξις. Neil (ad loc.) identifies τυρβάζω and its cognates as coarse colloquialisms (cf. *Pax* 1007 with Olson ad loc.).   **ἡμῖν:** The dative of interest is idiomatic (KG 1.423d; Smyth §1481, §1486a). The chorus compares Paphlagon to a fisherman who is looking out for tuna and shouting to his companions to get their nets ready. For a description of this practice, cf. Philostr. *Imag.* 1.13.8.   **τῶν πετρῶν:** I.e., the Pnyx, from where Paphlagon keeps watch for "approaching shoals of fish" (i.e., "allied tribute"); see Taillardat §723.

314–21. The first mesodic interlude; = 391–96. Meter: trochaic tetrameter catalectics.

314–16. τὸ πρᾶγμα: "Political business."   **καττύεται:** "Were cobbled up." The shoemaking metaphor plays on Cleon's tanning and leather operations. For the occupational metaphors, see Newiger 1957, 30.   **χορδεύματα:** "Sausage making."   **μοχθηροῦ:** I.e., of cheap, inferior quality.

318. μεῖζον ἦν δυοῖν δοχμαῖν: "Bigger than the width of two hands." δοχμή is an unofficial measurement of length. Paphlagon's leather is apparently of such low quality that it fails to retain its shape.

319-21. As Slave A momentarily assumes the persona of an Athenian citizen, "the speaker's servile status" is here "being forgotten for the sake of a joke" (Sommerstein 1981, ad loc.).

319. κατάγελων: Derisive, mocking laughter. For the recessive accent, cf. KB 1.321; Smyth §163a. The word and its cognates always denote laughter at the expense of someone; cf. 160–61n, καταγελᾷς.

321. Περγασῆσιν: Pergase, the name of two (Upper and Lower) small inland demes whose exact locations are unknown but are thought to be about eight miles north of Athens' walls; see Traill 1975, 38. **ἐμβάσιν:** Everyday shoes worn by simple people. Cf. *Nu.* 858 (where Pheidippides ridicules his father's shoes, ἐμβάδες) and *V.* 1157.

322-32. Strophe β = antistrophe β, 397–406. Meter: 322–25, cretics; 326–27, trochaic tetrameter catalectics (anaclasis—redistribution of long and short syllables—to accommodate the name at 327; i.e., - - [-δάμου]; see West 1982, 82); 328–29 = 402–3, dactylic to mark a break in sense and introduce a heightened emotional tone; 330, trochaic tetrameter catalectics; 331, iambic dimeters; 332, lecython (- ◡ -x - ◡ -). See Zimmerman 1985, 2:120; L. P. E. Parker 1997, 164.

322-25. *The chorus speaks to Paphlagon.* **ἄρα δῆτ':** "So then . . ." (*GP* 269). **ἀπ' ἀρχῆς:** "right from the start . . ." (i.e., "even before you were a politician"). **ἀναίδειαν:** Cf. 277n. **ῥητόρων:** Cf. 59–60n.

326-27. ἀμέργεις: "You pluck" or "shake down" (from olive trees). The metaphor is used of plucking profits (fruits) not only from the rich among the subject allies but also from among prosperous Athenians (cf. 258–60n on the metaphor of fig picking). **τῶν ξένων:** I.e., the prosperous citizens of Athens' subject allies, whom Cleon, so it seems, regularly intimidated and extorted for money and favors (*Pax* 639–40; *Av.* 1452–60). **πρῶτος ὤν:** "being foremost," both of ethnic Paphlagonians and of Athenian politicians; cf. Thucydides' description of Pericles as ὑπὸ τοῦ πρώτου ἀνδρὸς (2.65.9). **ὁ δ'Ἱπποδάμου:** The son of Hippodamus, a celebrated city planner from Miletus (*PAA* 538030; Arist. *Pol.* 2.5.1267b22–1268a14; Plu. *Mor.* 834a). Either Hippodamus or his son, Archeptolemus (*PA* 2384; *PAA* 210595), was granted Athenian citizenship; there was probably ancient confusion about which one. Following the Athenian victory at Pylos in 425/24, Archeptolemus brought from Sparta a negotiated peace offer that Cleon opposed (cf. 792–96; Th. 4.15–22, especially 4.22.2). In 411, Archeptolemus joined the oligarchic coup and was executed after the coup failed.

328–30. ἀλλ' . . . γὰρ: "But now . . ."; marking the presence of Sausage-seller (*GP* 101).   **μιαρώτερος:** Cf. 125–26n, 823.   **δῆλος . . . αὐτόθεν:** Cf. 324, ἀπ' ἀρχῆς ἐδήλους.

331–32. θράσει: The same accusation leveled against Paphlagon (304, 693) is here proudly attributed to Sausage-seller (181, 429).   **κοβαλικεύμασιν:** "in low-grade tricks."

333–34. Katakeleusmos. Meter: iambic tetrameter catalectics as in the epirrhematic sections. *The coryphaeus addresses Sausage-seller.*   **ὅθενπερ:** I.e., from the agora.   **νῦν:** "Now"; introduces a new direction in the confrontation (cf. 756 and *V.* 526, with the particle δή; *Nu.* 949, as here).   **οὐδὲν λέγει:** "means nothing"; a dismissive colloquialism (e.g., *Nu.* 644; *V.* 75, 1194; *Av.* 66 with Dunbar ad loc.; see Stevens 1976, 25).   **τὸ σωφρόνως τραφῆναι:** "to be raised wisely" (articular infinitive); i.e., good breeding is irrelevant in public life.

335–66. Epirrhema = antepirrhema, 409–40. Meter: iambic tetrameter catalectics.

335–39. In contrast to the two slave characters, who quarrel over who gets to speak last (13–20), the antagonists quarrel over who gets to speak first.

335. καὶ μὴν: "Very well," "sure"; a common opening for a speaker readily agreeing (or not) to an invitation or proposition (624), for marking a new item for consideration (970), or for the entrance of a new character on stage (691); cf. *GP* 355.   **οὑτοσὶ:** Sausage-seller points accusingly at Paphlagon.

336. οὐκ αὖ: "Not again"; i.e., "so again [you won't let me speak first]"). The particle points to an impatient or agitated question (e.g., 338; *V.* 942; *Av.* 993; *Lys.* 93; *Th.* 852).   **πονηρός:** "good-for-nothing," a trait that qualifies him to be a politician (180–81n).

338. μὰ τὸν Ποσειδῶ: As the most common oath in Aristophanes, swearing by Poseidon most often has no political significance, but here, in this contest of oath taking, Sausage-seller tops his rival's repetition of the Zeus oaths (336, 338 bis) by invoking Poseidon, patron god of both the knights and the comic hero (cf. 551–64). Although Paphlagon also swears by Poseidon later in the play (at 409 and 843), Sausage-seller ultimately gets the upper hand here and in the later scenes.

339. αὐτὸ: "But as regards this"; an accusative of respect. Cf. Neil ad loc. **περὶ τοῦ ... εἰπεῖν:** The genitive case (articular infinitive) is used regularly with verbs of fighting or contending (LSJ s.v. περί A.II.1). **πρῶτα:** Adverb.

340. οἴμοι, διαρραγήσομαι: "Alas, I'll burst!" **ἐγὼ οὐ παρήσω:** "I won't let you" (sc., λέγειν πρῶτα, "speak first").

341. πάρες πάρες ... διαρραγῆναι: "Let him, let him burst asunder!"; with dative of person and infinitive (LSJ s.v. A.IV.2).

342. τῷ καὶ πεποιθώς; "Trusting in what exactly?" Adverbial καί following an interrogative adds emphasis to the question (KG 2.255; Smyth §2884; López Eire 1996, 120). **ἔναντα:** Adverb with the genitive.

343–81. The antagonists in the confrontation draw on occupational imagery (tanning and sausage making).

343. λέγειν οἷός τε: Sc., εἰμί. **καρυκοποιεῖν:** "make a rich sauce"; i.e., "agitate, stir up political trouble" (cf. 66–67, 214; Sommerstein 1981, ad loc.). καρύκη is a blood-based sauce from Lydia (Pherecr. fr. 195).

344–45. ἰδού: Cf. 87n. **καλῶς γ᾽:** According to Dover (2002, 88), "since the adverbs καλῶς and χρηστῶς (at end of the sentence) are not coordinated it looks as if χρηστῶς carries the weight and καλῶς signals sarcasm" (cf. also Stevens 1976, 45). **πρᾶγμα προσπεσόν ... ὠμοσπάρακτον:** "a case fell [into your hands] already slaughtered"; the metaphor comes from butchering animals (Sommerstein 1981, ad loc.). **μεταχειρίσαιο:** μεταχειρίζειν regularly denotes administering public affairs (Th. 6.12.2, 6.16.6; Taillardat §670).

346. οἶσθ᾽ ὅ μοι πεπονθέναι δοκεῖς; "Do you want to know what you seem to me to have experienced?" I.e., "what I think you've experienced," spoken condescendingly. The phrase οἶσθ᾽ ὅ (cf. 1158) is apparently colloquial (Stevens 1976, 36). For πεπονθέναι, cf. V. 946; Ra. 718 with Dover ad loc.: "To represent someone as πάσχων [victim] rather than ποιῶν [agent] mitigates censure." **ὅπερ τὸ πλῆθος:** I.e., "what in fact most [experience when they make a public speech]."

347–50. δικίδιον: "A petty little case"; the diminutive expresses contempt. See Dover 2002, 88–89. **κατὰ ξένου μετοίκου:** A noncitizen. For the vulnerability of ξένοι (which included μέτοικοι) in a legal dispute with an Athenian citizen, see Harrison 1968, 188. The implication is that Paphlagon singles out defenseless foreign residents for his personal gain. **λαλῶν ἐν ταῖς ὁδοῖς σεαυτῷ / ὕδωρ τε πίνων:** "babbling to yourself in the streets and drinking water." Serious oratorical preparation was apparently associated with obsessive practice and with abstinence from drinking wine. Cf. 349 with van Leeuwen ad loc.; D. 19.46, for oratorical training. Cf. also Cratin. fr. 203, which argues against drinking water and in favor of drinking wine, for poetic inspiration; see Bakola 2010, 59–63. **μῶρε:** Cf. 162n. **τῆς ἀνοίας:** "what idiocy"; for the genitive, cf. 1–5n.

351–52. τί δαὶ . . . ; "Well then, what . . . ?" For the force of the particle, cf. 26–28n. **νυνί:** "even now"; a strengthened form of νῦν (KG 2.117). **τὴν πόλιν:** Prolepsis followed by a ὥστε clause (Smyth §2182). **ὑπὸ σοῦ μονωτάτου:** "by you above all others"; cf. 1165, προτεραίτερος, of Sausage-seller. **κατεγλωττισμένην:** "French-kissed"; here used primarily in the sense of being "overwhelmed verbally." Cf. *Ach.* 380, "tongue lash." For erotic kissing, cf. *Nu.* 51; *Th.* 131; Henderson 1991a, 181–82. For comic humor centered on the tongue, see Denniston 1927, 120. The tongue imagery foreshadows Paphlagon's claim to be a friend/lover (φιλόδημος) of Demos (732–34, 787, 821, 1163, 1341).

354–55. The focus on food anticipates the means for winning the favor of Demos and appointment as his steward (cf. 947–48, 959). **θύννεια θερμὰ:** "slices of cooked tuna." **ἀκράτου / οἴνου:** "of unmixed wine"; cf. 85–86n. **χοᾶ:** Cf. 95–96n. **κασαλβάσω:** "screw" (i.e., "sodomize"). **τοὺς ἐν Πύλῳ στρατηγούς:** Demosthenes, Eurymedon, and Nicias were the generals in command at Pylos before Cleon arrived (Th. 4.2–5). Paphlagon here momentarily identifies himself with Cleon (cf. 742–43).

356–58. ἐγὼ δέ γ': The pronoun and particle combination mark a lively retort and rejoinder (cf. *GP* 153). **ἤνυστρον βοὸς καὶ κοιλίαν ὑείαν:** Products of Sausage-seller's trade. **καταβροχθίσας:** "scarfing down"; a colloquial term for ravenous eating (cf. 826). Cf. Antiph. fr. 188.6, οἷοι καταβροχθίζειν ἐν ἀγορᾶι τὰ τεμάχη, "the kind of men who can scarf down fish slices in the agora." **ζωμὸν:** A meat broth that often implies overeating and drinking (*Nu.* 386; *Pax* 716; cf. also 360n).   **ἀναπόνιπτος:** "before wiping my hands." Greeks customarily washed their hands after eating (cf. *V.* 1217).   **τοὺς ῥήτορας:** Cf. 60.   ***Νικίαν λαπάξω:** read instead: Νικίαν ταράξω, "I'll harass Nicias." The paradosis has ταράξω, which continues the string of culinary metaphors. Wilson prints λαπάξω, "evacuate [the bowels]," on the grounds that it "matches κασαλβάσω for vigor and vulgarity." Thucydides (4.27–28) reports that Cleon harassed Nicias in the Assembly debate about Pylos.

359–60. ἓν δ᾽ οὐ προσίεταί με: "But one thing doesn't please me." For προσίημι with a personal object, cf. *V.* 742.   **τῶν πραγμάτων . . . τὸν ζωμὸν:** I.e., "the political gravy." For the culinary metaphor, see Taillardat §687.   **ἐκροφήσει:** "you'll slurp up." ῥοφέω is regularly used of ingesting meat broths, gravies, and thick soups (*Pax* 716; *V.* 811–12; fr. 208). Cf. 701, ἐκροφήσας (sc., σε); 905, μισθοῦ τρύβλιον ῥοφῆσαι; *Ach.* 278, εἰρήνης ῥοφήσει τρύβλιον; Taillardat §617, §686.

361. λάβρακας: A λάβραξ is a large, allegedly voracious sea bass (D. W. Thompson 1947, 140). The waters off Miletus were said to produce the largest and best; see Archestr. fr. 46.1–2 with Olson and Sens 2000, 182. Large fish are a luxury food in Greek comedy (Wilkins 2000, 294–304), and eating large fish is considered self-indulgent and even a sign of antidemocratic aspirations (e.g., at *V.* 488–99, Bdelycleon is accused of antidemocratic leanings because he buys a perch, ὀρφῶς, instead of anchovies, μεμβράδες; see Biles and Olson ad loc.). The reference to Miletus may allude to a reputed political scandal that involved Cleon soliciting bribes from wealthy Milesians (i.e., "big fish") in exchange for unsuccessfully opposing an increase in their annual tribute assessment in 424; cf. 930–40.   **κλονήσεις:** This verb is commonly used of winds and waves and metaphorically of epic and tragic heroes who carry off all before them (e.g., *Il.* 5.96, 15.324, 22.188; S. *Tr.* 146; *OC* 1244).

362. σχελίδας: "Sides [or ribs] of beef" which top Paphlagon's fish. Cf. Paphlagon's paltry fish offering, τέμαχος (1177) and Sausage-seller's counteroffer of meaty broth, ζωμοῦ κρέας, and tripe, γαστρὸς τόμον (1178–79). The chorus dances with "sides of beef" and other meats tucked under their arms at fr. 264; cf. also Pherecr. fr. 113.13, σχελίδες δ᾽ ὁλόκνημοι, "sides of bacon."   **ἐδηδοκώς:** An epic form for Attic ἐσθίω.   **ὠνήσομαι μέταλλα:** "I'll buy mining leases" (i.e., become rich). Sausage-seller seems to allude to the silver mines at Laureion in southeast Attica, which were leased by individuals who paid the state for mining rights (only the underground resources were regarded as state property). On the subject of mining leases as a whole, see Crosby 1950, 189–297. Perhaps not coincidentally, Paphlagonia seems to have been a good source of slaves for working the mines (*IG* ii² 1951.69, 145, dated 405 BCE; Str. 7.3.12); hence Aristophanes may here be hinting that Cleon, as a Paphlagonian slave, belongs in the mines with his fellow slaves. The Athenian general Nicias apparently made much of his fortune from the Laureion mines (cf. Plu. *Nic.* 4.2).

363. ἐγὼ δ' . . . γε: "But I . . ."; cf. 356.   **βουλὴν:** For the responsibilities of the Athenian Boule, see Rhodes 1972; for Aristophanes' treatment of the Athenian Assembly, see Rhodes 2004.   **κυκήσω:** Cf. κυκᾶν, 64–66n.

364. βυνήσω . . . πρωκτὸν ἀντὶ φύσκης: "I'll stuff your butt like a sausage." Threats of anal penetration are de rigueur in Attic comedy; see Henderson 1991a, 38–39.

365. κύβδα: "Bent over." For the attentive spectator, the image of dragging a subdued opponent to the threshold may suggest the scene in which Odysseus speculates about how the suitors might treat him (ἤν περ καὶ διὰ δῶμα ποδῶν ἕλκωσι θύραζε, *Od.* 16.276). In Aristophanes, κύβδα is always used in abusive or sexual contexts (cf. *Th.* 489 with Austin and Olson ad loc.).

366. νὴ τὸν Ποσειδῶ: The oath reinforces the statement (cf. 899, 1035, 1201).   **ἤνπερ γε:** "if, in fact, really . . ." The two particles strengthen the conditional (*GP* 487–88). Here, Slave A directly addresses Paphlagon; elsewhere, he refers to him in the third person (319–21, 375–81).   **ἕλκῃς:** From ἐξέλξω; the prefix ἐκ has been dropped which often happens when the compound form appears immediately above as it does here; cf. ἐξέλξω. 365.

367–81. Pnigos = antipnigos, 441–56. Meter: iambic dimeters.

367. οἷον: "How . . . !" On exclamatory οἷος, cf. KG 2.439.   **<(ἐ)ν> τῷ ξύλῳ:** "in a pillory" (394, 1049; cf. *Lys.* 10.16; And. 1.92); a generic term for an "anti-escape device" (Sommerstein 2001, 243).

368. διώξομαι: A legal term for "prosecute" (e.g., *Nu.* 1482, διωκάθω; *V.* 902, 1207, διώκων; *Ec.* 452, διώκειν; fr. 452, διώκης).   **δειλίας:** "cowardice"; genitive of charge (KG 1.381; Smyth §1375). What such a charge would mean legally is unclear. Perhaps it was a catchall term to cover evading military service or cowardice in the field (e.g., desertion, throwing away one's shield in flight, etc.); conviction on such offenses resulted in the loss of civil rights (cf. Lys. 14.16; And. 1.73–79 with Phillips 2013, 225–26). The comic stage routinely portrays demagogues as military cowards (e.g., 390; *Ach.* 664).

369–73. Occupational terms for tanning and sausage making dominate the exchange of threats, as each character tries to outdo the other. The line order is difficult; Sommerstein (1981, at 369–74; 2001, 239) suggests that one verse has been lost after 369 and another after 370.

369. βύρσα: "Hide, pelt" (104; *V.* 38; *Pax* 753). When used of human skin, the term is contemptuous (LSJ s.v. 3).   **θρανεύσεται:** From θρᾶνος, the word for a tanning bench on which an animal hide was stretched (schol. ad loc.).

370. δερῶ σε θύλακον κλοπῆς: "I'll flay you [into] a loot bag" (here, κλοπῆς substitutes for ἀσκός; a paraprosdokeion joke). The internal accusative expresses the result of the verb's action; cf. 768, κατατμηθείην τε λέπαδαν, "and may I be sliced up into harnesses" (KG 1.323). For the common phrase ἀσκὸν δέρειν, cf. Solon 33.7 *W*, ἀσκὸς ... δεδάρθαι; *Nu.* 442, ἀσκὸν δείρειν.

371. διαπατταλευθήσει χαμαί: "You'll be pegged and spread out on the ground [to dry]"; i.e., "You'll be spread-eagled on the ground." The audience may be reminded of the Persian practice of flaying victims alive and nailing their skins on a board for public display (Plu. *Art.* 17. 7; cf. Hdt. 5. 25.1).

372. περικόμματ᾽ ἔκ σου σκευάσω: "I'll make mincemeat out of you" (cf. 770); cf. *Nu.* 455, ἔκ μου χορδήν, "[turn me] into sausage." Sausage-seller's retort here is an exact metrical response to Paphlagon's threat at 371.

373. τὰς βλεφαρίδας σου παρατιλῶ: "I'll pluck out your eyebrows." Plucking bristles (from animal hides) is the work of tanners; for the image, see Taillardat §594. Likewise sausage making probably involved plucking bristles (pig) or feathers (fowl) too.

374. πρηγορεῶνα: A bird's crop (*Av.* 1113 with Dunbar ad loc.). Sausage-seller will deal with Paphlagon "like a butcher dealing with fowl" (Sommerstein 1981, ad loc.).

375–81. The sexual activities that Sausage-seller openly claims as his own practices become insults when they are linked with Paphlagon (cf. Hubbard 1991, 68).

376. πάτταλον: Wooden peg (*Th.* 222); cf. 371.   **μαγειρικῶς:** "like a butcher" (cf. *Ach.* 1015; *Pax* 1017). Before slaughtering an animal, the butcher jammed a wooden peg into the animal's mouth and grabbed its tongue, looking for signs of disease (Neil ad loc.). Perhaps also a double entendre in which peg = phallus; see Henderson 1991a, 123.

378. τὴν γλῶτταν ἐξείραντες: "Pulling out his tongue." As a politician, Paphlagon has a sexually "active" tongue that needs to be checked for disease. For sexual humor involving Paphlagon's tongue, see 352, 1034. Cf. 637 and 837, for Sausage-seller's.

379–81. εὖ κ᾽ ἀνδρικῶς: "Well and manly"; a set comic phrase (*V.* 153, 450; *Th.* 656).   **κεχηνότος / τὸν πρωκτόν:** "gaping in respect to his asshole" (i.e., "his gaping asshole"); a paraprosdokeion joke substituting "anus" (πρωκτός) for "mouth" (στόμα).   **χαλαζᾷ:** "hail" (*Nu.* 1127) and "hailstones" (*Ra.* 852); by extension, any small knot, hence a pimple or cyst in swine flesh (Arist. *HA* 603b21).

382–90. Antistrophe α = strophe α, 303–13.

382–86. ἦν ἄρα: "So there really are [temperatures]." Greek tends to stress the past existence of a fact (ἦν), English the present existence (cf. 1170; *GP* 36–37). L. P. E. Parker (1997, 162) notes that the opening line of the antistrophe confirms that the tide has turned in favor of Sausage-seller.   **καὶ λόγων:** Hermann's reading, καὶ <λόγοι τῶν> λογῶν, may be correct; see Sommerstein 2001, 239.   **ὧδ᾽ <– ◡ –>:** The final cretic is missing.

387–88. ἔπιθι: "Attack [him]."   **στρόβει:** "spin and twist [him]." There was also a lively dance called στρόβιλος, which featured positions and movements associated with wrestling (*Pax.* 864; Athen. 14.630a).   **μηδὲν ὀλίγον ποίει:** "do something not small" (i.e., "do something big"). The use of litotes here suggests that an important moment is at hand (cf. ὀλίγον . . . οὐδέν at Th. 2.8.1, concerning the combatants at the beginning of the Peloponnesian War, and 8.15.2, describing preparations to regain control of Chios).   **ἔχεται μέσος:** "he's caught in a waist lock"; a wrestling metaphor (*Ach.* 571; *Nu.* 1047; *Ra.* 469; *Ec.* 260; Taillardat §579). For the effectiveness of the hold, see Poliakoff 1987, 40.

389–90. μαλάξῃς αὐτόν: "You soften him"; alludes both to Paphlagon's character (τρόπους) and to a tanner's task of softening hides. Cf. Lind 1991, 57, 81.   **δειλὸν:** Cf. 368n.

391-96: The second mesodic interlude = 314-21. Meter: trochaic tetrameter catalectics. Sausage-seller takes up the chorus' attack on Paphlagon's corrupt and cowardly character.

391-94. οὗτος τοιοῦτος ὢν ἅπαντα τὸν βίον: I.e., his character is completely flawed. **κᾆτ':** "and yet"; with a finite verb after a participle to express incongruity (LSJ s.v. I.2). **ἀνὴρ:** Cf. 178n. **τἀλλότριον ἀμῶν θέρος:** "reaping another's crop"; i.e., taking credit for the achievements of another (sc., the Athenian general Demosthenes). ἀμῶν (reaping) is primarily an epic and tragic word, appearing only here in Aristophanes, perhaps as parody. **στάχυς:** "sheaves of wheat"; a metaphor for the "serried rows" or "harvest of Spartan prisoners" that Cleon "reaped" from capturing Sphachteria; see Taillardat §721. **ἐν ξύλῳ:** Cf. 367n. ***ἀφανεῖ:** read instead ἀφαύει, "he's drying [them] out." Cf. the joke on the Spartan prisoners' pale and emaciated appearance at *Nu.* 186 with Dover ad loc. Wilson's ἀφανεῖ, "he's winnowing them out." is the reading in R. **κἀποδόσθαι βούλεται:** He has plans to use the Spartan prisoners (held in Athens since their capture) as bargaining chips in peace negotiations (Th. 4.38-41). For the Athenian response to peace overtures, cf. 794-96.

395-96. Paphlagon is confident that he can bully the Council and the Assembly into supporting his private interests.

395-96. ὑμᾶς: I.e., you and the knights. **ζῇ:** "lives, exists." This sense of the verb seems to reflect everyday usage; see Fraenkel 1962, 48-49. The only other example of the metaphor is at *Lys.* 696, of Lampito. **τὸ τοῦ Δήμου πρόσωπον μακκοᾷ καθήμενον:** Demos (who stands in for the Athenian demos) is often portrayed as dim-witted and mesmerized by rhetorical display (*Ach.* 133), as are the spectators in the theater (e.g., 261-65, 651, 754-55, 1115-30, 1263, 1350-55). On μακκοᾷ, cf. also 62-63n.

397-408. Antistrophe β = strophe β, 322-34.

397-98. ὡς δὲ: Cf. 269-70n. **πρὸς πᾶν:** "completely." ***μεθίησι:** read instead μεθίστησι, "he changes [his color]." The paradosis is μεθίστησι (followed by Neil, Coulon and van Daele], and Henderson). Wilson, following Herwerden, prints μεθίησι.

400-401. εἴ σε μὴ μισῶ: An echo of the contemporary political term μισόδημος, "hatred for the demos" (cf. 508-11, where the coryphaeus declares that Aristophanes "hates the same men" as the chorus). For self-curses

in Greek drama, see Torrance 2014, 32n100.   ἐν Κρατίνου: Sc., οἴκῳ.
Cratinus (*PA* 8755; *PAA* 584385), son of Callimedes, gained prominence as
a leading comic poet of the preceding generation and is generally believed
to be the first "blame poet" of Old Comedy (i.e., first to have turned comedy
toward personal abuse and invective in the style of Archilochus; cf. T 17).
Over the course of his career, he won first prize six times at the City Dionysia
and three times at the Lenaea (*IG* ii^2 2325.C14, E.6 in MO, 166–67). He
competed in the same contest as *Knights* with his entry *Satyrs*, which took
second place. In the following year, he won first prize with *Pytine*, "Wine
Flask," at the City Dionysia, defeating Aristophanes' *Clouds*, which ranked
low (T 7c). Aristophanes routinely mocked him, as a washed-up drunk and
incontinent geezer, while he was alive (cf. 526–36; *Ach.* 848–53, 1173). After
Cratinus' death, however, Aristophanes put him on par with Sophocles (*Pax*
695–703; *Ra.* 357). On Cratinus' portrayal of himself as a drunk in *Pytine*, see
Biles 2002; Bakola 2010, 16–17. For intertextual rivalry between Aristophanes
and Cratinus, see Luppe 2000; Bakola 2010; Biles 2011, 97–166. In antiquity,
Cratinus, Aristophanes, and Eupolis were regarded as the premier poets
of Attic Old Comedy (Ar. T 63–66; Hor. *Sat.* 1.4.1–5).   κῴδιον: "little
blanket."   διδασκοίμην προσᾴδειν . . . τραγῳδίᾳ: "may I be taught to
sing the songs . . . in a tragedy."   Μορσίμου: (*PA* 10416; *PAA* 658815:
TrGF 29), son of the tragic poet Philocles, a second-rate tragic poet (cf. *Pax*
803, where the chorus celebrates the failure of Morsimus to qualify for entry
in the dramatic competition; *Ra.* 151; cf. also *Av.* 281 with schol.) and, in
Aristophanes' judgment, a second-rate physician (fr. 723). For a similar joke
on the horrors of second-rate tragic poetry, cf. Ephipp. fr. 16.1, Διονυσίου δὲ
δράματ' ἐκμαθεῖν δέοι (i.e., Dionysios I, tyrant of Syracuse).

403–4. δωροδόκοισιν ἐπ' ἄνθεσιν: Paphlagon gathers bribes (δωροδόκος)
like a bee collects nectar.   **φαύλως:** "easily," "casually" (as at 509, 1290–
95; *Pax* 25).   **ἐκβάλοις τὴν ἔνθεσιν:** Regurgitation is a favorite metaphor
of Aristophanes (e.g., 716, Paphlagon masticating foods for an infantilized
Demos; 1147–50, regurgitating stolen goods; *Ach.* 5–8, Cleon regurgitating
bribes).

406. "πῖνε πῖν' ἐπὶ συμφοραῖς": The quotation is from a victory ode by
Simonides (7 = *PMG* 512). On the double meaning of συμφορά, "fortune" and
"misfortune," see Kugelmeier 1996, 118–19.

407–8. Antikatakeleusmos (see glossary). Meter: two iambic tetrameter
catalectics.   **Οὔλιον:** *PA* 11496; *PAA* 750610; one of the sons of the
statesman Cimon (*PA* 8429; *PAA* 569795). He apparently had legal or political

trouble with Cleon, which explains his readiness to rejoice (βακχέβακχον ᾆσαι) at the downfall of Paphlagon. The manuscript has Ἰουλίου (son of Julius), probably a corruption dating from Roman times.   **πυροπίπην:** "wheat ogler"; a comic word for σιτοφύλαξ (LSJ s.v.), official inspectors appointed by lot to oversee the supply and marketing of wheat and bread (cf. 1009; Arist. *Ath.* 51.3; Cratin. fr. 484 with Olson, *FrC* 2018, 319–20). The inspectors were often blamed for increases in the price of grain (Lys. 22.5, 16).   **ἰηπαιωνίσαι:** A cry of celebration and thanksgiving for victory, success, and safety (cf. *Pax* 453, ἰὴ παιών ἰή; *Av.* 1763, ἰὴ παιών; *Lys.* 1291, ἰὴ παιών; cf. also 1318, παιωνίζειν τὸ θέατρον; Th. 2.91.2, οἱ . . . ἐπαιάνιζον, of Peloponnesian seamen about to enter battle); see Pulleyn 1997, 182–83.   **βακχέβακχον:** A joyful song to Dionysus, god of wine and theater, that begins with the words Βάκχε Βάκχε.

409–40. Antepirrhema = epirrhema, 335–66. Meter: iambic tetrameter catalectics.

409–10. οὔτοι: "There's no way . . ."; -τοι intensifies the negative oath (*GP* 543–44).   **ἀναιδείᾳ:** Cf. 277, 324–25, 1206.   **μὰ τὸν Ποσειδῶ:** Cf. 338n.   **ἀγοραίου Διὸς:** The patron god of the agora in all its sociopolitical aspects (see also 500). Sacrifices were apparently offered to Zeus Agoraios before the opening of the Athenian Assembly; see H. A. Thompson 1952, 93. To call a demagogue *agoraios* situates the source of his economic and political influence in the marketplace (see Connor 1971, 154–55; Ostwald 1986, 214–15.   **σπλάγχνοισι:** The choice innards of the sacrificial animal (i.e., heart, lungs, kidneys, liver, and spleen) that were roasted (Arist. *Part. an.* 667b1–6) and shared among ritual participants, with a portion reserved for the god (cf. *V.* 654; *Pax* 1039–40; *Av.* 518–19). The self-curse, "may I never share in the sacrifices to Zeus Agoraios," is self-fulfilling (cf. 1243–49).

411–14. ἔγωγε: "I certainly . . ." Affirmative -γε stresses Sausage-seller's confidence that he will outdo Paphlagon's "shamelessness" (*GP* 132).   **νὴ τοὺς κονδύλους:** "by the punches [and slashes of shears]."   **πολλὰ δὴ 'πὶ πολλοῖς:** "repeatedly"; cf. *V.* 1046. On δή with adjectives expressing indefinite numbers, see *GP* 205.iii.   **ἠνεσχόμην:** Depending on metrical needs, Aristophanes uses either a double or single augment (cf. *Pax* 347; fr. 632) with secondary tenses of ἀνέσχομην.   **μαχαιρίδων:** Most translators take this word to mean "knives," but it was also the Attic word for barber shears. According to Olson (2016, 775), Sausage-seller presumably hung around barbershops "with everyone else, but that proprietors occasionally struck him with tools of their trade, perhaps for verbal insolence, an attempt to filch from one of the customers, or the like." Cf. Eup. fr. 194, where the speaker, perhaps the slave Hyperbolus, mentions sitting in a barbershop pretending not to listen, perhaps to pick up information useful for slander or blackmail, unobtrusively; we owe the latter observation to Henderson. Typical meeting places for men to exchange gossip were barbershops (*Av.* 1440–43; Men. *Sam.* 510–13) and perfume markets (1375–77; Pherecr. fr. 70; Lys. 24.20).   ἢ μάτην γ': "or else for nothing" (emphatic γε; see *GP* 117).   ἀπομαγδαλιὰς: Small lumps of dough or soft bread used to wipe off one's hands after meals (cf. 819; Athen. 4.149D). The Spartans called these early napkins κυνάδες (dog bits), because they were often discarded on the floor for dogs to eat (Athen. 9.409 B); see Wilkins 2000, 35n134. Having been raised on such scraps, Sausage-seller boasts of an even baser past than his rival.   τοσοῦτος ἐκτραφεὶς ἦ: "I've grown so big." The perfect subjunctive is regularly formed periphrastically by the perfect active participle + copula (Smyth §691). *Sausage-seller presumably gestures to various parts of his costume.*

415–16. ἀπομαγδαλιὰς: The repetition as the first word in both lines sharpens the retort.   ὥσπερ κύων; Sc., σιτούμενος.   ὦ παμπόνηρε: "utterly vile"; a term of contempt for a social or intellectual upstart (1283; Neil ad loc.; cf. *Ach.* 854; *Ra.* 921).   βορὰν: Properly, food for animals ([A.] *Pr.* 583; S. *Ant.* 30; E. *Ph.* 1603).   κυνοκεφάλλῳ; "dog-faced baboon." Monkeys and other simians are traditional symbols of treachery and deceit (887; *Ach.* 120–21, 906–7; *V.* 1290–91; *Pax* 1064–65). See Keller 1909, 1:3–11; Taillardat §406. The word evokes the image of the Egyptian baboon god, Baba, whose appearance recalls a fierce and aggressive dog (Arist. *HA* 502a19–23). Here the penultimate syllable of κυνοκεφάλῳ is long by metrical necessity; cf. Hes. *Th.* 287 (of the monster Geryon), where the penultimate syllable of τρικέφαλον is lengthened, and 312 (of Cerberus), where the penultimate syllable of πεντηκοντακέφαλον lengthens.

417–20. ἄλλα . . . κόβαλα: "Other dirty tricks" (cf. 450; *Ra.* 104).   ἄν: With the imperfect, expresses repeated past action. See *MT* §249; Stevens 1976, 60.   ὥρα νέα, χελιδών: I.e., springtime (cf. *Pax* 800; *Th.* 1). Swallows are traditionally linked with the return of spring (Hes. *Op.* 568–69; Stesich., *PMGF* 211; Simon., *PMG* 597; *Carm. Pop.*, *PMG* 848.1–2).   οἱ δ' ἔβλεπον, κἀγὼ 'ν . . . ἔκλεπτον: For the reduction of καί + ἐγώ + a vowel (ἐν) to two syllables, cf. 647. Here Sausage-seller reminices about how, as a child, he would distract the cooks and steal meat from under their very noses; later he will use this same ploy of misdirection on Paphlagon, tricking Paphlagon into looking away so that he can steal Paphlagon's gift and present it as his own offering to Demos (cf. 1195–1202); see Anderson 1995, 33–35.

421-22. δεξιώτατον κρέας: "Most clever man" (cf. 457, γεννικώτατον κρέας). The word κρέας = "carcass," hence "body," "person" (LSJ s.v. 2) and perhaps a double meaning here of "penis." **σοφῶς γε προὐνοήσω:** προὐνοήσω: = προενοήσω, from προνοέω "you really cleverly thought ahead." The γε is exclamatory when alone in an apostrophe (*GP* 129). **ἀκαλήφας ἐσθίων πρὸ χελιδόνων:** "eating nettles before the swallows [return]"; sounds like a proverb. In early spring, nettles are not yet capable of stinging (Plin. *NH* 21.93).

423-24. καί . . . γ': "And furthermore." γε emphasizes the addition made by καί (*GP* 158). **εἰ δ' οὖν:** Sausage-seller acknowledges that he might be detected, but he seriously doubts it; see *GP* 465. **τὰ κοχώνα:** "buns"; slang for buttocks. The dual form, which could be either feminine plural or neuter plural, is colloquial, and its tone is often hypocoristic (i.e., baby talk). See, e.g., 726–27; *Nu.* 79–80; *Pax* 382; *Lys.* 872; *Ra.* 582; *Pl.* 1010–11.

426. οὐκ ἔσθ' ὅπως . . . οὐ: Cf. 238–39n. **τὸν δῆμον ἐπιτροπεύσει:** Sausage-seller is recognized as qualified to govern.

427-28. εὖ γε: "Well done!"; colloquial (cf. 470, 941, 1402). γε adds exclamatory emphasis to the adverb (*GP* 127). **ἀτὰρ:** Cf. 111. **'πιώρκεις θ' ἡρπακὼς:** Cf. 297–98n. **κρέας ὁ πρωκτὸς εἶχεν:** A joke on anal penetration and Sausage-seller's depravity (cf. schol. ad loc.); see Henderson 1991a, 129, 201.

429-31. Aristophanes applies storm imagery to Paphlagon throughout the play (430–41, 511). See Edmunds 1987b, 6–16. The metaphor is also in keeping with the legendarily violent storms of Paphlagon's native Paphlagonia (A. M. Bowie 1993, 61–62). **τοῦ θράσους:** Cf. 180–81n. **ἄμφω:** Sausage-seller and Slave A. **λαμπρὸς ἤδη καὶ μέγας καθιείς:** "swoop down [like] a really great wind." On the use of καθιέναι in this sense, cf. LSJ s.v. II; Taillardat §339, §344. Here ἤδη intensifies the preceding word (cf., e.g., 812, πολλῷ . . . ἤδη, "a lot more"; *Ach.* 315, δεινὸν ἤδη, "really terrible"; *Th.* 385, πολὺν ἤδη χρόνον, "for a really long time"; E. *Alc.* 747, πολλοὺς μὲν ἤδη, "in enormous numbers"); see KG 2.122–23.

432-41. Sausage-seller assumes the role of ship captain and Slave A that of crew member, as they weather Paphlagon's blustery storms; for the nautical imagery, see Taillardat §896.

432–33. ἐγὼ δὲ . . . γε: Cf. 356–58n.   **συστείλας γε τοὺς ἀλλᾶντας:** "shortening my sausages"; a paraprosdokeion joke for "shorten the sails" (*Ra.* 999–1003 with Dover ad loc.), as well as a metaphor for dealing with adversity and opposition.   **οὔριον:** "with a fair wind," i.e., "easily."   **κλάειν σε μακρὰ κελεύων:** "bidding you keep on crying" (i.e., "go to hell," "fare ill"); a colloquial, dismissive imprecation. Cf. *Ach.* 1130–31; *Pl.* 62. See Stevens 1976, 15–16.

434. κἄγωγ': "As for me," "I, for my part."   **παραχαλᾷ:** "it leaks."   **τὴν ἀντλίαν:** The bilge (the lowest internal part of the hull of a ship).

435–36. οὗτοι: Cf. 235–36n.   **μὰ τὴν Δήμητρα:** A favorite oath of Paphlagon (461, 698, 812); cf. 833, of Sausage-seller; 1021, of Demos. Note that men swear simply by Demeter in comedy; women add the adjective φίλην (cf. *Ach.* 708 with Olson ad loc.).   **καταπροίξει:** "you'll get away" + circumstantial particle (κλέψας). This verb is always second-person singular middle in Aristophanes (e.g., *Nu.* 1239–40; *V.* 1366; *Th.* 566).   **κλέψας Ἀθηναίων:** On κλέπτειν + genitive, see 109–10n.   **ἄθρει:** "be alert!" (*V.* 140–41; *Pax* 538–40; *Av.* 1196; *Th.* 607).   **τοῦ ποδὸς:** "the clew"; i.e., the lower corner of a sail, with a fitting for attaching a rope. See Morrison, Coates, and Rankov 2000, 257–58.

437. καικίας . . . συκοφαντίας: "Sycophantic wind"; a surprise. Cf. ὀρνιθίας = "bird wind" (*Ach.* 876–77). καικίας denotes storm-bearing northeast winds. The suffix -ιας is common with names of winds (Willi 2003, 67n41).

438–39. ἐκ Ποτειδαίας: Originally a Corinthian colony on the Chalcidic Peninsula, Potidaea became a member of the Delian League and a subject ally of the Athenian Empire. The Potidaeans revolted from Athens in 432 and were starved into submission after a two-year siege by Athenian forces. Sausage-seller's charge suggests that either Cleon was accused of demanding bribes not to prosecute the Athenian generals for accepting the surrender without authorization (*Th.* 2.70 with Hornblower 1991, ad loc.), or he denounced the generals, alleging that they had themselves taken bribes in return for the surrender; see Sommerstein 1981, ad loc.; Ostwald 1986, 210–11.   **δέκα τάλαντα:** A huge sum of money (cf. 442).   **τί δῆτα;** "What then?" is emphatic (*GP* 270).   **βούλει . . . σιωπᾶν;** "Are you willing to be quiet?" As Sommerstein (1981, ad loc.) notes, "Paphlagon admits that the charge just made against him is true." For the political corruption of Paphlagon-Cleon and his cronies, cf. 801–3, 834–35, 927–33; *V.* 669–72; *Pax* 644–48.

440. ἀνὴρ: "The gentleman"; used ironically of Sausage-seller.   **τερθρίους:** Ropes at the end of a sail yard that are used for "reefing" (slackening the ropes to reduce the area of a sail during rough weather). The word τερθρεία may also call to mind "rhetorical subtlety" (Neil ad loc.).

441–56. Antipnigos = pnigos, 367–81.

441–42. γραφὰς: Cf. 303–13n.   **<δωροδοκίας>:** The offense is omitted in the manuscripts, but the call for a specific charge is implied by Sausage-seller's impending threat against Paphlagon.   **ἑκατονταλάντους τέτταρας:** He threatens four separate indictments of Sausage-seller for soliciting bribes, with a fine of one hundred talents for each indictment. One talent = six thousand drachmas.

443–44. σὺ δ᾽ . . . γ᾽: A lively retort, cf. 356–58n.   **ἀστρατείας:** Genitive of the charge (cf. 368). Charges of draft evasion, desertion, and cowardice are comic stock-in-trade (e.g., *Nu.* 353–54; *V.* 15–19, 822–23, 1117–19; *Pax* 444–46, 673–78; *Av.* 1473–81).   **εἴκοσιν:** Refers to talents (442).   **κλοπῆς:** A (γραφή) κλοπῆς is an indictment for embezzlement or theft of public funds or property. See Cohen 1983, 30–33; Todd 1993, 283–84.

445–58. There are two different forms of ancestral *miasma* (pollution) in play here: (1) the desecration of religious space by the shedding of blood in the past and (2) the familial betrayal of the city and hence of the city's gods. Since *miasma* was treated as a kind of contagious and mortal danger to the whole community, it called for the expulsion of the originating cause; see R. Parker 1983, 3–5, 206.

445–46. ἐκ τῶν ἀλιτηρίων σε φη- / μι γεγονέναι: Paphlagon here alludes to the hereditary curse that the archon Megacles (*PA* 9688; *PAA* 636340) brought on his family, the Alcmeonids, for killing (contrary to sworn terms of surrender) the partisans of Cylon, who had sought refuge in the precinct of Athena Polias on the Acropolis when their coup d'état failed (Hdt. 5.71; Th. 1.126.8–12). The names of both the murderers and the conspirators were inscribed on a column on the Acropolis as forever cursed (Lycurg. *Leoc.* 117). The idea that a sausage seller could be descended from an aristocratic family of Athenian archons is imaginatively absurd.   **τῆς θεοῦ:** I.e., of Athena Polias.

448. τῶν δορυφόρων: Tyrants are typically portrayed as having personal bodyguards (A. *Cho.* 766–69; Th. 1.130.1, 6.57.1); Sausage-seller here links

Paphlagon's lineage to the bodyguards of the tyrant Pisistratus. Allegations of family histories of antidemocratic conspiracy were routinely made against political opponents to suggest that they planned to usurp popular sovereignty; see Henderson 2003a, 167–69.

449. βυρσίνης τῆς Ἱππίου: A wordplay on βύρσα, "an animal hide," and Μυρσίνη, the aristocratic wife of the tyrant Hippias (*PA* 7605; *PAA* 537810), son of Pisistratus (Th. 6.55.1), thereby connecting her pedigree to the family of the Paphlagonian tanner (cf. 786n).

450. κόβαλος: "Trickster." Cf. 417; *Ra.* 1015; *Pl.* 279; Phryn. Com. fr. 4.

451–52. ἰοὺ ἰού: "Ow, ow"; an inarticulate cry of pain and distress (cf. *Nu.* 1 [with Dover ad loc.], 1321; *Ra.* 653; *Pl.* 852). See Labiano Ilundain 2000, 219–20; Nordgen 2015, 226.   **οἱ ξυνωμόται:** Cf. 235–36n.

456. χὤπως κολᾷ: Sc., σκοπεῖ or the like. On the construction, see 217–21n. The future middle form in -άω of κολάζειν is contracted from κολάσει for the sake of the pun on κόλοις. See Peppler 1921, 157; Willi 2003, 249.

457–60. *Chorus to Sausage-seller.*   Meter: iambic tetrameter catalectics. **ὦ γεννικώτατον κρέας:** Cf. 421.   **σωτὴρ φανεὶς ἡμῖν:** Cf. 147–49n.   **πάντων:** Pleonastic with the superlative (cf., e.g., *V.* 605; *Av.* 514; Pl. Com. fr. 105.2).   **ποικίλως ... ἐν λόγοισιν:** "cleverly ... with words."   **πῶς ἄν ...;** "[tell us] how ..."; an example of a question in which the optative implies a virtual wish or command (KG 1.235–36; *AGPS* 54.3.8.A).   **ἐπαινέσαιμεν:** The verb can denote both formal public thanks (Th. 2.25.2) and informal praise (595), both senses are in play here.   **οὕτως ὥσπερ:** "just as"; i.e., "in a way that matches." Cf. S. *Tr.* 475.

461–97. Meter: iambic trimeter. This scene marks a turning point in the action and sets the stage for the first parabasis, "the stepping forward" (498–610, see glossary). Paphlagon responds to Sausage-seller and the chorus as if they were oligarchic conspirators (461–63) plotting with the Persian king and other enemies of the state to overthrow the democracy (477–79). *At 475–79, Paphlagon rushes off stage to inform the Boule of the dangers at hand. Sausage-seller soon follows after him (495).*

462–63. The construction metaphors are drawn from the technical language of carpentry, particularly the field of wagon building (464n); see Willi 2003, 68. The rhetorical flurry of metaphors on the part of Paphlagon may echo the historical Cleon's complaints of Athenian fascination with rhetorical display and mock his condemnation of style over substance (Th. 3.40.2–3).

464–71. Slave A worries that Sausage-seller lacks the skill to match Paphlagon's rhetorical wizardry; cf. also his concern at 183 over whether Sausage-seller is conscious of having anything good in his character.

465–67. οὔκουν . . . γ᾽: "Not, . . . at any rate!" (the negative form of γοῦν; see *GP* 422–23).   ἐν Ἄργει: Argos, a military power in its own right, was neutral in the war between Sparta and Athens. It was traditionally hostile to Sparta, and the renewal of a thirty-year treaty established between Argos and Sparta in 421/20 was in serious doubt because of a territorial dispute (Th. 5.14.4, 5.28.2; cf. also 5.43). Apparently, the Athenians had recently sent a delegation, which presumably included Cleon, to try to win over Argos (cf. 811–19).   πρόφασιν: "as a pretense." For πρόφασις as an "alleged reason" as opposed to an actual reason, cf. Th. 1.23.6 with Hornblower 1991, ad loc.   ἰδίᾳ δ᾽ . . . ξυγγίγνεται: "but privately he's getting together . . ." Aristophanes portrays Paphlagon's efforts as a cover for secret, self-serving negotiations with the Spartans for the release of the Spartan prisoner/hostages captured at Sphachteria.

464. The transposition of line 464 after 467 is based on a scholion which says the speaker "is afraid because Cleon had spoken all in carpentry expressions . . . and the Sausage-seller's reply contains no carpentry terms" (Sommerstein 1981, ad loc.). It is also possible that the line is an intrusion, as it is omitted altogether in some manuscripts.   οἴμοι: "Damn it"; expressing exasperated impatience.   ἐξ ἁμαξουργοῦ . . . ; "from wagon building?"

468–69. ἐφ᾽ οἷσίν ἐστι συμφυσώμενα: "On what terms these things are being forged (i.e., being contrived)"; an example of a "contemporary sophistic innovation," the so-called *schema Chalcidicum*, where a present verb form (συμφυσᾶται) is replaced by a perfect periphrastic construction (present participle + copula) but retains its present meaning (see Willi 2003, 152–53). For the forging metaphor (συμφορᾶν), see Taillardat §418.   ἐγᾦδ᾽: = ἐγὼ οἶδα (cf. 873–74), a common and apparently colloquial crasis; see Stevens 1976, 59.   γὰρ: Explanatory.   τοῖς δεδεμένοις χαλκεύεται: An allusion to the chains of the captured Spartan prisoners; cf. 391–94n.

470. εὖ γ᾽ εὖ γε: "Great, perfect!" Cf. 427–28n.   χάλκευ᾽ ἀντὶ τῶν κολλωμένων: Forging is superior to gluing in bonding strength and permanence.

471–74. Sausage-seller threatens Paphlagon and his cronies with a charge of treason; see 235–36. On the formal legal procedure (εἰσαγγελία), see Harrison 1971, 55n4; E. Harris 2013, 167–68.

471. ξυγκροτοῦσιν ἄνδρες: "The men are helping to hammer out"; continues the metallurgical metaphor.   **ἐκεῖθεν:** "from over there"; i.e., the men from Sparta. See Taillardat §418 for the forging metaphors.

473–74. ἀναπείσεις: The verb is a future active indicative, not conative; translate as "you will bribe." Ignore the reference to *Pax. Sausage-seller speaks to Paphlagon.*   **ὅπως ... ταῦτ' ... φράσω:** For the construction, cf. 222n.

475–76. μὲν οὖν: Cf. 13–14n.   **ἐρῶ:** "I will inform"; a reminder that Paphlagon is himself an informer.

477–79. τὰς ξυνόδους: Term commonly used of secret political meetings (e.g., Th. 3.82.6; And. 47; Pl. *Tht.* 173d).   **Μήδοις καὶ βασιλεῖ:** The reference would raise suspicion and fear of collusion with the Persians and of imminent tyranny, given memories of the Persian invasion and occupation of Athens in 480 (cf. *Th.* 335–39; Ostwald 1986, 357–58). From the beginning of the Peloponnesian War, both the Athenians and the Spartans had plans to gain Persian support; in fact, Athens was negotiating with Persia at the outbreak of hostilities (Th. 2.7.1, 2.67.1).   **ἐκ Βοιωτῶν:** The Athenian general Demosthenes and others had recently made secret contacts with democratic factions in Boeotia, a Spartan ally, with the aim of overthrowing the oligarchic government (Th. 4.76).   **συντυρούμενα:** "churning cheese together"; i.e., "making political trouble." Here Paphlagon rushes off stage to inform the Boule of the dangers at hand. Sausage-seller soon follows after him (495).

481. νὴ τὸν Ἡρακλέα: A common oath, perhaps motivated by Sausage-seller's mention of Boeotia, the birthplace of Heracles (cf. schol. ad loc.).   ***καταστορῶ:** read instead παραστορῶ: The scholiast (ad loc.) wonders whether this is a tanner's term for "skinning and tanning hides[?]." Wilson prints Herwerden's emendation καταστορῶ. *Exit Paphlagon.*

482–84. ἄγε δὴ: "Come now"; cf. 155–56n.   **ψυχὴν:** "spirit," "courage." **νυνὶ:** Cf. 351–52n.   **ἀπεκρύψω ... / εἰς τὰ κοχώνα τὸ κρέας:** Cf. the joke at 427–28n.

485–87. θύσει: Second-person singular middle future jussive (cf. KG 1.176.6; Smyth §1917).   **ἄξας:** "Dashing." The verb ἀίσσω, which is found mainly in epic, denotes rapid, javelin-like speed (*Il.* 5.657, 11.484, 17.460,

18.212).   **τὸ βουλευτήριον:** The council house was located in the agora (Camp 2010, 18–21).   **διαβαλεῖ:** "he'll make false charges"; cf. 44–45n.   **κράγον κεκράξεται:** The *figura etymologica*, a rhetorical figure in which words of the same etymological origin occur adjacently, is a colloquial intensifier; see Willi 2003, 252n104.

488. ὡς ἔχω: "Straightaway," "as I am" (cf. *Lys.* 376 with Henderson ad loc.; *Ec.* 533; Stevens 1976, 58).

490–97. The wrestling metaphors foreshadow the agonistic character of what follows in the parabasis.

490–91. ἔχε νυν: "Here [take this]"; cf. 50–51n. *Slave A offers Sausage-seller an oil flask.*   **ἄλειψον τὸν τράχηλον:** As if being coached for a wrestling match, Sausage-seller is advised to oil his neck in order to slip out of his opponent's hold in the wrestling ring. This comic advice runs counter to the actual practice, as wrestlers would be expected to scrape oil off their bodies to allow for a firmer grip (cf. Luc. *Anach.* 1–2; Poliakoff 1987, 15).   **τουτῳί:** I.e., oil.   **ἐξολισθάνειν:** "to slip out of," "escape" (cf. *Pax* 141; *Ec.* 286–87).   **τὰς διαβολάς:** A pun on the legal term διαβολή, "slander," and the wrestling term, διαλαβή, "hold and take down" (see 261–63n)

492. ἀλλ' εὖ λέγεις: "Great idea"; the implication is that he will do just that (*AGPS* 69.31.1.H).   **παιδοτριβικῶς:** "like a coach."   **ταυταγί:** The deictic suffix -γί for -ι (from γ[ε] + ι) is comic.

493. τί δαί; Cf. 351–52n.

494. ὦ τᾶν: Colloquial; Stevens (1976, 42) identifies it as "ostensibly a polite form of address used for an equal or superior but very often with a tone of condescension and impatience."   **ἐσκοροδισμένος μάχῃ:** Sausage-seller is primed with garlic like a fighting cock (cf. 946). Garlic and its by-products are connected to fierce and bellicose natures; see Taillardat §378. The cockfighting metaphor continues through 497. *Exit Sausage-seller.*

496–97. διαβάλλειν: Cf. 6–7n.   **τοὺς λόφους κατεσθίειν:** "devour his comb," as if a fighting cock. The term λόφος suggests a military joke on the plumes or crest of a warrior's helmet. For jokes on λόφος as a military term, cf. *Av.* 279, 287 with Koenen 1959.   **χὤπως ... ἥξεις:** For the construction, cf. 221–22n.   **τὰ κάλλαι':** "wattles"; i.e., the beard-like fold of colorful skin hanging from the neck of the rooster.

498–610. Parabasis (see glossary) consisting of the kommation (see glossary), in anapestic tetrameters, marking the departure of the actors at the start of the parabasis (498–506); the speech of the coryphaeus (507–50), also in anapestic tetrameters with a pnigos in iambic dimeters in the last four lines; the strophe (551–54); the epirrhema (565–80); the antistrophe (581–94); and the antepirrhema (595–610). For the form and history of the parabasis, see Sifakis 1971, 33–70. Note that the poetic succession, in which Aristophanes presents himself as the culmination of the genre, parallels the Sausage-seller's political succession to power in the opening scene (128–43); see Biles 2011, 221–32.

498–500. ἀλλ᾽ ἴθι χαίρων: "Go, happily"; a set parabatic opening phrase (*Nu.* 510; *V.* 1009; *Pax* 729; cf. *Ach.* 1143).   πράξειας / κατὰ νοῦν τὸν ἐμόν: "may you act in accord with our intent" (cf. *Pax* 762, πράξας κατὰ νοῦν); see Collard 2018, 160.   Ζεὺς ἀγοραῖος: See 409–10n.

502. στεφάνοις κατάπαστος: "Bespangled with garlands/crowns." The image (cf. 967–69) evokes the bestowal of a public honor worthy of athletic champions or esteemed leaders (e.g., Plu. *Per.* 28.4, στεφάνοις ἀνέδουν . . . ὥσπερ ἀθλητήν, of Pericles; Th. 4.121.1, χρυσῷ στεφάνῳ ἀνέδησαν . . . ὥσπερ ἀθλητῇ, of the Spartan general Brasidas).

503–6. For the call for the spectators' attention, cf. *V.* 1010–14; Pherecr. frr. 84, 204; Eup. fr. 42. Praise of the audience's critical expertise seems ironic (cf. *Nu.* 520–25; *V.* 1010–14; *Ra.* 674–78, 1109–18).   ὑμεῖς: The audience.   προσέχετε τὸν νοῦν: "Pay [full] attention"; cf. 1014, 1064.   τοῖς ἀναπαίστοις: Refers to the second major part of the parabasis as "the anapests," although the meter is not always anapestic (cf. Hubbard 1991, 18).   παντοίας . . . Μούσης: "of every kind of Art."   πειραθέντες: "[you] who've had experience."   καθ᾽ ἑαυτούς: "in your own right." The phrase is emphatic at line end and, as Neil suggests (ad loc.), may be a retort to those who questioned why Aristophanes took so long to request a chorus (i.e., produce a play) under his own name (512–14).

507–9. εἰ μέν τις ἀνὴρ τῶν ἀρχαίων κωμῳδοδιδάσκαλος: "If some comic producer of the old [days]" (cf. 526–36n). κωμῳδοδιδάσκαλος refers to the author, director, and producer of the comedy (*Pax* 736–38). The terms for "producer" and "author" are here embedded in the noun (cf. *Pax* 734, κωμῳδοποιητής, with Olson ad loc.; *Av.* 912–14).   λέξοντας ἔπη πρὸς τὸ θέατρον παραβῆναι: "to step forward to make a speech to the audience" (cf. *Ach.* 629; *Pax* 735). For τὸ θέατρον, cf. 232–33n.

510–11. τοὺς αὐτοὺς ἡμῖν μισεῖ: "He hates the same men as us." The verb, which is here focused on comic rivals, echoes the political sentiments of the chorus (cf. 400–401n).   **λέγειν τὰ δίκαια:** Aristophanes' self-presentation (like the self-presentation of comic poets in general) rests on claims of being a fearless public educator and courageous benefactor who is committed to justice and the true interests of the city (*Ach.* 497–501, 633–45, 655–56, 661–64; *V.* 648–51, 1036–37; *Pax* 759–60; *Ran.* 686–88; cf. *Lys.* 648). For these kinds of self-presentation in Aristophanes, see Bremmer 1991, 127–34.   **γενναίως:** "bravely," "nobly" (cf. 577).   **πρὸς τὸν Τυφῶ:** I.e., code for Cleon. For Paphlagon as a monstrous opponent representing chaos, see 127–43n.   **ἐριώλην:** "whirlwind" (cf. 429–31n; *V.* 1148).

512–16. At least three earlier plays of Aristophanes were produced by others. Why would the poet wait until now to introduce himself as the author and the producer of this play? As a fledgling and circumspect poet, and in light of the competitive successes of his previous plays, he apparently thought it best to learn the ropes first and now sensed the opportune moment to take full responsibility for presenting his work under his own name (513). For a review of the question, see Rosen 2010, 237–38. Regarding Aristophanes' motives for having others produce and receive public recognition for later plays that he wrote (e.g., *Birds* and *Lysistrata*, which were produced by Callistratus; *Wasps* [cf. Dover at *Nu.* 530–51], *Amphiaraus*, *Frogs*, and *Plutus*, by Philonides), we can only speculate that he, like other comic poets of his day, simply did not want to bother with the many production details, such as costuming, directing actors, arranging music, set construction, stage business, and the like; see Olson, *FrC* 2017, 56–58.

512–14. ἃ: "As to what . . ." The neuter plural relative pronoun (idiomatic) qualifies the following principal clause (LSJ s.v. IV.2 ὅς, ἥ, ὅ).   **θαυμάζειν ὑμῶν φησιν πολλοὺς . . . / καὶ βασανίζειν:** "he says that many of you [i.e., theatergoers] were wondering and were questioning" (cf. 1212; *Ach.* 110; *Ra.* 802). For the use of present infinitives in direct discourse, see *MT* §683; Smyth §1866a.   **ὡς οὐχὶ πάλαι χορὸν αἰτοίη καθ᾽ ἑαυτόν:** "How come he didn't apply for a chorus long ago in his own name." The poet/producer was required to "apply for a chorus" (i.e., a performance) with the appropriate archon in charge of each of the major dramatic festivals. For information about these festivals, see the present book's introduction.   **ἐκέλευε:** The poet, like a hipparch, issues orders to his "troops."   **γὰρ:** Explanatory (*GP* 60).   **ἀνήρ:** "the gentleman" (cf. 176–78n).

515–16. ὑπ' ἀνοίας: "Because of foolishness." The preposition is causal, and its object "designates some condition of the subject's . . . circumstances which cause him to act in a certain manner" (Poultney 1936, 195–96).   **τοῦτο πεπονθώς:** "being in this position."   **κωμῳδοδιδασκαλίαν:** "producing a comedy" (cf. 507–09n).

517. πολλῶν γὰρ δὴ πειρασάντων: Genitive absolute. In Aristophanes, πειρᾶν often means "to force one's attention upon," "make a pass at" (e.g., *V.* 1025, young boys; cf. also *Pax* 763; *Pl.* 149–50, prostitutes; see Henderson 1991a, 158). The combination γὰρ δή emphasizes the point: "for certainly" (*GP* 243).   **αὐτὴν ὀλίγοις χαρίσασθαι:** "she [the comic muse] has granted sexual favors to few." For the use of χαρίζεσθαι in the sense "to grant sexual favors," cf. LSJ s.v. A.3. See also Dover 1978, 83; Henderson 1991a, 160. Comedy is here personified as a courtesan, ἑταίρα, and would-be lover, available to only a few (ὀλίγοις), select suitor-poets. This is one of the earliest extant examples in which the relationship between an artist and his work is spoken of in erotic terms (see Sommerstein 2001, 244).

518–40. Speaking on behalf of Aristophanes, the coryphaeus notes the difficulty of being a comic producer, sketches a history of the development of Attic comedy, and complains of the fickle tastes of the Athenian audience, who routinely dismiss poets whom they recently admired. Both Olson (2007, 16–22) and Storey (2010, 179–225) provide concise introductions to the history of fifth-century Attic Comedy.

518. ἐπετείους τὴν φύσιν ὄντας: "being fickle by nature." Cratinus (fr. 25) expresses a similar attitude about spectator tastes: ἐτήσιοι γὰρ πρόσιτ' ἀεὶ πρὸς τὴν τέχνην, "for you always approach my art year by year."

520–21. τοῦτο μὲν: The ordinal πρῶτον is understood from the context (*GP* 376–77).   **ἄπαθε:** = ἃ ἔπαθε.   **Μάγνης:** A comic poet (*PA* 9651; *PAA* 630950) active from the 470s, who won eleven victories at the City Dionysia (*IG* ii² 2318.3, 2325C.8; MO, 166), which seems to have been a record.   **πολιαῖς:** Supply θριξί.   **νίκης . . . τροπαῖα:** Victory in the dramatic competition is likened to military victory on the battlefield (cf. 1334, τοῦ (ἐ)ν Μαραθῶνι τροπαίου). The victory at Marathon was commemorated both at Marathon and on the Acropolis in Athens. At Marathon, there was a large funerary mound (tumulus) where the Athenians who died in battle were buried. On the Acropolis, the Athenians erected a marble Ionic column topped by a Nike figure to commemorate the victory. See Hdt 6.94–140; Vanderpool 1966, 93–106.

522–23. The scholion (at 522) reports that Magnes used such vocalizations and costuming in his comedies, but it seems much more likely that the actions of choruses or characters in his plays are being ascribed to the poet himself; e.g., Sommerstein (2001, 244) points to "*Frogs* 13–15 where Phrynichus, Lycis, and Ameipsias are said to 'carry luggage' in their plays, meaning that they often have scenes featuring luggage-carrying slaves." The interpretation of the participles (ψάλλων καὶ πτερυγίζων καὶ λυδίζων καὶ ψηνίζων) as referring or alluding to titles of plays written by Magnes was probably invented by ancient critics to make sense of the passage; see Spyropoulos 1975, 247–54.

522–24. ψάλλων: "Plucking," as a string of a musical instrument (cf. *Av.* 218, ἀντιψάλλων; Anacr., *PMG* 373.3; Hdt. 1.155.4)   πτερυγίζων: "flapping [like a bird]."   λυδίζων: "Lydizing," apparently a reference to songs sung in the Lydian mode (cf. Cratin. fr. 276.4–5). For the Lydian mode, see West 1992, 174–75, 181–82.   ψηνίζων: "buzzing" (cf. ψήν, a gall insect).   βαπτόμενος βατραχείοις: "dyeing himself [or his clothing] with frog colors"; an apparent reference to an animal chorus of actors costumed or dyed like frogs in one of the comedies by Magnes. For animal choruses in Aristophanes, see Rothwell 2007, 102–82.   ἐπὶ: Temporal with the genitive (LSJ s.v. A.II).

525. ἐξεβλήθη: "He was thrown out." Cf. D. 19.337, where the audience drives [the actor] from the stage with hisses and catcalls (ἐξεβάλλετ᾽ αὐτὸν καὶ ἐξεσυρίττετ᾽ ἐκ τῶν θεάτρων).   τοῦ σκώπτειν ἀπελείφθη: On the articular infinitive in the genitive case with a verb of separation, see Poultney 1936, 117. If the reference is to a failed comedy of Magnes that is still fresh in the minds of the audience, his career may have lasted until the 430s (see Storey 2010, 185).

526–36. To place Cratinus between the almost certainly dead Magnes and Crates (τοὺς προτέρους τῶν ποιητῶν, 519) suggests that he is a senile hanger-on from the last generation (cf. Biles 2001, 196–97; Ruffell 2002, 143). For the professional rivalry between Aristophanes and Cratinus, cf. 400–1n.

526–28. εἶτα: "Then," "on top of that" (here answering τοῦτο μέν at 520).   ῥεύσας: "gushed, effused." The metaphor is taken from a river in flood (cf. Taillardat §504).   ἔρρει: "used to flow." Hubbard (1991, 74n35) notes that "the use of the imperfect verb ἔρρει as also possibly the present of ἔρρω ('goes to perdition . . .') [is] aptly descriptive of Cratinus' present condition."   διὰ τῶν ἀφελῶν πεδίων: "across level plains."   τὰς δρῦς καὶ τὰς πλατάνους καὶ τοὺς ἐχθροὺς: "oaks and plane trees and his enemies" [i.e., his comic rivals]. An adaptation of a Homeric simile of a raging river, a metaphor for Homeric heroes in combat (*Il.* 5.87–92, 11.492–95, of Ajax). In Cratinus' *Pytine*, produced in 423, someone compares his poetry to a Homeric river (Ἰλισὸς ἐν τῇ φάρυγι, fr. 198.3–5) that inundates everything in its path, an image that represents the force of Cratinus' iambic invective (cf. Rosen 1988, 38–39).

529–30. ᾆσαι . . . ἐν συμποσίῳ: Guests at symposia held a branch of laurel or bay as they each, in turn, sang generally moralizing or patriotic drinking songs (*scolia*). Cf. *Nu.* 1364–65; *V.* 1225–26; *Lys.* 631–32.   **"Δωροῖ συκοπέδιλε":** "Goddess of Bribery with fig-leaf sandals." Δωρώ is personified "Bribery" (from δῶρον), and συκοπέδιλε is a pun on "sycophant." The quotation refers to a song taken from Cratinus' *Run-Aways* (fr. 70, perhaps produced close to *Knights* in 424; see Bakola 2010, 174n169) that was sung at symposia; apparently, it mocked someone for being a bribe taker and a sycophant.   **"τέκτονες εὐπαλάμων ὕμνων":** "Builders of Dexterous Songs"; a second song also attributed to Cratinus' *Run-Aways* (cf. schol. at fr. 70). τέκτων, which is properly used of carpenters' work, here = "poet" (cf. Pi. *P.* 3.113; *N.* 3.4).   **ἤνθησεν:** I.e., he flourished for only a short time (cf. *Nu.* 897, ἀνθεῖ, of novel ideas; 962, ἤνθουν, of traditional education).

531–33. παραληροῦντ': "Jabbering."   **ἐκπιπτουσῶν τῶν ἠλέκτρων:** "with his [lyre] pegs falling out."   **τῶν θ' ἁρμονιῶν διαχασκουσῶν:** "and with gaping joints." Cratinus' physical condition is compared to the pegs of a worn-out wooden lyre that can no longer hold a tune (τοῦ τόνου οὐκέτ' ἐνόντος): his "teeth" (pegs) are falling out, his strength is exhausted, and his body is deformed by old age. There may also be a hint that Cratinus' "ship" (poetry) is sinking, as ἁρμονίαι are a ship's tenon joints, crucial to keeping it afloat (*Od.* 5.361–62; see Morrison, Coates, and Rankov 2000, 183).

534–36. Κοννᾶς: "Conn-ass" (Henderson's translation); an ad hoc nickname for Connus (*PA* 8697; *PAA* 581470), the musician and citharode teacher of Socrates (Pl. *Euthd.* 272c, 295d; *Mx.* 235e–236a). Here, he teaches the lyre. His name came to be synonymous with mindlessness and lost talent (cf. *V.* 675 with Biles and Olson ad loc.). Connus was the subject of individual comedies by Phrynichus (fr. 6) and Ameipsias (T ii; frr. 7–10).   **"στέφανον . . . αὖον":** "withered crown," withered because he has not won first prize in a while.   **"δίψῃ δ' ἀπολωλώς":** also a dig at Cratinus for his alleged penchant for drinking.   **ἐν τῷ πρυτανείῳ:** Cf. 164–67n. The scholia (ad loc.) report that the quotations are adapted from the proverb "A Delphian man, wearing a garland and all but dead of thirst." Aristophanes' portrayal of Cratinus as a heavy drinker is expanded and reformulated in Cratinus' self-presentation in his comedy *Pytine* (Biles 2002, 147–54; Bakola 2010, 16–17). **ληρεῖν:** "[he's] talking drivel"; cf. 295n. **λιπαρόν:** "sleek, glistening with oil" (*Od.* 15.332; *Nu.* 1002; *Ec.* 652). ***παρὰ τῷ Διονύσῳ:*** Read instead παρὰ τῷ Διονύσου, "next to [the priest of] Dionysus"; Elmsley's text. For the dative ellipsis (colloquial), see 77–79n.

537-40. Κράτης: *PA* 8739; *PAA* 583995. His career, which fits between those of Magnes and Cratinus, flourished from ca. 450 to the late 430s. Aristotle (*Po.* 1449b7–9) reports that Crates was the first poet to move away from simple invective and create "plots and stories" (καθόλου ποιεῖν λόγους καὶ μύθους). Crates is also said to have begun his career as an actor for Cratinus and only later to have become a poet (schol. 537a = T 3). Crates is credited with three victories at the City Dionysia (*IG* ii² 2325C.16; MO, 167). Aristophanes characterizes Crates' work as "effortlessly summoned up" (fr. 347.3, ἀπόνως παρακεκλημένον). **στυφελιγμούς:** "abuses." Admitting that Crates enjoyed occasional success, Aristophanes adds that Crates' productions were cheaply staged and insipid and that, like Magnes and Cratinus, Crates fell out of favor with the tastes of a fickle theatrical audience because he was unable to sustain the power of jesting (i.e., making jokes and fun of someone, τοῦ σκώπτειν). **σμικρᾶς δαπάνης:** "small expense." **ἀπὸ κραμβοτάτου στόματος:** "from his dainty palette" (Henderson's translation). **μάττων ἀστειοτάτας ἐπινοίας:** "kneading most witty ideas." Cf. fr. 347.4, where Crates' poetry is said to be composed of thousands of other such things to raise a laugh (ἄλλα τε τοιαῦθ᾽ ἕτερα μυρί᾽ ἐκιχλίζετο); see Taillardat §753. For the image of the comic poet or statesman (cf. 815–16, of Themistocles) as a skilled chef of ideas (ἐπίνοια), see Reckford 1987, 127–28. ***χοῦτος μέντοι μόλις:*** Read instead χοῦτος μέντοι μόνος: "and he alone ..." (cf. 188–89n, for καὶ ... μέντοι). Wilson (2007b, ad loc.) prints μόλις, suggested by van Leeuwen. For a defense of the paradosis μόνος "as driving home the sense in which the poets stand alone against the audience," see Biles 2011, 105n31. **τοτὲ μὲν πίπτων, τοτὲ δ᾽ οὐχί:** "sometimes falling, sometimes not," summarizes Crates' simple, unembellished style.

541-42. ταῦτ᾽ ὀρρωδῶν: "Fearing these things" (cf. the defecation joke on ὀρρωδῶν at 125–26n). **πρὸς τούτοισιν:** "in addition to these things." **ἐρέτην:** "oarsman." **πηδαλίοις ἐπιχειρεῖν:** "trying his hand at the tillers." Triremes had a pair of steering oars, one for port side, the other for starboard, to help maintain the course when the bow "lifted" out of the water under full pressure or because of rough seas (cf. Morrison, Coates, and Rankov 2000, 173–74).

542–46. The three stages of his apprenticeship may be understood metaphorically to refer to progressive naval service in the major positions aboard a trireme: (1) before 427, when Aristophanes wrote passages or scenes for other poets; (2) between 427 and 425, when he wrote but did not produce plays himself; and (3) his current stage (cf. Mastromarco 1979, 172–73; Halliwell 1980, 39). Whether these three stages actually correspond to specific stages of the poet's career is not certain, and Hubbard (1991, 76n42) reminds us that the details at *Eq.* 541–44 can just as well be a "general reference to the poet's assumption of progressively greater responsibility for the details of production." The nautical metaphor, by linking the experiences of Aristophanes with the oarsmen who rowed the ships of the Athenian navy, suggests that the poet was as important to the health of the state as was the navy.

543–44. κᾆτ᾽ ἐντεῦθεν: "And from that point." κᾆτ᾽ = καὶ εἶτ(α). **πρῳρατεῦσαι:** "to serve as bow officer," whose duties included correcting bow-seated rowers whose stroke was out of cadence, relaying instructions from the helmsman, and keeping an eye on weather conditions.   **κυβερνᾶν:** "to serve as helmsman," who was in charge of navigation under oar and sail (cf. Morrison, Coates, and Rankov 2000, 111–13).

545–46. σωφρονικῶς . . . εἰσπηδήσας: "Leapt discretely, cautiously" (cf. 599, εἰσεπήδων ἀνδρικῶς, of the knights' horses). On the popularity of adverbs in -ικῶς and adjectives in -ικός, see 17–18n. Wilson (2007b, ad loc.) observes that a verb would seem to be needed after the first adverb "in order to achieve the required translation of the transmitted text." Sommerstein (2001, 240) accepts the emendation of Ademollo (1994, 177–80), οὐκ for κοὐκ, "making the line mean literally 'because, in a self-controlled way, he did not leap in foolishly and talk nonsense.'"   **ἐφλυάρει:** "spout gibberish," like Cratinus does (531, 536).   **πολὺ τὸ ῥόθιον:** "a big splash" (i.e., "a rousing cheer").   **ἐφ᾽ ἕνδεκα κώπαις:** The interpretation of "eleven oars" is controversial. Sommerstein (1981, ad loc.) understands the number as referring metaphorically to the tongue ("cheers") and ten fingers ("applause") of each spectator. Lech (2009, 19–26) argues that the "eleven oars" recall the victory of Phormio (mentioned explicitly at 562–64) and his eleven triremes on the gulf of Naupactus in 429 (Th. 2.90.5, 2.91.1) and that this may also be an echo of a lost ode performed at the celebration of Phormio's victory. In addition, Lech notes that, as Phormio and his eleven ships prevailed because of their superior military skills, Aristophanes' superior artistic skills will similarly prevail in this dramatic competition. We favor Lech's interpretation.

547-50. Pnigos in iambic dimeters.   **θόρυβον . . . Ληναΐτην:** "festive Lenaean cheer [of approval]"; a reference to the festival in which the play was performed (cf. *Ach.* 504, οὑπὶ Ληναίῳ τ᾽ ἀγών); perhaps also a pun on νῆἶτην, "nautical" (see Blaydes ad loc.).   **ὁ ποιητὴς ἀπίῃ χαίρων / κατὰ νοῦν πράξας:** cf. 498-500n.   **λάμποντι μετώπῳ:** "shiny forehead," an unexpected substitution for "face" or "countenance" (cf. Pax 771-74) and perhaps an allusion to Aristophanes' baldness (cf. Eup. fr. 89, referring to Aristophanes as "baldy," τῶι φαλακρῶι).

551-64. Strophe = antistrophe, 581-94. Meter: primarily iambo-choriambic and aeolo-choriambic. The strophe and antistrophe (fourteen lines each) fall into four metrical sections. The first two sections of each stanza (551-58 = 581-88) are composed of iambo-choriambic dimeters (- ⏑ ⏑ - × - ⏑ -) with an aristophanean (- ⏑ ⏑ - ⏑ - -) ending each section (555, 558 = 585, 588); the third section, in ionics (559-60 = 589-90), takes the form - - - ⏑ ⏑ - - ⏑ ⏑ - - ; the last section (561-64 = 591-94) consists of three glyconics (- × - ⏑ ⏑ - ⏑ -) and a pherecratean (- - - ⏑ ⏑ - -). Cf. Zimmermann 1984, 207-9; L. P. E. Parker 1997, 166-68. Parker suggests that the prominence of aeolo-choriambic rhythms in this play may "possibly reflect some cult connection with Poseidon Hippios" (72).

This choral song praises Poseidon as the patron of both the chorus of knights (and the knights in general) and the navy. It also identifies Poseidon as a friend and supporter of the poet, whose professional occupation was just described in nautical terms. The image of Poseidon in this song complements that of Athena Polias and Nike in the antistrophe, which characterizes the chorus as "conspirators" plotting to overthrow Paphlagon.

551-52. ἵππι᾽ ἄναξ Πόσειδον: The chorus begins its song by calling upon Poseidon as ἵππι᾽ ἄναξ, a title that associates him with both horses in general and knights in particular (cf. *Nu.* 83, νὴ τὸν Ποσειδῶ . . . τὸν ἵππιον, sworn by Pheidippides). Poseidon ἵππιος was jointly worshipped with Athena ἱππία on an altar at Colonus just outside of Athens (Paus. 1.30.4); cf. S. schol. at *OC* 711. On the close relation of Poseidon ἵππιος to the Athenian knights, see Siewert 1979. Cf. the exclamation ἄναξ Πόσειδον at *V.* 143, the choral invocation ὁ ποντομέδων ἄναξ πατήρ at *V.* 1532-33, and the vocative ὦ Ποντοπόσειδον at *Pl.* 1050.   **χαλκοκρότων ἵππων κτύπος:** Refers to the sound (κτύπος) of horses' hooves striking the ground (*Il.* 10.535; S. *El.* 713-14). Xenophon (*Eq.* 3.1) says that the test of a horse's quality was the cymbal-like "ringing" of its hooves on the ground although ancient Greeks did not shoe their horses (cf. Spence 1993, 41-42). During this song, we might imagine the chorus imitating the movements and sounds of horses by striking their feet/hooves on the ground and throwing back their heads in a neighing motion.

554–55. κυανέμβολοι: "Dark rams"; an allusion to the ἔμβολον, the trireme's formidable bow ram of bronze (*Ra.* 1318), which weighed around two hundred kilograms (ca. 440 pounds). Morrison, Coates, and Rankov (2000, 204–5) provide an illustration (no. 60); see also Casson 1994, 74, illustration 59.   **μισθοφόροι τριήρεις:** "payload bearing triremes"; refers both to the pay given to the oarsmen in the fleet (1065–66, 1366–67) and to the revenue that triremes collected from the subject allies to pay the seamen's wages (1070–71).

556–58. μειρακίων θ᾽ ἅμιλλα λαμ- / πρυνομένων ἐν ἅρμασιν: "Contests of youths shining forth in chariots." The knights were wealthy young men, the group most likely to be chariot-racing enthusiasts; see, for example, Pheidippides, himself a knight or associated with them, who was devoted to horses and chariot racing (*Nu.* 14–16, 25–32).   **βαρυδαιμονούντων:** "being deeply unlucky"; an Aristophanic coinage.

559–62. The accumulation of epithets (χρυσοτριαίν᾽, μεδέων, Γεραίστιε), a common feature of prayers, adds a lofty and serious tone to the invocation (cf. *Lys.* 341–49); see Kleinknecht 1937, 69.   **δεῦρ᾽ ἔλθ᾽ εἰς χορόν:** The adverb + imperative is formulaic in prayers calling for the deity's presence (cf. 583–85, 591; *Lys.* 1263, 1271; *Th.* 319). In Aristophanes, choruses regularly invite gods to join their dances (e.g., 583–86; *Ach.* 665–66; *Nu.* 564–65; *Pax* 775–76; *Th.* 1136–39; *Ra.* 324–27, 384–85, 397–400, 674–75), but the tone and content of this choral song especially stand out for their parallels with kletic hymns, "summoning calls," of cult poetry (cf. Fraenkel 1962, 191–99).   **χρυσοτρίαιν᾽:** The trident, like the dolphin, is a regular attribute of Poseidon in cult statues (Paus. 10.36.8; cf. *PMG* 939; *LIMC* 7.2, s.v. "Poseidon").   **δελφίνων:** Metonymy for the sea; perhaps a wordplay on δελφίς, the name of a naval weapon; see 762n.   **μεδέων:** The ancient epithet μεδέων/μεδέουσα is customarily applied to the tutelary deity of a special place; see 583–85n.   **Σουνιάρατε:** "Poseidon prayed to at Sounion"; i.e., Poseidon as he was worshipped in a temple at Sounion, a celebrated promontory at the southeastern tip of Attica, where trireme races were staged at a festival in his honor (Hdt. 6.87; Lys. 21.5). The term is parodied at *Av.* 868, "Hawk of Sounion" (ὦ Σουνιέρακε). For the temple of Poseidon at Sounion, see Paga and Miles 2016; Athena was also worshipped there (Barletta, Dinsmoor, and Thompson 2017).   **Γεραίστιε:** The name is formed from a port on the southern tip of Euboea, where there was an ancient sanctuary of

Poseidon.   **παῖ Κρόνου**: "son of Cronos"; stresses the sanctuary's antiquity (cf. *Od.* 3.177–79). The scholiast at Pi. *O.* 13.159 mentions the celebration there of a festival of Poseidon called the Gerestia.

562–64. Φορμίωνι: Phormio (*PA* 1498; *PAA* 963060), son of Aesopius, was an Athenian admiral who won memorable naval victories, including the defeat of a numerically superior Spartan fleet in the Corinthian Gulf in 429/28 (Th. 2.68.7). Aristophanes treats Phormio as a tough and disciplined fighter (e.g., *Pax* 347–49; *Lys.* 801–4; fr. 397, without context). He is also represented as one of the central characters in Eupolis' *Taxiarchs*, in which the admiral teaches the god Dionysus, presented as a bungling recruit, about military life; for the play, see Storey 2003, 246–60; for Phormio's career, see Olson, *FrC* 2017, 175. Phormio probably died in the spring of 428 (Th. 2.103); he was certainly dead by 411 BCE (*Lys.* 801–4 with Henderson ad loc.).   **φίλτατ᾽**: A frequent epithet in Aristophanic hymns and prayers; see Willi 2003, 20.   **Ἀθη- / ναίοις πρὸς τὸ παρεστός**: "to the Athenians in the present situation"; i.e., in the war generally and, more specifically, in the successful joint cavalry/marine operations in Corinthian territory (cf. 595n).

565–80. The epirrhema (565–80), balanced metrically by the antepirrhema (595–610), is recited by the coryphaeus, who speaks on behalf of the chorus. Meter: trochaic tetrameter catalectics. The chorus, which praises its ancestors as extraordinary, promotes itself as a champion of victory (cf. *Nu.* 575–94; *V.* 1071–90). The praise applies equally to the poet; see Hubbard 1991, 33n75.

565–66. εὐλογῆσαι: The word suggests a set speech or eulogy (e.g., *Ach.* 372; *Ec.* 454; Isoc. 12.206); cf. Neil ad loc.   **τοὺς πατέρας**: I.e., the generation of the Marathon veterans, who represent, for Aristophanes and other contemporary authors, the great and glorious achievements of the past (cf. 1321–23; *Ach.* 178–81; *Nu.* 985–96; Hermipp. fr. 75; Eup. frr. 106, 233; Hdt. 9.27.5; Th. 1.73.4–5).   **ἡμῶν**: Reflexive pronoun (KG 1.569).   **ἄνδρες**: Cf. 176–78n.   **τῆσδε τῆς γῆς ἄξιοι**: Cf. 577, 1333–34n.   **τοῦ πέπλου**: Cf. 1180n. The robe carried to the Acropolis in the quadrennial procession at the Great Panathenaea and presented to the ancient wooden cult statue of Athena Polias there. The peplos was embroidered with scenes depicting the Gigantomachy, the battle of the gods versus the giants, and thus symbolized the victory of Athenian/Hellenic civilization over monstrous non-Greek forces (e.g., the monstrous Paphlagon); R. Parker (2005, 265n54) explains that "it was, as it were, the seal of the contract between the goddess and the city." For the peplos, see Barber 1992, 103–17; for the Panathenaic procession, see Simon 1983, 39, 55–72; Neils 1992a, 13–27.

567–68. The chorus stresses the common interests and patriotic heritage of the aristocratic knights, hoplite soldiers, and oarsmen. **[ἐν] πεζαῖς μάχαισιν ἔν τε:** To omit the preposition with the first of two datives is typical of high poetic style (cf. 610n; *Ach.* 532; *Av.* 739–40); see KG 1.550. **ναυφάρκτῳ:** "ship-fenced"; first attested in A. *Pers.* 1029, recalling the Greeks at Salamis, and again in E. *IA* 1259, concerning the heroes about to sail to Troy. **στρατῷ:** A rare word in comedy (elsewhere only in *Ach.* 156; see Olson ad loc.). Cf. the phrase ναύφ[αρκτ]οι στρατιᾶι at *IG* i³ 365.30. **ἐκόσμησαν πόλιν:** "adorned/honored the city"; cf. Th. 2.42.2, from Pericles' funeral eulogy, αἱ τῶνδε καὶ τῶν τοιῶνδε ἀρεταὶ ἐκόσμησαν, "the excellence of these men and men like them adorned [τὴν πόλιν]."

570. ἀμυνίας: "Steadfast," "on guard." Cf. 576–77, "fight for the city" (τῇ πόλει . . . ἀμύνειν); 790, "standing up for the demos" (τῷ δήμῳ . . . ἀμύνων).

571–72. πέσοιεν εἰς τὸν ὦμον . . . μὴ πεπτωκέναι: A wrestling metaphor. In a match, when a contestant's shoulders touched the ground, it was considered a takedown. Because the referee had to see the fall, contestants whose shoulders merely brushed the sand of the wrestling ring could quickly shake off the dust, deny the fall, and continue the match (Poliakoff 1987, 169n3). For application of the wrestling metaphor to rhetorical skills, cf. Plutarch *Per.* 8.4, where a political rival complains, Ὅταν . . . ἐγὼ καταβάλω παλαίων, ἐκεῖνος ἀντιλέγων ὡς οὐ πέπτωκε, νικᾷ καὶ μεταπείθει τοὺς ὁρῶντας, "whenever I take him [Pericles] down wrestling, that man argues that he did not take a fall; he prevails and changes the minds of those who saw him fall." The knights' message is that "our fathers" never gave up but quickly picked themselves up off the ground, denied they were taken down, and fought on to victory. **ἄν:** With a past indicative (a common colloquial construction in Aristophanes; see Stevens 1976, 60), to highlight the frequency of past action (KG 1.211–12; Smyth §1790).

574. τῶν πρὸ τοῦ: I.e., the past generation. **σίτησιν:** Cf. 164–67n. **Κλεαίνετον:** Cleon's father (*PA* 8460; *PAA* 574420 = 574425) and successful businessman with slaves to work and run his tannery operations (schol. at 44), who was wealthy enough to serve as a choregos (see glossary) for his tribe's entry in the dithyrambic competition at the City Dionysia of 459 (*IG* ii² 2318.144; MO, 52). Unlike the generals of his father's day, Cleon is neither honorable nor public-minded. Old Comedy is full of praise for the integrity and moral superiority of past generations (τῶν πρὸ τοῦ) and censure for the present one (cf. *Ra.* 721–26; Cratin. fr. 256; Eup. frr. 219, 384.3–8, with Storey 2003, 345–48).

575. προεδρίαν: Honorary seating in the front row at public festivals and important events awarded to recognize service to the polis. At 702, Paphlagon swears an oath by his "front-row seat."

577. προῖκα: As an adverb, "freely," "gratis"; i.e., "for the common good" (cf. 679; *Nu.* 1426; Pl. *R.* 346e). **γενναίως:** Cf. 507–11n. **θεοῖς ἐγχωρίοις:** "for our native gods," preeminent of whom is Athena; cf. *Nu.* 601, ἥ τ᾽ ἐπιχώριος ἡμετέρα θεός.

578-80. καὶ πρὸς: "Moreover, in addition"; colloquial (cf. Stevens 1976, 57). **τοσουτονί:** I.e., what follows. **ἤν ποτ᾽ εἰρήνη γένηται καὶ πόνων παυσώμεθα:** Perhaps a contemporary slogan or phrase expressing opposition to prolonging the war unnecessarily (cf Th. 5.16.10); see Boegehold 1982, 149–51. **ἡμῖν κομῶσι:** "for our hair." Long hair (also mentioned at 1121) was a contemporary fashion among wealthy knights at Athens (*Nu.* 14–16) and was popularly regarded as a sign of snobbery (*Nu.* 545), as well as of antidemocratic and pro-Spartan sympathies (e.g., *V.* 463–66; *Av.* 1280–82; *Lys.* 560–61; cf. Lys. 16.18). The charge levied against the knights of being antidemocratic would be more pointed because of the association of long hair (and perhaps excessive facial hair) with Spartans and their sympathizers, cf. *V.* 474–76); see Millis 1997, 577–78. **ἀνεστλεγγισμένοις:** Either "for scraping with strigils" or "wearing tiaras." A *strigil* is a tiara or gilded leather headdress or, alternately, a curved metal tool used to remove oil or perspiration from the body in bathing or after exercise at the gymnasium (MacDowell 1995, 94n29). Van Leeuwen's emendation of ἀν- instead of ἀπ- is preferable (cf. Wilson 2007b, ad loc.).

581-94. Antistropher = strope, 551-64. The language of the song closely echoes contemporary language denoting factional strife, thus suggesting a kind of comic "conspiracy," involving Athena as well as the chorus and poet, in keeping the city safe from the likes of Paphlagon-Cleon and securing victory for the poet in the dramatic competition; see Hubbard 1991, 60–87; Anderson 1995, 12–14.

581. Ὦ πολιοῦχε: Aristophanes regularly uses this poetic epithet as a synonym for Athena Polias (*Nu.* 601-2; *Av.* 826-28; *Lys.* 344-45; cf. *Th.* 318-19, 1139-40). **Παλλάς:** An epic title and name of Athena as she stands armed and ready to defend the citadel and the city. The etymology of the word is given in the scholia at *Il.* 1.200; see also Koenen and Merkelbach 1976, 16-17; Burkert 1985, 140. The Athenian Pallas Athena is not the war goddess of epic poetry but, rather, a kind of idealized "civic emblem" for the Athenians (Neils 1992b, 37).

582–85. The introduction of Athena in her familiar guise of goddess of the citadel and patron of Athens is elaborated by the appeal to her as μεδέουσα χώρας (585). Indeed, the appeal to this aspect of the goddess suggests that Athens is in mortal danger and highlights the critical role of Aristophanes' poetry in keeping the city safe.

583–85. πολέμῳ τε καὶ ποιη- / ταῖς δυνάμει: The unexpected placement of ποιηταί (poets) between the abstract nouns πόλεμος (war) and δύναμις (power) playfully implies that poets (especially Aristophanes) are part of Athena's invincible arsenal that protects the city.   **μεδέουσα χώρας:** μεδέουσα is an ancient cult title of Athena Polias attested in several inscriptions, including the so-called Themistocles Decree (cf. 763n). Just as Poseidon is master of the sea (δελφίνων μεδέων, 560), Athena is mistress of the land. In Aristophanes, the epithet μεδέουσα occurs once elsewhere, of Aphrodite as mistress of her renowned cult places (*Lys.* 834).

587–90. μάχαις: Usually refers to military contests but can be used to denote agonistic competitions (Pi. *O.* 8.58); the leap from an athletic to a dramatic competition for a prize is not great.   **ἡμετέραν ξυνεργὸν:** "our helpmate" (cf. *Lys.* 346, ξύμμαχον, of Athena). For the belief that the deity will literally be an ally in a time of need, see *Lys.* 349 with Wilamowitz-Moellendorff 1964, ad loc.; A. *Ag.* 811 with Fraenkel 1950, ad loc.; E. *Med.* 395–98; *Hipp.* 522–24; *Ion.* 48.   **Νίκην:** Here personified; associated with victory in war and success in athletic and dramatic competitions (Hamdorf 1964, 58–59). When the chorus prays for Nike to "hasten here" (δεῦρ᾽ ἀφικοῦ, 586) and "make herself visible" (φάνηθι, 591), the audience might well have thought of the lifesize image of Nike standing in the right hand of the statue of Athena Parthenos on the Acropolis (1168–70; Zimmermann 1985, 2:208; Sommerstein 2001, 244).   ***Χαρίτων:** Read instead χορικῶν: "of choruses." This is the paradosis, which Biles (2011, 107n43) defends on the ground that "the adjective is perhaps most naturally taken to refer to the chorus themselves as the relative clause builds on Nike's support of them . . . and plays off expressions like τῶν τραγικῶν χορῶν (fr. 156.9)." Wilson (2007b, ad loc.) prints Χαρίτων, a proposal of Wilamowitz-Moellendorff. For adjectives in -ικός, cf. 17–18n.   **ἑταίρα:** "companion" and, in this context, "partisan." See Calhoun 1913, 4–7, especially at 5n2, 6n7; Connor 1971, index, s.v. *hetaireiai.*   **τοῖς τ᾽ ἐχθροῖσι:** Such "enemies" here include foreign entities as well as homegrown demagogues like Cleon and the poet's comic rivals, all of whom—some in fact, others metaphorically—are treated as threats to the security of the city (Edmunds 1987b, 39–41).   **στασιάζει:** "[who] takes sides." The terms ξυνεργός and ἑταίρα can be neutral, but their association here with the polemical στασιάζει introduces a political dimension. The choice of the word ἐχθροῖς (political enemies) to describe the chorus' opponents completes the joke. Aristophanes enlists the aid of Poseidon, Athena, himself as poet, Nike, the chorus of knights, and the audience (592), all as members of a political club, or ἑταιρεία, that is "plotting" to oust Paphlagon (Cleon) from power; see Anderson 1995, 12–14.

592–94. οἷς ἀνδράσι τοῖσδε: I.e., both to the knights in the audience and the chorus of knights; anticipates a double victory, one in the war with Sparta and the other in the theatrical competition.   **πά- / ση τέχνη:** "by all mean[s]." The expression "makes an imperative or its equivalent into an urgent plea" (Dover at *Nu.* 885n).   **νί- / κην:** I.e., victory over the rival dramatic chorus; cf. *Lys.* 1293, ὡς ἐπὶ νίκη, "as for victory."   **εἴπερ ποτέ:** A formulaic phrase used in prayers in kletic hymns and based on the religious concept of reciprocity and remembrance, *da quia dedisti*, "give since you have given"; i.e., "it's really urgent this time" (Pulleyn 1997, 33).

595–610. The antepirrhema has a lighter tone than the epirrhema (565–80). The knights' praise of their fathers and their anthropomorphized horses (ὥσπερ ἡμεῖς οἱ βροτοί, 601) is self-praise as well as praise of the audience (i.e., the Athenian demos); see Hubbard 1991, 81n52.

595. ἃ ξύνισμεν τοῖσιν ἵπποις: The chorus refers to Nicias' successful expedition against Corinthian territory (Solygia; cf. 604), in which two hundred cavalry distinguished themselves in battle (Th. 4.42).   **ἐπαινέσαι:** Cf. 460, ἐπαινέσαιμεν.

596–97. ἄξιοι δ᾿ εἴσ᾿ εὐλογεῖσθαι: Cf. 565–66n.   **γὰρ δὴ:** Cf. 517n.   **εἰσβολάς:** Sorties aimed at harassing enemy intrusions into Attica (Th. 2.19.2, 2.22.2, 2.31.3, 3.1).

598–99. τὰν: = τά ἐν.   **⟨δ᾿⟩:** Balances the μέν clause.   **ἱππαγωγοὺς:** Horse transports modified from triremes (Th. 2.56.2, 4.42.1). See the illustration of a trireme conversion to a horse transport in Morrison, Coates, and Rankov 2000, 227–30, fig. 70.   **εἰσεπήδων ἀνδρικῶς:** Cf. 266–68n, ἀνδρείας χάριν, of the cavalrymen; 545, εἰσπηδήσας, of the poet.

600. πριάμενοι: Sc., οἱ μέν.   **κώθωνας:** A drinking cup often associated with soldiers' campaign equipment (e.g., Theopomp. Com. fr. 55; Eub. fr. 56.3; Archil. 4.6W); see Sparkes 1975, 128–29. The vessel can also be used as metonymy for the symposium (see W. J. Slater 1976, 168; Davidson 1997,

66–67). Lech (2017, 599–606) suggests a joke here on the horses (i.e., cavalry) boarding the transports "manfully" (ἀνδρικῶς, 599) with their drinking cups, as if they were about to embark on a drinking adventure rather than a military expedition.   **οἱ δὲ:** For the ellipse of οἱ μέν, cf. E. *HF* 636, ἔχουσιν, οἱ δ᾽ οὔ. The idiom is especially common in poetry (*GP* 166).   **σκόροδα καὶ κρόμμυα:** Garlic and onions are standard military and naval provisions (*Ach.* 550, 1099; *Pax* 1129; X. *Anab.* 7.1.37).

601–3. εἶτα: As at 526.   **κώπας:** "oar handles." Cf. 545–46n. **ἐμβαλόντες:** "put the oar blade [into the water]"; a rowing term. Cf. *Ra.* 203–6, where Charon explains to Dionysus how to row (ἐμβάλῃς); X. *HG* 5.1.13, where the Lacedaemonian sailors refuse to row (οὐδέ . . . ἤθελον οἱ ναῦται . . . ἐμβάλλειν).   **ἱππαπαῖ:** An equine rendition of the rowers' cry, ῥυππαπαῖ (cf. *V.* 909; *Ra.* 1073 with Dover ad loc.; Labiano Ilundain 2000, 377).   **ληπτέον μᾶλλον:** "take [the oar]"; i.e., "pull harder." The verbal adjective often omits ἐστί (KG 1.447; Smyth §944b). The use of verbal adjectives (-τέος/-τέα/-τέον) was the contemporary linguistic style; see Willi 2003, 146–48.   **ἐλᾷς:** ἐλαύνειν is used for both "rowing" and "riding."   **ὦ σαμφόρα:** Horses were often branded, as a mark of their pedigree, with the Dorian letters *san* (ϡ), for σαμφόρα (cf. *Nu.* 122, 1298, where Strepsiades pretends a horse-dealing creditor is a horse), or *koppa* (ϙ), for κοππατία (*Nu.* 23, 438; fr. 43).

604–5. ἐξεπήδων τ᾽ εἰς Κόρινθον: Cf. 595n, 598–99n.   **οἱ νεώτατοι:** Just as younger troops prepared meals, foraged for food, and readied a bivouac for the veterans on a campaign, young colts tend to the grunt work of setting up camp and foraging for fodder (βρώματα) for their senior messmates.   **ταῖς ὁπλαῖς:** The generic term for the hooves of horses and other cloven-footed domestic animals.   **εὐνὰς:** "camp bed" (Th. 3.112.3, 4.32.1, 6.67.1).   **μετῆσαν:** "went after," "went to fetch" (cf. *Ach.* 727–28; *Nu.* 801; *Pax* 274).

606–7. παγούρους: The common crab (Arist. *HA* 525b5; Xenarch. fr. 8.2).   **ποίας Μηδικῆς:** "Median clover/alfalfa"; a premier fodder crop (Hdt. 4.53.2–3) said to have been imported into Greece at the time of the Persian invasion under King Darius (Plin. *NH* 18.144).   **θύραζε:** "ashore" (cf. *Il.* 16.408, of fish drawn out of the sea; *Od.* 5.410, of Odysseus emerging from the sea).

608–10. Halliwell (1982, 153) notes the relevance of *PMG* 892, a symposiatic drinking song, "scolion," (*scolion*) featuring a crab who talks to a captured snake about the importance of friends being straightforward and not thinking crooked thoughts. **Θέωρος:** *PA* 7223; *PAA* 51360; mentioned as a parasite, political flatterer, and crony of Cleon (*Nu.* 399–400; cf. *V.* 42–43 with MacDowell ad loc.), qualities that easily account for Aristophanes' mention of him here. The claim in the scholia (ad loc.) that Theorus was a voracious consumer of seafood (ἰχθυόφαγος) is probably based on this passage. **δεινά γ':** "It's really terrible!" For the neuter plural instead of singular form, cf. KG 1.66–67; *AGPS* 44.4.2.A. For the force of γε with the adjective or adverb, cf. 427–28n. **Πόσειδον:** The Corinthian crab prays to the Corinthians' tutelary god, who was closely associated with Athena in Corinth as at Athens (551–64n). Cf. Pi. *O.* 13.81–82; Yalouris 1950. **μήτε γῆ μήτ' ἐν θαλάττῃ:** For the omission of the first ἐν, see 567–68n. The phrase echoes a poem of Timocreon, μήτε γῆι μήτ' ἐν θαλάσσηι (*PMG* 731.1); see Kugelmeier 1996, 68–72.

611–15. The chorus welcomes Sausage-seller with a series of mostly unresolved iambs which may parody the elevated and emotive language of tragedy.

611. *Enter Sausage-seller.* **ὦ φίλτατ' ἀνδρῶν:** "dearest of men" (cf. 147–49n). **νεανικώτατε:** an adjective that indicates "qualities associated with youth: of persons 'lively, impetuous,' in a good sense or in a bad sense 'rash, insolent'" (Stevens 1976, 49); may also refer to contemporary rhetorical style (Neil ad loc.).

614. ἄγγειλον: Sausage-seller's report (624–82) is modeled on the messenger speech of tragedy. **ἠγωνίσω:** The verb is a second-person aorist middle, not an imperative.

615. τί δ' ἄλλο γ'; "What else but . . . ?"; a set phrase. See Collard 2018, 145–46. **Νικόβουλος:** "Victor before the Council"; a common Athenian personal name composed of νική, "victory," and βουλή, "Council" (cf. *LGPN* s.v.); here a pun rather than a reference to a particular individual.

616–23. Strophe = antistrophe, 683–90. Meter: trochees and cretics; the first two and last four verses are trochaic, the middle section mainly cretic-paeonic (see Zimmermann 1987, 3:13; L. P. E. Parker 1997, 170–72). In the strophe, the chorus congratulates Sausage-seller as a speaker of words and a doer of deeds (as if he were a Homeric hero with an elite education; cf. *Il.* 9.442, of

Phoenix as heroic educator); in the antistrophe, the chorus warns and exhorts him to be ready for more confrontations with Paphlagon.

616–17. ἄξιόν γε πᾶσιν: "It is worthwhile for all . . . !" ἄξιον + dative (rather than genitive) is common in Aristophanes (e.g., *Ach.* 8, 205; *Nu.* 474 with Dover ad loc.; *Av.* 548); the particle is exclamatory, as at 124.   **ἐπολολύξαι:** "to let out a cry of joy and celebration." The onomatopoetic verb is customarily uttered at the successful completion of a venture or a triumph (cf. 1327; *Lys.* 240 with Henderson ad loc.)

620–22. ὡς ἐγώ μοι δοκῶ / κἄν . . . διελθεῖν: "I think I could . . ."; i.e., "I'd be willing to . . ." (*Ach.* 994; *Av.* 671; *Lys.* 115–16).   **πρὸς τάδ':** "therefore" (cf. 760; *Pax* 305).   **βέλ- / τιστε, θαρρήσας λέγ':** "my excellent man, speak boldly." Here, the chorus uses the vocative as tactical praise to get Sausage-seller to "think and act in a way desired" (Dover 2002, 89–90).

624–82. The scene, a report of the offstage meeting of the Boule, contains one of two lengthy set speeches (excluding those of the coryphaeus in the two parabases). Briefly, the chorus and audience hear that because Sausage-seller decisively outdid his rival in terms of deceit, fraud, and corruption in front of members of the Boule and so incited their rage against Paphlagon that Paphlagon was physically removed from the meeting, and his enemies no longer fear him; see Sommerstein 2009, 164–65. Revermann (2006, 126) suggests that Sausage-seller's "vivid narrative prepares for, as well as pre-enacts, the shouting contests between him and the Paphlagonian that are to follow."

624. γ': "Certainly"; sharpens the invitation to relate his account (*GP* 119–20).

626–27. ἔνδον: I.e., the Bouleuterion.   **ἐλασίβροντ' ἀναρρηγνὺς ἔπη:** "break out thunderous words" (cf. Pi. fr. 180, ἀναρρῆξαι τὸν ἀχρεῖον λόγον, "blurt out a useless word"), as expected of a politician known for his rhetorical bombast (cf. 134–37n).   **τερατευόμενος:** "talking nonsense." The term and its cognates denote ridiculous speech and ideas (cf. *Nu.* 317–18; *Lys.* 762; *Ra.* 834). The stem τέρας- befits the portrayal of Paphlagon as a monster.   **ἤρειδε:** "he was hurling forth" (sc., ἔπη).   **κατὰ:** + genitive of the persons under attack (see Poultney 1936, 174).

628–31. κρημνοὺς: "Huge crags"; i.e., "gigantic phrases" (cf. *Nu.* 1367, where the tragedian Aeschylus is dismissed as a κρημνοποιόν, "crag maker"; and cf. *Ra.* 929 where his poetic language is described as ῥήμαθ' ἱππόκρημνα, "neck-breaking words."   **ἐρείπων:** "throwing down"; Brunck's proposal (Wilson

2007b, ad loc.). **ξυνωμότας λέγων:** Cf. 235–36n. **πιθανώταθ':** =
πιθανώτατα, "most persuasively." Cf. Th. 4.21.3, τῷ πλήθει πιθανώτατος,
of Cleon's political influence with "the multitude." **ψευδατραφάξυος:**
"pseudo-orach." Eating this plant (Pliny *NH* 20. 219) could make one's face
blanch. **κἄβλεψε νᾶπυ:** "and the Council was looking mustard." For this
colloquial use of βλέπειν, cf. *Ach.* 95, ναύφαρκτον βλέπων, "looking like a
warship"; *Ra.* 562, ἔβλεψεν εἴς με δριμύ, "he gave me a nasty look"; Taillardat
§385. **τὰ μέτωπ' ἀνέσπασεν:** "furrowed their brows," affecting a serious
and important air (LSJ s.v.).

632–33. ὅτε δὴ: = "precisely when . . ." The particle intensifies the temporal
force of the clause (*GP* 219). **ἐνδεχομένην τοὺς λόγους:** "[the Boule] was
approving his words" (cf. Hdt. 5.92.1; Th. 3.82.7). **τοῖς φενακισμοῖσιν:**
"by his cheating, deception"; frequently in the plural.

634–36. Sausage-seller prays to personified aspects of his own character and
cites past experiences to help him win over the Boule; cf. Slave A's ad hoc
libation to personified "Stupidity" (Κοάλεμος) at 221. For the prayer parody,
see Kleinknecht 1937, 60–61.

634–37. Σκίταλοι: "Gods of Lust and Vulgarity." The word might derive
from σκιταλίζειν, "to be lustful, lascivious" (cf. Longus 3.13) or might be
related to the name of a wicked fuller named Sciton (*PAA* 824360; Pherecr. fr.
266); for the name, see Frisk 1960–72, s.v. This occupation was malodorous,
since fullers would reek of urine, the usual cleaning solvent in their line
of work. **Φένακες:** "Gods of Cheats" (cf. 633, φενακισμοῖσιν). **ἦν
δ' ἐγώ:** "I said"; a colloquial Attic formula (cf. *Lys.* 514; Cratin. fr. 205),
especially common in Plato (*Ap.* 20b; *Phd.* 61C; *Cra.* 383b). **Βερέσχεθοι:**
"Gods of Stupidity." Of unknown etymology, the word is glossed as
"stupidity" (*POxy* 1801.45), but "we have no way of knowing whether
the gloss is based on any evidence or whether it is pure conjecture"
(Sommerstein 1981, ad loc.). **Κόβαλοι:** "Gods of Swindlers" (cf. 269–70n,
ἐκκοβαλικεύεται). **Μόθων:** "God of Rascals" (cf. *Pl.* 279–80, ὡς μόθων
εἶ . . . κόβαλος / . . . φενάκεις, of Cario). **θράσος:** "brazen" (cf. 180–
81n, θρασύς). **γλῶσσαν:** Here used metonymically (and pejoratively) of
rhetorical skills (cf. *Nu.* 424, 1013, 1018).

637–38. This sequence of unresolved iambs establishes a quasi-tragic tone for
these lines that makes the substitution of "fart" for "sneeze" at 639 all the more
surprising and funny. Cf. the unresolved iambs at 611–15n.

638–39. ταῦτα φροντίζοντι: "As I was pondering these [words]"; dative participle of interest (cf. Smyth §1474).   **ἐκ δεξιᾶς ἐπέπαρδε:** "farted on the right." The verb (perfect for the present tense; see LSJ s.v.) is a surprise substitution for "sneezed on the right" (ἐκ δεξιᾶς ἐπέπταρε), an involuntary action thought to foretell a favorable omen (cf. *Od.* 17.541–47; Plu. *Themis.* 13.2; Catullus 45.8–9); cf. the fart of the infant god Hermes at *h. Hom. Merc.* 293–98 (with Vergados 2012, 434, 441–43; Katz 1999, 315–16). This surprising substitution is an excellent example of a paraprosdokeion joke.   **καταπύγων ἀνήρ:** "some pathic." In this context, καταπύγων is associated with pathic homosexuality, but it can also be used as a general term of abuse with males and females (e.g., *Lys.* 137, 776, fr. 128; Cratin. fr. 259, a personification). See Henderson 1991a, 209–10.

640–42. The series of double entendres establishes that Sausage-seller has a characteristic that makes him fit for public service: an anus widened by frequent penetration.   **προσέκυσα:** "I made obeisance [to the fart-omen]."   **κᾆτα:** = καὶ εἶτ(α) "and then"; perhaps colloquial when used in a temporal sense (López Eire 1996, 206–10; Dover 1997, 76–77).   **τῷ πρωκτῷ θενών:** "banging open with my butt" (cf. 77–79n, on ὁ πρωκτός and submission to anal penetration as a prerequisite for a successful political career).   **τὴν κιγκλίδ᾽:** The κιγκλίς was a movable bar at the entry gates (675) to the law courts and Bouleuterion (fr. 216; *V.* 124, 775). The word derives from the name for the wagtail, a bird whose habitual tail wagging reminded some of the constant swinging of the gate; see Arnott 2007, 96–97 (cf. also fr. 29, which refers to making an old man's rump shake like a wagtail: ὀσφὺν δ᾽ ἐξ ἄκρων διακίγκλισον ἠύτε κίγκλου / ἀνδρὸς πρεσβύτου).   **κἀναχανὼν μέγα / ἀνέκραγον:** "and opening [my mouth] wide, I shouted out." The root κραγ- is overwhelmingly associated with Paphlagon elsewhere in the play (cf. 134–37n).   **ὦ βουλή:** This was the regular form of address before the Council; see Dickey 1996, 180–81.

643–56. The city's traditional reward given to the bearer of good news was a garland or crown (e.g., Plu. *Dem.* 22; *Mor.* 184A), which is now part of Sausage-seller's stage costume.

644–45. γὰρ: Explanatory (*GP* 60).   **ὁ πόλεμος κατερράγη:** "the war broke out" (cf. *Ach.* 528, τοῦ πολέμου κατερράγη). On the image of war "breaking out" like a violent storm, see Taillardat §635.   **ἀφύας:** Common small fish, variously translated as "sardines," "anchovies," "herring." Those caught in the bay of Phaleron, southwest of the city, were a favorite Athenian dish (*Ach.* 900–903; *Av.* 76–77; fr. 521; Eub. 75.4, a

personification).   **ἀξιωτέρας:** "cheaper"; cf. 645, 895–96; *V.* 491–92;
Pherecr. fr. 67.

645–82. Food, whether cheap fish or elaborate dishes, is essential to Sausage-
seller's success in securing the favor of Demos (cf. 1152–1223).

646–50. τὰ πρόσωπα διεγαλήνισαν: "They calmed their faces" (schol. ad
loc.). The verb evokes an image of calm seas (γαλήνη: *Od.* 5.451–53, 7.319–20,
10.93–94; Arist. *Top.* 108b25) or calm winds (*Od.* 12.168–69); see Taillardat
§337.   **ἐστεφάνουν μ᾽ εὐαγγέλια:** "they were ready to crown me [for
bringing] good news." εὐαγγέλια is an internal accusative (cf. *Pl.* 764–66;
Plu. *Sert.* 11.4; KG 1.321; Smyth §1620). In Attic, εὐαγγέλια is always in the
plural.   **κἀγὼ ᾽φρασα:** = καὶ ἐγὼ ἔφρασα.   **αὐτοῖς:** I.e., members of
the Boule.   **ἀπόρρητον ποιησάμενος:** "making it an unspeakable secret"
(LSJ s.v. II.2). The word ἀπόρρητον usually refers to religious secrets (*Ec.*
442–43; X. *An.*7.6.43); with this one word, Sausage-seller renders the secret
ridiculous.   **ταχύ:** With ξυλλαβεῖν.   **τοὐβολοῦ:** Genitive of value
(cf. 682, 945). Such a cheap price also makes the speech laughable.   **τῶν
δημιουργῶν:** Craftsmen (here potters) selling similar products tended
to keep their shops and stalls in the same quarters of the agora (cf. 852–
53n).   **τρύβλια:** Cf. 905; bowls used for holding fish (*Av.* 76–77), for
mixing and mashing (*Pl.* 1108), and for serving and holding soups, broths,
porridges, and the like. Confiscating these bowls would cripple the market
for small fish, as customers would lose the means to transport them; the
councilors could then buy them up for a reduced price.

651. ἀνεκρότησαν: "They shouted [with approval]."   **πρὸς ἔμ᾽:** Wilson
(2007b, ad loc.) comments that the emphatic form of the pronoun stresses
the fact that "the audience gaped, not that they looked at him, rather than
Paphlagon (contrast 633)."   **ἐκεχήνεσαν:** "gaped in amazement."

652–56. ἄρα: "Of course"; indicates a logical connection between Paphlagon's
perception (ἐπινοήσας) and the realization (εἰδὼς) that he needs to make
a more attractive proposal than that of his rival (*GP* 36). See Stevens 1976,
44.   **ἡ βουλή:** The Boule is authorized to approve state sacrifices and
festivals (cf. Aeschin. 3.160).   **γνώμην ἔλεξεν:** See 266–68n.   **ἄνδρες:**
Paphlagon addresses the Boule in less formal terms than Sausage-seller
does; cf. 640–42n.   **ἐπὶ συμφοραῖς ἀγαθαῖσιν εἰσηγγελμέναις:** "in
honor of the happy events just announced." εἰσαγγέλλειν is administrative
vocabulary associated with official public announcements (cf. *Th.* 597, τὸ
πρᾶγμα τουτὶ δεινὸν εἰσηγγέλλεται, of a male infiltrator into the exclusively

female ecclesia; Th. 8.79, εἰσηγγέλλετο αὐτοῖς ἡ ἐν τῇ Σάμῳ ταραχή, of political disturbance on Samos).   **εὐαγγέλια θύειν:** "sacrifice in honor of the happy reports." Paphlagon treats Sausage-seller's announcement (643) like a report of a military victory (cf. X. *HG* 1.6.37; Isoc. 7.10) rather than the ridiculous proclamation that it actually is.   **ἑκατὸν βοῦς:** A "hecatomb"; i.e., a sacrifice of a hundred oxen, common in Homeric epic but a comic exaggeration here as it was rare in Athens, reserved primarily for the celebration of the Panathenaic festival.   **τῇ θεῷ:** To Athena, as at the Panathenaic festival.

657. ἐπένευσεν εἰς ἐκεῖνον: "Nodded toward him."

658–62. ὅτε δὴ: As at 632.   **βολίτοις:** "with cow dung"; a scatological surprise. Cf. *Ach.* 1025–26, μ' ἐτρεφέτην ἐν πᾶσι βολίτοις, "the pair (of oxen) supported me in all the cow dung"; Cratin. fr. 43, βόλιτα χλωρά . . . πατεῖν, "to walk on fresh cow dung."   **διηκοσίῃσι βουσὶν:** "with two hundred bulls." The doubling of the hecatomb means more meat for the demos.   **ὑπερηκόντισα:** "I outshot [him]"; a military metaphor (e.g., *Av.* 363; *Pl.* 666; cf. *Av.* 825, καθυπερηκόντισαν; Diph. fr. 67.5 ὑπερηκοντικῶς); see Taillardat §582n6.   **τῇ δ᾽ Ἀγροτέρᾳ:** Artemis Agrotera, "Huntress," is a goddess of the open countryside and thus goddess of the hunt. Preceding the battle of Marathon, the Athenians vowed to sacrifice a yearling goat to her for every enemy they killed (cf. *Lys.* 1262–63 with Henderson ad loc.). Their sacrifice of five hundred goats is a compromise number, as Persian casualties were much higher (e.g., Hdt. 6.117.1 reports sixty-four hundred).   **κατὰ χιλίων . . . χιμάρων:** "a thousand goats." κατά + genitive of the thing or person vowed is idiomatic (cf. *Ra.* 101; *Th.* 5.47.8). The sanctuary and temple of Artemis Agrotera were in the suburb of Agrai, southeast of Athens (Paus 1.19.6); see Camp 2001, 105–6.   **γενοίαθ᾽:** = γενοίατο (third-person plural optative; cf. *Nu.* 1199; *Pax* 209; *Av.* 1147; *Lys.* 42).   **ἑκατὸν τοὐβολοῦ:** "a hundred per obol."

663–64. ἐκαραδόκησεν εἰς ἔμ᾽: "Looked expectantly toward me." The pronoun form is emphatic.   **ἐφληνάφα:** "he was babbling" (cf. *Nu.* 1475).

665–69. οἱ πρυτάνεις: Cf. 299–302n.   **τοξόται:** State-owned slaves, often of Scythian origin, who were used as police to enforce the will of public officials (And. 3.5). They carried whips, bows, and quivers and, under orders, could forcefully remove disruptive individuals from public assemblies and spaces (cf. *Ach.* 54–55; *Ec.* 143, 258–59; Pl. *Prt.* 319c).   **ἐθορύβουν:** "they were yelling"; an onomatopoetic word (cf. θόρυβος and cognates) used to describe noisy crowds, especially at assemblies and law courts (e.g., 547; V. 622; Pl. *Ap.* 17d, 20e). **ἀφύων:** The accent distinguishes the noun ἀφύη, "small fish," from the adjective ἀφυής, "stupid," "dumb"; cf. the same pun at Luc. *Pisc.* 48. **ἑστηκότες:** "standing [up]"; an "intensive" perfect denoting the members' excited emotional state over the fishes' bargain prices (Smyth §1947a). **δ᾽... γ᾽:** A lively continuation (*GP* 155-56). **ἠντεβόλει:** For the double augment, cf. *Ach.* 147; fr. 39; Rutherford 1881, 83-84; Smyth §451. **ἵν᾽... πύθησθ᾽:** The subjunctive in secondary sequence in a final clause often imparts vividness (cf. 1181-82); see *MT* §321. The Boule members are too fixated on the lower price of fish to care about the claim of Paphlagon-Cleon, who actively opposes any citizen who would advocate peace with Sparta (cf. 326-27n). **ἄτθ᾽** = ἄττα. **ὁ κῆρυξ:** By custom, the herald conveyed formal communications between states at war (cf. *Lys.* 980-1013, where the arrival of the clueless Spartan herald is the first step toward peace negotiations). Porson's proposal of πάλιν instead of λέγων (the consensus of the codices) is attractive with the verb of motion, as it emphasizes that the Spartan herald has come back again. Thucydides (4.41.3-4) reports that the Spartans continued (πολλάκις) to send embassies to Athens after the capture of their troops on Sphachteria in the hope of making peace and gaining their release, but that their proposals were always rebuffed (cf. 794-96n; *Pax* 664-67).

670-73. ἐξ ἑνὸς στόματος: "With one voice" (cf. Pl. *R.* 364a, πάντες γὰρ ἐξ ἑνὸς στόματος). **ἅπαντες ἀνέκραγον:** "all shouted back." Cf. *Ach.* 178-83, where elderly Acharnian farmers all shout (ἀνέκραγον πάντες) at Amphitheus when he brings back a peace treaty from Sparta. Here, the Boule gives Paphlagon a taste of his own medicine (i.e., shouting). **νυνὶ...;** "Now...?" **γ᾽:** "yes"; cf. *GP* 136: "in assenting, the second speaker echoes a word from the previous speaker." **ὦ μέλε:** "sir"; a common colloquial form of address of unknown etymology (see Dickey 1996, 160). Its tone may be indignant, as here (cf. *V.* 1400; *Av.* 1216, 1257), or patronizing (cf. 1337; *Nu.* 1192-94; *Av.* 1360). **ᾔσθοντο:** Sc., the Spartans. **παρ᾽ ἡμῖν:** "among us"; i.e., "here [in the city]." **ὁ πόλεμος ἑρπέτω:** "let the war drag on." The phrase "was probably a wartime slogan" (*Lys.* 129 with Henderson ad loc.).

674-75. τοὺς πρυτάνεις ἀφιέναι: "That the magistrates adjourn [the Boule]." The call to adjourn the Boule was apparently something that could regularly happen; cf. the call to let the jurors off early at *V.* 595 (τὰ δικαστήρι᾽ ἀφεῖναι πρώτιστα μίαν δικάσαντας). **ὑπερεπήδων τοὺς δρυφάκτους:** "they were leaping over the railings." **πανταχῇ:** "pell-mell"; i.e., they were too excited about the prospect of cheap small fish to file through the gates (641n) in an orderly way.

676–79. Having recommended that the councilors corner the market on bowls (647–50), Sausage-seller corners the market on condiments.

676–77. ὑποδραμών: "Overran"; i.e., "cut in ahead." Cf. 1161, where Sausage-seller warns Paphlagon, ὑποθεῖν οὐκ ἐῶ, "don't cut in," as they start to race toward the house of Demos.   **γήτει':** "Onions" (Theophr. *HP* 7.4.10); cf. *V.* 496, where it is used to spice "small fish" (ἀφύαι).

679–82. προῖκα: "Gratis."   **ὑπερεπύππαζον:** "they cheered"; πυππάξ = "bravo!" (cf. Pl. *Euthd.* 303a; *Com. adesp.* fr. 417).   **ὥστε ... ἐλήλυθα:** The indicative marks the actual fact of the matter.   **ἀναλαβών:** "after winning [them] over."

683–90. Antistrophe. In the strophe (616–23), the chorus congratulated and invited Sausage-seller to recount what happened in the Boule. Here, the chorus reminds him of his outstanding "qualifications" and exhorts him to stand tall in the confrontations that follow. L. P. E. Parker (1997, 171–72) notes, "In content, the song belongs to a type characteristic of plays which make a major feature of a formal contest" (cf. also Dover 1972a, 66–68).

683. τοι: "You know"; colloquial (*GP* 540).   **χρὴ τὸν εὐτυχοῦντα:** "foretell your succeeding."

685–87. κεκασμένον: "Excelling" (perfect for present tense). The word occurs only here in comedy and parodies epic; cf. *Il.* 4.339, κακοῖσι δόλοισι κεκασμένε, "you, excellent in evil wiles"; *Od.* 4.725, παντοίης ἀρετῇσι κεκασμένον, "excelling in all virtues."   **δόλοισι ποικίλοις:** "with clever schemes" (cf. 459, τὸν ἄνδρα ποικίλως ... ἐν λόγοισιν, of Sausage-seller; 758, ποικίλος γὰρ ἀνήρ, of Paphlagon).   **ῥήμασίν θ' αἱμύλοις:** "with flattering words."

688–90. ὅπως ἀγωνιεῖ φρόντιζε: For the construction, cf. 217–22n.   **συμμάχους:** "allies, partisans" (cf. Nike as ξυνεργόν at 588–90; Athena as ξύμμαχον at *Lys.* 346).   **εὔνους:** "well-disposed"; i.e., "allies." Cf. 748, 779, 788, 874. Here, the term, which became popular in the 420s reflects the language of political discourse and connotes devotion to the democracy (cf. the expression εὔνοια τῷ δήμῳ); see Connor 1971, 103–5.   **ἐπίστασαι πάλαι:** "you've long known."

691–93. *Enter Paphlagon.* **οὑτοσὶ:** The chorus gestures toward Paphlagon, an action that could also draw attention to Cleon if he happened to be present in the theater (cf. 202–3n). **κολόκυμα:** A hapax legomenon (see glossary). The term seems to denote "long swells," a sign of impending storms at sea (*Il.* 14.16–17), and is here used metaphorically for Paphlagon's swelling threats; see Taillardat §343. **δὴ καταπιόμενός με:** "no doubt, swallowing me whole," as if Paphlagon were the man-eating whirlpool Charybdis. The particle adds a sarcastic and indignant tone (*GP* 230). **μορμώ:** "Boo!"; an interjection (cf. Theoc. 15.40, Μορμώ, δάκει ἵππος, "Boo, Bogey! horse bites," with Gow ad loc.). Mormo was a female bogey monster who hated children and was thus invoked to frighten them; cf. *Ach.* 581–82, where μορμόνα is substituted for the expected word γοργόνα in a paraprosdokeion joke about the boss on the shield of Lamachus. Comic Mormo masks were displayed in the theater of Dionysos (frr. 31, 130). On Mormo and other goblin figures, see Patera 2015, 106–44. Sausage-seller's joke implies that only children fear the likes of Paphlagon. **τοῦ θράσους:** On the genitive, see 1–5n.

694–95. τῶν αὐτῶν . . . / ψευδῶν: "Of the same lies"; a surprise substitution for "qualities," "strengths," or the like. **διαπέσοιμι πανταχῇ:** "may I fall apart into pieces everywhere."

696–97. ἥσθην . . . ἐγέλασα . . . / ἀπεπυδάρισα . . . περιεκόκκασα: "I'm delighted, . . . I laugh at, . . . I say 'coo-coo' [to you]"; aorists of instantaneous action. Of actions that have just been felt, the actor speaks as if they had already taken place (KG 1.164; *MT* §60). **ψολοκομπίαις:** "thunderous boasts"; i.e., "blowhard noise." **μόθωνα:** Apparently a lascivious and contorted dance that involved kicking the buttocks with the soles of the feet (schol. ad loc.), "a motif common in the κόρδαξ, the characteristic dance of Old Comedy" (Lawler 1944, 32).

698–99. οὔτοι μὰ τὴν Δήμητρα: For the oath, cf. 435–36n. **εἰ . . . ἐκφάγω:** Citing this passage, Goodwin (*MT* §454) writes, "This Homeric use of the simple εἰ with the subjunctive in future conditions was allowed by poetic license in a few passages of the Attic drama, chiefly in tragedy, even in the dialogue." **ἐκ τῆσδε τῆς γῆς:** I.e., "out of Athens."

700–701. εἰ μὴ 'κφάγῃς: The repetition mocks Paphlagon's threat. **κἄν:** = καὶ ἄν, "even if." **ἐκροφήσας:** Cf. 359–60n.

702. νὴ τὴν προεδρίαν τὴν ἐκ Πύλου: Cf. 575–77n. For Aristophanic oaths that invoke nondivine objects (e.g., 411–12 of Sausage-seller), see

Sommerstein 2014, 318–19n21. In addition to reserved front-row seating at the theater and elsewhere, Cleon enjoyed lifetime meals at public expense (cf. the joke at 164–67n).

703–4. ἰδού: "Indeed."   **οἶον:** "How."   **ἔσχατον θεώμενον:** Where nonentities were seated. For the seating arrangement of the theater of Dionysus as a kind of "map of the body politic," see Winkler 1990, 40–42.

705. ἐν τῷ ξύλῳ δήσω σε: Cf. Paphlagon's threat at 367.

706–7. ὡς ὀξύθυμος: "How fierce!"; perhaps an aside to chorus and audience (cf. Neil ad loc.).   **φέρε:** "Here." Cf. 113–14n.   **ἐπὶ τῷ φάγοις ἥδιστ᾽ ἄν;** "what would you most enjoy eating?"   **βαλλαντίῳ:** "money bag, purse"; i.e., "bribes" (cf. 1197). Purses were needed because Greek clothing did not normally feature pockets. The joke plays on proffering bribes for protections against Paphlagon's attacks.

708. τοῖς ὄνυξι: "With my [finger]nails." Paphlagon eviscerates his victim like the mythical monster Echidna; cf. *Ra.* 473–74, ἔχιδνά θ᾽ ἑκατογκέφαλος, ἣ τὰ σπλάγχνα σου / διασπαράξει, "one hundred-headed Echidna, who shall claw through your guts." For Echidna, cf. Hes. *Th.* 295–332.

709. τἀν πρυτανείῳ σιτία: Cf. 164–67n.

710. ἕλξω σε πρὸς τὸν δῆμον: "I'll drag you before the people," i.e., "drag you into court"; a technical legal term (cf. *Nu.* 1004, 1218).   **ἵνα δῷς μοι δίκην:** "so that you'll pay a price to me." The phrase δοῦναι δίκην has a legalistic tone but is used idiomatically here for "you'll pay a price," i.e., "you'll be sorry" (cf. *Nu.* 1242; *V.* 1332–33; *Th.* 465–66; Hdt. 3.69.2).

711. διαβαλῶ τε πλείονα: "And I'll outslander you." Cf. 6–7n.

712–13. πόνηρε: "You loser"; an antonym of ἀγαθός, "good, worthwhile, noble" (see Dover 1994, 52–53, 64–65).   **ἐκείνου:** Refers to Demos.   **καταγελῶ:** Paphlagon, as a quintessentially corrupt and self-serving politician, mocks, deceives, and laughs at clueless Demos. But see Demos' vow at 1313 never again to allow Paphlagon to make a fool of him (i.e., the Athenian demos).

714. ὡς σφόδρα: "So sure." σφόδρα lends an "affirmative charge to the whole sentence" and is probably colloquial (Dover 1987, 57–59).

715. γὰρ: Explanatory.   **οἷς ψωμίζεται:** "on what tidbits he is fed." Paphlagon feeds the people tidbits of "food" (i.e., money), while he keeps the lion's share of the "feast" for himself; presumably, the "bits" he feeds to the people are in the form of jury pay (cf. 50–51n, 797–98n).

716–18. The metaphors of chewing and feeding both speak to Demos' identity as an old man and infantilize him, as the verbs denote chewing to soften food or breaking food into small pieces to feed an old man or an infant (e.g., *Lys.* 18–19, παιδίον / . . . ἡ δ᾽ ἐψώμισεν; *Th.* 692, τοῦτο [sc., παιδίον] . . . σὺ ψωμιεῖς; Theophr. *Char.* 20.5, τὸ παιδίον τῆς τίτθης . . . μασώμενος σιτίζειν).   **κᾆθ᾽:** = καὶ εἶτα.   **ὥσπερ . . . γε:** "Sure, just like"; the particle strengthens ὥσπερ (*GP* 124).   **ἐντίθης:** Cf. 50–51n.   **τριπλάσιον:** Cf. 285n.   **κατέσπακας:** The gnomic perfect is used to describe a general truth based on a recurring fact. See *MT* §§154–55; Smyth §1948.

719–20. δεξιότητος: "Cleverness." In Aristophanes, contemporary abstract nouns ending in -ότης are often associated with intellectual fashion (e.g., *Nu.* 153, τῆς λεπτότης τῶν φρενῶν, "subtlety of thought"; *V.* 1059, ὀζήσει δεξιότητος, "[your clothes] will smell of cleverness"; *Ra.* 1181, τῆς ὀρθότητος τῶν ἐπῶν, "precision of diction"; cf. also Th. 3.37.3, Cleon's denunciation of the Athenian fondness for δεξιότης).   **ποιεῖν τὸν δῆμον εὐρὺν καὶ στενόν:** "make demos wide and narrow"; a double entendre for anal penetration (see Henderson 1991a, 211).

721. πρωκτός: Here personified. Cf. 77–79n. Cf. also *Nu.* 193–95, where the personified πρωκτοί of bent-over students study astronomy.   **τουτογὶ σοφίζεται:** "comes up with that [trick]." Cf. Arist. *Pol.* 1297a15, σοφίζονται πρὸς τὸν δῆμον, "They [sc., politicians] devise many arguments in regard to the people." For the deictic suffix -γί, cf. 492n.

722. ὦ 'γάθ᾽: Here, probably sarcastic. Cf. 69–72n.   **καθυβρίσαι:** Cf. also 726–27n.

723–24. οὐδὲν κωλύει: "Nothing prevents it." The penultimate syllable of κωλύει (long by nature) is shortened, as at 972 (also at line end).   **βάδιζε:** "hurry up." Paphlagon apparently lingers on the stage, less confident of success than when he rushed off to the Boule (481).   **μηδὲν ἡμᾶς ἰσχέτω:** "Let nothing stop us." The phrase is recycled (also at line end) at *V.* 1264.

725. *Paphlagon knocks at Demos' door.*   **πάτερ:** An affectionate form of address to an elder who is not a relative; see Dickey 1996, 79–80.

726–27. δῆτ': "Yes, absolutely"; an echo and emphatic confirmation of Paphlagon's words (*GP* 276).   **ὦ Δημίδιον ⟨ὦ⟩ φίλτατον:** "O dearest little Demos"; affectionate diminutives (cf. 1199, ὦ Δημίδιον; 1215, ὦ παππίδιον). In comedy, diminutives are generally used in attempts to cajole or impress the addressee (e.g., 1199; *Ach.* 475–78; *Pax* 382; *Lys.* 872–73; see Dickey 1996, 5); here, it has a condescending tone (see Landfester 1967, 52).   **περιυβρίζομαι:** "I'm really insulted." The prefix περι- is an intensifier (LSJ s.v. περί F.IV). Paphlagon portrays himself as a victim of *hybris* (cf. 722), an offense that assaults the dignity and honor of a person and, by extension, of an entire community; such offense is legally actionable (γραφὴ ὕβρεως). See MacDowell 1978, 129–32; Fisher 1992, 36–82. *Enter Demos.*   Here he wears the mask of a peevish old man (ἀκράχολος, 41), a pair of worn-out shoes (ταῖς ἐμβάσιν, 870), a well-worn himation (inferred from a chiton Sausage-seller offers him at 882–83), and a gray wig (τὰς πολιάς, 908). For his change in costumes at the beginning, middle, and conclusion of the play see Stone 1981, 360–1.

728–29. τίνες οἱ βοῶντες; Ordinarily, a house servant, not the master of the house, would answer a knock at the door (cf. *Av.* 57–58 with Dunbar ad loc.).   **εἰρεσιώνην:** A harvest wreath of laurel or olive branches, decorated with wool fillets, seasonal fruits, and small jars of oil and honey and displayed on the doors of private houses as offerings to Apollo, especially as part of the Panopsia and Thargelia festivals; the wreaths would remain on display for the remainder of the year (see Parke 1977, 76). Demos accuses the "intruders" (his own slaves) of having torn down his wreath. On the Panopsia and Thargelia festivals, see Simon 1983, 76–79.

730–31. τίς ... ἀδικεῖ σε; "Who's insulting you?" If, as suggested by Kugelmeier (1996, 158–90), the question echoes a love poem of Sappho (fr. 1.19–20, τίς σ', ὦ / Ψάπφ', ἀδικήει), it may account for Paphlagon's response at 732, ὁτιὴ φιλῶ σ'.   **διὰ σὲ τύπτομαι:** Cf. 266, δι' ὑμᾶς τύπτομαι.   **τουτουί:** He points accusingly at Sausage-seller.   **τῶν νεανίσκων:** "young upstarts." The term is often used historically to describe young knights, classified as rash, arrogant, and troublesome (cf. Th. 8.69.4, νεανίσκοι, a team of troublemakers employed by the Four Hundred; Th. 8.92.6, τῶν ἱππέων νεανίσκοι, as aides of Aristarchus; X. *HG* 2.3.23–24, νεανίσκοις οἵ ... ἐδοκοῦν ... θρασύτατοι εἶναι, as henchmen of the Thirty). Cf. the occasional use of the cognate adjective νεανικός to denote "impetuous and rash" youthful behavior; see Stevens 1976, 49.

732. φιλῶ σ': Paphlagon's profession of love for Demos (773, 791, 799, 821; cf. 1341–42) is transmuted into erotic love for a decrepit old man and thus subject to public scorn (Wohl 2002, 87–88, 90).   ἐραστής: To be a "lover" of the demos (cf. φιλόδημον 787) implies idealized love and devotion to the city (e.g., Th. 2.43.1, ἐραστὰς γιγνομένους αὐτῆς; cf. also A. *Eu.* 852, γῆς τῆσδ' ἐρασθήσεσθε).

733–40. Sausage-seller here reproaches Demos for falling for the wrong kind of lovers, precisely the type that he himself was meant to typify; see Dover 1994, 36. For a similar complaint of boys bestowing favors on anyone who provides them with money and material goods, rather than on those who truly love them, cf. *Pl.* 153–59. The passage typifies Aristophanes' and Thucydides' principal complaint about popular sovereignty: that it is for sale in exchange for immediate favor. For the features of demagoguery in comedy, cf. Eup. fr. 384 with Storey 2003, 344–45).

733–35. *Demos speaks to Sausage-seller.*   ἐτεόν; Cf. 32– 33n.   ἀντεραστής: "rival lover."   τουτουί: Sausage-seller gestures at Paphlagon.   σ' εὖ ποιεῖν: "treat you well," as a lover was expected to do (cf. 741; see also his pederastic courtship gift, λαγῷ[α], at 1192).   καλοί τε κἀγαθοί: Cf. 185–87n.

736. τουτονί: The accumulation of deictics (τουτουί at 731 and 733) suggests a lively jury trial.

739–41. λυχνοπώλαισι: An allusion to Hyperbolus (cf. 1303–15).   βυρσο- πώλαισι: Shorthand for Cleon, to whom the two remaining occupations may also allude; e.g., he is earlier referred to as a cobbler and maker of cheap shoes (315–21).   τί δρῶν; = τί ποιῶν;

742–43. The text is corrupt.   *τοὺς στρατηγούς: Read instead τὸν στρατηγόν. The singular form, attested as a manuscript reading and favored by Sommerstein and Henderson, seems preferable, since Nicias (but not Demosthenes) was in Athens at the time. Wilson (2007b, ad loc.) favors τοὺς στρατηγούς (Brunck's suggestion), on the grounds that both generals, Demosthenes and Nicias, served at Pylos.   ὑποδραμών: "running under"; i.e., "circumventing," "getting the jump on" (cf. ὑποδραμών, 676–77n; ὑποθεῖν, 1161).   ἐν Πύλῳ: "at Pylos." Wilson (2007b, ad loc.) rejects the paradosis ἐκ Πύλου, as he does "not believe that ὑποδραμών took a genitive." He concludes, "If there is something wrong with the rare word ὑποδραμών it would be better to substitute for it not a commoner word like ἀποδραμόντων but another rare one; Kock's ὑποτρεμόντων is worth considering."   τοὺς Λάκωνας: The Spartan prisoners taken captive at Pylos (cf. 391–94n).

744–45. περιπατῶν: "strolling around"; i.e., looking for opportunities.
ἑτέρου τὴν χύτραν ὑφειλόμην: "I filched another's cooking pot" (cf. 778). On the cooking pot (χύτρα), see 1173–74n.

746–49. Paphlagon is confident that the Assembly favors him, and his influence seems to be, at least to him, secure and unassailable (contrast Sausage-seller's expression of despair at this development, at 752–55).   **ποιήσας . . . ἐκκλησίαν:** "summoned an Assembly"; cf. Neil ad loc.   **σοι / εὐνούστερος:** "more devoted, more well-disposed to you." The expression εὔνοια τῷ δήμῳ reflects the language of political discourse and connotes devotion to the democracy; cf. 688–90. The pamphleteer of the "Old Oligarch" implies that εὔνοια was a quality of any πονηρός who wanted to stand up and address the Assembly ([X.] *Ath.* 1.6–8).   **'ν τῇ Πνυκί:** Cf. 40–42n.

751. ἀλλ᾽ εἰς τὸ πρόσθε: "Forward." The imperative is understood from the transition, marked by ἀλλ[ά], from argument to required action (*GP* 14–15); the use of this adverb in the prepositional phrase is a contemporary stylistic feature (e.g., *Ach.* 43, 242; *Th.* 645; Hdt. 8.89.2; S. *Aj.* 1249; E. *Hipp.* 1228; Pl. *Prt.* 339d).   **παρεῖν(αι) εἰς τὴν Πύκνα:** The phrasing recalls the formal language used by the herald to summon citizens to the real Assembly. Cf. also πάριτ᾽ εἰς τὸ πρόσθεν at *Ach.* 43 and *Ec.* 129.

752–55. *All move from the house into the orchestra, where Demos takes his seat on the Pnyx.*   Sausage-seller, distressed by this development, complains that Demos sits dim-witted and at "home" (cf. 395–96); Demos himself seems to be clueless about what is going on under his own nose (cf. 40–70, 85–100).

οἴμοι κακοδαίμων: Cf. 234n.   **δεξιώτατος:** "most clever, most sophisticated" (cf. 228–29n).   **τῆς πέτρας:** The Pnyx.   **κέχηνεν:** "Gaping [stupidly]" (cf. 261–63n).   **ἐμποδίζων ἰσχάδας:** "chafing, mashing figs with the feet"; i.e., "chewing on [dried] figs." The meaning of this phrase is unclear. The interpretation given here follows that of Molitor (1980), who combines the understanding of the Alexandrian critic Aristarchus that ἐμποδίζων means "chewing" with the report of Symmachus, a second-century commentator, that beekeepers provided their bees with mashed figs for food when inclement weather kept them in their hives (schol. ad loc.). According to Symmachus, the method for mashing figs was either by rubbing or chaffing them with the feet, metaphorically a process of "mashing" or "chewing," hence linked with the notion of "gaping."

756-941. Demos sits as judge of who is more disposed to him and thus most deserves to wear his steward ring, which authorizes the wearer to manage his household affairs. The scene transforms theatrical space into "political space" with a parody of the traditional prayer offered at the opening of the Athenian Assembly, and it concludes with Sausage-seller wishing his rival would choke to death on his own "food" (i.e., financial gain, corruption).

756-60. Choral song introducing agon II. Strophe = antistrophe, 836-40. Meter: five iambic tetrameter catalectics, with the second and third lines (757-58) omitting the first syllable of the third foot (metron), which turns it into a Euripidean (e.g., 758, ∪ - ∪ - ∪ - ∪ - | - ∪ - ∪ - -). See Zimmermann 1985, 2:122; L. P. E. Parker 1997, 172-73.

νῦν δή: Cf. 333-34n.   **πάντα . . . κάλων ἐξιέναι:** "let out the all rope[s]"; i.e., "spread full sail." See Taillardat §344. The metaphor of setting sail to face impending storms and conflicts (cf. 429-34) may parody Euripidean tragedy (cf. E. *Med.* 278, ἐχθροὶ γὰρ ἐξιᾶσι πάντα δὴ κάλων; *HF* 837, ἔλαυνε κίνει, φόνιον ἐξίει κάλων; *Tr.* 94, ὅταν στράτευμ᾽ Ἀργεῖον ἐξιῇ κάλως; see Newiger 1957, 29).   **λῆμα:** "Courage, resolve"; primarily poetic vocabulary (LSJ s.v.).   **ἀφύκτους:** "inescapable"; a wrestling term (e.g., *Nu.* 1047, μέσον . . . ἄφυκτον, of the Worse Argument holding his opponent in an "inescapable waist lock" [Taillardat §579]). See Poliakoff 1987, 33-53.   **ποικίλος . . . ἀνήρ:** "The cunning, skillful, devious man," as is Sausage-seller himself (cf. 459, εὖ τὸν ἄνδρα ποικίλως τ᾽ ἐπῆλθες ἐν λόγοισιν).   **κἀκ τῶν ἀμηχάνων πόρους εὐμήχανος πορίζειν:** "contriving ingenious ways out of impossible situations." Cf. [A.] *Pr.* 59, δεινὸς γὰρ εὑρεῖν κἀξ ἀμηχάνων πόρον. For wordplay on πορίζειν, πόρος, and cognates, cf. *Ec.* 236, πορίζειν ⟨δ᾽⟩ εὐπορώτατον; Alexis fr. 236.5-6, εὐπόρους / ἐν τοῖς ἀπόροις.   **ὅπως ἔξει . . . εἰς:** "you go forth . . . against"; for the construction, cf. 217-21n.   **πολὺς καὶ λαμπρός:** "a full force wind"; cf. 429-31n.

761-835. Agon II, part 1. Meter: anapestic tetrameter catalectics (761-835), followed by a pnigos in anapestic dimeters (824-35). This formal epirrhematic agon (see glossary) has two halves. The second half is in iambic tetrameter catalectics (841-910) with an iambic pnigos (911-40). Sommerstein (1981, 761-835) notes that two other Aristophanic comedies have an agon that is divided in two halves, each in different meters, *Clouds* (959-1023, 1034-1104) and *Frogs* (905-91, 1004-98), and that "each time the anapestic meter is assigned to the more dignified of the two contestants" (the "Better Argument" and Aeschylus respectively). He speculates that here the anapestic meter "is assigned (at least momentarily) to Paphlagon, who is defeated by Sausage-seller precisely because the latter is *more* vulgar and base than he is."

762. τοὺς δελφῖνας: This is the earliest attested poetic reference to the δελφίς, a heavy, lead-weighted, dolphin-shaped naval weapon hung over the yardarm and dropped onto the deck of an enemy vessel to cause it to sink (cf. Pherecr. fr. 12; Th. 7.41.2).   **τὴν ἄκατον παραβάλλου:** "bring the boat alongside" (cf. *Ra.* 269, παραβαλοῦ τῷ κωπίῳ, "bring [her] alongside with the oar"). The ἄκατος was a small rowboat that could serve as a lifeboat in case a ship had to be abandoned. The line seems to mean "see that you are fully prepared for combat" (Sommerstein 1981, ad loc.); see Taillardat §583.

763–68. Paphlagon parodies the ritual prayer offered at the convening of the Athenian Assembly (cf. *Th.* 331–51; *Ec.* 170–72; see Kleinknecht 1937, 54–56; Horn 1970, 44) and then utters a self-curse to take effect should his claims be proved wrong (767–68).

763–65. τῇ ... δεσποίνῃ Ἀθηναίᾳ: This honorific title adds a tone of authenticity to the prayer, as it reflects the form of address Athenians used for Athena and certain goddesses in prayers and cultic performances (Henrichs 1976, 261–66). It is also the customary address used in dramatic contexts by tragic heroes and favorites of Athena in both dialogue and prayers (e.g., S. *Ai* 38, Odysseus; E. *Suppl.* 1227, Theseus; E. *Cyc.* 350, Odysseus; *Rh.* 608, Odysseus), and used by servants to address the mistress or master (δεσπότης) in domestic contexts (e.g., 960; *Ra.* 1; E. *Hipp.* 89 with Barrett ad loc.). Elsewhere in Aristophanes, Athena is addressed as δέσποινα by Trygaeus in *Peace* (271) and by the chorus of old men in *Lysistrata* (317).   **τῇ τῆς πόλεως μεδεούσῃ:** "the mistress of the city"; at Athens, Athena Polias. The title recalls the knights' earlier invocation of the goddess as μεδέουσα χώρας, "mistress of the land" (585). Paphlagon probably draws on the title's historic and patriotic associations with Themistocles, architect of Athenian naval expansion in the 480s and the mastermind of the Greek victory over the Persians at the battle of Salamis (cf. 810–12n). Athena was worshipped under the cult title Ἀθηναιῶν μεδέουσα by the Aegean subject states of Athens (e.g., *IG* i³ 1492–95, Samos; 1491, Cos; 37.15, Colophon; 1454, Eteocarpathian koinon). See Anderson and Dix 1997; 2004.   **εὔχομαι:** The *vox propria* for a prayer and a vow (Burkert 1985, 69, 73).   **περὶ τὸν δῆμον / τὸν Ἀθηναίων:** A formulaic phrase denoting the Athenian people (cf. *IG* i³ 37.45, 43.5, 106.3). Cf. 830–35n.   **βέλτιστος ἀνήρ:** "most outstanding man" (cf., of Sausage-seller, 873, περὶ τὸν δῆμον ἄνδρ' ἄριστον; 944, ἀγαθὸς πολίτης; cf. also 176–78n).   **Λυσικλέα:** Cf. 132n.   **Κύνναν:** Cynna, a notorious Athenian prostitute (*PAA* 588743), compared to Cleon at *V.* 1032 and *Pax* 755.   **Σαλαβακχώ:** Salabaccho, another notorious Athenian prostitute, said to be less vile than the demagogue Cleophon (*Th.* 805). Paphlagon is fated to trade insults with prostitutes; cf. 1397–1401.

766–68. μηδὲν δράσας: Paphlagon shamelessly admits that he is undeserving of the public honors the city has bestowed on him, which is precisely the view expressed at 709 and 1402–5.   **σε μισῶ:** I.e., "I hate the demos" (cf. 400–401n).   **περί σου μάχομαι μόνος:** Paphlagon repeats this assertion in the oracle at 1038 about a lion (himself) fighting a swarm of gnats (i.e., rival politicians), just as he reasserts being a "lover of Demos" (cf. 732n).   **ἀντιβεβηκώς:** "resisting."   **λέπαδνα:** "leather straps"; an accusative of result (Smyth §1579). The metaphor comes from the leather trade, as his rival's metaphors come from butchers' work.

769–72. Paphlagon's conditional self-curse prompts Sausage-seller to utter a stronger and more detailed self-curse of his own. On competitive conditional self-cursing in Greek literature, see Konstantinidou 2014, 33–34.

σε φιλῶ: Cf. 732n.   **κατατμηθεὶς:** "cut up"; the repetition mocks Paphlagon's self-curse (767–68).   **ἐψοίμην ἐν περικομματίοις:** "may I be boiled in mincemeat." Cf. 372, where Sausage-seller declares, περικόμματ᾽ ἔκ σου σκευάσω.   **ἐπὶ ταυτησὶ:** "on this butcher's block" (cf. 152, τοὐλεὸν; 1165, τράπεζαν).   **ἐν μυττωτῷ:** "in a tasty sauce"; (cf. *Pax* 247, καταμεμυττωτευμένα, = a mash of grated cheese, garlic, honey, and leeks).   **τῇ κρεάγρᾳ:** The metal claw-like hook often used to remove meat from boiling water (cf. *V.* 1155–56); see Sparkes 1975, 131.   **τῶν ὀρχιπέδων:** ὄρχεις = testicles (Henderson 1991a, 124–25); in Aristophanes, the term occurs mostly in threats and violent sexual contexts (e.g., *Nu.* 713, τοὺς ὄρχεις ἐξέλκουσιν; *Av.* 442, ὀρχίπεδ᾽ ἑλκεῖν; *Lys.* 363, τῶν ὄρχεων λάβηται; *Pl.* 955–56, ἕλξει θύραζ᾽ αὐτὸν λαβὼν / τῶν ὀρχιπέδων).   **Κεραμεικόν:** The "Potters' Quarter" can refer both to a section of the city located in the northwest area of the agora (where potters' workshops were concentrated) and to Athens' major cemetery (cf. *Av.* 395–96). Here, the term refers to the graveyard.

773–76. σε φιλῶν: Cf. 732n.   **πολίτης:** Emphatic at line end.   **πρῶτα μὲν:** "first of all"; πρῶτα and πρῶτον are often used with μέν *solitarium* (i.e., without the balance of a δέ clause) when the speaker has no further point in mind or when there is no further point to be made (cf. *Nu.* 224 with Dover ad loc.; *GP* 382).   **ἡνίκ᾽ ἐβούλευον:** "When I was a member of the Boule." Among the responsibilities of the Boule were enforcing the collection of taxes and punishing defaulters (Arist. *Ath.* 48.1); in their capacity as Boule members, Cleon and other demagogues (e.g., Hyperbolus, Pl. Com. fr. 182) would have exerted influence on the process. A precise date for Cleon's tenure in the Boule is uncertain, but 428/27, the year in which the εἰσφορά (war tax) was substantially increased (923–24n), is a reasonable conjecture;

see Ostwald 1986, 204–205n23.   **χρήματα πλεῖστ᾽ ἀπέδειξα:** "I showed greatest profits."   **ἐν τῷ κοινῷ:** "in the public accounts" (cf. Th. 1.80.4, [χρήματα] ἐν κοινῷ ἔχομεν).   **στρεβλῶν:** This extremely painful form of torture involved binding the victim to the rim of a wheel-like device and gradually stretching the body and limbs until they broke (cf. *Pax* 452 with Olson ad loc.).   **μεταιτῶν:** "shaking them down," as a price for avoiding prosecution. Cf. *V.* 915–16, where the "Dog of Cydathenaeum" (i.e., Cleon) complains that the dog Labes failed to give the former (the prosecutor) a share of the stolen goods and should be condemned for thus harming the public interest.   **τῶν ἰδιωτῶν:** "individuals"; i.e., "people without much influence" (*Pax* 751; *Ra.* 458–59 with Dover ad loc.).   **σοὶ χαριοίμην:** "[so long as] I could please you. " For the future optative (representing a future indicative) as "quasi-oblique," cf. Neil ad loc.

777–78. τοῦτο μέν … οὐδὲν σεμνόν: "Well, that's nothing special." Here, the demonstrative with μέν *solitarium* (i.e., without the balance of a δέ clause) highlights the contrast between Sausage-seller's boast and that of Paphlagon (cf. 1216, αὕτη μέν; *GP* 381–82).   **τοὺς ἄρτους … τοὺς ἀλλοτρίους** "others' loaves"; i.e., "others' property." The antagonists provide Demos with goods that they themselves stole from others (417–20, 744–45, 1195–1201).   **παραθήσω:** Cf. 52–53n.

779–80. φιλεῖ σ᾽: Cf. 732n.   **διδάξω:** "I'll explain" (cf. *Nu.* 382; *V.* 519; *Av.* 548).   **ἀλλ᾽ ἢ διὰ τοῦτ᾽ αὔθ᾽:** = αὔτο, "except for this very" (*GP* 26).   **σου τῆς ἀνθρακιᾶς ἀπολαύει:** "he benefits from your fire." The image is of Paphlagon leisurely sitting by the fire and warming himself.

781. διεξιφίσω: Perhaps "outdueled," "fought to the death[?]"; the verb's precise meaning is unclear. The simplex form (ξιφίζειν) means "to do the sword dance" (Cratinus fr. 234, ξίφιζε καὶ πόδιζε καὶ διαρρικνοῦ, "do the sword dance and foot dance and twist").   **Μαραθῶνι:** The victory of the vastly outnumbered Athenians over Persian invaders at Marathon was the archetypical great deed of the past, and its veterans, the Μαραθωνομάχαι, were regarded as national heroes (*Ach.* 179–81; *Nu.* 985–86). The Marathon reference puts Demos in his eighties at least. At the only other reference to Marathon in the play, a rejuvenated Demos is restored to his past glory and deemed "worthy of the city" (cf. 565–66n) and "the trophy at Marathon" (1334).

782–85. μεγάλως: Cf. 151n.   **ἐγγλωττοτυπεῖν:** "to strike our tongues"; a minting metaphor (-τυπεῖν). Cf. 1379, γνωμοτυπικός, "clever at coining maxims." ἐπὶ ταῖσι πέτραις: The Pnyx (cf. 313, 754, 956). οὐχ ὥσπερ ἐγώ: "unlike me, . . ." The comparative clause is idiomatic (KG 2.575). ῥαψάμενός σοι τουτὶ: "having sown for you this here [cushion]." If the cushion was of leather, as Neil (ad loc.) suggests, it was probably "lifted" from the gear Paphlagon brought on stage. κᾆτα: "and then" (cf. 640–42n). μαλακῶς: "gently." *Demos slowly lowers himself onto the cushion.* τὴν: Sc., πυγήν. Σαλαμῖνι: The great Athenian naval victory over the Persian fleet in 480 (Hdt. 8.56–63).

786-87. ἄνθρωπε: Originally a neutral address to completely unknown persons, it "became possible to use as an insult [when] speaking to known addressees" (Dickey 1996, 152); Henderson (ad loc.) translates it as "my man." μῶν ἔκγονος εἶ . . . τις . . .; "Surely you're not a descendant . . . ?" For the form ἔκγονος (not ἔγγονος), cf. *Hipp.* 447–50 with Barrett ad loc. Demos implies that any politician who aspired to win his favor might claim to be a descendant of one of the "tyrant slayers." Ἁρμοδίου: Harmodius (*PA* 2232; *PAA* 203425) and his companion Aristogeiton (*PA* 1777; *PAA* 168195) assassinated Hipparchus, a son of the tyrant Pisistratus, the brother of Hippias (449), and thereby came to be memorialized as tyrant slayers and heroes of the democracy. Cleon apparently claimed Harmodius as an ancestor, and he may have been related by marriage to the sister-in-law of Harmodius of Aphidna (*PA* 2234; *PAA* 203430), the tyrannicide's kinsman, who, like Cleon, enjoyed the honor of free meals in the Prytaneum (*IG* i³ 131.5–7; Sommerstein 2001, 245). Symposiastic drinking songs (*scolia*; see 529–30n) celebrated the tyrannicide. γέ τοι: a colloquial idiom that gives "a reason, valid so far as it goes, for accepting a proposition" (*GP* 550). τοὔργον ἀληθῶς γενναῖον καὶ φιλόδημον: "your truly noble and demos-loving deed." The term φιλόδημος appears in the formal language of interstate relations as early as 447/46 BCE (cf. *IG* i³ 37.48, Athens and Colophon) but is attested for the first time in a literary text here; see Connor 1971, 101–2, 106.

788. ὡς . . . γεγένησαι: "So, you've become . . ."; probably spoken contemptuously. θωπευματίων: "tidbits of flattery"; a diminutive uttered contemptuously.

789. καί . . . γὰρ: "Well, . . . in fact." For postponement of γάρ, cf. 32–33n. μικροτέροις: The comparative and superlative forms of the adjective often "imply contempt" (Neil ad loc.). δελεάσμασιν: "bait"; a synonym for δόλος, "deceit" (schol. ad loc.). For the fishing imagery, see Taillardat §395.

790–91. καὶ μὴν: "Indeed." Cf. 335n.   **που:** here "used ironically by a speaker who is quite sure of his ground" (*GP* 491).   **ἀνὴρ:** a favorite term of Paphlagon for his self-description (176–78n).   **περὶ τῆς κεφαλῆς περιδόσθαι:** "to bet my head [on it]." περί + genitive (in Homer, a genitive alone) defines what is at stake in the bet; cf. *Ach.* 772–73; *Il.* 23.485; *Od.* 23.78; KG 1.377.

792–809. Demos and the Athenian demos are here spoken of as one and the same; see Newiger 1957, 37.

792–93. Beginning with the Spartan incursions of 431, many Athenians, forced to evacuate the countryside, had to live in makeshift shelters wherever they could find space inside the city walls (Th. 2.14–17, 52). There is a bit of historical distortion here, as the situation had changed after the seasonal Spartan invasions ceased, following the Athenian capture of Spartan troops at Sphacteria in 425.

ἐν ταῖς φιδάκναισιν / καὶ γυπαρίοις καὶ πυργιδίοις: "in their little barrels, lean-tos, and garrets." For the accumulation of diminutives, see also 98–100.   **ἔτος ὄγδοον:** "in the eighth year"; by inclusive reckoning, from 431 to 424 BCE.

794–96. καθείρξας αὐτὸν: "Having shut him in."   **βλίττεις;** "are you taking his honey." Cf. *Av.* 498, ἀπέβλισε; *Lys.* 475, ἀπέβλισε; Pl. *R.* 564e, βλίττει; see Taillardat §534, §722. This accusation is elaborated at 801–9; cf. *V.* 664–85.   **τὴν εἰρήνην:** Archeptolemus (326–27n) likely helped to negotiate and then support acceptance of Spartan peace proposals to the Assembly, which was sovereign in matters of war and peace (*IG* i³ 105.36).   **τὰς πρεσβείας:** Cf. ὁ κῆρυξ ... περὶ σπονδῶν (665–69n).   **ῥαθαπυγίζων:** "Slapping their butts." If there was a game or dance in which participants slapped their buttocks with their hands and/or feet (cf. schol. ad loc.; Pollux 9.122, 126), the point would be that someone else's butt is being slapped/kicked.   **αἵ τὰς σπονδὰς προκαλοῦνται:** "who propose a treaty" (sc., embassies). Cf. 1392–93, where Paphlagon is said to have concealed peace proposals (here personified as girls) from Demos.

797–98. ἵνα γ᾽ Ἑλλήνων ἄρξῃ πάντων: "Yes, so he could rule over all Greeks." In affirmative statements and questions, the particle adds "something to the bare affirmation which is not expressed but implied" (*GP* 133–34). The expression recalls the imperial ambitions that Slave A expressed to Sausage-Seller at 169–74. Cf. also the description of the rejuvenated Demos (i.e., the Athenian demos) as τῆς γῆς τῆσδε μόναρχον, "monarch of this land," at 1329–30, as well as the address to him as ὦ βασιλεῦ τῶν Ἑλλήνων, "O king of the Greeks," at 1333.   ἐν Ἀρκαδίᾳ: Conquest of Arcadia, landlocked and in the heart of the Peloponnese, would require victory over the Spartan army, a highly unlikely scenario, despite the recent success at Pylos; cf. Hyperbolus' alleged plans to conquer Carthage (1300–1315 with Anderson 2003). For Athenian imperial involvement in the Peloponnese, cf. Th. 5.29.

47.   πεντωβόλου: The extension of the empire would mean additional revenue and thus, he suggests, an increase in daily jury pay from three (50–51n, 800) to five obols, the equivalent of daily pay for a Boule member (Arist. Ath. 62.2).   ἠλιάσασθαι: "to act as a juror in the Heliaea" (cf. Lys. 380). The Heliaea (ἡλιαία), one of many fifth-century courts that required large juries (often up to a thousand or more members), is used here to refer to the courts and to jury duty in general (e.g., 255, 897-98; Nu. 863; V. 88–90; Av. 109–10). Contemporary inscriptions record the word and its cognates without aspiration (Lewis, IG i³ 40.75, 71.14 spiritus aspera abest).

799–800. ἢν ἀναμείνῃ: "If he's patient."   πάντως: "in any case"; intensifies the verb (cf. Ach. 956; Nu. 1352 with Dover's text, ad loc.).   αὐτὸν θρέψω 'γὼ καὶ θεραπεύσω: "I'll nourish and attend to him." Throughout the play, Paphlagon identifies himself as patron, protector, and benefactor of the jurors (cf. 50–51, 255–57, 1019; cf. 896–98).   εὖ καὶ μιαρῶς: "fairly and foully"; cf. 256, δίκαια κἄδικα, "justly and unjustly."

801–8. Paphlagon–Cleon needs the war to continue, for a return of peace might cause the people to conclude that the war had not been worth the sacrifice of life and property, to turn their anger against Paphlagon, and to seek his prosecution. Thucydides (5.16.1) writes that Cleon "thought if quiet were restored he would be more manifest in his villainies and less credited in his calumnies" (C. F. Smith's translation). Cf. also the people's anger and resentment against Pericles, whom they blamed for taking them to war and whom they held responsible for their misfortunes (Th. 2.59.2, 2.65.2–4).

801–4. ἵνα γ' ἄρξῃ: A sarcastic response to 797.   δωροδοκῇς: Cf. 438–39n.   παρὰ τῶν πόλεων: "from the subject allies" (cf. Ach. 506, 642).   ὑπὸ τοῦ πολέμου καὶ τῆς ὀμίχλης: "under the fog of war" (Henderson's translation).   ἃ πανουργεῖς μὴ καθορᾷ σου: "so that he doesn't perceive what wicked things you're doing." For the construction, see KG 1.362; Smyth §1361; AGPS 47.10.8.A.   μισθοῦ: "jury pay"; an elaboration to the claim of Sausage-seller's rival at 800.

805–9. εἰ: On the absence of ἄν with the subjunctive in the conditional clause, cf. 698–99n.   **εἰς ἀγρὸν:** "back to his field," i.e., "his farm" (cf. 1394–95; *Ach.* 32).   **χῖδρα:** Groats boiled and served as a kind of soup (fr. 918).   **στεμφύλῳ:** "pressed olive cake" (cf. *Nu.* 45; fr. 408).   **εἰς λόγον ἔλθῃ:** "comes into conversation"; i.e., "comes to eat".   **τῇ μισθοφορᾷ:** "with public pay"; i.e., pay for jury or military service.   **παρεκόπτου:** "you were cheating," "swindling" (cf. 859; *Nu.* 639–40). Cleon and politicians like him offer token wages to distract Demos from noticing what he is rightly owed (cf. *V.* 682–95).   **εἶθ᾽:** = εἶτα; "Then," as at 208.   **ἥξει σοι δριμὺς ἄγροικος:** "he'll come to you, a fierce rustic." The dative of interest (here personal) with a verb of motion is usual in poetry (Smyth §1475). The adjective δριμύς is applied to fiercely temperamental old men, πολὺ δριμύτατος (*V.* 277–80), and jurymen, δικαστὴν δριμύν (*Pax* 348–49); see Taillardat §§356–57.   **κατὰ σοῦ:** "[to vote] against you."   **τὴν ψῆφον:** "voting pebble"; used for voting and counting by dropping into one of two urns (*Ach.* 375–76; *V.* 95–96, 109–10, 656, 675, 987, 1205–7; *Lys.* 270; *Ra.* 1263).   **ἰχνεύων:** "hunting down"; i.e., ostracizing. For the metaphor, see Taillardat §731.   **ὀνειροπολεῖς:** Cf. 1090, ἐγὼ [sc., Paphlagon] εἶδον ὄναρ.   **περὶ αὐτοῦ:** "about him"; reading proposed by Herwerden. The manuscripts read σ(ε)αυτοῦ.

810–12. οὔκουν . . . δῆτ᾽; Cf. 17–18n.   **ταυτί:** I.e., what has just been said.   **διαβάλλειν:** Cf. 261–63n.   **πρὸς Ἀθηναίους καὶ τὸν δῆμον:** Cf. 273n; cf. also 764. Neil (ad loc.) suggests a metatheatrical nod to the audience.   **νὴ τὴν Δήμητρα:** Cf. 435–36n.   **Θεμιστοκλέους:** Cf. 763–65n. For Paphlagon's attempts to assimilate himself to a new and better version of Themistocles, see Edmunds 1987b, 40–41, 46–47, 72; Anderson 1989. Paphlagon suggests that the defeat and capture of Spartan forces stranded on the island of Sphacteria and the Athenian naval victory of Themistocles over the Persians at Salamis are equally significant achievements.

813. ὦ πόλις Ἄργους, κλύεθ᾽ οἷα λέγει; "O city of Argos, hear the things he says?"; a parody of a quotation from Euripides' *Telephus* (*TrGF* fr. 713; cf. also *Pl.* 601). When treated as a collective, πόλις sometimes patterns with a plural verb form (KG 1.53). The Euripidean tragedy featured an exiled beggar-king, Telephus, dressed in rags and seeking refuge in Argos. For a review of what is known of the tragedy, see Olson 2002, liv–lxi. The quotation may also remind the audience of Themistocles' ostracism, exile, and initial residence in Argos (Th. 1.135.3); for the many surviving ostracism ballots against Themistocles (dated ca. 472/71), see Broneer 1938, 231–43.   **Θεμιστοκλεῖ ἀντιφερίζεις:** Neil (ad loc.) suggests that ἀντιφερίζω, "being an Epic word," is probably a parody (cf. *Il.* 21.357, 488; Hes. *Th.* 609).

814. εὑρών: Thiercy (1997, 1051–52) substitutes πύργων, "fortifying," for εὑρών, "found," on the grounds that Themistocles oversaw the rebuilding of fortifications after the Persian Wars (817–18; cf. also schol. ad loc.); see Wilson 2007b, ad loc.   **ἐπιχειλῆ:** "up to the brim [with wine]" (cf. Pollux 5.133). Maar (1996, 562–63) argues that the metaphor (μεστὴν εὑρών ἐπιχειλῆ) alludes to Themistocles providing the city with a complete meal (i.e., wine, Piraeus cake, 815; fish, 816) by organizing and rebuilding the Piraeus walls and thus expanding the area of the city (Th. 1.93.3–8); Paphlagon-Cleon, by contrast, tried to make Athens smaller (817).

815–16. καὶ πρὸς τούτοις: Cf. 541–42n.   **ἀριστώσῃ:** "for her [sc., πόλις] second meal"; i.e., a substantial midday meal.   **τὸν Πειραιᾶ προσέμαξεν:** "he kneaded / closely attached the Piraeus [to the city]." Already prosperous, Athens benefited further from Themistocles' development of the port of the Piraeus and rebuilding of city fortifications (Th. 1.93.3–7). The kneading image may recall the barley cake kneaded at Pylos that Paphlagon falsely claimed as his own work (54–56). For the culinary metaphor, see Taillardat §687.   **ἰχθῦς καινοὺς παρέθηκεν:** "he served new fish"; refers to Themistocles' initiatives in the development of the Piraeus harbor, expansion of the navy, and consequent increase in foreign trade for the empire. For a catalog of goods imported into Athens because of Athenian control of the sea, see Hermippos fr. 63; cf. also the allusion to the material benefits of empire in Pericles' funeral oration (Th. 2.38.2).

817–19. μικροπολίτας: "Small communities."   **διατειχίζων:** "building cross walls." Cleon's power and influence depend on promoting communal strife; cf. V. 41, τὸν δῆμον ἡμῶν βούλεται διιστάναι, "he wants to set our Athenian people at variance."   **χρησμῳδῶν:** Cf. 61.   **ὁ Θεμιστοκλεῖ ἀντιφερίζων:** The words of Paphlagon at 813 are here repeated derisively.   **κἀκεῖνος μὲν φεύγει:** Themistocles was charged with treason (consorting with the Persian king) and condemned to permanent exile (Th. 1.135–36), and his remains were forbidden to be interred at Athens (Th. 1.138.5). In the following century, his reputation was rehabilitated, and his tomb was publically honored in the Piraeus (Plu. *Them.* 32.4).   **Ἀχιλλείων:** "Achillean cakes"; a fine barley cake or bread served to diners in the Prytaneion (schol. ad loc.). Cf. Pherecr. fr. 137.3–4 (a catalog of the good life), ποταμοί . . . / . . . Ἀχιλλείοις μάζαις κοχυδοῦντες, "rivers . . . rush forth with Achillean cakes."   **ἀπομάττει:** "you wipe off [your hands]," as if the Prytaneion cakes were disposable napkins (cf. 411–14n and Poultney 1936, 88 for the genitive with a verb of "enjoying, reaping the benefits of").

821–22. σε φιλῶ: Cf. 732n.   **παῦ παῦ':** The final short syllable (-ε) of the first imperative is "cut off" (apocope) before an initial consonant. See KB 1.176–77; Smyth §75D. For the imperatival repetition, cf. 247–48n.   **οὗτος:** A colloquial vocative used in an impatient command; cf. Stevens 1976, 37.   **σκέρβολλε:** "verbally abuse, scold" (?); a rare word occurring only here. Hesychius equates it with κερβολέω = κερτομέω, "taunt."   **πονηρά:** Contrast Paphlagon's χρηστά (811).   **πολλοῦ δὲ πολύν . . . χρόνον:** "far too long." For the strengthening force of the genitive, cf. *Nu.* 915, θρασύς . . . πολλοῦ, "pretty brazen"; *Ra.* 1046, πολλὴ πολλοῦ, "really hard"; KG 1.387).

823. μιαρώτατος: "He's total slime" (cf. 125–26n).   **Δημακίδιον:** "my sweet little Demos"; a colloquial diminutive containing the comic element -ακ/ξ- and the affectionate -ιδιον.

824–35. Pnigos. Meter: anapestic dimeters.

824–27. καυλοὺς / τῶν εὐθυνῶν: "Stalks of the audits." καυλός is literally "the stem of a plant" (cf. 894–95n). For εὔθυνα, cf. 258–60n.   **ἐκκαυλίζων:** "stripping the stalks" (i.e., helping himself to public funds). Although the word might be an Aristophanic coinage, it could just as easily be a pedestrian term that does not get attested in literature.   **καταβροχθίζει:** Cf. 356–58n.   **μυστιλᾶται:** "he sops up with bread"; this refers to pieces of bread hollowed out in the middle (cf. 1168–70) and used as ladles for sopping up soups and broths, such as ἔτνος and ζωμός (1178–79; *Pl.* 627; Pherecr. fr. 113.5). The word is here used metaphorically to describe Paphlagon's voracious appetite; Taillardat §708.   **δημοσίων:** "public funds."

828–29. οὐ χαιρήσεις: "You'll be sorry" (cf. 235–36n).   **κλέπτονθ' / αἱρήσω:** "I'll convict you of stealing" (cf. *Nu.* 591, Κλέωνα . . . ἑλόντες . . . κλοπῆς).   **τρεῖς μυριάδας:** Sc., drachmas.

830–35. θαλαττοκοπεῖς καὶ πλατυγίζεις: "Splashing and slapping" water with oar blades feathered (i.e., with the blades flat on the water); a nautical metaphor for ineptitude (Taillardat §530, §532).   **μιαρώτατος ὢν περὶ τὸν δῆμον / τὸν Ἀθηναίων:** περὶ τὸν δῆμον / τὸν Ἀθηναίων is a formulaic phrase in state inscriptions (cf. Lewis, *IG* i³ fasc. iii, s.v. δῆμος); contrast Paphlagon's claim at 764–65, περὶ τὸν δῆμον τὸν Ἀθηναίων γεγένημαι / βέλτιστος ἀνήρ.   **νὴ τὴν Δήμητρ':** Cf. 435–36n.   **ἢ μὴ ζῆν:** "or may I die [if I fail to prove my case]." Cf. *Nu.* 1255, ἢ μηκέτι ζῴην ἐγώ; *Lys.* 531, μή νυν ζῴην. The optative is here used both to express a wish and as a form of oath (KG

1.227; *AGPS* 54.3.1.A).   **δωροδοκήσαντ᾽ ἐκ Μυτιλήνης:** Cleon implicitly leveled this charge (κέρδει ἐπαιρόμενος, "incited by gain") against Diodotus in the Assembly debate over the execution of the Mytilenians in 427 (Th. 3.38.2 with Hornblower 1991, ad loc.).   **μνᾶς τετταράκοντα:** Wilson (2007b, ad loc.) notes that the text may be corrupt, with μύριοι abbreviated by the letter *mu* (= minas), but that "the regular use of such abbreviations is much commoner in MSS of technical content than literary texts." One mina = one hundred drachmas (Arist. *Ath.* 10.2).

836–40. Antistrophe = strophe, 756–60.   **ὦ πᾶσιν ἀνθρώποις φανεὶς μέγιστον ὠφέλημα:** "O greatest benefactor revealed to all mankind." Cf. 149, σωτὴρ τῇ πόλει καὶ νῷν φανείς (addressed to Sausage-seller). Here, it perhaps parodies [A.] *Pr.* 613, ὠφέλημα θνητοῖσιν φανείς; see Rau 1967, 188.   **ζηλῶ σε τῆς εὐγλωττίας:** "I envy you for your glibness." ζηλῶ σε + causal genitive is a favorite Aristophanic construction (cf. *Ach.* 1008; *V.* 1450–52, the respective comic heroes; *Th.* 175; S. *El.* 1027; E. *IA* 677; Poultney 1936, 124). For εὐγλωττία, "glibness, ready tongue," cf. *Nu.* 445.   **εἰ γὰρ ὧδ᾽ ἐποίσε:** "if you'll keep attacking thus" (an emotional future condition; cf. 67–68n.).   **μέγιστος Ἑλλήνων:** "greatest of the Greeks" (cf. 178, ἀνὴρ μέγιστος, of Sausage-seller).   **τὰν τῇ πόλει:** = τοῖς πράγμασι (political affairs); cf. 187, εἰς τὰ πράγματα.   **ἔχων τρίαιναν:** "having trident [in hand]"; a veritable Poseidon (559) who will harass and rule over the subject allies (τῶν ξυμμάχων). See Anderson 1995, 14–15. The trident is a trademark of Poseidon.   **πολλὰ χρήματ᾽ ἐργάσει:** "you'll earn a lot of money" (cf. Hdt. 1.24.1; Pl. *Hp. mi.* 282d).   **σείων:** "shaking." The verb σείειν, recalling Poseidon as "the earth shaker," is used metaphorically to denote political intimidation, extortion, and blackmail (cf. *Pax* 639, τῶν δὲ συμμάχων ἔσειον [sc., politicians] τοὺς παχεῖς καὶ πλουσίους; fr. 228, ἔσειον, ᾔτουν χρήματ(α); Antiph. 6.43, ἑτέρους τῶν ὑπευθύνων ἔσειε; Taillardat §704).

841–940. Agon II, part 2. Meter: iambic tetrameter catalectics (841–910) followed by a pnigos in iambic dimeters (911–40).

841–42. μὴ μεθῇς τὸν ἄνδρ᾽: "Don't let your man go." Like a coach, the coryphaeus shouts encouragement to his athlete.   **σοι λαβὴν δέδωκεν:** "he's given you a grip"; a wrestling metaphor (cf. *Nu.* 551, παρέδωκεν λαβήν, with Dover 1968, 126n). There is perhaps an ad hoc joke here, suggesting that he has got him "by the balls." For λαβή (haft or handle) used in a sexual sense, see Henderson 1991a, 122.   **κατεργάσει:** "you'll overpower him," i.e., "take him down." Wrestlers begin their match in standing positions; see illustrations in Poliakoff 1987, 33–52.   **πλευρὰς ἔχων τοιαύτας:** "having such a chest."

A broad, deep chest was a notable feature of a good wrestler; cf. *V.* 1192–94 with Biles and Olson ad loc.

843–46. *Paphlagon speaks to the chorus.*   **οὐκ, ... ταῦτ᾽ ἐστί πω ταύτῃ:** "that's not how it is in this case" (cf. *Pl.* 399, οὐκ ἔστι πω τὰ πράγματ᾽ ἐν τούτῳ). **ὦγαθοί:** Cf. 69–72n.   **ἐμοὶ:** Emphatic, stressed further by position at line opening.   **τοιοῦτον ἔργον:** I.e., the capture of Spartan forces on Sphacteria.   **ἁπαξάπαντας:** "once and for all"; a contemporary comic coinage (cf. *Pax* 106, 247, 542, 655).   **ἐπιστομίζειν:** "to bridle mouths shut"; an equestrian term (Taillardat §497).   **τῶν ἀσπίδων τῶν ἐκ Πύλου τι λοιπόν:** The bronze shields captured from the Spartans at Sphacteria—some of which were displayed as trophies in the Stoa Poikile in the agora (Paus. 1.15.5), others of which may have been affixed as votives (ἀνατεθῆναι, 849) to the Athena Nike bastion on the Acropolis—celebrated Cleon's triumph and, by extension, symbolized his current political influence; see Lind 1991, 67. One of the captured bronze shields, identified by inscription as "one of those captured by the Athenians from the battle of Pylos" (Shear 1937, 347–48), was discovered in a cistern in 1936. The topographical prominence of the bastion display could provide a context for this reference by suggesting that Paphlagon-Cleon and his cronies, who routinely accuse rivals of antidemocratic conspiracy, plan to arm themselves with these shields, "ready for use" (849), to occupy the Acropolis and stage a coup d'état; see Lippman, Scahill, and Schultz 2006, 557–60.

847–49. ἐπίσχες: "Hold it [on those shields]"; cf. Smyth §466b for the form. Fraenkel (1962, 49–50) thought the punctuation should come after the imperative, not after ἀσπίσιν.   **λαβὴν γὰρ ἐνδέδωκας:** "for you've given me a hold" (cf. 841; *Nu.* 1047).   **εἴπερ φιλεῖς τὸν δῆμον:** Cf. Paphlagon's claim at 732.   **αὐτοῖσι τοῖς πόρπαξιν:** αὐτοῖσι in the instrumental dative is pleonastic and idiomatic (KG 1.433–34; Smyth §1521, §1525; Stevens 1976, 52–53). The inner surface of a *porpax* shield featured a detachable bronze strip or armband (*porpax*), through which the warrior inserted his left forearm to hold the shield (cf. Snodgrass 1967, 40, plate 18). This kind of shield was especially associated with Sparta (cf. *Lys.* 106, where the Spartan women use the participle πορπακισάμενος to describe their husbands' readiness for battle); see Colvin 1999, 247–48. Critias reports (88B 37 DK) that Spartans removed the armband of their shields when in their homes because of their distrust of the helots.

851. σοι: Unaccented because in poetry, enclitics are normally not allowed to stand directly after a sense pause, unless the preceding words form a vocative or a parenthetic interjection (cf. *Pax* 20–23 with Olson ad loc.; KB 1.348–49).   **μὴ 'κγένηται:** = ἐξῇ; "it won't be allowed [to punish (κολάσαι)]"; i.e., "you won't be able . . ." (cf. *Pax* 345, ἐκγένοιτ' ἰδεῖν). For the impersonal use of ἐκγίγνομαι, cf. LSJ s.v. III.

852–54. στῖφος: "Mass array," "phalanx." The noun is often used of military forces (A. *Pers.* 20, 366; Hdt. 9.57.1, 9.70.4).   **βυρσοπωλῶν / νεανιῶν:** "young leathermongers"; i.e., brash and aggressive (νεανιῶν) supporters of Cleon. Rhodes' view (1994, 93) that political allies and supporters may have sat together as an organized bloc in the Assembly (like merchants selling similar products in the agora) is doubtful (cf. Hornblower 2008, at Th. 6.13.1).   **περιοικοῦσι:** "live around." It seems probable that the stands of dealers in leather, honey, and cheese were located in the same quarters of the agora, near the Stoa Poikile and close to tanneries in Cleon's deme (*IG* ii² 1556.5–6); see Lind 1991, 94–131. The verb περιοικεῖν, "to live/be next to," is neutral in itself, but given the allusion to Sparta (846–49), there may be a joke here on Cleon's supporters being as subservient to him as *perioikoi* were to the Spartans.   **τοῦτο δ' εἰς ἕν ἐστι συγκεκυφός:** "This has bent together into one"; i.e., "they put their heads together in this." The verb συγκύπτειν has a conspiratorial ring (cf. Hdt. 3.82.4, οἱ γὰρ κακοῦντες τὰ κοινὰ συγκύψαντες ποιεῦσι, "evildoers conspire together to harm the common good"; van Leeuwen ad loc.). For the use of language of partisanship and conspiracy, see 587–90n.

855–57. βριμήσαιο: "You snort," "growl."   **βλέψειας ὀστρακίνδα:** "you're looking like the potsherd game." Olson and Seaberg explain, "The suffix -ίνδα was used in Attic to form 'adverbs of games'" (*FrC* 2018, 289–90). In the potsherd game, two opposing teams drew a line on the ground; one player then threw to the ground a potsherd glazed on one side but not on the other; depending on how the potsherd fell, one team ran away as the other team pursued (Pl. Com. fr. 168; cf. Pl. *Phdr.* 241b). Pollux (9.111–12) reports that a player who was caught had to sit out and was dubbed an *onos*, "donkey." A surviving ostracism ballot inscribed "Agasias son of Phanomachus is a donkey" is perhaps a joke turning ostracism into an adult version of the potsherd game; see Bicknell 1986. The possibility of ostracism, although rare in the second half of the fifth century, was always present (Arist. *Ath.* 43.5); see Forsdyke 2005, 144–204.

νύκτωρ: It was thought that antidemocratic conspirators typically initiated their plans under cover of darkness (e.g., Th. 6.27.1, the response to the nighttime "mutilation of the Hermes").   **τὰς εἰσβολὰς τῶν ἀλφίτων:** A paraprosdokeion joke substituting "gateways of the grain market" (τὰ ἄλφιτα, the Piraeus) for "gateways of the citadel" (the Acropolis); for seizure of the citadel as a prelude to a coup d'état, cf. 445–46n, 843–46n.   **ἂν ... ἂν:** Cf. 17–18n.

858–59. οἴμοι τάλας: "Oh no!"; a stock interjection of surprise, alarm, despair, disgust, etc. (cf. 887, 1200; López Eire 1996, 149; Sommerstein 2009, 22–23).   **γὰρ:** Explains the interjection (*GP* 80).   ***πονηρέ:** Read instead πόνηρε: "you no-good." Wilson (2007a, ad loc.) prints πονηρέ, but the view that πονηρος means "bad" when accented oxytone but "unfortunate" when accented proparoxytone lacks scholarly consensus; see Dover 2002, 85–86.   **παρεκόπτου:** Cf. 805–9n.   **κρουσιδημῶν:** "shortchanging the demos"; a parody of κρουσιμετρέω, "shortchanging measurements."

860–63. ὦ δαιμόνιε: "My dear man"; an ostensibly friendly colloquial and deferential form of address found frequently in comedy (e.g., *Nu.* 38; *V.* 962; *Av.* 961; *Th.* 64; *Ra.* 44) but absent in tragic and lyric poetry of the classical period. In Aristophanes, the address is used in "rebuking, admonishing, or pleading with a respected person, always with an element of deference" (Sommerstein 1977, 272; cf. Dickey 1996 141–42).   **μὴ τοῦ λέγοντος ἴσθι:** "don't believe [what] he's saying"; idiomatic (cf. S. *OT* 917, ἀλλ᾽ ἐστὶ τοῦ λέγοντος; KG 1.372b).   **ὅστις ... μ':** The shift from ὅστις to με instead of ὅντινα is idiomatic; cf. Hermipp. fr. 46.3–4, πέμπειν δὲ Νόθιππον ἑκόντα·/ εἷς γὰρ μόνος ὢν, "to send Nothippus as a volunteer, for he alone."   **ξυνωμότας:** Cf. 235–36n.   **κέκραγα:** "[but] I screamed out," as presumably he did against the two "plotting" slaves at 235–39. The image of Paphlagon-Cleon screaming about his loyalty to the democracy and accusing his political opponents of antidemocratic conspiracy recurs in fourth-century Athenian political discourse. Sommerstein (2001, 246) quotes [D.] 25.64, "He [Aristogeiton: *PA* 1775; *PAA* 168145] shouts at every meeting of the Assembly: 'I alone am loyal to you; all the others are in a conspiracy,'" and [D.] 25.40, "some folk say he's the people's watchdog."

864–67. Aristotle (*HA* 8.2 = 592a6) reports that most eels fed and thrived in clear drinkable water, hence those fishing for eels would stir and muddy the water to arouse them. Eels were a prized delicacy, and the most prized came from Lake Copais in Boeotia (*Ach.* 879–80; *Pax* 1003–5, last in a list of Boeotian delicacies; *Lys.* 35–36). In the parabasis of *Clouds* (559), Aristophanes complains that his joke comparing Cleon with an eel fisher was stolen and applied by another poet to Hyperbolus; presumably the "other poet" made more of the image, which Aristophanes resented (cf. Dover at *Nu.* 559n).

ὅπερ γάρ ... πέπονθας: "Which very thing ... you've experienced." θηρώμενοι: Used of fishing as well as hunting. For the image's political associations, see Taillardat §705. καταστῇ: "is calm"; of water, wind (cf. *Ra.* 1003), and, by extension, political situations (cf. Neil ad loc.). τὸν βόρβορον: Cf. 303–13n.

868–69. τοσουτονί: "This one thing." On the accumulation of deictics (τουτῳὶ, 869; τουτὶ, 872; τονδὶ, 881; τουτονὶ, 883), see 736n. σκύτη: Leather hides. κάττυμα: Piece of leather, presumably the sole of a shoe (cf. 314; *Ach.* 301).

870–72. ἐμβάσιν: Cf. 321n. οὐ δῆτα μὰ τὸν Ἀπόλλω: "absolutely not, by Apollo" (cf. 13–14n). οὖν δῆτ᾽ ...; Cf. 17–18n. τουτὶ: "this pair of shoes [ζευγος ... ἐμβάδων]."

873–74. *Demos puts on the shoes.* ἐγῴδα: Cf. 469. περὶ τὸν δῆμον ἄνδρ᾽ ἄριστον: Cf. 764–65, περὶ τὸν δῆμον / ... βέλτιστος ἀνήρ. The phrase parodies inscriptional language used to thank public benefactors in state decrees (e.g., *IG* i³ 182.4 [ἀνὴρ ἀγαθὸς περὶ [ἐς] τὸν δῆμον], 65.10, 96.16, 102.7, 114.6). εὐνούστατόν τε τῇ πόλει: Cf. 688–90n. τοῖσι δακτύλοισιν: "to my toes!"; an unexpected bathos.

875–77. τοσουτονὶ δύνασθαι: "Can mean this much"; Paphlagon uses deictics only here and at 891 (τοδί). ἐμοῦ δὲ μὴ μνείαν ἔχειν: "yet you have no memory of me." ἔπαυσα τοὺς βινουμένους: "I stopped the buggers." Passive homosexuality is a running joke about ambitious politicians (cf. 77–79n, 638–42). Γρῦπον: Grypus, a plausible but unknown man's name meaning "Hooknose" (Dover 1972b, 24). ἐξαλείψας: "erased from the rolls." The conviction of a citizen for male prostitution could result in disenfranchisement. Cf. Aeschin. 1 passim; Dover 1989, 33–34; 1994, 215–16; Halperin 1990, 88–112.

878–80. οὔκουν ... δῆτα ...; "Well ... in that case ...?" Note the accumulation of negatives by Sausage-seller regarding Paphlagon's shortcomings (οὐκ, 879; οὐχί, μὴ, 880; οὐπώποτ᾽, 882; οὐκ, 888) and by Demos (οὐπώποτ᾽, 882; οὐ, 886; οὐκ, 892), whereas Paphlagon (in this exchange) utters a negative only to complain about his treatment (οὐχ, 890). σε ... πρωκτοτηρεῖν: "you scope out asshole[s]." κοὐκ ἔσθ᾽ ὅπως: Cf. 238–39n. φθονῶν ἔπαυσας: "you stopped out of jealousy" (i.e., fearing they would become rival politicians).

881–83. χιτῶνος: A garment that was folded and draped over the shoulders and often belted or sewn at the side. It is a regular piece of comic costuming; see Stone 1981, 146, 171–72.   **ἀμφιμασχάλου:** A sleeved woolen chiton that covered the shoulders and the body below the neck, for warmth in winter (χειμῶνος ὄντος); cf. Pl. Com. fr. 255.

884–86. τουτονὶ: Sc., ἀμφιμάσχαλον. Perhaps the chorus of knights supplied Sausage-seller with this garment, as it seems unlikely that either he or Paphlagon had carried it onstage earlier.   **Θεμιστοκλῆς οὐπώποτ' ἐπενόησεν:** οὐπώποτ' echoes Sausage-seller at 882. The verb ἐπινοεῖν, like its cognates, implies innovative thinking (cf. ἐπίνοια, 89–91n; νόημα, 1202–4n).   **καίτοι:** "and yet"; introduces surprise or doubt about the appropriateness of the preceding comment (*GP* 556).   **ὁ Πειραιεύς:** Cf. 815.   **ἔμοιγε μέντοι:** "but as I see it."   **ἐξεύρημα:** "inventive policy/plan" (cf. Th. 1.93.3–7, of Themistocles; cf. also Papachrysostomou, *FrC* 2016, 102).

887. οἴμοι τάλας: "Alas!"   **πιθηκισμοῖς:** "with monkey business" (cf. 415–16n).   **με περιελαύνεις:** "you're corralling me" cf. 290, περιελῶ σ' ἀλαζονείαις, now turned to complaint and grievance.

888–89. πίνων ἀνὴρ: Like a symposiast (cf. *Ach.* 985; *V.* 1198; Pl. Com. fr. 51.2).   **χεσείη:** "[has] to take a shit," presumably urgently.   **τοῖσιν τρόποις τοῖς σοῖσιν . . . χρῶμαι:** "I'm using/borrowing your own methods."   **ὥσπερ βλαυτίοισι:** "as if a pair of little slippers." The phrase is here used in a metaphorical sense "to emphasize a deception by Paphlagon" (Stone 1981, 232). Guests attending banquets would leave a pair of slippers (βλαῦται) by the door of the host's house in case they should need to use the latrine (cf. Pl. *Smp.* 174a, where Socrates takes his best pair for dining at the house of Agathon). Latrines were often simply limed pits located at the side of the courtyard door (cf. *Pax* 99–100; Eub. fr. 52.3, ἐπὶ ταῖς θύραις); see H. A. Thompson 1959, 101–2.

890–918. What follows is the first of three contests between Paphlagon and Sausage-seller: the first to determine who is better at pandering to Demos, the second to learn who has the best oracles concerning Demos' future (997–1099), and the final contest to show who best satisfies the culinary preferences and appetites of Demos (1151–1263).

890–91. θωπείαις: "In flattery"; especially, shameless fawning over gullible targets (47–48, 788, 1115–17; *Ach.* 633–35; *V.* 563; cf. also Pl. *R.* 426c).

Paphlagon takes off his cloak and tries to put it on Demos. **τοδί:** Sc., τὸ ἱμάτιον. Verbs of clothing routinely take two objects in the accusative, one of a person and the other of a thing (Smyth §1628). **οἴμωζ':** "be damned." The imperative is used as a curse (e.g., *Ach.* 1035; *Ra.* 257 with Dover ad loc.). **ὦ πονήρ':** The accent of the oxytone is here thrown back to the penult because of elision (KB 1.332–33; Smyth §174). *Paphlagon again tries to put the cloak on Demos.* **ἰαιβοῖ:** "Ugh"; a comic interjection expressing revulsion. Cf. 957; Labiano-Ilundain 2000, 80–81; Nordgren 2015, 215.

892. οὐκ ἐς κόρακας ἀποφθερεῖ . . . : "Go to the crows and be damned" (i.e., "go to hell"); cf. *Nu.* 789, verbatim. The κόραξ is a raven. Dover, noting that this curse (ἐς κόρακας) is "a violently abusive exclamation . . . expressing a wish that the person so addressed may lie unburied and be eaten by ravens," observes (at *Ra.* 187) that "like swear-words in most languages, it is constantly used without regard for its literal sense." For the raven feeding on dead bodies (cf. *Th.* 941–42; A. *Ag.* 1472–74), see D. W. Thompson 1936, 159–64. ἀποφθερεῖν = ἰέναι with a curse. The verb and its compounds, a colloquial idiom when used as an imperative, emphasize anger, impatience, and dismissiveness (e.g., *Ach.* 460; *Nu.* 789; *Pl.* 598). Cf. Stevens 1976, 17–18; López Eire 2000, 16–17. **βύρσης κάκιστον ὄζον:** Cf. *V.* 38, ὄζει κάκιστον τοὐνύπνιον βύρσης σαπρᾶς, where "the dream [of a dragon] smells most horribly of a rotten hide [= Cleon]." Urine was the universal solvent in industrial processes such as tanning and fulling; water would cause the hide to shrink and could not be used to remove the odor. For smells as often indicative of status, behavior, personal preferences, and such in Aristophanes, see Taillardat §748; Lilja 1972, 120–48. This is the play's final reference to Paphlagon as a tanner (cf. Lind 1991, 73).

893. ἐπίτηδες: "Deliberately"; a widely attested colloquial adverb (e.g., 896, 1184; *V.* 391; *Pax* 142; *Th.* 546; Xenarch. fr. 7.10, ἐξεπίτηδες), often anticipating, as here, a purpose clause (cf. *Pax* 931–32; *Ec.* 116–17; Hdt. 7.168.3; Lys. 1.11). **ἵνα σ' ἀποπνίξῃ:** "so that he can smother," "choke." The use of ἵνα with the subjunctive in secondary sequence stresses that the purpose conceived in the past remains in the present (KG 2.380–81; Smyth §2197b).

894-95. ἐπεβούλευσέ σοι: "He plotted against you." The verb is primarily prosaic (e.g., Hdt. 1.24.2; Th. 1.82.1, 6.54; Lys. 1.44; Pl. *Smp.* 203b). Aristophanes notably uses it in the parody of the Assembly's traditional curses against enemies of the state (*Th.* 335–51); see Kleinknecht 1937, 33–40; Horn 1970, 106–15. **τὸν καυλὸν:** "stalk" (824); properly, of the silphium, a wild flowering plant (now probably extinct) that flourished in the North African city of Cyrene (Plin. *NH* 22.48). The stalk itself was eaten as a vegetable (Eub. fr. 6.3) and used as a seasoning (*Av.* 533–34, 1579, 1585; *Ec.* 1171); milky juice extracted from its stalk had various medicinal uses (e.g., relief of flatulence [898] and bowel evacuation; cf. Theophr. HP 6.3.1).   ἄξιον: "cheap," "inexpensive"; silphium was imported from Cyrenaica and was generally expensive (cf. *Pl.* 925 with Sommerstein 2001, 195). It apparently became temporarily cheap, for unknown reasons, shortly before *Knights* was produced in 424.   μέντοι: = "sure [do]"; signals eager assent in echoing οἶσθα (*GP* 401).

897–98. ἡλιαίᾳ: For the Heliaea, cf. 797–98n.   **βδέοντες:** "farting"; for crepitation, cf. 115–17n.

899. νὴ τὸν Ποσειδῶ: Cf. 366n.   **ἀνὴρ Κόπρειος:** "a man from Shitville"; an occasional joke on the name of a small coastal Attic deme, Kopros, which was located in the area of Eleusis (see Vanderpool 1953; Traill 1975, 52). For wordplay involving deme names in Old Comedy, cf. 77–79n.

900. οὐ . . . δήπου . . . ; "Surely not?"; marks a surprised or incredulous question (*GP* 267).   **ὑμεῖς:** I.e., Demos and (presumably) the imaginary demesman.   **(ἐ)γένεσθε πυρροί:** "turn yellow/brown" (the color of feces); caused by wet flatulence soiling his clothes or from some other related incident (cf. *Ra.* 307–8; *Ec.* 328–30, 1060–62).

901. Πυρράνδρου τὸ μηχάνημα: "A scheme of Pyrrhander"; perhaps a proverb used for the sake of the pun on πυρρός. A contemporary person with this same name is attested (*IG* i³ 1190.8), but, beyond his name, nothing is known of him.

902. βωμολοχεύμασιν: "With clownish, buffoonish [tricks]" (cf. 1194; *Pax* 748; *Ra.* 358 with Dover ad loc.).   **ταράττεις:** Perhaps continuing the scatological joke; cf. *Nu.* 386–87, ἐταράχθης / τὴν γαστέρα, "stirred up my gut," from indigestion brought on by consuming pea soup (ζωμός).

903. ἡ . . . θεός: Athena Polias. For Athena's support and guidance of Sausage-seller, see Anderson 1995, 22–38.   **ἀλαζονείαις:** "with nonsense" (cf. 290 for the nonsense; 269 for the practitioner).

904–5. παρέξειν: "I will provide" (and keep on providing). Note that Paphlagon promises Demos future benefits, whereas Sausage-seller focuses on immediate ones.   **ὦ Δῆμε:** Cf. 50.   **μηδὲν δρῶντι:** "for doing nothing."   **μισθοῦ τρύβλιον:** "bowl of [jury] pay"; see Taillardat §688.   **ῥοφῆσαι:** Cf. 359–60n.

906–7. κυλίχνιον: "little cup."   **ἑλκύδρια:** "small ulcers" of the skin (Hp. *Art.* 63; Theophr. *Char.* 19.3). For diminutives applied to Demos, see 726–27n).   **ἀντικνημίοις:** "shins."

908. τὰς πολιάς . . . σοὐκλέγων: "plucking out your gray hair"; cf. fr. 416.1–2, ἐκλέγει τ' ἀεὶ / ἐκ τοῦ γενείου τὰς πολιάς, "he's always plucking gray hair from his beard."   **νέον ποιήσω:** "I shall make [you] young"; a foreshadowing of the magical rejuvenation of Demos at 1325–28.

909. κέρκον λαγῶ: "Hare's tail"; a hint at the pederastic courtship gift for Demos at 1198–99.   **τὠφθαλμιδίω:** "both sweet little eyes." The diminutive form is colloquial Attic (López Eire 1996, 137–44).   **περιψῆν:** "to wipe all around."

910–11. ἀπομυξάμενος: "After blowing your nose."   **μου πρὸς τὴν κεφαλὴν ἀποψῶ:** "wipe it on my head"; an invitation befitting sycophants and slaves (cf. Petron. *Sat.* 27.6).   **ἐμοῦ μὲν οὖν:** "On me!" The phrase repetition suggests demonstrative gestures.

911–40. Antipnigos; meter: iambic dimeters.

912–18. Service as trierarch (lasting for one year) was a public duty (liturgy) imposed on wealthy citizens (cf. *Ra.* 1065 with Dover ad loc.). For the appointment and responsibilities of the trierarch, see Morrison, Coates, and Rankov 2000, 109, 120–26.

912–14. ποιήσω τριη- / ραρχεῖν: "I'll make you commander of a trireme."   **ἀναλίσκοντα τῶν / σαυτοῦ:** "spending your own money." The genitive is partitive with ἀναλίσκω (Poultney 1936, 78d).   **παλαιὰν ναῦν:** "an aged trireme," thus needing costly maintenance and repairs.

916–18. διαμηχανήσομαι: Cf. the description of Paphlagon as a master at contriving ways out of impossible situations for himself: κἀκ τῶν ἀμηχάνων πόρους εὐμήχανος πορίζειν (see 758–59n).   **σαπρὸν:** "rotted" (for a personified trireme, cf. 1308).

919–22. παφλάζει: "Sputtering"; a play on Cleon's dramatic pseudonym. The verb properly refers to boiling water and, by extension, to bombastic oratory (*Pax* 313–15, of Cleon; Timocl. fr. 17, of an orator).   **παῦε παῦ':** Cf. 247–48n.   **ὑπερζέων:** "he's boiling over." Paphlagon is imagined to be a kind of cooking pot or liquid that boils over (cf. Eub. fr. 108.2, λοπὰς παφλάζει βαρβάρωι λαλήματι, "a stew pot sputtering with barbarian nonsense").   **τῶν δαλίων:** Bentley's conjecture; a diminutive of δαλός, "a firebrand" (see Olson at *Pax* 959n).   **ἀπαρυστέον:** "must be skimmed off." Cf. 601–3n, on verbal adjectives.   **τῶν ἀπειλῶν:** "threats"; a surprise substitution for "froth," "scum," or the like.   **ταυτηί:** "with this here." The demonstrative points to a feminine noun, likely a word for a ladle (e.g., 1091, ἀρύταινα) or a pouring vessel (e.g., *Ach.* 245–46, ἐτνήρυσις).

923–24. δώσεις . . . καλὴν δίκην: "You'll pay a pretty price."   **ἱπούμενος:** "crushed," "trapped." The noun ἱπος originally denoted a fuller's press or a mousetrap (Archil. 235 W; Pollux 7.41, 10.135).   **εἰσφοραῖς:** An extraordinary war tax levied on wealthy Athenians. The εἰσφορά of 428, which raised an amount as high as two hundred talents (Th. 3.19.1 with Hornblower 1991, ad loc.), was probably followed by others. Cleon was perhaps especially zealous about levying εἰσφοραί during this period; see Sommerstein 1981, ad loc.

925–26. εἰς τοὺς πλουσίους: "Among the wealthy."   **ὅπως ἂν ἐγγραφῇς:** For the construction, see 80–81n. The threat to enroll Sausage-seller in the wealthier class indicates that εἰσφοραί were levied as a progressive tax (Sommerstein 1981, ad loc.). As a general with the authority to control the lists of those liable to this tax (cf. Harrison 1971, 32), Cleon would have been able to influence the levying of tax rates, which probably unnerved wealthier citizens; cf. 223–24, καὶ γὰρ οἵ τε πλούσιοι / δεδίασιν αὐτόν.

928–32. εὔχομαι: Governs the accusative subject + infinitives ἐφεστάναι at 930 and σπεύδειν at 934.   **σοι:** The dative pronoun is regular with verbs of prayer or wishing (KG 1.410; *AGPS* 48.7.14.B).   **ταδί:** "the following."   **τάγηνον:** A flat-bottomed pan used to hold hot coals for grilling (Sparkes 1962, 129).   **τευθίδων:** "squid" (cf. the curse involving grilled and sizzling squid at *Ach.* 1156–61).   **σίζον:** "sizzling" is onomatopoetic for the sound of frying food (cf. *Ach.* 1158 with Olson ad loc.).   **γνώμην ἐρεῖν:** Cf. 266–68n.   **περὶ / Μιλησίων:** Perhaps a reference to a recent political scandal involving Cleon, corruption, and the Milesians (cf. 361n).

934–40. σπεύδειν ὅπως τῶν τευθίδων / ἐμπλήμενος: "You rush having stuffed yourself with squid . . ." (cf. *V.* 1127, ἐπανθρακίδων ἐμπλήμενος, "filled myself on fish fry"). **φθαίης ἔτ᾽ . . . ἐλθών:** "hurrying to get (there) first . . ." (KG 2.76; Smyth §1873, §2096). **πρὶν φαγεῖν:** Sc., σε. **ἀνὴρ:** = ὁ ἀνήρ. Wilson (2007b, at 237) notes, "One would have expected τις be used, and σέ τις would have been satisfactory." Presumably, "the man" is one of Paphlagon's cronies. **ἐ- / σθίων ἐπαποπνιγείης:** "may you choke on it [i.e., corruption]." ἐπαποπνιγείης is a conjecture of Elmsley; see Wilson 2007b, at 940.

941. εὖ γε: Cf. 427. **νὴ τὸν Δία καὶ τὸν Ἀπόλλω καὶ τὴν Δήμητρα:** A prose oath; Zeus, Apollo, and Demeter were the conventional triad for oaths of particular solemnity, including those sworn by Athenian jurymen (D. 52.9; Pollux 8.122; cf. Sommerstein 2014, 338–39). Aristophanes uses prose elsewhere for prayer parody (*Ach.* 237, 241; *Av.* 864–88), official announcements (*Ach.* 43, 61), and legal quotations and decrees (*Av.* 1035–41, 1661–66).

943–48. ἀγαθὸς πολίτης: "Good citizen"; i.e., one who is devoted, in this context, to the interests of the demos (see Connor 1971, 47–49). **οἷος οὐδείς . . . ἀνὴρ γεγένηται:** "such as no man has been" (cf. Th. 1.138.2, μεγὰς καὶ οἷος οὐδείς, of Themistocles). **χρόνου:** = πολλοῦ χρόνου or δὶα χρόνου (Poultney 1936, 109). **τοῖσι πολλοῖς τοὐβολοῦ:** "for the many [worth] an obol," i.e. "for the common folk." The suggestion is that although they pretend otherwise, contemporary politicians regard those whom they claim to serve as essentially worthless (cf. *V.* 666–68). **ἐσκορόδισας:** Cf. 494n. **τὸν δακτύλιον:** The ring that authorizes the wearer, ταμίας or ἐπίτροπος, to manage financial and domestic affairs on behalf of the master. The position was often entrusted to a freedman or slave or to the wife (*Lys.* 495; cf. also *Ec.* 210–12). **ἔχε:** See 50–51n.

949–50. εἰ μή μ᾽ ἐάσεις ἐπιτροπεύειν: Emotional future condition; cf. 67–68n.

951–53. οὐκ ἔσθ᾽ ὅπως: Cf. 238–39n. **οὑτοσὶ:** Demos shows the ring to Sausage-seller. **οὑμός:** = ὁ ἐμός. **γοῦν:** "at any rate"; introduces a statement that is partial proof for the preceding statement (*GP* 451–52). **ἀλλ᾽ ἦ . . . ;** The particle combination "puts an objection in interrogative form, giving lively expression to a feeling of surprise or incredulity" (*GP* 27). **φέρ᾽ ἴδω:** Cf. 118–20n. **σημεῖον:** The seal of the signet ring (cf. *V.* 585; *Lys.* 1198–99 with Henderson ad loc.).

954–56. δημοῦ βοείου θρῖον ἐξωπτημένον: "A fig leaf wrapped with beef fat" (cf. *Ach.* 1101–2; *Ra.* 133–34). Note the pun on δημός and δῆμος.   **ἀλλὰ τί;** "Well then, what?" ἀλλά (colloquial?) introduces a question "following a rejected suggestion or supposition" (*GP* 9).   **λάρος:** The seagull was a stock symbol of gluttony and rapaciousness (e.g., *Nu.* 591, Κλέωνα τὸν λάρον δώρων ἑλόντες καὶ κλοπῆς; *Av.* 567, Ἡρακλέει . . . λάρῳ); see Taillardat §714.   **ἐπὶ πέτρας:** The Pnyx (cf. 313, 754, 783).   **δημηγορῶν:** "giving speeches in the Assembly" (cf. δημαγωγία, 190–93n). This is the first colloquial attestation of this verb (see Olson, *FrC* 2017, 336–37).

957–59. αἰβοῖ τάλας: "Yuck, disgusting" (cf. 858, 891, ἰαιβοῖ; *Pax* 544).   **Κλεωνύμου:** This man (*PA* 8680; *PAA* 579410) is a popular target of Aristophanic abuse, being smeared at least once in every extant play from 425 to 414, for a total of seventeen insults. He was an ally of Cleon and an apparent mover of decrees or amendments in the 420s; cf. *IG* i³ 61.34 (430/29–424/23 BCE), 68.5.27 (426/25), 69.3 (426/25], 70.5 (425/24). He is presented here as an embezzler and elsewhere as a glutton (1289–99; *Ach.* 88–89) or a coward who threw away his shield in flight from battle (*Nu.* 353–54; *V.* 15–19; *Av.* 1473–81; Eup. fr. 352). Storey (2010, 224) believes that the charge of cowardly retreat is likely true, but it seems more probably a case of comic exaggeration; see Sommerstein 2001, 230. To discard one's shield in flight from combat was punishable by loss of citizenship (And. 1.74; see also Storey 1989).   **τουτονὶ:** Presumably refers to the genuine signet ring (954).

960. μὴ δῆτά πώ γ': "Not yet, no"; an impassioned negative command (*Nu.* 696; *Lys.* 36; *GP* 276).   **ὦ δέσποτ':** Cf. 763–65n.

963–64. μολγὸν γενέσθαι δεῖ σε: "You're destined to become a leather wineskin" (cf. *Nu.* 442). The phrase seems to allude to a pair of oracles comparing Athens to a storm-tossed but unsinkable wineskin (Plu. *Thes.* 24.5). The word μολγός (south Italian) is substituted for the ἀσκός of the oracles; cf. frr. 103 (conjectured) and 308, both of which seem to allude to the same oracle. Rusten (2011, 294n29) notes, "If there is also an allusion to Cleon in the reference to leather or tanning, it would suggest a date [of the oracle] before Cleon's death in 422."   **κἄν γε τουτῳί:** The tone of the (slightly altered) repetition is dismissive. Sausage-seller perhaps points to Paphlagon's leather phallus.   **ψωλὸν:** "scalped cock"; refers to circumcision, which the Greeks regarded as genital mutilation and a barbarian custom (e.g., *Ach.* 158–63; Hdt. 2.37.2). See Henderson 1991a, 110, 218.   **μέχρι τοῦ μυρρίνου:** "up to the pubic bush." For μύρτον, "myrtle berry," as a slang for pubic hair, see Henderson 1991a, 134.

965–66. οἱ . . . λέγουσιν: Sc., χρησμοί.   **ἐστεφανωμένον ῥόδοις:** Cf. *Nu.* 1330, where Pheidippides bids his father to "strew him with lots of roses" (πάττε πολλοῖς τοῖς ῥόδοις). Roses were associated with love, praise, victory, and special celebrations.

967–69. οὑμοὶ δέ γε: Cf. 356–58n.   **ἀλουργίδα:** A luxurious purple robe once commonly worn by the upper classes, especially by the generation of Marathon fighters (Ath. 12.512b–c, quoting Heraclides of Pontus, a student of Plato). Here, it complements the offer of a garland of roses (στεφάνη).   **κατάπαστον:** Cf. 502n.   **στεφάνην:** A diadem, often of precious metal, suggesting a promise of wealth and luxury befitting a monarch (1329–32).   **ἅρματος:** A four-horse chariot associated with formal processions (*Nu.* 69–70) and chariot racing (*V.* 1427–29).   **διώξεις Σμικύθην:** "you'll pursue Smicythe [and husband] into court." διώκειν can mean both "pursue" and "prosecute." The male form of the individual's name, Smicythus, is here put in its feminine form (cf. Cleonyme for Cleonymus at *Nu.* 680). A Smicythus (*PA* 12773; *PAA* 826440) is mentioned as active in the 420s, both as councilor in 427/26 (*IG* i³ 66.3) and as the secretary to the treasury of Athena in 424/23 (*IG* i³ 301.17, 302.28.37, 303.41.102). Our Smicythus could be either of them, or one and the same person, or neither, as the name was not uncommon (cf. Lewis, *IG* i³ fasc. iii, s.v.).   **κύριον:** The defense of "Smicythe" will be mounted by her κύριος (i.e., a legal guardian and representative of a woman or a minor in the courts), since a woman could not take part personally in legal proceedings (cf. Harrison 1971, 84n4). Henderson (ad loc.) suggests that the phrase Σμικύθην καὶ κύριον was possibly a "legal tag, since Smicythe was also a common female name."

970–72. ἔνεγκ᾽ . . . ἰών: "go and get . . ."; a colloquialism.   **οὑτοσί:** Paphlagon.   **πάνυ γε:** "absolutely!" (cf. 22–23n).   **ἰδού:** Cf. 121n.   **νὴ τὸν Δί᾽:** The oath strengthens Sausage-seller's compliance.   **οὐδὲν κωλύει:** Cf. 723. *The contestants go into the house to fetch their oracles.*

973–84. Strophe = antistrophe, 985–96. Meter: glyconic; each four-line period consists of three glyconics (- × - ⏑ ⏑ - ⏑ -) and a pherecratean (- ⏑ - ⏑ ⏑ - -). The chorus offers mock praise of Cleon and applauds his anticipated destruction; see Storey 2010, 224. Here the chorus members speak as knights who hate Cleon for their own reasons (not the same as those of the poet and Sausage-seller or the other classes who are cited in the play and also hate/fear Cleon).

973–80. ἥδιστον φάος ἡμέρας: φάος (here uncontracted poetic) can mean both "light" and "source of joy" or "deliverance" (cf. *Ach.* 1184–85). The quotation apparently comes from an unknown tragedy of Euripides (schol. ad loc.); see Rau 1967, 188.   **παροῦσι:** "those who are present"; i.e., the "audience." The precise meaning of the term is uncertain. Wilson (2007b, ad loc.) writes, "Editors seem to agree that the contrast is between residents and visitors . . . 'Audience' is how one would naturally take it."   **τοῖσιν εἰσαφικνουμένοις:** "visitors"; i.e., people who visit Athens for a longer or shorter period to conduct public or private business, including attending the dramatic festival, but who do not intend to stay (Neil ad loc., citing Pl. *Meno* 92b and *Leg.* 8.848).   **Κλέων:** Mentioned only here in the comedy. L. P. E. Parker (1997, 176) writes that "the audience can have no doubt about whom the Paphlagon was meant to represent, but the explicit identification makes a climax, and also makes the song into a self-contained anti-Cleon ditty suitable for performance at drinking parties."

977–81. καίτοι: Cf. 884–86n.   **οἵων ἀργαλεωτάτων:** "of the most bothersome." The construction, οἵος + superlative, is primarily poetic (KG 1.27–28 lists examples). The adjective ἀργαλέος, which is common in archaic poetry (e.g., *Il.* 11.812; Hes. *Th.* 718; Sol. fr. 4.38W) but does not occur in tragedy, "seems to have acquired a colloquial flavor in Attic" (Dover at *Nu.* 455n; cf. also Dover 1987, 226–27).   **ἐν τῷ δείγματι:** "in the sample/ emporium of lawsuits." δεῖγμα was a kind of mart or emporium, often located in ports and featuring various goods for sale (e.g., X. *HG* 5.1.21, of the Piraeus). Here, the phrase is used metaphorically of the gathering place for the business (τῶν δικῶν) of the old jurists and seems specifically to refer to the monument in the agora of the ten Eponymoi, where public notices, including impending lawsuits, were posted (cf. D. 21.103); see Shear 1970, 145, 203–4.   **ἀντιλεγόντων, / ὡς:** "arguing that" (cf. Hdt. 8.77.1, ἀντιλέγειν ὡς; Th. 8.24.5, αὐτοὺς ἀντιλέγοντας . . . ὡς).

982–84. μέγας: "A big shot"; cf. 176–78n.   **ἤ- / στην:** Third-person dual of εἰμί.   **σκεύει χρησίμω:** "two useful tools"; nominative duals.   **δοῖδυξ οὐδὲ τορύνη:** The pestle and ladle were used, respectively, to grind and mash, stir and agitate. τορύνη is a variant on the verb ταράττειν, "stir up, agitate, cause trouble." Aristophanes describes Cleon (*Pax* 268–70) and the Spartan general Brasidas (*Pax* 281–84), both recently deceased, as "pestles" that the character War had hoped to use to pound Greece into mortar. Both generals were killed in the same campaign, in 422 BCE. Note that Thucydides' description of Cleon meeting a coward's death in that campaign is probably a slander (5.10.9); cf. Hornblower 1996, ad loc.

985–90. ἀλλὰ καὶ: Marks a progression to a new item (*GP* 22).   **τῆς ὑομουσίας / αὐτοῦ:** "of his piggish music"; i.e., "his pig education." Cleon regarded those who were well educated with suspicion and distrust (Th. 3.37.3–5). For Sausage-seller's education, cf. 188–93.   **ξυνεφοίτων:** "classmates" (φοιτᾶν = "go to school"). Cf. *Nu.* 916; Pl. *Euthd.* 272c; D. 18.265.   **Δωριστὶ:** "in Doric mode." The mode was widely associated with a manly and dignified character and was used commonly in the choral songs of tragedy (West 1992, 172–84).   **ἀρ- / μόττεσθαι:** "tuning." The passage suggests that tuning was the first lesson taught to schoolboys when they were learning to play the lyre.   **θαμὰ:** "often"; elevated poetic diction (cf. Neil ad loc.; *Av.* 234; *Th.* 952; Pl. 1166).   **λύραν:** A stringed instrument with a sounding board formed from a tortoise shell. The kithara is a more elaborate version of the instrument; see West 1992, 51–60.

992. τὸν κιθαριστὴν: "The kithara teacher." For Athens as a citharodic center, see Power 2010.

996. Δωροδοκιστί: The reason for his devotion to this particular mode is explained by the pun on "Dorian" and "bribe taking," δωροδοκεῖν.

997–1099. *Enter Paphlagon with a bundle of scrolls.*   In this contest, Sausage-seller and Paphlagon compete to show who has the best oracles about their master's destiny. The competition concludes with each contestant reciting his own dream oracle of Athena (1090–95). Deciding that Sausage-seller is "wiser than Glanis" (Γλάνιδος σοφώτερος, 1097), Demos is about to entrust stewardship of his household to Sausage-seller (1096–99), when Paphlagon begs for one more chance to win Demos over, thus beginning the final and decisive, food-serving contest (1151–1252).

997–98. ἰδού, θέασαι: "See, look!" When ἰδού is imperatival, a verb is added to show that the person being addressed should "look and see" (e.g., ἰδοὺ θεᾶσθε, *Ach.* 366; ἰδού. θεῶ, *V.* 1170; ἰδού, θεᾶσθε, *S. Tr.* 1079; ἰδού, θέασαι, *E. HF* 1131).   **ἅπαντας:** Sc., χρησμούς. Observing that Aristophanes nowhere satirizes any other politician for exploiting oracles, MacDowell (1995, 111) concludes that "the likeliest explanation of [such satire's] inclusion in *Horsemen* is that Kleon had in fact read out oracles in the Assembly on at least one or two occasions"; see also Muecke 1998, 268. *Enter Sausage-seller with a bigger load of scrolls.*   **οἴμ':** For the use of the interjection to express a speaker's emotional state, see López Eire 1996, 67–68; Nordgren 2015, 208.   **χεσείω:** "I'm going to shit." Scatological jokes generated by physical exertion (in this case, because of carrying the oracles) are stock-in-trade among the comic poets (cf. *Ra.* 3–10); see Henderson 1991a, 190.

999–1001. λόγια: For popular interest in prophecies and oracles at the beginning of and throughout the Peloponnesian War, cf. Th. 2.8.2 and 8.1.1, where the demos blames the oraclemongers and soothsayers who had prophesied that the Athenians would conquer Sicily (cf. also Dunbar at *Av.* 958–91).   **κιβωτὸς:** A lidded wooden chest or box with a lock, used to hold official documents (cf. Thomas 1989, 80), clothing (*V.* 1055–57), supplies (*Pl.* 711–12), household equipment (Eup. fr. 218.4), and money (Lys. 12.10). For the political aspects of oracles that are locked away and kept private, see 1011–13n.   **ὑπερῷον:** An upstairs room or an attic in a house (cf. *Ec.* 697–99; *Pl.* 811).   **ξυνοικία:** A tenement or boardinghouse (cf. *Th.* 273 with Biles and Olson ad loc.; Th. 3.74.4).

1002–4: γάρ: Idiomatic; signals a transition to a fresh point (*GP* 81–82).   **Βάκιδος:** "of Bacis" (cf. 123n).   **Γλάνιδος:** A kind of shad or sheatfish. Here, the name is a play on the assonance between the final syllables of the seers' names (Βάκιδος/Γλάνιδος). See Weinrich 1929.   **γεραιτέρου:** Older, more ancient, and, thus, of greater authority.

1005. περὶ Ἀθηνῶν, περὶ Πύλου: Hiatus with περί is allowable (KB 1.197) before a short vowel (e.g., περὶ ἐμοῦ, *Ra.* 87) and, more often, before a long vowel (e.g., περὶ εἰρήνης, *Ach.* 39; περὶ ἡμᾶς, *Nu.* 97; περὶ ἀνδρῶν, *Lys.* 858). In lines 1005–10, περί occurs a total of twelve times; this repetition makes the passage even more emphatic.

1007–10. φακῆς: A hearty lentil soup often associated with the diet of the common people (e.g., *V.* 811–13; *Pl.* 1004–5; cf. 192; Pherecr. fr. 26; Strattis fr. 47.2; Antiph. fr. 185.5). On the lentil in comedy, see Wilkins 2000, 13–16.   **σκόμβρων:** Salted and pickled mackerel, a common import from the Hellespont (cf. Hermipp. fr. 63.5, ἐκ δ᾽ Ἑλλησπόντου σκόμβρους καὶ πάντα ταρίχη).   **μετρούντων:** Official inspectors of weights and measures (cf. 407–8n, πυροπίπης).   **τὸ πέος οὑτοσὶ δάκοι:** [the oracles bid him to] "bite off his own cock" (Henderson 1991a, 38–39).

1011–13. ἄγε νυν: Singular is used here without regard to the actual number of persons addressed (cf. *V.* 211–12; López Eire 1996, 26).   **ὅπως...ἀναγνώσεσθε:** "read [them] aloud." On the construction, cf. 217–21n. Neither Paphlagon nor Sausage-seller is likely to be "literate" (cf. 118–54n). Nagy (1990, 171), noting the connection between the command and the "box" (κιβωτός, 1000), imagines that in reading aloud, "we see a metaphor for the making public of what is potentially kept private by the tyrannical mentality."   **ἐν νεφέλησιν αἰετὸς γενήσομαι:** "I shall become an eagle amid the clouds" (cf. the same verse with minor variation at *Av.* 978; cf. also fr. 241). The scholiast (at 1013) quotes the oracle in full: εὔδαιμον πτολίεθρον Ἀθηναίης ἀγελείης, / πολλὰ ἰδὸν καὶ πολλὰ παθὸν καὶ πολλὰ μογῆσαν, / αἰετὸς ἐν νεφέλῃσι γενήσεαι ἤματα πάντα, "blessed polis of Athena, driver of the spoils, having seen much and suffered much and toiled much, you shall become an eagle amid the clouds forever."

1014-95. The mix of dactylic hexameters and commonplace iambic dialogue (1070–79) gives the scene a humorous touch. The hexameters, previously restricted to the recitation of the actual oracles (106–69), here occur as part of the dialogue (1051–60, 1080–95).

1014-20. ἄκουε δή νυν: A favorite introductory formula of Euripides (*IA* 1009, 1146; *Supp.* 857; *Ph.* 911, 1427; *HF* 1255; *Or.* 237, 1181; cf. also *Av.* 1513 with Dunbar ad loc.). For δή with the imperative, see 21n.   **φράζευ:** (cf. *Pax* 1099) reflects the opening word of the oracles attributed to Bacis (Hdt. 8.20.2); cf. *Pax* 1099.   **Ἐρεχθεΐδη:** "son of Erechtheus" (cf. 1030); = "Athenian." Erechtheus, like Cecrops (1055) and Aegeus (1067), was an early Athenian king. After his death, he was worshipped, along with Athena, on the Acropolis (*Il.* 2. 546–51); see Simon 1983, 51–52.   **λογίων ὁδόν:** "path of prophecies"; a common poetic metaphor (cf. ὁδὸν λόγων, *Pax* 733; ὁδὸν . . . μελέων, *Av.* 1374; ὁδὸν λόγων, Pi. *O.* 1.110; γλώσσης ἀγαθῆς / ὁδόν, A. *Eu.* 988–89). See Taillardat §74n14.   **Ἀπόλλων:** In this scene, the expected oracles of Bacis and Glanis originate at Delphi (presumably to enhance their authority); cf. 217–21n.   **ἐξ ἀδύτοιο:** The innermost chamber of Apollo's temple, housing the throne from which the Pythia reported the god's responses (Pi. *O.* 7.32; A. *Eu..* 29; E. *IT* 973, 1252–57; *Ion* 662).   **διὰ τριπόδων ἐριτίμων:** "through golden tripods." The phrase is lifted from a description of tripods that stood at the entrance to Apollo's temple at Delphi (*h. Hom. Ap.* 443). Here, Apollo, rather than the Pythia, "shrieks" (ἴαχεν) his response directly to the inquirer, who either enters or stands at the threshold of the inner sanctum. In the ancient tradition, perhaps supported by geological studies, the chasm located in the inner sanctum, was said to emit intoxicating vapors, which inspired the Pythia's pronouncements; see Spiller, Hale, and De Boer 2002.   **σῴζεσθαι:** His first oracle calls on Demos to keep him (Paphlagon) safe (1023–24).   **ἱερὸν κύνα καρχαρόδοντα:** "saw-toothed sacred dog." καρχαρόδους is a Homeric epithet for dogs (*Il.* 13.198). It is also used of Cleon at *V.* 1031 (= *Pax* 754). For politicians calling themselves "watchdogs of the people," cf. *V.* 895–97; D. 25.40; Plu. *Dem.* 23.4.   **μισθὸν:** Refers to jury pay (804, 905), to tribute collected from the subject allies (1070–72), and to official fines and confiscations (1352–

54). **κἂν μὴ δρᾷ ταῦτ᾽, ἀπολεῖται:** A self-curse (cf. 410, 767–68, of Paphlagon; 832–35, of Sausage-seller). **σφε κατακρώζουσι:** "squawking against him" (cf. 287, κατακεκράξομαί σε κράζων). The pronoun σφε is singular. **κολοιοί:** "jackdaws"; perhaps alludes to Pi. *N.* 3.80–82, κραγέται δὲ κολοιοί, where jackdaws cackle [at an eagle]. On the identification of Paphlagon with an eagle, cf. also 197–201n.

1021. μὰ τὴν Δήμητρ᾽: Cf. 435–36n.

1023–24. ἀπύω: "I roar," "howl" (cf. ὑλακτεῖν of barking dogs, *V.* 904.). In Attic, the verb form (= epic ἠπύω) is found only in tragedy (e.g., [A.] *Pr.* 593; S. *Aj.* 887; E. *Hec.* 154) and here is perhaps mock-epic (cf. *Il.* 14.398–99, ἄνεμος . . . / ἠπύει, a simile of warriors in combat). Cf. Wilson 2007b, ad loc.   **σοὶ:** Emphatic.   **ὁ Φοῖβος:** A stock epithet of Apollo; cf. also Λοξίας (1047, 1072) and Λητοΐδης, "son of Leto" (1081).

1026–27. ὥσπερ θύρας: "As if by [the] doors".   **λογίων:** Cf. 1014–20n.   **παρεσθίει:** "he nibbles, gnaws at"; with the genitive (LSJ s.v.).   **ἐμοὶ:** Emphatic.   **ὀρθῶς:** Neil (ad loc.) identifies this as the "critic's word for a correct reading or rendering of a text."

1028–29. πρῶτα λήψομαι λίθον: Demos acts to defend himself as if against an actual dog attack.   **ὁ χρησμὸς ὁ περὶ τοῦ κυνὸς δάκῃ:** On the metaphor, see Newiger 1957, 24.

1030–34. φράζευ, Ἐρεχθεΐδη: Cf. 1014–20n.   **Κέρβερον:** The identification of Cleon with the dog that guards the entrance to the underworld was popular on the comic stage (*V.* 894–97; *Pax* 313–14; Plato Com. fr. 236).   **ἀνδραποδιστήν:** "kidnapper"; in particular, one who kidnaps and sells captives into slavery. The epithet perhaps alludes to Cleon's action regarding Mytilene in 427, when he proposed to execute all its male citizens and enslave the women and children (Th. 3.36.2, ἀποκτεῖναι . . . τοὺς ἅπαντας Μυτιληναίους ὅσοι ἡβῶσι, παῖδας δὲ καὶ γυναῖκας ἀνδραποδίσαι).   **κέρκῳ σαίνων:** "wagging his tail [at you]" (cf. 48–49n).   **τοὔψον:** "supper"; i.e., public funds.   **ποι ἄλλοσε:** = πρὸς ἄλλο τι, "in another direction."   **τοὐπτάνιον:** = τὸ ὀπτάνιον   **λήσει:** Cf. Sausage-seller's trick for stealing in the agora (418–20), as well as his theft of the hare (1195–1201).   **κυνηδὸν:** "dog-like"; adverb (cf. *Nu.* 491 with Dover ad loc.).   **τὰς λοπάδας . . . διαλείχων:** "licking the dishes." Henderson (1991a, 144) suggests a joke that "compares Cleon to a dog at work on the personified cities in an obscene fashion [i.e., "licking the dish" =

cunnilingus] while Demus [*sic*] sleeps." **τὰς νήσους**: I.e., subject allies in the Aegean; a surprise substitute for a kitchen item of some sort.

1035. νὴ τὸν Ποσειδῶ: Cf. 366n. The construction: "is the standard Aristophanic oath when the space to be filled from the head of the line extends to the penthemimeral caesura" (Olson at *Ach*. 560); a penthemimeral caesura is one that occurs "after the first position of the third foot" (West 1982, 198).   **πολύ γ'**: "a lot better!" Exclamatory γε often occurs following an adjective; ellipsis of ἐστι is common with adjectives (*GP* 126–27).

1036-40. Paphlagon's oracle alludes to the Pythian prophesies of the birth of Cypselus, future tyrant of Corinth (Hdt. 5.92.β3), and to Agariste (Hdt. 6.131.2; Plu. *Per.* 3), who bore the Athenian statesman Pericles a few days after dreaming that she gave birth to a lion (Hdt. 6.131.2; Plu. *Per.* 3). **ὦ τᾶν**: Cf. 494n.   **λέονθ'**: = λέοντα; refers to Paphlagon himself.   **πολλοῖς κώνωψι μαχεῖται**: "He'll fight against many gnats" (i.e., rival politicians; cf. 59–60). The verse "alludes to an Aesopic fable (255 Perry) in which a gnat challenged a lion to single combat, and the lion, vainly trying to lay hold on the gnat, succeeded only in injuring himself and eventually had to admit defeat" (Sommerstein 2001, 247).   **ὥς τε περὶ σκύμνοισι βεβηκώς**: "as if protecting his cubs" (cf. 767, ἀντιβεβηκώς, of Paphlagon protecting the demos; cf. also *Od.* 20.14, ὡς δὲ κύων ἀμαλῇσι περὶ σκυλάκεσσι βεβῶσα).   **σὺ φύλαξαι**: Aorist middle imperative (cf. Smyth §669).   **τεῖχος . . . ξύλινον**: An allusion to the "wooden walls" of the Delphic oracle that Themistocles famously interpreted (Hdt. 7.141.3–3).

1041-44. μὰ τὸν Ἀπόλλω 'γὼ μὲν οὔ: Cf. 13–14n.   **ἔφραζεν ὁ θεός**: "the god meant."   **σῴζειν ἐμέ**: The pronoun is emphatic. The salvation theme introduced at 147–49 is here turned on its head (cf. 1017).   **ἀντὶ τοῦ λέοντός εἰμί**: The preposition ἀντί denotes equivalence (LSJ s.v. A.iii): "I'm the lion's counterpart."   **Ἀντιλέων**: This name of an early tyrant of Chalcis (Arist. *Pol.* 1316a.29–32) is a pun on ἀντὶ τοῦ λέοντος (1043). Cf. *V.* 1232–35, where Cleon is compared to the tyrant Pittacus of Mytilene in an adapted line of an Alcaeus fragment (fr. 141.3–4).

1045-48. ἀναδιδάσκει: Cf. 152–53n.   **ἑκών**: "deliberately."   **σιδήρου τεῖχος**: The stocks (cf. 367) were sometimes reinforced with iron rings (Hdt. 9.37.2) to clamp head, hands, and feet in separate holes as public punishment (cf. *Nu.* 591–92; Cratin. fr. 123).   **ὁ Λοξίας**: Cf. 1072. Apollo Loxias (Loxias = "Oblique") is associated with intentionally obscure and ambiguous oracles.   **τουτονί**: "this here man."

1050: ταυτὶ ... τὰ λόγι': "These here oracles."   **ἤδη:** "soon enough"; cf. 210n.

1051–55. φθονεραί ... κορῶναι: "Envious ravens" (cf. Pi. *O.* 2. 86–88, the pair of ravens squawking at the eagle; cf. also 285, 287, 1020).   **ἰέρακα:** The hawk is Apollo's sacred bird.   **συνδήσας Λακεδαιμονίων κορακίνους:** I.e., the Spartans captured at Sphachteria and imprisoned in Athens (cf. 391–94n); κοράκινος can mean either the black-winged raven (fr. 500) or cheap fish (Henderson at *Lys.* 560). If the latter, Paphlagon here equates the capture of the Spartan troops on Sphachteria with a haul of tiny fish, a clever insult against the Spartans.   **γέ τοι:** "in any case"; restrictive (*GP* 551).   **Παφλαγών ... μεθυσθείς:** An apparent allusion to the famous vow of Cleon to kill or capture the Spartans on Sphacteria within twenty days, if given the command at Pylos (cf. 1079; Th. 4.27–28). The Athenians regarded Cleon's vow as laughable (Th. 4.28.5, τι καὶ γέλωτος τῇ κουφολογίᾳ), and many were astonished that he succeeded (Th. 4.39.3).   **Κεκροπίδη:** "son of Cecrops"; = "Athenian" (cf. 1014–20n).   **κακόβουλε:** "ill-advised." Note the alliteration of κε-, κρο-, κα-, κό-.   **τοῦθ' ... μέγα τοὔργον;** "this great deed"; an "oracular" dig at Cleon's success.

1056–57. A quotation from the *Little Iliad* (Allen fr. 2 = schol. at *Eq.* 1056), in which two Trojan girls are overheard arguing about whether Ajax or Odysseus had the greater achievements. One of the girls favored Ajax, because he retrieved Achilles' body from the battlefield. The other, inspired by Athena (Ἀθηνᾶς προνοίᾳ), replied that even a "woman could carry a load when a man has put it on her back, for she'd shit if she should fight."

1057. χέσαιτο: Presumably from fear (on the effect of fear on the bowels, cf. 222–24n). The absence of ἄν in the potential optative is presumably normalized by the ἄν of the preceding μαχέσαιτο (cf. *Ra.* 574 with Dover ad loc.). Neil (ad loc.) suggests that "the form χέσαιτο is a comic datismos" (cf. 115–17n).

1059. ἔστι Πύλος πρὸ Πύλοιο: Equals half a hexameter line and thus may be lifted from an oracle. Paphlagon cites the verse to remind the listeners of the Athenian victory at Pylos and thereby glorify himself.

1060–61. πυέλους: A pun on Πύλος. The πύελος is a large tub with a drain, used for baths, food processing, etc. (cf. *V.* 141; *Pax* 843; *Th.* 562; Ginouvès 1962, 47–48.).   **φησὶν:** Sc., ὁ θεός (1048) or ὁ χρησμός (1025).   **καταλήψεσθ(αι):** The verb suggests a military operation (cf.

Lys. 624, καταλαβεῖν τὰ χρήματα, from Athena's treasury; Th. 1.126.5, κατέλαβε τὴν ἀκρόπολιν).   **ἐν βαλανείῳ:** "at the bathhouse"; Paphlagon's final destination (1401).   **ἄλουτος:** "without a bath." Bathing was often preliminary to special occasions (cf. 50–51n).   **τήμερον:** Neil (ad loc.) writes, "The tragic rhythm [of the verse] is counteracted by the colloquial [form] τήμερον."

1062. Many editors reject this line as an explanatory note, arguing that it is "weak, repetitive and anticlimactic" and that "its past tense . . . is in contradiction with the future tense" (Sommerstein 1981, ad loc.). But the line stands in all the manuscripts and is extant in both papyri (Wilson 2007b, ad loc.).

1063–64. ἀλλ' . . . γάρ: "But [never mind]," "anyway" (*GP* 102–3).   **οὑτοσὶ:** The deictic (understood as a stage direction) suggests that Sausage-seller brandishes the oracle scroll.   **πάνυ:** Cf. 22–23n.

1065–66. ἀναγίγνωσκε: "Keep reading aloud." The present imperative has a durative aspect (Smyth §1864).   **μισθὸς:** Naval pay (cf. 1078–79, 1366–67). Daily pay for crews, which numbered around two hundred per ship (Hdt. 8. 17; Th. 6.8.1, 8.29.2; Morrison, Coates, Rankin 2000, 107–26), was likely around six obols, which is equal to one drachma (cf. *V.* 1188–9 with MacDowell ad loc.; Th. 6.31.3 with Hornblower 2008, ad loc.).

1067–69. Αἰγεΐδη: "Son of Aegeus" (cf. 1015); = "Athenian." **κυναλώπεκα:** "fox-dog." Cf. Paphlagon's self-description as a dog at 1017–34.   **λαίθαργον:** "secretly biting." The scholiast (at 1068) quotes a proverb: σαίνεις δάκνουσα καὶ κύων λαίθαργος εἶ, "you're a fawning, biting, nipping dog."   **κερδώ:** "wily thief."   **πολύιδριν:** "crafty"; epic diction (*Od.* 2.346, 15.459, 23.82; Hes. *Th.* 616; fr. 43(a) 57).   **Φιλόστρατος:** Nothing is known of him other than that his nickname was κυναλώπηξ, "fox-dog" (*Lys.* 957–58).

1070–72. ναῦς . . . / . . . ἀργυρολόγους: I.e., Athenian triremes dispatched to collect tribute among the allies and sometimes accompanied by a military force (Th. 2.69.1, 3.19.1; Hornblower 1991, ad loc.).   **οὑτοσί:** Paphlagon.   **Λοξίας:** Cf. 1047.

1073–74. πῶς δὴ . . . ; "How then?" The particle intensifies the question (*GP* 210–11).   **ὅπως;** Cf. 128–29n.   **ἡ τριήρης ἐστὶ χὠ κύων ταχύ:** Cf. the parody of oracular interpretations at 207–8.

1076–77. ἀλωπεκίοισι: "fox cubs." For foxes eating grapes and damaging vineyards, cf. Theoc. 1.45–49.   **ὅτιὴ βότρυς τρώγουσιν:** "because they eat grapes." Troops brought limited supplies of provisions with them on campaign; after those provisions ran out, they either relied on supply ships and available markets or turned to stealing and plundering from local residents (cf. *V.* 235–39, 354–55; *Ra.* 1074–75; Th. 4.45.1; Casson 1994, 70–71).

1078. εἰέν: "Now then"; a colloquial interjection "introducing a transition to a fresh point by a backward glance at what has been established" (Stevens 1976, 34). Cf. López Eire 1996, 93; Nordgren 2015, 221. Here it is *extra metrum* (outside the meter).

1079–81. ἡμερῶν τριῶν: "Within three days" (on Cleon's promise, cf. 1051–55n). Three days of rations were apparently standard for recruits called up for military service (cf. *Ach.* 197 with Olson ad loc.; *Pax* 312).   **εἶπε:** "[Apollo] bids you . . ."   **Λητοΐδης:** Cf. 1023–24n.   **Κυλλήνην:** Cyllene is a settlement and harbor in Elis on the western Peloponnese (Liv. 27.32.2; Plin. *NH* 4.6,13); that settlement's name is here chosen for the sake of the pun on κυλλή, "curved [hand]."

1082–83. ποίαν Κυλλήνην; "Crooked-hand indeed!?" On the colloquial use of ποῖος with the repetition of the previous speaker's word, cf. 162–63n.   **ὀρθῶς:** Cf. 1026–27n.   **φησ᾽:** Sc., Paphlagon.   **κυλλῇ:** "crooked [hand]"; alludes to habitually taking bribes (cf. schol. ad loc.) and also plays on the image of a beggar extending an empty upturned hand (κοίλῃ χειρί) to accept alms. For corrupt politicians extending an open hand to accept bribes, cf. *Th.* 936–37, πρὸς τῆς δεξιᾶς, ἥνπερ φιλεῖς / κοίλην προτείνειν, ἀργύριον ἤν τις διδῷ, "by the right hand which you like to extend cupped, if anyone might give silver."

1084–87. οὐκ ὀρθῶς φράζει: "He got it wrong."   **τὴν Κυλλήνην γὰρ ὁ Φοῖβος / εἰς τὴν χεῖρ(α) ὀρθῶς ᾐνίξατο:** "for Phoebus correctly used the riddling word 'Κυλλήνην' to refer to the hand" (cf. *Pax* 47, ἐς Κλέωνα τοῦτ᾽ αἰνίσσεται, "it's a riddle about Cleon"). On the close association of riddles with oracles, cf. 196n.   **Διοπείθους:** Diopeithes (*PA* 4309; *PAA* 363105) was a well-known oraclemonger (cf. *Av.* 988 with Dunbar ad loc.; Phryn. Com. fr. 9; Amips. fr. 10; Telecl. fr. 7), a political opportunist (*V.* 380; cf. Connor 1963, 115–16), and probably the mover of an impiety decree aimed at the philosopher Anaxagoras (Plu. *Per.* 32.2–5; but see Dover 1976, 39–40). Sommerstein (2001, 247) suggests that he "may be the man described in Eupolis fr. 264 (from *Prospaltioi*, produced in 429) as 'lame in hand.'" The latest mention of this man is in the late fourth century (Xen. *HG* 3.3). **ἀλλὰ γάρ:** "But here." The combination stresses what Paphlagon sees as decisive. **αἰετὸς ὡς γίγνει . . . βασιλεύεις:** "you'll become an eagle [cf. 1013], and you'll be king." In prophecies, a future event may be regarded as present (cf. 1089; KG 1.138; Smyth §1882).

1088-89. καὶ γὰρ ἐμοὶ: "And I [have] one too!" The phrase occurs often with ellipsis of a verb (cf. 1092; *GP* 109–10). **τῆς Ἐρυθρᾶς . . . θαλάσσης:** In Aristophanes' day, the "Red Sea" denoted the modern Red Sea, the Persian Gulf, and the Indian Ocean (*OCD*[4] s.v. "Red Sea"). **χὤτι:** = καὶ ὅτι **ἐν Ἐκβατάνοις:** The capital of Media and the summer residence of the Persian king (X. *An.* 3.15.5l; *Cyr.* 8.6.22). On Athenian imperial ambitions in *Knights*, cf. 173–74n and 1300–1315n. The prophecy declares that Athens is to seize and occupy Ecbatana as an outpost of the Athenian Empire; cf. the joke about Sparta becoming the Athens of the Peloponnese that is told at the end of *Lysistrata* (Anderson 2011/12). **ἐπίπαστα:** Cf. 103–4n.

1090-95. The dream oracles are significant in the contest for the steward's ring of Demos, as they reveal the characters of the rival dreamers and their competing conceptions of Athena, patron deity of the city. Paphlagon presents the goddess as a kind of bath attendant, but as occurs so often in the play, Sausage-seller seizes the opening to "top" Paphlagon; Sausage-seller's Athena remains a bath attendant but retains her traditional tutelary position, descending from the Acropolis with her special bird, the owl, in hand, to bestow immortality on Demos and to scorn Paphlagon and render him repulsive (see Anderson 1991).

1090-91. ἐγὼ εἶδον ὄναρ: For dreams and dream divination in ancient Greece, see Dodds 1951, 103–11, 117–21; Mikalson 1983, 39–49; Struck 2005. For the political role of oracles and dreams in Aristophanes, see Smith 1989; Muecke 1998, especially 267–72. **ἡ θεὸς αὐτὴ:** Athena Polias, as at 446, 903, 1169, 1173, 1185, 1203. **ἀρυταίνῃ:** A bath attendant's ladle. According to Theophrastus (*Char.* 9.8), one ladle could hold enough water to douse the bather. In a fragment by Aristophanes (450), a bath attendant has ladles large enough to move customers around (βαλανεὺς δ᾽ ὠθεῖ ταῖς ἀρυταίναις). Bath attendants were notoriously unsavory characters (e.g., 1403; *Ra.* 710; *Pl.* 955–56; cf. Pl. *R.* 1.344D; Ginouvès 1962, 212). Paphlagon's oracle unwittingly anticipates his destined occupation (1400–1401). **πλουθυγίειαν:** An apparent Aristophanic coinage for denoting blessings of every kind and number (*V.* 677; *Av.* 731).

1092–95. ἐκ πόλεως: "from the Acropolis." On the omission of the article, cf. 266–68n.   **γλαῦξ αὐτῇ ᾿πικαθῆσθαι:** For images of the owl settled on the goddess, see *LIMC* 2.1, no. 976; 2.2, especially nos. 187, 206. The owl of Athena is a harbinger of victory at Salamis (Plu. *Them.* 12.1).   **κατασπένδειν κατὰ τῆς κεφαλῆς:** "pour a libation over the head [of Demos]." Casabona (1966, 252) understands σπένδομαι as expressing the idea of contact.   **ἀρυβάλλῳ:** Unlike the ἀρύταινα, which is associated with bathwater, the ἀρύβαλλος is connected with scented water applied after the bath; see Ginouvès 1962, 214n1.   **ἀμβροσίαν:** Associated with peace (e.g., *Ach.* 196) and pleasing odors (e.g., *Il.* 14.170–77; cf. Lilja 1972, 58–59). As food of the gods (the relationship here with νέκταρ is confused or reversed; cf. *Pax* 723–24), it possesses powers of renewal and strength (e.g., *h. Hymn Dem.* 235–43; Pi. *P.* 9.63; Theoc. 15.106–9); cf. also the rejuvenation of Demos at 1326–28.   **σκοροδάλμην:** "garlic brine"; evokes foul and repulsive odors (cf. the single other mention in the play, at 199, δὴ τότε Παφλαγόνων μὲν ἀπόλλυται ἡ σκοροδάλμη, "the garlic brine of the Paphlagons shall perish").

1096. ἰοὺ ἰού: "Yippee, Yippee"; a cry of joy and enthusiasm (*Nu.* 1171; *Pax* 345; *Av.* 193, 819, 1510). Cf. López Eire 1996, 85–86.

1098–99. ἐμαυτὸν ἐπιτρέπω: Cf. 1259, Ἀγορακρίτῳ τοίνυν ἐμαυτὸν ἐπιτρέπω. On Aristophanes' use of ἐπιτρέπειν (entrust) and its cognates, see Newiger 1957, 47–48.   **γεροντaγωγεῖν κἀναπαιδεύειν:** "to guide me in old age and reeducate me"; an apparent parody of a verse from Sophocles' *Peleus* (*TrGF* fr. 487), γεροντaγωγῶ κἀναπαιδεύω; cf. also *Com. adesp.* fr. 740, γεροντaγωγῶν κἀναμισθαρνεῖν διδούς, with Rau 1967, 189.

1100–1. μήπω γ᾿, ἱκετεύω: "Not yet, please."   **κριθὰς:** Barley grain used for making cakes, breads, and the like (cf. Pl. *R.* 372b).

1103–4. Θουφάνους: Thuphanes (*PA* 7074; *PAA* 515900) was apparently a petty bureaucrat (ὑπογραμματεύς) and crony (κόλαξ) of Cleon; cf. schol. ad loc.   **ἀλλ᾿:** "Instead" (cf. 85–86n).   **ἄλφιτ᾿ . . . ᾿σκευασμένα:** barley groats prepared for baking; see Moritz 1949, 117.

1105–6. μαζίσκας . . . διαμεμαγμένας: "barley cakes already made"; cf. *Av.* 463, διαμάττειν. Note also the alliteration with "μ" at 1166–68.   **μηδὲν ἀλλ᾿:** "nothing except"; cf. KG 2.487.

1107–10. ἀνύσατε: Adverbial (cf. 71, 119).   **ὅ τι περ ποιήσεθ᾿:** "[with] whatever you're going to do." ποιήσεθ᾿= ποιήσετε. The conditional relative clause + future indicative (in place of the subjunctive) expresses "a present intention or necessity" (*MT* §527).   ὁπότερος . . . σφῷν: σφῷν = genitive dual; cf. 1207, ὁπότερός ἐστι νῷν.   ἄν . . . ἄν: The repetition of the modal with the subjunctive is apparently pleonastic (KG 1.248).   τῆς Πυκνὸς τὰς ἡνίας: For the metaphor "reins of the Pnyx" (i.e., "governance of the city"), cf. *Ec.* 466, τῆς πόλεως τὰς ἡνίας; Pl. *Plt.* 266e, τὰς τῆς πόλεως ἡνίας; Plu. *Per.* 11.4, τῷ δήμῳ τὰς ἡνίας; see Taillardat §669.   οὐ δῆτ᾽: Cf. 726–27n.

1111–50. Lyric duet between the chorus and Demos (1111–20 = 1121–30 = 1131–40 = 1141–50). Meter: aeolo-choriambic. Each song has two stanzas, alternating between three or five telesilleans (× - ◡ ◡ - ◡ -) with a reizianun (◡ ◡ - ◡ ◡ - -) at the end of each sequence of telesilleans. See L. P. E. Parker 1997, 176–80.

1111–14. καλήν γ᾽ / . . . ἀρχήν: "A really fine empire!" (for exclamatory γε, cf. 1035n).   ὅτε: "since."   πάντες ἄν- / θρωποι: "all mankind."   ἄνδρα τύραννον: For the Athenian Empire conceived as a kind of "tyranny," cf. Th. 2.63.2, 3.37.2. The right of the Athenian demos to absolute power at home and abroad is taken for granted; see Henderson 2003a, 160–61.

1115. εὐπαράγωγος: "Easily duped, credulous." Cf. Cleon's complaint (Th. 3.38.6–7) about the fascination of the Athenian demos with rhetorical displays.

1119–20. ὁ νοῦς . . . / παρὼν ἀποδημεῖ: For the metaphor of a character as physically present but with his mind on "vacation," cf. *Ach.* 396–99; *V.* 92–93.

1121–30. Demos declares that while politicians may think him stupid and easily manipulated, he plays along, fattening them up to swat them down one at a time; see Landfester 1967, 68–69. L. P. E. Parker (1997, 178) writes, "The song is highly significant in the play (and unique in Aristophanes) in offering an interpretation of the action which the audience would otherwise have no reason to think of."

1121–24. Cf. *Nu.* 575–95; for the Athenian belief that they might be deceived by unscrupulous leaders but that they would eventually come to their senses, sometimes with divine guidance, see Ostwald 1986, 226–27.   ἔνι: For ἔνεστι.   ἑκών: Cf. 1045–48n.

1125–40. For the remainder of the song, Demos and the chorus sing as if Paphlagon is an offering to be fattened for sacrifice rather than a fearsome monster; see Sommerstein 2009, 166.

1126. βρύλλων: The verb apparently imitates an infant's cry (βρῦ) for a drink (cf. *Nu.* 1382 with Dover ad loc.). For Demos being treated and fed like a child, cf. 716–18n.   **τὸ καθ᾽ ἡμέραν:** "daily [jury pay]."

1128. προστάτην: Sc., τοῦ δήμου or the like; denotes a protector and leader of the people and was commonly applied to Cleon and politicians like him (*Ra.* 569 Cleon; *Pax* 683–84 Hyperbolus; Th. 3.75.2 [leaders of Corcyra], 8.89.3 [politicians in Athens]). See Connor 1971, 110–15.

1130. ἄρας: "Lifting him up," like a wrestler throwing an opponent to the ground (cf. *Ach.* 565; Poliakoff 1987, 23).

1131–32. οὕτω μὲν: "In that case" (cf. *Av.* 656, 1503).   **πυκνότης:** "cunning," with a pun on Πνυκί (1137).

1134–36. πάνυ πολλή: "Really a lot."   **ἐπίτηδες:** Cf. 893n.   **ὥσ- / περ δημοσίους τρέφεις:** "you raise them like public victims."

1139–40. παχύς: "Fat," "plump," "wealthy" (cf. *V.* 288, 639; *Pax* 639; Hdt. 5.30.10; Taillardat §543).   **θύσας ἐπιδειπνεῖς:** Like a sacrificial animal or scapegoat (cf. 1402–5n and Bagordo, *FrC* 2016, 214–15).

1141–42. σοφῶς / αὐτοὺς περιέρχομαι: "I cleverly circumvent them."

1144.   ἐξαπατύλλειν: "Dupe," "outtrick." On the verb form, which is attested elsewhere only at *Ach.* 657, cf. Peppler 1921, 153. Olson (at *Ach.* 656–58) describes it as "a contemptuous colloquial form of ἐξαπατάω . . . (also of the Athenian people being taken in by demagogues)."

1146–50. οὐδὲ δοκῶν ὁρᾶν: "I pretend not to see" (cf. *Pax* 1051; *Pl.* 837; E. *Hipp.* 463).   **ἀναγ- / κάζων . . . ἐξεμεῖν:** "forcing [them] to vomit." In Aristophanes, emesis is associated not only with excessive drinking and eating but also with political corruption (cf. 404, Paphlagon; *Ach.* 6–8, Cleon; fr. 625, a politician [?]); see Taillardat §71.   **κεκλόφωσί μου:** Cf. 109–10n.   **κημὸν:** A wicker funnel placed at the opening of a voting urn to ensure secret balloting (cf. *V.* 99, 754–55; *Th.* 1031). On voting procedures in Athenian courts, see Harrison 1971, 164–66; Todd 1993, 132–33.   **καταμηλῶν:** "using as a probe"; to induce vomiting (cf. Phryn. Com. fr. 66, ἔμει καταμηλῶν, "inserting the probe he vomits").

1151–1263. *Enter Sausage-seller and Paphlagon, each carrying a large basket of food.* The pattern observed in the two earlier contests continues: Paphlagon is continuously outdone by his rival. What differs in this contest is that nearly all of the food offerings are connected somehow to Athena, who, although not a stage character herself, plays the decisive role in Sausage-seller's triumph.

1151. ἄπαγ᾿ ἐς μακαρίαν ἐκποδών: "Get out of the blessed way." ἐς μακαρίαν is a surprise substitute for the common curse formula ἐς κόρακας (cf. 892). Sommerstein (2009, 75) explains, "It sounds like a blessing, but as its contexts here and elsewhere show, it is intended and perceived as a curse; for οἱ μακάριοι could mean the 'dead' (cf. Ar. fr. 504.9–11)." **σύ γ᾿, ὦ φθόρε:** "you [get out of the way], you wretch."

1152–55. μέντοι: "certainly." The particle has an emphatically assentient force (*GP* 399). **τρίπαλαι:** "for a thrice long time ago." **εὐεργετεῖν:** "to be a public benefactor" (e.g., *IG* i³ 1454.7–8 [445–30 BCE], 102.28 [409 BCE], 101.35 [409–407 BCE]). **δεκάπαλαί γε καὶ δωδεκάπαλαι / καὶ χιλιόπαλαι καὶ προπαλαιπαλαίπαλαι:** Cf. *Pax* 242–43, τρὶς ἄθλιαι καὶ πεντάκις / καὶ πολλοδεκάκις, of the mash-up recipe prepared by the personified stage character War.

1158–61. οἶσθ᾿ οὖν ὃ δρᾶσον; A (colloquial) rhetorical question: "Do you know what you should do?" (cf. *Pax* 1061; *Av.* 54, 80; E. *Hec.* 225; Stevens 1976, 36; López Eire 1996, 107). **εἰ δὲ μή, φράσεις γε σύ:** "If not, you're going to tell [me]"; cf. *Pax* 1061. **βαλβίδων:** βαλβῖδες "were a row of flat stones set into the ground . . . that served as toe-holds for the (standing) start" at one end of a running track (Biles and Olson at *V.* 549). *During the next several lines the competitors rush in and out of the house of Demos to retrieve serving implements and foods.* **τουτονί:** He gestures toward Paphlagon. **ἐξ ἴσου:** "fairly." **ἄπιτον:** "You will go!"; a dual imperative (i.e., "Ready!"). **ἰδού:** "Indeed." **θέοιτ᾿ ἄν:** "You can run!" The potential optative with ἄν has the force of a mild command (*MT* §237). **ὑποθεῖν οὐκ ἐῶ:** "I won't let you cut in." ἐῶ is present with a future sense; cf. Pl. Com. fr. 46.6–7, οὐκ ἐῶ / παίζειν, "I won't let you play" (also at the start of a competition).

1162–63. ἀλλ᾿ ἦ: "Well then." The particle is used affirmatively (cf. *GP* 28; Wilson 2007b, ad loc.). **μεγάλως εὐδαιμονήσω:** "I'll be mighty happy." Cf. 151, μεγάλως εὐδαιμονεῖς, of Sausage-seller. **θρύψομαι:** "I'll play coy." The word is used of lovers pretending to refuse a favor or request (cf. Eup. fr. 393, ὡραιζομένη καὶ θρυπτομένη, "preening herself and flirting"; X. *Smp.* 8.4, ἐπισκώψας ὡς δὴ θρυπτόμενος, "joking as though flirting").

1164–65. ὁρᾷς: Cf. 92.   **δίφρον:** A δίφρος, a simple footstool, seems inappropriate for dining, since the usual and certainly more comfortable and customary position for symposiastic dining was to recline and not sit (Lynch 2011, 77). On a secondary level, there may also be a joke on Paphlagon as a διφροφόρος, a service position reserved for women (*Ec.* 734; Hermipp. fr. 25; Nicopho. fr. 7; Stratt. fr. 7); cf. Cratin. fr. 32, where Lycurgus (*PA* 9449; *PAA* 611320) is mocked as a διφροφέρων in a procession of Isis.   **προτεραίτερος:** "firster."

1166–67. μαζίσκην . . . / . . . μεμαγμένην: A μαζίσκη is a small cake kneaded out of barley grain (ὀλαί), which was thrown toward an altar or sprinkled near an animal as a preliminary to its "assent" to being sacrificed (e.g., *Od.* 3.441; Hdt. 1.132.1; *Pax* 948, 959–60); see Stengel 1910, 13–33. The offer of cake (perhaps motivated by Sausage-seller's promise of fully kneaded barley cakes at 1105) is here given as if an appetizer for what customarily follows the sacrifice, a serving of meat. Mere possession of the cake implies that Paphlagon must have lifted it from the sacrificial altar at Pylos (54–55) and thus committed sacrilege (ἱεροσυλία; see Anderson 1995, 23–24).

1168–70. Sausage-seller copies Paphlagon's alliteration with "μ" (1166–68, μαζίσκην . . . μεμαγμένην), topping it with his own (μυστίλας μεμυστιλημένας), and he uses a similar prepositional arrangement, but with ὑπό (1169) instead of ἐκ (1167). Sausage-seller's offerings, here and throughout the competition, draw attention to the material benefits that Athena provides the Athenians at home, whereas Paphlagon's Athena is a fearsome deity entirely engaged in military matters.

μυστίλας: Cf. 824–27n.   **τῇ χειρὶ τῇλεφαντίνῃ:** "with her chryselephantine hand" alludes to the great Athena Parthenos statue, which was over seven times life-size and held in its right hand a likeness of Nike that was nearly six feet tall. On the appearance, construction, and dimensions of the Parthenos statue, see Lapatin 2001, 62–79.   **ἆρ':** Indicates that Demos is genuinely surprised by the size of Athena's finger (KG 2.320.6); the predicate position of μέγαν further stresses that the depression was made by a large digit (*GP* 37).   **πότνια:** An ancient honorific title reserved for mortal mistresses of the house and certain goddesses, particularly Athena of Athens (e.g., *IG* i³ 607, 619, 718, 832, 872, all metrical dedications on the Acropolis).   **δάκτυλον:** A double entendre based on Athena's "big finger" and the shape and resemblance of certain breads and pastries to the female pudenda; thus Athena here becomes a kind of lesbian parthenos who stimulates herself (see Anderson 2008b). On comic exploitation of the resemblance of certain pastries and breads (e.g., ἐλατήρ, μᾶζα, μυστίλη, πλακοῦς, πότανα) to the female pudenda, see Henderson 1991a, 144.

1171–72. ἔτνος: A pea or bean soup that was a favorite dish of gluttons (e.g., *Ra.* 62–63 of Heracles). On sexual jokes based on the association of μυστίλαι, ἔτνος, and ζωμός (1174) with female anatomy, see Anderson 2008b, 178–79.   **εὔχρων καὶ καλόν:** "nice and tasty." The soup's color and appearance suggest divine approval (e.g., at *Lys.* 205, Kalonike interprets the rich "blood" color (εὔχρων) of the sacrificial "victim" as a sign of divine approval; see Casabona 1966, 317–21).   **ἐτόρυνε:** The image of Athena with a spoon for stirring (τορύνη, 984) recalls Paphlagon's activities as a political agitator (64–66n. On ζωμός used metaphorically for political affairs, cf. 359–60n.   **Πυλαιμάχος:** "Fighter at the Gates"; a rarely attested epithet (Stesich., *PMGF* 242, of Ares; Callim. 638, of Athena) adduced for the sake of the geographical pun on Pylos; i.e., Paphlagon's Athena is the "Fighter at Pylos." Absurdly, the image turns Athena into a kind of messmate at Pylos who uses her finger as a stirring spoon. On the structural significance of Athena's epithets in plays of Aristophanes, see Anderson 1995.

1173–74. These lines draw on a famous verse of Solon (4.1–4W) in which Athena, guardian of the city (ἐπίσκοπος) extends her sheltering hands (χεῖρας ὕπερθεν ἔχει) so as to protect her subjects from greedy and unscrupulous leaders (like Cleon).   **ἐναργῶς:** "manifestly" (cf. *Il.* 20.131, θεοί . . . ἐναργεῖς; *Od.* 16.161, θεοί . . . ἐναργεῖς; A. *Th.* 135–36, Ἄρης . . . / ἐναργῶς).   **ἐπισκοπεῖ:** Solon's elegy is the earliest example in Attic poetry of ἐπισκοπεῖν used of a protecting deity. For use of that term to refer to other deities in Athenian drama, cf. S. *Ant.* 1148 (Bacchus); E. *IT* 1414 (Poseidon).   **χύτραν:** A common cooking pot (Sparkes 1962, 130) and a surprise substitution for the χεῖρας of Solon's elegy.   **ζωμοῦ:** A thick meat-based soup customarily served along with meats, sausage, and tripe (1178–79) at public festivals. ζωμός is used metaphorically for the mandatory tribute of the subject allies. Demos' rhetorical question suggests that he appreciates Athena's soup as a pun on plundering the allied states.

1176. φανερῶς: "Clearly"; acknowledging the political implications of the absence of Athena's protecting hand and tangible benefits (i.e., Athens without its subject states).

1177. τέμαχος: A simple slice of fish. The pun on τέμνω (cut, wound) and τέμαχος suggests that the only cutting Athena did at Pylos was done to a fish. τέμαχος also suggests a martial pun, as if the word were a compound based on -μαχος (cf. πυλαιμάχος). On Paphlagon-Cleon voraciously "gobbling up" various fish as a representation of "his usurpation of power," see Davidson 1993, 57–59.   **Φοβεσιστράτη:** "Terror of Armies"; an ad hoc Aristophanic coinage playing on Athena's aegis, which was bordered by tassels and snakes, fastened by the gorgoneion (an elaborate pin featuring a frontal gorgon), and used to incite panic and terror in the ranks of the enemy (cf. *Il.* 5.733–42; *Od.* 24.528–29; cf. also Hes. fr. 343.18 MW = 294.18 Most, αἰγίδα . . . φοβέστρατον).

1178–80. Ὀβριμοπάτρα: "Daughter of a Mighty Father"; a well-attested epithet of Athena in epic, relating to the story of her birth, fully armed, from the head of Zeus (*Il.* 5.747, 8.391; *Od.* 1.101, 3.135, 24.540; Hes. *Th.* 587). The epithet draws attention to the intimate bond between Athena and Zeus, who defend the city together in Solon's elegy (lines 1–2).   **ἐφθὸν ἐκ ζωμοῦ κρέας:** "meat boiled from soup." Sacrificial victims were routinely boiled and distributed to the public at state festivals (*Pax* 715–17; Hdt. 1.59.1; *IG* ii² 334.21–25).   **χόλικος ἠνύστρου:** On Sausage-seller's trade specialties, cf. 356–58n. The foods are metaphors for Athena's protection of her city.   **καλῶς γ':** "really well." The particle underscores the force of the adverb (*GP* 127).   **τοῦ πέπλου:** Cf. 565–66n. According to Sommerstein (1981, ad loc.), "Demos supposes that Athena has given a dish of tripe in gratitude for this [peplos] offering!"

1181–82. ἡ Γοργολόφα: "Goddess of the Gorgon Plumes"; an ad hoc comical formation (note the pun on Γοργώ/γοργός). The epithet alludes to the crest of Athena's helmet as an additional instrument of terror and is an example of a war epithet that is absurdly out of proportion to the food offering. Athena γοργολόφα also recalls the characterization of the pro-war general Lamachus as γοργολόφας at *Ach.* 566–68; see Anderson 1995, 27.   **ἐκέλευε:** Athena gives commands, as if a στρατηγός.   **ἐλατῆρος:** A broad flat cake (cf. *Ach.* 245–46) that was pounded (ἐλαύνειν) into shape. Paphlagon puns on ἐλατήρ in the sense of "rower" (ἐλαύνειν = "to row") to impress Demos with his nautical devotion (cf. 1065–66 for Demos' interest in the navy).   **ἐλαύνωμεν:** On the subjunctive in secondary sequence, see 665–69n, ἵν[α] . . . πύθησθ(ε). The idea seems to be that he and Demos can row well together by consuming "rower cake."

1183–87. Sausage-seller's Athena offers Demos foods that not only reflect the work of Sausage-seller's trade but are confusing, inedible, and linked to warships.

τί τούτοις χρήσομαι / . . . ; On the use of the future instead of the subjunctive in deliberative questions, cf. *MT* §68.   τοῖς ἐντέροις: "intestines," here offered as a comic substitution for the σπλάγχνα, the inner organs of the animals that were enjoyed only by the circle of sacrificial participants; cf. R. Parker 2011, 151–53. Paphlagon foreswore claims to the σπλάγχνα if he proved less shameless than his rival (see 409–10n).   ἐπίτηδες: Cf. 893n.   ἐντερόνειαν: The precise meaning of this hapax legomenon is unknown, but it must be a pun on some internal structure of triremes (e.g., frame timbers, gunwales, etc.); see Frisk 1960–72, s.v. ἔντερα; Morrison, Coates, and Rankov 2000, 181n5; Sommerstein 2001, 247.   ἐπισκοπεῖ: Cf. 1173–74n.   τὸ ναυτικόν: The joke is that Athena sends Demos "intestines" because they give strength to the body of the ship, the ἐντερόνεια, yet they are suitable only for dumping into the ship's "belly." For the sake of the joke, Athena's support for the navy is momentarily converted into contempt for it and the naval war.   πιεῖν: An imperatival infinitive.   τρία καὶ δύο: Ancient Greeks drank their wine diluted with water, and the ratio of three parts water to two parts wine was considered very potent. Hesiod (*Op.* 596) recommends a three-to-one ratio for moderate drinkers; Aristophanes' one-to-one ratio causes even the god Hermes to feel the effects (*Pl.* 1132). In statements concerning the ratio of water and wine mixtures, water usually comes first, wine second; see Page 1955, 308. For mixtures of wine and water from comedy, see Ath. 10.426b–427c.

1188–89. ὡς ἡδύς: Sc., οἶνος. Dover (1987, 47) notes, "The masculine gender . . . shows that 'the wine you are giving me' is understood from the previous line."   ἡ Τριτογενής: An ancient epithet of Athena (*Il.* 4.515; *Od.* 3.378; *h. Hom. Ath.* 4; Hes. *Th.* 895; *Sc.* 197), commonly explained as coming from the location of her birth at or near a body of water called Trito (Hdt. 4.180.3; Paus. 8.26.6, 9.33.7; cf. also *Lys.* 347, Athena as a firefighter). Sausage-seller puns on the element τρι- (three) for the sake of the joke on the three-to-one ratio of water and wine.   ἐνετριτώνισεν: "tripartified"; an ad hoc coinage.

1190. πλακοῦντος πίονος . . . τόμον: "Slice of rich flat cake." These cakes were often baked with honey and served as appetizers or savories at symposia. For a list of typical cakes served at symposia, cf. Athen. 14.643e–644; Wilkins 2000, 308–11. The term τόμον, "slice," is used mostly of sausages (e.g., Cratin. fr. 205; Pherecr. fr. 113.8; Mnesim. 4.14) and cheese (Eub. fr. 148.2).

1192. λαγῷ': Sc. κρέα or the like. Hare flesh was a delicacy consumed on festive occasions (*Ach.* 1005–6; *Pax* 1196) and was especially hard to find in wartime. It was also a traditional pederastic courtship gift (cf. *ARV²* 284, 362, 471; Dover 1989, 92). Here the patriotic sense of the word φιλόδημος is transformed into erotic love (cf. 786–87n).   ἀλλ᾽ ἐγώ: The attentive spectator might wonder at Paphlagon's exclusive access to such delicacies and associate these possessions with wartime contraband (cf. *Ach.* 873–80, a list of contraband, including hare's meat, in the possession of a Theban merchant whose city was hostile to Athens).

1193–94. οἴμοι: "Damn it."   ὦ θυμέ: The address to one's heart is poetic (*Ach.* 450, 480; Archil. fr. 128.1W; Thgn. 695, 877; E. *Med.* 1056); see Dickey 1996, 187.   βωμολόχον ... τι: "some buffoonish trick" (cf. 902n).

1195–1202. Cf. 418–20, where Sausage-seller uses the same ploy to distract his opponent.

1195–97. *Paphlagon produces a hare.*   ὁρᾷς τάδ᾽ ...; "Do you see this [τὰ λαγῷα]? " (cf. 94).   κακόδαιμον: Cf. 6–7n.   ἐκεινοί: He points in the direction of the agora (stage left).   ἀργυρίου βαλλάντια: "purses of silver," with which to bribe Paphlagon; see 706, where Sausage-seller proffers a similar bribe (βαλλαντίῳ) for his own protection.

1198–1201. *Paphlagon drops the hare in his excitement.*   ποῦ, ποῦ; "where, oh where?"   τί δὲ σοὶ τοῦτ᾽; "what's it to you?"; a colloquial formulaic expression (*Lys.* 514; *Th.* 498; *Ec.* 520–21). See Stanton 1973, 89.   ξένους: "ambassadors."   ὦ Δημίδιον: Cf. 726–27n.   ἀδίκως: The theft of the hare is presented as just retribution for the theft of the cake "kneaded at Pylos" (54–57);   ὑφήρπασας: Cf. 54–57n.   νὴ τὸν Ποσειδῶ: That this is the play's final reference to Poseidon as well as to Pylos is fitting, because the contest for the stewardship of Demos is settled and because Paphlagon's attempt to take credit for the Athenian victory at Pylos is rendered laughable.   καὶ ... γάρ: "for, in fact" (*GP* 110–11).   τοὺς ἐκ Πύλου: "the men from Pylos"; Paphlagon took (undeserved) credit for their capture (cf. 54–57n).

1203–4. τὸ μὲν νόημα τῆς θεοῦ, τὸ δὲ κλέμμ᾽ ἐμόν. "The idea was Athena's, the theft mine" (cf. 107–8n). Sausage-seller's improvisation recalls the ingenuity of Athena's favored hero Odysseus, who also prevails through a combination of his own daring and her divine guidance. The line is perhaps paratragic with the surprise substitution of κλέμμα for τοὔργον δ᾽ or the like, but its source (if any) is unknown; cf. Neil ad loc.   ἐγὼ δ᾽ ἐκινδύνευσ᾽: "I took the risk" (i.e., brought the siege at Sphacteria to completion). The manuscripts assign the second half of the line (ἐγὼ δ᾽ ὤπτησά γε.) to Sausage-seller, but he did not "roast" meat at Pylos, and Demos directs his reply at 1205 to Paphlagon rather than to Sausage-seller.

1205–6. **οὐ γὰρ ἀλλὰ:** "For, in fact " or "for, really"; colloquial (Collard 2018, 106–7). **ὑπεραναιδευθήσομαι:** "I'm getting outbrazened" (cf. 397, ἀναιδεύεται). Cf. the hopes of the chorus that Sausage-seller will outdo Paphlagon in brazenness, at 276–77, 330–32, 382–85.

1208. **ἀνὴρ ἀμείνων:** Cf. 765, βέλτιστος ἀνήρ (765).   **τὴν γαστέρα:** A surprise substitution for τὴν πόλιν.

1211–13. **κίστην:** A small, lidded wicker basket that could be used as a storage case (*V.* 529), especially to carry food (*Ach.* 1085–86; *Pax* 666; *Lys.* 1183–84; *Th.* 284–85).   **σιωπῇ:** I.e., "quietly, without a word."   **βασάνισον:** Cf. 512–14n.   **ἔνι:** Cf. 17–18n.   **κἀμέλει:** = καὶ ἀμέλει, "and don't worry," "rest assured"; colloquial (López Eire 1996, 104–5).

1214–16. *Demos opens Sausage-seller's basket.*   **οὐχ ὁρᾷς:** cf. 92n.   **κενήν:** a stark contrast to Paphlagon's full basket at 1218.   **παππίδιον:** "Daddy"; cf. Δημίδιον at 726 and 1199. N. W. Slater (1999, 366) suggests that Sausage-seller turns his empty basket over for added effect.   **αὕτη μὲν:** On μέν *solitarium* (i.e., without the balance of a δέ clause) with the demonstrative pronoun, cf. 777–78n.   **ἡ κίστη τὰ τοῦ δήμου φρονεῖ:** "the basket understands the interests of demos!" The expression τὰ . . . φρονεῖ has a partisan color, cf. *Pax* 640, "φρονεῖ τὰ Βρασίδου"; Hdt. 2.162.6, τὰ ἐκείνου ἐφρόνεον; Th. 5.84.1, τὰ Λακεδαιμονίων φρονεῖν ἔλαβε.

1217. **βάδιζε:** "Come . . ." The verb is "exceedingly common in comedy . . . [but] is very rare in tragedy and other serious poetry and is thus presumably colloquial" (Olson at *Ach.* 393); cf. also Collard 2018, 182.   **δεῦρο:** "over here" (cf. 147–49n).

1218–20. **ὁρᾷς <τάδ᾽>:** Cf. 1195.   **οἴμοι:** "Oh my"; cf. 97, 183–84, 1218-20.   **τῶν ἀγαθῶν ὅσων:** "how many tasty goodies!" ὅσον often occurs in exclamations expressing size or number (Stevens 1976, 21).   **ὅσον τὸ χρῆμα:** "the size of!" χρῆμα is used periphrastically with the genitive (cf. *Ach.* 150; *Nu.* 2; *Av.* 826).   **τυννουτονί:** "teeny-tiny"; colloquial. Aristophanes is fond of the word τύννος (e.g., *Ach.* 367; *Nu.* 392, 878; *Th.* 745; *Ra.* 139).

1221-22. τοιαῦτα μέντοι: "Yes, precisely such things." μέντοι with the demonstrative pronoun is emphatic (*GP* 400).   **προσεδίδου μικρὸν:** "he was giving a small share."   **παρετίθει τὰ μείζονα:** As befits a glutton (cf. the seal of Paphlagon's signet ring at 956).

1224-25. μιαρέ: Cf. 125-26n.   **δή . . . ;** "so, how?"; an indignant question (*GP* 236).   **ἐγὼ δέ τυ ἐστεφάνιξα κήδωρησάμαν:** "But I garlanded you and gave you presents" (Doric dialect). The scholiast (at 1225) identifies the line as a quote from Eupolis' *Helots* (fr. 147), which featured Doric dialect spoken by helots putting a garland on Poseidon. Sommerstein (1980, 51–53) points to the use of the verb κήδωρησάμην at Eup. fr. 89 as further evidence of intertextual rivalry between Aristophanes and Eupolis (see also Kyriakidi 2007, 14–16, 192–94; Olson, *FrC* 2017, 273–76). On the professional relationship between Aristophanes and Eupolis, see Biles 2011; Kyriakidi 2007, 209–15. The use of Doric dialect hints that Paphlagon is an untrustworthy Spartan helot.

1227-28. στέφανον: The garland is ceremoniously transferred to the head of Sausage-seller (τουτῳί), who "immediately offers it to 'Hellenic Zeus' as a victory dedication" (1253) in a "gesture of gratitude" (Biles 2011, 128).   **μαστιγία:** "whipping boy" (cf. *Lys.* 1240, to a slave; *Ra.* 501, perhaps a personal insult, see Dover ad loc.).

1229-30. Πυθικὸς: Refers to Delphi as the source of Paphlagon's oracle (cf. 1036-40, where he, in his oracle to Demos, refers to the tripods in the sanctuary of Apollo there).

1231. τοὐμόν γε φράζων ὄνομα: "Yes, specifying my name." For the force of γε here, cf. 797-98n.

1232-52. This scene parodies the oracular recognition scenes of tragedy in which the oracle a character receives at the beginning of a play foretells a fate the character comes to recognize as having been fulfilled at the end (e.g., S. *OT* 1121-85; Eur. *Ba.* 1271-89). See Rau 1967, 170-73; Landfester 1967, 76-77. Neil (ad loc.) observes that the parody is heightened by this passage's rhythm, which is intentionally comic in only a few lines.

1232-36. ἐλέγξαι . . . / εἴ τι ξυνοίσεις: "to test whether you'll agree with it."   **τεκμηρίῳ:** Cf. 32-33n.   **ἐκπειράσομαι:** With the genitive of person and the accusative of thing.   **ἐφοίτας:** Cf. 988, where the chorus jokes that Cleon had a "pig's education."   **εἰς τίνος διδασκάλου;** "to [the school] of what teacher?" εἰς with an accusative ellipsis of a word for "house," "temple," or the like is colloquial (*V.* 123; *Lys.* 1064, 1211; *Pl.* 621).   **εὔστραις:** The "singeing pits" where a slaughtered pig's bristles were removed (schol. ad loc.).   **κονδύλοις:** "knuckles." Beatings are a regular feature of a harsh upbringing (411–12; *Nu.* 1409–10; *V.* 254–8; *Pax* 122–23 with Olson ad loc.).   **ἡρμοττόμην:** A musical term often associated with education; on musical education in ancient Greece in general, see West 1992, 36–38.

1237-39. πῶς εἶπας; "How's that you say?"   **ὥς μοὒ χρησμὸς ἅπτεται φρενῶν:** "how the oracle grabs hold of my heart." The line suggests a tragic model (cf. Blaydes ad loc.).   **εἶέν:** "Now then" (cf. 1078).   **ἐν παιδοτρίβου:** The παιδοτρίβης was a physical education trainer for students (Dover 1968, lix).   **δὲ:** The late position of the normally postpositive particle is regular following a preposition phrase without the article at clause beginning (KG 2.268; GP 185–86).   **πάλην:** Ordinarily refers to "wrestling style or tactics," but Sausage-seller, raised in the agora, interprets the word to mean "trick" or "ploy." Sommerstein (1981, ad loc.) notes that "this sense is not attested elsewhere for *palê* but is common for the cognate *palaisma* (e.g. *Frogs* 689; Aeschine[s] 3.205)."   **ἐπιορκεῖν καὶ βλέπειν ἐναντία:** "swear an oath and look directly [in the eye]"; a mark of shamelessness (e.g., *Ra.* 1474; S. *OT* 1371–74; cf. 298, κἀπιορκῶ γε βλεπόντων).

1240-42. Φοῖβ᾽ Ἄπολλον Λύκιε: "Phoebus Apollo of Lycia"; a quotation from Euripides' *Telephus* (*TrGF* fr. 700), which recounts the story of the exiled Mysian king Telephus, who disguised himself as a beggar and sought refuge at the Argive temple of Apollo Lykeios (Paus. 2.19.3). Like Telephus, Sausage-seller turns out to be nobler than he at first appeared (146–47, ἀλλ᾽ ὁδὶ προσέρχεται / ὥσπερ κατὰ θεὸν εἰς ἀγοράν). The tragedy is widely quoted by Aristophanes (cf. 810–12n). Boegehold (1999, 69) suggests that Sausage-seller prepares the spectators for the parody—either through an introductory stance or by body language—to "amplify its effect." The invocation is also a prayer parody (see Kleinknecht 1937, 92) and may be a play on the Athenian cult of Apollo Lykeios, whose precinct served as the main training ground for the cavalry and hoplites (*Pax* 356 with Olson ad loc.; X. *HG* 1.1.33; see also R. Parker 2005, 402, 405).   **ἐξανδρούμενος:** Apparently, tragic diction (cf. E. *Ph.* 32, ἐξανδρούμενος; *Suppl.* 703, ἐξηνδρωμένος; cf. also *Ion* 53, ἀπηνδρώθη); see Neil ad loc.   **καί τι καὶ:** "and sometimes even" (*GP* 294).   **βινεσκόμην:** "I was getting fucked." The use of the unaugmented past tense in σκ- gives a "Homeric tone to a very obscene word" (Dover 1997, 87n36). This is the only example in Aristophanes of an omitted augment in comic dialogue, which more commonly occurs "in para-epic hexameters or in some parodic or high-flown lyric passages" (Willi 2003, 247). On the obscene force of βινεῖν, see Henderson 1991a, 152. On sexual perversity and male prostitution as a comic prerequisite to political success, see 77–79n.

1243–46. οὐκέτ᾽ οὐδέν εἰμ᾽ ἐγώ: "I am a nothing now." The phrase is perhaps paratragic (cf. *V.* 997; S. *El.* 677; E. *Alc.* 387; *Andr.* 1077; *Hel.* 1194).   **ὀχούμεθα:** The use of plural for the first-person singular is a stylistic affectation (KG 1.83–84). For the marine metaphor "we ride at anchor," see Taillardat §874. The similarity between this line and fr. 156.11 (ἐπὶ λεπτῶν ἐλπίδων ὠχεῖσθ᾽ ἄρα, "you ride on slender hopes") suggests either a tragic quotation (cf. *TrGF adesp.* 55) or simply a reflection of tragic language; see Farmer 2017, 208.   **ἐν ἀγορᾷ:** Where good-for-nothings congregate.   **'πὶ ταῖς πύλαις:** A pun on Pylos and perhaps a reference to the Sacred Gate located just outside the northwest walls of the city, near and close to the Ceramicus; see Lind 1991, 175–84.

1247. τὸ τάριχος: "Dried fish." The word's gender is variable (e.g., masculine in fr. 207; cf. Willi 2003, 253).

1248–49. οἴμοι, πέπρακται τοῦ θεοῦ τὸ θέσφατον: "Alas, the god's prophecy has been done"; a paratragic quotation from Sophocles (fr. 885a).   **κυλίνδετ᾽ εἴσω τόνδε τὸν δυσδαίμονα:** An allusion to the eccyclema (see glossary) in answer to Paphlagon's command. The verse appears to parody either Euripides' *Bellerophon* (*TrGF* fr. 311, κομίζετ᾽ εἴσω τόνδε δυσδαίμονα), with the substitution of κυλίνδετ[ε], or his *Sthenoboea* (*TrGF* 671.1, κομίζετ᾽ εἴσω τήνδε). Boegehold (1999, 69–70), taking the commands as a "stage direction," suggests that the actor would have raised a hand and used body language to signal to the audience that "something outside the action was about to transpire."

1251–52. σε δ᾽ ἄλλος τις … / … εὐτυχὴς δ᾽ ἴσως: *Paphlagon tosses his garland to Sausage-seller and collapses on the eccyclema.*   Paphlagon's farewell to the garland parodies the farewell of the heroine to her marriage bed (λέκτρον) in Euripides' *Alcestis* (181–82, σὲ δ᾽ ἄλλη τις γυνὴ κεκτήσεται, / σώφρων μὲν οὐκ ἂν μᾶλλον, εὐτυχὴς δ᾽ ἴσως).   **κεκτήσεται:** The future perfect implies the immediate consequence or certainty of an action accomplished in the future (cf. 1370–71; KG 1.179; Smyth §1956).   **κλέπτης … ἄν:** Sc., ὤν. On the ellipsis of a verb form with modal ἄν, see KG 1.243; *MT* §227.

1253. Ἑλλάνιε Ζεῦ, σὸν τὸν νικητήριον: Cf. 1227–28n. The address to Hellenic Zeus, patron of all Greeks (Hdt. 9.7.2; cf. Burkert 1985, 130), implies that Cleon's defeat is a victory for all of Hellas (not just for Athens) and particularly for Aristophanes in this dramatic competition. Ἑλλάνικος (the Doric form of the epithet) is also a cult title of Zeus on Aegina (Pi. *N.* 5.10; *Pae.* 6.125) and may allude to Aristophanes' family owning property and residing there (*Ach.* 652–54 with schol. at *Ach.* 378). The verse may be a citation from tragedy (Rau 1967, 173n10).

1254–56. Some manuscripts attribute these lines to the coryphaeus, but cf. 177–78, where Slave A first tells Sausage-seller that he is destined to become a "big-shot man" (ἀνὴρ μέγιστος).

1254. ὦ χαῖρε, καλλίνικε: "Hail, fair victor." This shout or chant (in full, τήνελλα καλλίνικος) was often used to mark both athletic triumphs (e.g., [Archil.] fr. 324W; Pi. *O.* 9.1–4) and nonathletic ones (e.g., *Ach.* 1227, 1228, 1233; *Av.* 1764); the word τήνελλα is said to be "an imitation of some sound of pipe playing" (schol. at *Av.* 1764).

1255–56. ἀνὴρ: Cf. 176–78n.   **αἰτῶ . . . / ὅπως ἔσομαι:** For object clauses with ὅπως after verbs of asking, entreating, exhorting, commanding, and forbidding, see KG 2.373; *MT* §355.   **Φᾶνος:** Phanos (*PA* 14078; *PAA* 916585), a crony and drinking companion of Cleon (*V.* 1220); his name is used here for the sake of puns on φάνειν and "sycophant" (cf. 300, φανῶ σε τοῖς πρυτάνεις; Kanavou 2011, 63).   **ὑπογραφεὺς δικῶν:** "signer of indictments." This is not an official executive officer but rather an administrative clerk, a notary, whose signature authorized legal accusations on behalf of another (schol. at 1256).

1257–58. ἐμοὶ δέ γ': As at 356.   **Ἀγοράκριτος:** Not a name of any known Athenian, although it is attested outside of Athens (e.g., Paus. 9.34.1 mentions a contemporary Parian sculptor by that name who was a pupil of Phidias).   **ἐν τἀγορᾷ . . . κρινόμενος:** By combining the elements ἀγορά (marketplace) and κριτος (disputant), Sausage-seller comically etymologizes his name to mean "disputant in the marketplace." The audience would also recognize and appreciate the proper alternative meaning of the name, "chosen by the assembly"; *agora* can, in its archaic sense, mean "assembly," and the element -κριτος (from κρίνομαι) can mean "to be chosen." The latter interpretation befits Sausage-seller's transformation from lowlife to the champion of Demos / the demos. See Kanavou (2011, 49–51) for deliberately ambiguous Aristophanic names that rely on context to be comprehensible.   **γὰρ:** Causal; implies that he acquired the nickname from his upbringing in the agora (181, 217–18, 293).   **ἐβοσκόμην:** "I supported myself" (cf. 255–57n).

1259–60. τοίνυν: "Well then" (cf. 30–31n).   **παραδίδωμι τουτονί:** As if he's handing over an enemy of the state (cf. LSJ s.v. A.2).

1261. καὶ μὴν ἐγώ: "Indeed, I will."

1263. Κεχηναίων: An ad hoc coinage combining κεχηνότῶν, "of the slack-jawed, clueless" and Ἀθηναίων, "of the Athenians." The motif of a sausage-seller ends here; transformed into the character Agoracritus, the actor serves as an honest advisor/steward of Demos, following the second parabasis (1264–1315). *The eccyclema bearing Paphlagon is withdrawn as Demos and Sausage-seller go into the house.*

1264–1315. Second parabasis. While Agoracritus "rejuvenates" Demos, the chorus fills in the time with attacks on four people: Thumantis (ode, 1264–73), Ariphrades (epirrhema, 1274–89), Cleonymus (antode, 1290–99), Hyperbolus (antepirrhema, 1300–1315). The meters for the strophe and antistrophe are dactylo-epitrite; the epirrhematic sections are in trochaic tetrameter catalectics.

1264–73. Strophe = antistrophe, 1290–99. Meter: dactylo-epitrite which comprises sequences of hemiepes (- ᴗ ᴗ - ᴗ ᴗ -), a link syllable, and cretics (- ᴗ -) with an ithyphallic (- ᴗ - ᴗ - -) as the final unit of the stanza (cf. Sommerstein 1981 at 1264; L. P. E. Parker 1997, 180–82). Dactylo-epitrite was a favorite meter of Pindar (cf. West 1982, 69–76). The song depends on literary and metrical allusions for its effect with some unusual aspects, such as the absence of personal abuse, especially at the beginning. In this instance, the avoidance of personal abuse is ironic (Neil ad loc.).

1264–66. τί κάλλιον ἀρχομένοισιν ἢ καταπαυομένοισιν / ἢ θοᾶν ἵππων ἐλατῆρας ἀείδειν . . . ; "What is more noble for beginning or ending [our song] than what [we] drivers of swift horses sing?" The ode adapts the meter and language of the beginning of a Pindaric processional ode to the cult of Leto and Artemis (fr. 89a); see Kugelmeier 1996, 92–94. Aristophanes here renders the direct object of the Pindaric ode (θοᾶν ἵππων ἐλάτειραν ἀεῖσαι, "to sing of the driver of swift horses") into the subject of his song; see Fraenkel 1962, 204–7.

1267–68. Λυσίστρατον: Lysistratos (*PA* 9630; *PAA* 618290) belonged to the deme of Cholargos, located to the northwest side of the city (Traill 1975, 47). Aristophanes refers to Λυσίστρατος as impoverished (*Ach.* 855) and as a practical joker and a philologue (*V.* 787–95, 1308–13; fr. 205.1–2). Since

Λυσίστρατος is a common Athenian name (there are ninety-five other examples in *LGPN* s.v.), it is impossible to distinguish between this individual and other men of the same name.   **Θούμαντιν:** Nothing is known of this man (*PAA* 515550) except that Hermippus (fr. 36) portrays him as poor and emaciated.   **ἀνέστιον:** "without a hearth" (cf. *Pax* 1097; *Il.* 9.63).

1270-73. καὶ γὰρ οὗτος: Cf. 250.   **ὦ φίλ᾽ Ἄπολλον:** "Beloved Apollo." The invocation is suggestive of a religious hymn (Kleinknecht 1937, 109n2; Horn 1970, 46).   **θαλεροῖς δακρύοις:** characteristic epic and tragic vocabulary (e.g., *Il.* 2.266, 6.496, 24.9, 24.794; E. *IA* 39-40).   **ἁπτόμενος φαρέτρας:** "clutching the quivers." Thumantis is imagined as a supplicant clinging to a statue of Apollo the "Far Shooter" (ἑκηβόλος).   **Πυθῶνι δίᾳ:** "at divine Pytho"; locative dative without a preposition (see Willi 2003, 251-52). The phrase is probably quoted or adopted from Pindar (e.g., *P.* 7.11, Πυθῶνι δίᾳ; *O.* 2.49, Πυθῶνι). Whether Thumantis had visited Delphi in the recent past, as a suppliant or in any other capacity, is uncertain but possible as Thucydides (4.118) does mention that there was a truce guaranteeing passage to Delphi during the Peloponnesian War.   **μὴ κακῶς πένεσθαι:** "[praying to] not be wretchedly poor." The act of clutching Apollo's quivers in supplication rather than grasping his knees or chin is comic parody (Kleinknecht 1937, 109n2).

1274-89. Epirrhema; = 1300-1315. Meter: trochaic tetrameter catalectics.

1274-86. Situating the epirrhema in the iambographic tradition in which the use of abusive language is a convention of the genre (as it is of comic drama) justifies the abuse of Ariphrades (one of the πονηροί); Rosen (1988, 77) concludes, "If it is an 'honorable thing' (τιμή 1275) to make fun of Ariphrades with the obscene diction of 1284-86, then the abuse of Cleon too is honorable."

1274-75. λοιδορῆσαι: Cf. 89-90n.   **τοῖσι χρηστοῖς:** Cf. 191-93.   **ὅστις:** Sc., τούτῳ as antecedent.

1276-79. μὲν οὖν: "Well then."   **ἄνθρωπος:** = ὁ ἄνθρωπος.   **αὐτὸς:** "on his own accord" (KG 1.653; Smyth §1209a).   **ἔνδηλος:** "well-known." This ancient variant for εὔδηλος appears in comedy only here; see Olson at *Ach.* 1130.   **οὐκ ἂν ἀνδρὸς ἐμνήσθην:** "I wouldn't mention a man [as I am doing now]"; an example of *praeteritio* (i.e., calling attention to something by seeming to disregard it).   **νῦν δ᾽ ... γὰρ:** "But as it is." As Boegehold (1999, 70) imagines, "a movement of the head signifying 'no' could easily

accompany the adversative phrase, 'but as it is.'"   Ἀρίγνωτον: Arignotus
(*PA* 1612; *PAA* 162000), son of Automenes, was a celebrated citharode player
(*V.* 1277–78).   οὐδεὶς ὅστις οὐκ ἐπίσταται: I.e., "everyone knows."   τὸ
λευκὸν οἶδεν ἢ τὸν ὄρθιον νόμον: "[if] he can tell white from the orthion
mode"; i.e., if he knows good music from bad. The "orthion mode" was a high-
pitched cithardic mode/tuning ascribed to the musician and poet Terpander
(West 1992, 352n119). Aristophanes here plays on the common phrase, τὸ
λευκὸν ἢ τὸν μέλαν οἶδεν (literally, "he knows white from black"; see schol. ad
loc.), which meant "if he had half a brain" (Sommerstein 1981, ad loc.).

1280–83. οὖν: Cf. 80–81n.   ἀδελφὸς αὐτῷ: In addition to
Ariphrades, there was a third brother, name unknown, who was an actor
(*V.* 1279).   Ἀριφράδης: Ariphrades (*PA* 2201; *PAA* 202305) was a
contemporary rival comic poet who made fun of tragic poets (Arist. *Po.*
1458b31–32, Ἀριφράδης τοὺς τραγῳδοὺς ἐκωμῴδει). Aristophanes attacks
Ariphrades as a devotee of cunnilingus (*V.* 1280–83; *Pax* 883–85; fr. 926),
particularly for engaging in this practice at brothels (*V.* 1280–83) and "thus
overdoing it in the poet's eyes" (Henderson 1991a, 52).   ἀλλὰ τοῦτο μὲν
καὶ βούλεται: Ariphrades is not only a πονηρός but a shamelessly willful
one. Cf. a similar description of the contemporary politician Epichares at
And. 1.95: ὁ πάντων πονηρότατος καὶ βουλόμενος εἶναι τοιοῦτος, "He was
most wicked of all men and he was willing to be such."   οὐ γὰρ οὐδ᾽ ἂν
ᾐσθόμην: "I wouldn't even have noticed"; sc., "if he hadn't been so utterly
wicked" or the like.   παμπόνηρος: "utterly depraved" (cf. 415).   ἀλλὰ
καὶ: As at 985.   προσεξηύρηκέ τι: "he invented something [new]."

1284–87. αἰσχραῖς ἡδοναῖς λυμαίνεται: "He sullies [his tongue] with
disgusting pleasures." The implication is that contact with the female
pudenda defiles his mouth (R. Parker 1983, 100–101).   κασωρείοισι: =
κασαλβίοισι; i.e., "brothels" (schol. ad loc.).   δρόσον: "dew"; a euphemism
for sexual secretions (Henderson 1991a, 145). For "dew" in Greek poetry
and religion, see Boedeker 1984.   μολύνων τὴν ὑπήνην: "befouling his
beard" (Henderson 1991a, 175, 185).   κυκῶν τὰς ἐσχάρας: "stirring up
their hotboxes." ἐσχάρα, which normally means "hearths," here refers to
the labia (schol. ad loc., τὰ χείλη τῶν γυναικείων αἴδιον; Henderson 1991a,
143).   Πολυμνήστεια: Apparently, songs performed with instrumental
accompaniment (cf. Cratin. fr. 338, καὶ Πολυμνήστει᾽ ἀείδει, μουσικήν τε
μανθάνει, "and he sing songs of Polymnestus and learns music"). Polymnestus
is traditionally identified as a seventh-century musician (citharode) and
composer from Colophon (Alcm., *PMG* 145; Pi. fr. 188). How Ariphrades was
"acting like Polymnestrus" is unclear, as no evidence (excluding this passage)

suggests that the latter's music was considered lude or undignified or, for that matter, whether his literary biography is reliable; see Olson and Seaberg, *FrC* 2018, 109–10.   **ξυνών**: "being intimate." συνεῖναι is a stock euphemism for sexual intercourse (cf. *V.* 475 wih Henderson 1991a, 159).   **Οἰωνίχῳ**: A musician mentioned in an anonymous comic fragment (*Com. adesp.* 396).

1288–89. Following the comments of the scholia (ad loc.), some ancient scholars connected a similarly phrased imprecation near the end of an epirrhematic passage (dated to 412 BCE) in Eupolis' *Demes* (fr. 99.33–34, ὅστις οὖν ἄρχειν τοιούτους ἄνδρας α̣[ἱρεῖται / ποτε μήτε πρόβατ' αὐτῶι τεκνοῖτο μήτε γῆ κ[αρπὸν φέροι) to that poet's claim that he had a hand in the composition of *Knights* (fr. 89), and those scholars subsequently concluded that Eupolis, not Aristophanes, authored the entire second parabasis of this comedy; see Storey 2003, 281–88.

1290–99. Antistrophe = strophe, 1264–73. Like the strophe, the antistrophe parodies lyric verse and draws on mock-epic language to ridicule the notoriously insatiable appetite of Cleonymus. In the strophe, the chorus had prayed to Apollo to save Thumantis from starvation; here, the chorus implores Cleonymus not to consume all the food, leaving the singers to starve.

1290–93. **πολλάκις ἐννυχίαισι φροντίσι**: "Often with thoughts at night." The motif of restless ruminating nights perhaps parodies Euripides' *Hippolytus* (375–76, νυκτὸς ἐν μακρῷ χρόνῳ / . . . ἐφρόντισ(α), "in the long passage of night, I [sc., Phaedra] have pondered"; cf. Rau 1967, 120, 189).   **διεζήτηχ' ὁπόθεν**: "I have thoroughly inquired where [on earth]." This is the first attestation of the compound form of the verb (repeated at *Th.* 439). The simplex form often appears in contexts of scientific investigation or philosophical inquiry of some sort (Pl. *Ap.* 23b; *Men.* 73d; *Theat.* 201a; X. *Mem.* 1.1.15).   **Κλεώνυμος**: See 957–59n.

1294–99. **ἐρεπτόμενον**: "Feeding on," "chomping." The verb is found mostly in epic, where it is often applied to animals (*Il.* 2.776, 5.196, of horses; *Od.* 19.553, of geese).   **τῶν ἐχόντων ἀνέρων**: "of wealthy men"; ἀνέρων in place of the normal ἀνδρῶν is epic diction.   **ἂν ἐξελθεῖν** . . . / . . . **ἀντιβολεῖν ἄν**: The infinitives with ἄν here represent an iterative (not potential) action (*MT* §210).   **ἀπὸ τῆς σιπύης**: "from the feed bin" (Pl. 806; Pherecr. fr. 151).   **ὦ ἄνα**: "O Lord." This lofty and ancient vocative (ἄναξ) is used primarily for gods, kings, and heroes. In Aristophanes, the addressee is generally a deity (e.g., *Nu.* 264; *V.* 875–76), but it can also be a mortal, as here (cf. also *Pax* 90); see Dickey 1996, 102–3.   **πρὸς γονάτων**:

"by your knees"; a set phrase (probably paratragic here) for a supplicant
seeking protection (*Ach.* 414; *Pax* 1113; E. *Med.* 709–10; *Hipp.* 607). For the
act of supplication, see Gould 1973, especially 75–77.

1300–15. Antepirrhema = epirrhema, 1274–79. The chorus leader reports
the conversation he overheard among gossiping triremes assembled (like
gossiping women) to discuss their opposition to Hyperbolus' plan to send an
expedition of one hundred ships against Carthage (598–99n). The triremes'
personification recalls the personification of the knights' horses as rowers in
the fleet, in the antepirrhema of the parabasis (595–610). When read together,
these two passages connect the interests of the knights and navy. The triremes
are not simply talking ships but also represent the female perspective on
Athens' wealth and security; see Anderson 2003. Cratinus' *Pytine*, produced in
the year following *Knights*, may also have featured a female chorus of triremes
(fr. 210) and probably attacked (fr. 213) Aristophanes for using the materials
of Eupolis. Aristophanes' *Merchant Ships* also had a "female" chorus.

1300–1. φασὶν ἀλλήλαις ξυνελθεῖν . . . εἰς λόγον: The personified triremes-
women assemble as if for a public debate (εἰς λόγον), to exchange gossip at
their communal gathering place. On gossip as an activity through which
public opinion was nourished and disseminated, see Hunter 1994, 96–119;
S. Lewis 1996, 10–23.   **τριήρεις:** Also mentioned at 279, 555, 1073–74,
1185, 1353; cf. *Pax* 538–40, where Aristophanes personifies cities (πόλεις,
also a conveniently feminine noun) as incessant talkers.   **γεραιτέρα:** The
senior speaker of an imaginative "assembly" (cf. LSJ s.v. γεραιός). The notion
of women holding a quasi-political assembly is developed more fully in
Thesmophoriazusae and *Ecclesiazusae*.

1302–4. παρθένοι: "maidens"; a double meaning playing on the
personification. For the association of nautical imagery and terminology
with sexual congress, see Henderson 1991a, 164–65.   **ἡμῶν ἑκατὸν εἰς
Καρχηδόνα:** "A hundred of us [to go] to Carthage." The Athenians harbored
imperial ambitions in Sicily and the western Mediterranean for some time
(cf. 173–74n; Th. 3.86.3–5). Whether this passage refers to a real proposal by
Hyperbolus to send a new expedition to the west is unknown. The triremes
are not opposed to imperialism per se, as they are after all its main tools. But
they reject expansionist adventures such as the conquest of Carthage (cf.
Th. 1.144.1, 2.65.7, for Pericles' policy to tend to the navy and not seek to
extend the empire during the war).   **ὀξίνην:** "sour-tasting." The adjective
is usually applied to vinegary wine (Hermipp. fr. 88; Diph. fr. 83) and, by

extension, characterizes Hyperbolus' "hawkish" policies (cf. *V.* 1082, of fighting spirit). Ὑπέρβολον: Hyperbolus (*PA* 13910; *PAA* 902050), son of Antiphanes of the deme Perithoidas, was a wealthy lamp merchant (739) who first came into prominence as a prosecutor in the law courts (cf. *Ach.* 846–47). After the death of Cleon, he emerged as a leading demagogue and, thus, a prime target for comic abuse (cf. Olson at *Pax* 681). Ostracized in 417/16 through the combined efforts of Nicias and Alcibiades (Plu. *Nic.* 11.3–4; *Alc.* 13.4–5; see Rosenbloom 2004), Hyperbolus was murdered on the island of Samos during the oligarchic coup of 411 (Th. 8.73.3).

1305–6. ἀνασχετόν: "It was intolerable." ἥτις ἀνδρῶν ἆσσον οὐκ ἐληλύθει: "One who had not come near men." The language evokes her virginal status as a trireme without a crew (ἀνδρῶν) and as a female without a man/husband (ἀνδρός).

1307–10. ἀποτρόπαι᾿: "Averter [of Evil]"; an epithet of Apollo (*V.* 161; *Av.* 61; *Pl.* 359, 854) and stock cry of alarm. ὑπὸ τερηδόνων: "by ship worms," an especially destructive insect for wood (Theophr. *HP* 5.4.4–5). σαπεῖσ᾿: The adjective σαπρός is often applied to old women and aging whores (e.g., *Ec.* 884, 926, 1098–99; Hermipp. fr. 9). Paphlagon's earlier threat to appoint Sausage-seller as trierarch of an ancient ship with rotten sails (σαπρόν, 918) anticipates this passage. καταγηράσομαι: καταγηράω denotes age of human beings, not of inanimate objects (LSJ s.v.). Its use here amounts to a declaration of spinsterhood; not only will the trireme refuse to submit to marriage, but she will grow old without bearing children, and there will be no new generation of triremes. The life expectancy of a trireme is estimated to have been about twenty years (Morrison, Coates, and Rankov 2000, 199–200). οὐδὲ . . . γε: Here, marks a change in subject (*GP* 156). Ναυφάντης γε τῆς Ναύσωνος: Nauphantes, "Shipshape," is probably a comic invention rather than a real name of a trireme. The use of the patronymic implies that this trireme and her trireme-maiden companions (παρθένοι) come from respectable families. The name of her "father," Nauson, is attested in Athens as a slave's name (*IG* i³ 1032, 275; 405 BCE). ὦ θεοί: A colloquial oath attested in comedy and tragedy in the classical period (e.g., *Ach.* 1058; *Th.* 905; S. *Ph.* 779; E. *Hel.* 72; *Or.* 385). ἐκ πεύκης . . . καὶ ξύλων: "of pine and timbers." Pine was the principal timber used in the construction of triremes (cf. E. *Med.* 4; Pl. *Lg.* 4. 705c; Theophr. *HP* 5.7.1–5), because it is more resistant to decay than other woods and because its lighter weight allows for greater boat speed (Morrison, Coates, and Rankov 2000, 179–81).

1311–12. καθῆσθαι: As if a suppliant (cf. Hdt. 5.63.1; in an oracle, 7.140.2).   **τὸ Θησεῖον:** The Theseum was a refuge for fugitive slaves and people of low status who were fearful of men in power (cf. fr. 577; Plu. *Thes.* 36.2–3). In "fleeing," the triremes would seek escape from Hyperbolus (Christiansen 1984, 23).   **πλεούσας:** "sailing." Her mode of locomotion, qua ship, is comically transformed into pedestrian flight to the sanctuary of Theseus.   **'πὶ τῶν Σεμνῶν θεῶν:** Sc., ἱερόν. The shrine of the Semnai, "August Goddesses" (called the Erinyes or Eumenides), lay close to the Panathenaic Way, between the Areopagus and the Acropolis, and was an ancient sanctuary for suppliants (*Th.* 224; Th. 1.126.1; Paus. 7.25.1); see R. Parker 1996, 298–99. The wheeled ship carrying Athena's peplos in the Panathenaic procession anchored near the shrine of the Semnai (Paus. 1.29.1); see Travlos 1971, 423, fig. 540.

1313–15. ἐγχανεῖται: Refers to wide-mouthed, mocking laughter, usually directed at a person (cf. Biles and Olson at *V.* 719–21).   **πλείτω:** Third-person singular imperative.   **ἐς κόρακας:** Cf. 892n.   **σκάφας:** "skiffs," with a pun on the meaning "tub" or "bowl."   **καθελκύσας:** "Dragging to the sea," as if launching a trireme (*Ach.* 544–45; E. *Hel.* 1531).

1316–34. Meter: anapestic tetrameter catalectics. The scene parodies prayers for a divine epiphany (cf., e.g., *Nu.* 263–66, the arrival of Air, Aether, and Clouds; *Av.* 1706–19, the arrival of Peistetairos and Basileia). See Kleinknecht 1939, 59–60; Horn 1970, 27.

1316–18. *Enter Sausage-seller, dressed in new clothes.*   **εὐφημεῖν χρὴ:** "be silent." The command for silence is routinely uttered before a "solemn" occasion or significant activity (e.g., *Ach.* 237, 241; *Nu.* 263; *V.* 868; *Pax* 96, 434; *Av.* 959; *Th.* 39, 295). The solemn occasion here is the singing of the paean (1318).   **μαρτυριῶν ἀπέχεσθαι / καὶ τὰ δικαστήρια συγκλῄειν:** "to refrain from [calling] witnesses and close up the law courts." The rejuvenation of Demos calls for special celebration and thanksgiving; historically, the law courts (Paphlagon's seat of power in the play) were suspended on festival days ([X.] *Ath.* 3.8). There is also a tongue-in-cheek suggestion that litigation is a "polluting activity" that prevents participants from taking part in religious rituals (at 1332, the "stink" of the law courts is contrasted with the smell of myrrh and ambrosia).   **παιωνίζειν:** To sing a paean (hymn) in honor of the god Paean (who is often associated with Apollo) calls for a ritual shout or song of thanksgiving for victory, success, or salvation (cf. the paeonic cry of thanksgiving at 408).   **τὸ θέατρον:** Cf. 232–33n.

1319–20. ὦ ταῖς ἱεραῖς φέγγος Ἀθήναις: "O light of holy Athens." Sausage-seller is addressed as if a god or conquering hero returning home (cf. 149; *Pl.* 640, μέγα βροτοῖσι φέγγος, of Asclepius); see Taillardat §679.   **ταῖς νήσοις:** Cf. 169–70n.   **ἐπίκουρε:** "defender [of the islands]."   **φήμην ἀγαθὴν:** "good report" (cf. *V.* 864, of a propitious song).   **ἐφ᾽ ὅτῳ:** "whereby" (KG 2.505 A3; Smyth §2279).   **κνισῶμεν ἀγυιάς:** The phrase has strong religious connotations (cf., e.g., *Av.* 1232–33, ἐπ᾽ ἐσχάραις / κνισᾶν τ᾽ ἀγυιάς, where Iris complains of burnt offerings being withheld; *D.* 21.51, κατὰ τὰ πάτρια καὶ κνισᾶν ἀγυιάς, where the city is filled with the odor of burnt offerings as an ancestral tradition).

1321. The magical rejuvenation of Demos by means of boiling plays on Sausage-seller's professional expertise in preparing and cooking flesh. The rejuvenation also calls to mind the story of Medea successfully rejuvenating Jason's father, Aeson, in the same way (*Nostoi* fr. 6 Allen; Ov. *Met.* 7.159–293); see Rau 1967, 189. The story of Medea boiling and destroying Peleus also lurks in the background (schol. ad loc.). On rejuvenation as a symbol of felicity, see Olson 1990.

1321–23. ἀφεψήσας: "having boiled down" (cf. Taillardat §49).   **καλὸν:** "handsome."   **καὶ ποῦ . . . ;** "And where?" The idiom signals the speaker's need for more information as well as a degree of incredulity (*GP* 310).   **ἐπινοίας:** Cf. 89–90n.   **ἐν ἰοστεφάνοις . . . ταῖς ἀρχαίαισιν Ἀθήναις:** "in violet-crowned Athens of old." Cf. Pi. fr. 76, a well-known dithyramb in praise of Athens' role in the Persian Wars. The Athenians took such pleasure and pride in the song's celebratory epithets that they made Pindar their πρόξενος and rewarded him with a cash prize (Isoc. 15.166). The colorful and fragrant garlands befit a happy and victorious personified city (Kugelmeier 1996, 104).

1324. σκευήν: The Ionian fashion or style that Demos here wears (1331–32n). Thucydides (1.6.3) writes, Ἰώνων τοὺς πρεσβυτέρους κατὰ τὸ ξυγγενὲς ἐπὶ πολὺ αὕτη ἡ σκευὴ κατέσχεν, "this fashion obtained for a long time among the older men of the Ionians owing to their kinship."

1325–26. Ἀριστείδῃ: Aristides (*PA* 1695; *PAA* 165170), Miltiades (*PA* 10212; *PAA* 653820; mentioned again at *Eq.* 1387), and Themistocles (cf. 763–65n, 811–12) were Athenian heroes of the Persian Wars. The miraculous rejuvenation of Demos "manages to achieve two seemingly contradictory things at the same time: a nostalgic shift back to the glorious days of Aristides and Miltiades . . . and an invigorating shift forward into the audience's present

and new future" (Revermann 2006, 120–21).   ἀνοιγνυμένων ψόφος:
Creaking doors signal that someone is about to enter the comic stage (e.g.,
Ra. 603–4; Men. Dys. 586).   ἤδη: "really [loud]," adds emphasis (cf.
429–31n).   προπυλαίων: The scene suddenly shifts to the Propylaea, the
western gate of the Acropolis. The Propylaea (and Athena) are also featured at
Lys. 265; see Anderson 1995, 39–51.

1327–28. ὀλολύξατε: Cf. 616–17n.   ἵν᾽: "where."   κλεινὸς: Elevated
poetic vocabulary (Neil ad loc.).

1329–30. ὦ ταὶ λιπαραὶ καὶ ἰοστέφανοι . . . Ἀθῆναι: Cf. 1323. The scholiast
notes that λιπαραί is especially fitting because Athens was famous for its
olives; but Dover (at Nu. 299) notes that "Pindar uses λιπαρός of many other
places."   τὸν τῆς Ἑλλάδος . . . μόναρχον: Context determines whether
the term μόναρχος, neutral in itself, should be understood in a negative
or positive sense (cf. 797, of Paphlagon; E. Supp. 351–52). In Aristophanes
Athenian supremacy during the Peloponnesian War takes several forms (e.g.,
Pax 1082, κοινῇ τῆς Ἑλλάδος ἄρχειν, Athenian/Spartan hegemony; Lys. 1296–
1321, the supremacy of Athens' patron goddess in the Spartan pantheon; cf.
Anderson 2011/12).   τῆς γῆς τῆσδε: Cf. 566.

1331–32. The rejuvenated Demos, wearing a new mask (cf. 1324n),
emerges from the gates of the Propylaea.   For the mask, see Stone
1981, 44; Compton-Engle 2015, 47–48.   ὅδ᾽: "here."   ὁρᾶν: Sc.,
ἐστι.   τεττιγοφόρας: "wearing a τέττιξ." The golden hairpin shaped like
a grasshopper was identified with upper-class dress but fell out of fashion
shortly after the Persian Wars (cf. Nu. 984; Th. 1.6.3).   ἀρχαίῳ σχήματι
λαμπρός: "radiant in the old fashion"; i.e., long hair and an ornate himation
draped over an ankle-length linen chiton (see Stone 1981, 403).   οὐ
χοιρινῶν ὄζων ἀλλὰ σπονδῶν: "smelling not of law courts but of libations."
χοιριναί, literally "mussel shells," were sometimes used in place of voting
pebbles in the law courts (V. 333; Pollux 8.16). "Smelling of libations" refers
to festive celebrations and peace treaties (e.g., Ach. 195–99).   σμύρνῃ
κατάλειπτος: "anointed with myrrh" (cf. 1092–95, on the rejuvenation of
Demos with ambrosia; Pax 860–62, rejuvenation of Trygaeus with myrrh).

1333–34. χαῖρ᾽: "Hail." The verb and its cognates are often used in kletic
hymns to express joy (cf. Pulleyn 1997, 16–55, on χάρις in prayers).   ὦ
βασιλεῦ τῶν Ἑλλήνων: Cf. 1330.   σοι ξυγχαίρομεν: "we rejoice with you."
Here, the phrase is liturgical (cf. Pax 1317–18); see Kleinknecht 1939, 64–
65.   τῆς γὰρ πόλεως ἄξια πράττεις καὶ τοῦ ᾽ν Μαραθῶνι τροπαίου: The

generation of Athenians who fought at Marathon in 490 (Μαραθωνομάχαι, *Ach.* 181) were treated like heroes (cf. 565–66n), and their historic victory came to be regarded as justifying Athens' claim to wealth and empire (cf. *V.* 707–11 with MacDowell at 711).

1335–83. Shocked and ashamed to have been so stupid and gullible (1355), Demos vows to correct past abuses, tend to the security of the city, and restore the moral and ethical values associated with Athens in the days of Aristides and Miltiades.

1335–38. ὦ φίλτατ' ἀνδρῶν: Cf. 611n.   δέδρακας . . . ἀφεψήσας: Cf. 1321.   ἐγώ; "Who, me?" Cf. 168.   ὦ μέλ': Cf. 671.   γὰρ: Explanatory: "for [if you did] . . ."

1339. τί δ' . . . ; "And what . . . ?" At the opening of a question in dialogue, δέ "denotes that the information [the speaker] already possesses is inadequate," and "usually there is a note of surprise, impatience or indignation" (*GP* 173–74).   πρὸ τοῦ: "before, in the past." Cf. 573–74.   κάτειπε: Often suggests "disclosing information that may be harmful" (Neil ad loc.).

1340–42. πρῶτον μέν: Cf. 1366; "does its standard Aristophanic duty by beginning the process of offering support for the preceding assertion" (Olson at *Pax* 739–40).   ἐραστής εἰμι σὸς φιλῶ τέ σε / καὶ κήδομαί σου: For ἐραστής in its patriotic sense; cf. 732n.

1344. ἀνωρτάλιζες κἀκερουτίας: "You used to flap your wings and toss your horns" (cf. Taillardat §332). Sausage-seller perhaps flaps his arms like a rooster (a traditional courtship gift; cf. 1192) and tosses his head for emphasis.   ἐγώ; "I did?"

1345–49. ἀντὶ τούτων: "In return for these things"; cf. 1404.   τί φής; "what do you say!?" The exclamatory question is *extra metrum* (as at *Nu.* 235 and *Av.* 414 with Dunbar ad loc.)   τὰ δ' ὦτα . . . ἐξεπετάννυτο / ὥσπερ σκιάδειον: On the comparison of a human ear to a parasol, see Taillardat §78.   δ' . . . γ': "Yes, and . . ."; marks continuity with Sausage-seller's earlier train of thought that was interrupted by Demos (*GP* 154).   ἀνόητος . . . : Cf. 545, κοὐκ ἀνοήτως to describe Aristophanes.

1350–52. νὴ Δί': "Indeed, by Zeus" (cf. 26–28n).   λεγοίτην: Sc., ἐν τῇκκλησίᾳ (1340); optative dual.   ῥήτορε: Nominative dual.   ποιεῖσθαι ναῦς μακράς: "to build long ships."   καταμισθοφορῆσαι τοῦθ': "to use it [i.e., the same sum] for state pay." "For the use of offers of wages to influence public debate," see Olson at *Ach.* 656–58n.

1354–55. οὗτος: "Hey, you . . ."; cf. 821–22n.   **κύπτεις:** For the gesture of hanging one's head (thereby avoiding eye contact) in consciousness of mistakes, cf. *Th.* 930 with Austin and Olson ad loc.; Cairns 1993, 352.   **τοι:** "for sure" or the like. The particle reveals his emotional state (cf. *GP* 541). Citing this passage and 1121–30, Ostwald (1986, 226–28) remarks, "If someone can show the people that they have been deceived by unscrupulous leaders, they can come back to their senses."

1358–60. βωμολόχος ξυνήγορος: "Foolish advocate." For the adjective, cf. 902; on its uses in Aristophanes and Old Comedy in general, see Dover at *Ra.* 358n. A ξυνήγορος is either an advocate who speaks in court on behalf of a litigant or, as here, a special prosecutor appointed to conduct trials for serious offenses against the state (see MacDowell at *V.* 482–83; Todd 1993, 94–95; Phillips 2013, nos. 302, 371, 391). Aristophanes routinely speaks unfavorably of ξυνήγοροι (e.g., *Ach.* 685–86, 703–5, 715–16; *Nu.* 1089–90; *V.* 482–83; frr. 205.9, 424).   **τοῖς δικασταῖς ἄλφιτα:** "groats for the jurymen." The primary meaning of ἄλφιτα in Aristophanes is "roughly milled grain" (Moritz 1949, 117n5); here, the term is substituted for "jury pay," in a paraprosdokeion joke.   **εἰ μὴ καταγνώσεσθε ταύτην τὴν δίκην:** "unless you shall convict in this case." The future indicative is emphatic and common in a conditional sentence "containing a strong appeal to the feelings, or a threat or warning" (*MT* §447).

1362–63. εἰς τὸ βάραθρον: The deep rocky pit (just outside the city walls) into which condemned criminals judged to be enemies of the demos were sometimes thrown; whether they were alive or dead is unclear (Hdt. 7.133; X. *HG* 1.7.20; Pl. *Grg.* 516d). Here, as often (e.g., *Nu.* 1448–50; *Ra.* 574; Alex. fr. 159.1; Men. *Dys.* 394, 575), the expression is used colloquially, as a violent threat. For the pit's location, see Pl. *R.* 4.439e; Judeich 1931, 140. On Athenian capital punishment in general, see Barkan 1936, 54–62.   **Ὑπέρβολον:** Cf. 1302–4n. The body weight of Hyperbolus, a notorious and presumably overweight glutton (956–58), is imagined as accelerating his descent.

1364–65. τουτί: "That's the way" (Henderson's translation).   **τὰ δ' ἄλλα:** "as for the rest [of your policies]."

1366–67. Half of an oarsman's pay (cf.1065–66n for the naval pay rate) was withheld until his tour of duty ended, to ensure that he returned to ship from ports of call; this amount was paid when the ship returned to the Piraeus (Th. 8.45.2; cf. Morrison, Coates, and Rankov 2000, 119–20). **ʼντελῆ:** The regular word for payment in full. It was considered disgraceful if oarsmen (or soldiers) did not receive their pay when it was due (cf. *Ach.* 161–62). The normal daily rate of hoplite pay until at least 413 was one drachma (cf. Th. 3.17.4 with Hornblower 1991, ad loc.).

1368. πολλοῖς γ' ὑπολίσφοις πυγιδίοισιν: "to a lot of flattened butts." The joke arises from the blistering of oarsmen's backsides from rowing long stretches on hard benches; blisters were (and still are) a common problem for distance rowers (cf. *Ra.* 236, where Dionysus, lacking a seat cushion, complains of blisters as he is rowing across the Styx. **ἐχαρίσω:** A gnomic or empirical aorist for a primary tense (cf. ἔβλαψεν at 190) and a pederastic joke (cf. 517n, χαρίσασθαι).

1369–71. ὁπλίτης: Hoplites, heavy infantrymen, formed the main corps of the contemporary Greek armies; they provided their own armor and weapons. The common interests and shared civic bonds of the hoplites, the sailors of the imperial fleet, and the cavalry troops drawn from the knights are a recurring theme in the play (cf. 567–68n). **καταλόγῳ:** Refers to the muster role for military service (Arist. *Po.* 1303a7–10). The names of citizens being called up for military service were posted on public notice boards set up in front of the statue of the tribes' eponymous heroes in the agora; see Thompson and Wycherley 1972, 40–41. **κατὰ σπουδὰς:** "through political influence." **οὖπερ ἦν τὸ πρῶτον ἐγγεγράψεται:** "he'll remain registered where, in fact, [he was registered] first."

1372. ἔδακε: "Bites"; gnomic aorist, here used metaphorically for causing emotional pain (López Eire 1996, 152–53; Taillardat §296). **πόρπακα:** Cf. 847–49n. **Κλεωνύμου:** Cf. 957–59n.

1373–74. ἀγοράσει . . . ἐν ἀγορᾷ: Frequenting the agora was a mark of idleness (cf. schol., ἀγοράζοντας· ἐν ἀγορᾷ διατρίβοντας; Cratin. fr. 257; *Lys.* 556); it was also frowned on for moral reasons (cf. *Nu.* 991, 1003,

where the "Better Argument" advises Pheidippides to stay away from the
agora).   ἀγένειος: Aristophanes regularly ridicules beardless men as
effeminate (cf. *Nu.* 355 with Dover ad loc.).   Κλεισθένης: Cleisthenes
(*PA* 8525; *PAA* 575540–45) is a regular target of Aristophanic abuse (*Ach.*
118–19; *Nu.* 355; *Av.* 829–31; *Lys.* 621–23; 1092; *Th.* 574–654, as a stage
character; fr. 442), especially as a feminized character (*Ra.* 48, 57, 422–24; fr.
422).   Στράτων: Strato (*PA* 12964; *PAA* 839265); other than his mention,
likewise beardless, again with Cleisthenes at *Ach.* 122 and fr. 422, nothing
further is known of him.

1375–80. Demos, describing who will be most affected by his reforms,
parodies young men who exchange gossip in fashionable "sophistic" style. Cf.
Dover 1997, 119; Rosen 1988, 29n70.

1375–77. τὰ μειράκια: A common term for young men (Dickey 1996,
72–76).   τἀν τῷ μύρῳ: Metonymy for the perfume market (KG 2.1.12).
Athenian men typically gathered to socialize and engage in gossip at perfume
markets (Pherecr. fr. 70.3; Lys. 24.20; cf. Buxton 1994, 11–12) and barber
shops (*Av.* 1440–41; Lys. 24.20; Men. *Sam.* 509–13).   στωμύλλεται:
"chatting," "prattling on." The word (and its cognates) is attested only in
Comedy (*Ach.* 579; *Nu.* 1003; *Pax* 995; *Th.* 1073–74; *Ra.* 1071, 1310 [of birds])
and is presumably colloquial; see Peppler 1921, 152–53.   Φαίαξ: Phaeax
(*PA* 13921; *PAA* 911410), son of Erisistratus of Archarnae (Plu. *Alc.* 13.1–2;
D.L. 2.63), was an orator and prominent political figure. In 422, he served on a
diplomatic mission to Sicily, where he persuaded the normally anti-Athenian
Locrians to make a treaty with Athens (Th. 5.4–5). Along with Alcibiades
and Nicias, he helped engineer the ostracism of Hyperbolus in 416 (Plu. *Alc.*
13). Eupolis (fr. 116) describes Phaeax as excellent at chatting but utterly
ineffective at (public) speaking (λαλεῖν ἄριστος, ἀδυνατώτατος λέγειν).
Phaeax disappears from the historical record after 416.   δεξιῶς τ᾽ οὐκ
ἀπέθανεν: "he cleverly [avoided] death." Apparently, Phaeax won an acquittal
on a capital charge at a trial held sometime in 425 (cf. And. 4.36–37).

1378–80. συνερκτικός: "Cogent" (cf. συνείρω, "connect closely").
περαντικός: "conclusive" (cf. the phrase περαντικὸς λόγος, a kind of
syllogism, at *Stoic.* 277).   γνωμοτυπικὸς: "clever at coining maxims"
(LSJ s.v.).   κρουστικός: "impressive."   καταληπτικός τ᾽ ἄριστα
τοῦ θορυβητικοῦ: "superb at checking the outrageous [politician]." On the
accumulation of adjectives in -ικός, see 17–18n.

1381. οὔκουν καταδακτυλικὸς . . . ; "Surely you're not flipping off?" The word δάκτυλος is commonly used as an obscene gesture of contempt (cf. *Nu.* 652–54, κατὰ δάκτυλον, where Strepsiades remarks that, as a boy, he used to raise his [middle?] finger in a vulgar gesture to Socrates; see Henderson 1991a, 213.

1382-83. κυνηγετεῖν: Hunting, as an aristocratic pastime suitable for young "intellectuals," was thought to have good physical and mental effects on young men (X. *Cyn.* 12.7–9; *Cyr.* 8.1.34–36). **παυσαμένους ψηφισμάτων:** "[make them] stop passing decrees" (cf. *Lys.* 704, κοὐχὶ μὴ παύσησθε τῶν ψηφισμάτων τούτων, of the obsession of the male chorus with passing decrees).

1384-91. *Enter a slave boy with a campstool.* The rejuvenated and sexually energized Demos is happy to indulge his desires with any attractive female or available boy. Indeed, he is overcome with lust at the prospect of sexual enjoyment with the boy slave. For the audience, an adult male's pederastic desire for a boy was regarded as natural; see Dover 1994, 213–16.

1384-86. ἐπὶ τούτοις: "With those things in mind." **ὀκλαδίαν:** A foldable campstool carried by a slave for his master's convenience. Ancient commentators identify it as one of the luxuries enjoyed by the generation of Marathon fighters (Ath. 12.515c); cf. also the folding chair, δίφρος ὀκλαδίας, kept in the Erechtheum and said to be the work of the mythical Daedalus (Paus. 1.27.1). A boy with such a stool appears on an amphora by Exekias (*ABV* 145.13 = Vat. 344). **παῖδ᾽ ἐνόρχην:** "a well-hung boy" (Henderson's translation). **τοῦτον ὀκλαδίαν ποίει:** "make him your folding seat"; i.e., bend him over and enjoy him sexually (cf. Henderson 1991a, 158).

1387. μακάριος: "A happy man." **εἰς τἀρχαῖα δὴ καθίσταμαι:** "I am restored to the good old ways!" The placement of δή intensifies both the prepositional phrase and the verb.

1388-89. φήσεις γ᾽: "You'll say so for sure." The particle is affirmative (*GP* 130–31). **τὰς τριακοντούτιδας / σπονδάς:** Likely alludes to the peace treaty between Athens and Sparta (Th. 1.115.1), as thirty years, essentially a generation, was the standard duration for treaties between states in fifth-century Greece (Hdt. 7.149.1; Th. 5.14.4; cf. also *Ach.* 194–200, peace treaty offered Dicaeopolis). **δεῦρ᾽ ἴθ᾽:** "Come here." For the phrase, cf. *Ec.* 737, 739. *Enter two personified treaties—mute, nude, and costumed as girls.* **αἱ Σπονδαί:** The "treaties" are personified as mute girls (at least two) for Demos to fondle. Personified, mute, and nude female characters are a regular feature of celebratory scenes in Aristophanes (e.g., *Ach.* 989; *Lys.* 1114, Διαλλάγη, "Reconciliation" [see Newiger 1957, 107–8]; *Pax* 523, Ὀπώρα and Θεωρία, "Harvest" and "Holiday"). Female nudity was represented by male actors wearing female masks and outfitted with breasts and pubic hair. Zweig's (1992) argument for real slaves or prostitutes playing these female roles is unlikely, as it assumes that they were allowed to participate in an official way in the dramatic festival; see Vaio 1973, 379n48.

1390–92. ὦ Ζεῦ πολυτίμηθ᾽: "O much honored Zeus" is a stock exclamation of astonishment and delight (*Av.* 667; fr. 336.1; Pherecr. fr. 166).   **κατατριακοντουτίσαι:** "to push in my 'boat pole' thirty times"; an obscene joke on the peace treaty of thirty years; an apparent Aristophanic coinage; see Taillardat §194. The ability of the rejuvenated Demos to perform the sex act many times in succession confirms his youthful virility (cf. *Ach.* 993–94; *Av.* 1254–56).   **οὐ γὰρ:** "Don't you realize . . ."; conveys surprise or indignation that the previous question was even asked (cf. *Ach.* 576; *V.* 863; *GP* 79–80).

1393–95. ἵνα . . . λάβῃς; See 893n.   **νῦν οὖν:** Colloquial (cf. 69–72n).   **εἰς τοὺς ἀγροὺς / . . . ἰέναι:** "go to your farm"; cf. 805.

1396. εἴφ᾽: = εἴπε.

1397–1401. οὐδὲν μέγ᾽ ἀλλ᾽ ἤ: "Nothing big except" (*GP* 26).   **ἐπὶ ταῖς πύλαις:** Cf. 1246.   **μόνος:** I.e., alone by himself and without friends.   **τὰ κύνεια μιγνὺς τοῖς ὀνείοις *τρώγμασιν:** Read instead πράγμασιν, "mixing dog meat with asses' affairs"; a paraprosdokeion joke, substituting πράγμασιν for κρέασι or the like (cf. Taillardat §706). For whores (πόρναι) and public baths as representing moral corruption, see *Nu.* 990–97, where the Δίκαιος Λόγος advises that a well-raised young man should avoid the agora, baths, and πόρναι (cf. also *PMG* 905, a drinking song in which the whore and a male bath attendant are said to bathe in the same tub). Note that the shouting matches that Paphlagon will hold at the city "gates" replace his combat at the "gates of Pylos."   **κἀκ τῶν βαλανείων . . . τὸ λούτριον:** I.e., the runoff from the public baths.

1402–5. ἐπενόησας: Cf. 89–90n.   **ἀντὶ τούτων:** As at 1345.   **εἰς τὸ πρυτανεῖον:** Cf. 167, 280–81.   **φαρμακός:** "scapegoat." For the Athenian Thargelia, a festival of purification and renewal dedicated to Apollo, two individuals, ritual embodiments of public danger and communal pollution, were selected as scapegoats for public abuse and exile from the city. The treatment of Paphlagon as a scapegoat is entirely appropriate, as his exile from politics will benefit the city. For the ritual, see Hippon. fr. 6–10, 104, 109 W; Burkert 1985, 82–84; R. Parker 2005, 481–83.

1406. ἕπου: Sc. μοι.　　βατραχίδα: For a man's chiton that has been died a pale green, cf. 523, βαπόμενος βατραχειοῖς (referring to a comedy by Magnes). According to the scholia (at 1406), the βατραχίς was richly ornamented with floral designs; see also Stone 1981, 176–77. Elsewhere, the garment is mentioned as worn by women and dedicated by them to Artemis Brauronia (*IG* ii² 1514.16, 48). Bennet and Tyrrell (1990, 251) suggest that putting on the robe transforms Sausage-seller "visually into an embodiment of fertility and reawakening of life," which they contrast with the harvest wreath (*eiresione*) that has fallen to the ground (729).

1407. If the chorus sang a traditional celebratory song (which here is doubtful), it was not transmitted in the manuscript tradition; contrast the transmission of the concluding lyrics composed by Aristophanes in *Wasps*, *Peace*, and *Birds*. Indeed, the departure of Demos and the comic hero, surely walking together toward the agora and Prytaneion, can leave little doubt in the mind of the audience that Demos and Sausage-seller are on their way to a celebration feast (Biles 2011, 129–32).

1407-8. ἐκφερέτω τις: "Someone carry him out!" The verb is commonly used of carrying out the corpse for burial (e.g., *Il.* 24.786; Hdt. 7.117; Antipho *Orator* 6.21).　　οἱ ξένοι: I.e., both the subject allies in general and specifically their wealthy citizens whom Cleon and his associates intimidated, blackmailed, and extorted for personal gain (e.g., 324–27, 802–4, 832–35, 1070–72; *V.* 669–77; *Pax* 635–48). The emphasis given to οἱ ξένοι as the final word of the play is perhaps a dig at Cleon (and his followers) for their apparent attempt to prosecute Aristophanes for an alledged critical portrayal of the demos in the presence of the city's subject allies, οἱ ξένοι, in *Babylonians* in 426.

Demos, Sausage-seller, the slave boy, the personified peace treaties, and the chorus of knights exit on one side; Paphlagon, now equipped as a sausage seller, is carried off in the other direction.

GLOSSARY

agon. A formal debate between antagonists, during which the chorus interjects with short speeches. It is characterized by a metrical balance between songs recited by the chorus and epirrhematic verses recited by the antagonists, and all accompanied by dance. The traditional structure of the agon is: an opening choral song (the strophe), a speech (the eppirrhema) by one of the antagonists usually in trochaic tetrameter, a second choral song (the antistrophe), and a speech by the second antagonist usually with the same number of lines and metrical pattern as the first epirrhema. *Knights* (as well as *Clouds* and *Frogs*) deviates from this structure by including a second agon that features epirrhematic speeches with different metrical patterns. The definition and terminology for the agon is the work of modern scholars.

anapest. A metrical unit ($\smile\smile-$) that is commonly used in the parabis in which "the poet speaks directly to the audience through the chorus or the chorus-leader, or the chorus sing for themselves, or their leader speaks in character" (Olson 2007, 20). To introduce the parabis, Aristophanes will often say "here come the anapests."

antepirrhema. A spoken passage in the same style and meter as the epirrhema.

antistrophe. A choral song in lyric meters and with dance steps, corresponding metrically (not always exactly) to the strophe. The antistrophe is sometimes referred to as the "antode."

apostrophe. An exclamatory rhetorical figure of speech when a speaker breaks off and addresses someone directly in the vocative.

choregos (pl. choregoi). A wealthy citizen designated by the state to recruit, train and costume the chorus for the dramatic festivals. Choregoi were selected according to tribe affiliation; no tribe could be represented by more than one choregos. The coryphaeus was the leader of the chorus.

City Dionysia. The major annual dramatic festival of Dionysus, normally held in late March or early April. The conventional date for the first production of comedies at the City Dionysia is 487/86 (cf. *IG* ii[2] 2325.C in MO). This city festival is distinguished from the Rural Dionysia, a deme festival, that featured a phallic procession (cf. Olson 2002, at *Ach.* 241), music, and, in some (but not all) demes, dramatic contests (cf. *DFA*[2], 42–54).

deme. A territorial unit, effectively a kind of village. The city of Athens and its countryside were divided into 139 demes (Traill 1975, 42, 76).

dithyramb. A choral song with dancing in honor of Dionysus. The origin of the dithyramb is unclear, but it seems to have begun as a cult performance connected to the god. According to the Marmor Parium (see below), dithyrambic choruses of men and boys were added to the City Dionysia in 510–508 BCE (*FGrH* 239 A 46).

eccyclema. A platform or cart that could be pushed out through the central door of the skene (see below) and onto the stage, to give the audience a glimpse of action having taken place inside a building.

enjambment. The running on of a thought from one verse line to the next without syntactic break.

epirrhema. A speech or dialogue in tetrameter usually sung by the chorus and directly following a strophe or antistrophe. The epirrhema may be recited by the coryphaeus (the chorus leader, as always in the parabasis), another character (as always in the agon), or interrupting characters (cf. Sommerstein 2019, s.v.).

epirrhematic agon. A succession of choral stanzas (i.e., strophes and antistrophrs), accompanied by dance and metrically balanced by epirrhematic verses recited by the participants following the stanzas.

exodos. Marks the exit of the chorus from the orchestra and of the actors from the stage. During the exodos, the chorus may call for audience approval, comment on the concluding actions of the play, and happily sing of the feasting and songs that will follow.

hapax legomenon. A word that is attested just once in the written record of a language.

hypothesis. An ancient summary of a play. The earliest examples are datable to the Hellenistic period, after 300 BCE.

katakeleusmos. A formal element of the parados and agon of Old Comedy, often a couplet sung in the same meter as the epirrhema and antepirrhema respectively, initiating or activating a debate by calling each party to state his or her case. The katakeleusmos is commonly introduced with ἀλλά as a break-off formula (e.g., *Eq.* 761–62; *Ach.* 364–65; *Nu.* 476–77, 959–60; *V.* 346–47; *Pax* 601–2).

kommation ("little song"). A short transitional choral song sung between the moment the actors leave the stage and the start of the parabasis proper.

Lenaea. A dramatic festival of Dionysus, held in January/February, in which, right from the beginning, comic performances may have been more important than tragic performances; in the fifth century, only two tragic poets competed, each competing with two tragedies but no satyr play. Cf. *DFA*, 25–42.

Marmor Parium. A fragmentary inscribed marble stele found on the island of Paros that lists political, military, historical, and literary events, chronologically but not always accurately, from the time of Cecrops, the legendary first king of Athens, to 264/63 BCE, presumably the date or approximate date of the inscription.

mesodic. A metrical interlude between choral stanzas. See, for example, eight trochaic tetrameter lines between strophe α (303–13) and strophe β (322–34).

metatheater. Moments in the play when characters or even the chorus will step out of the immediate dramatic context and speak directly to the audience, refer to their costumes or the stage setting, mention that they are actors and not the characters they play, or otherwise force the audience and actors to look away from the action of the play and remember where they actually are.

metron. A metrical unit, also referred to as a foot.

parabasis (pl. parabases). A structural element unique to Old Comedy (also called the "anapests"), in which the chorus may step out of character to address the audience and to advocate for the poet, singing in a range of meters (see παραβῆναι, *Eq.* 507; cf., in the present book's commentary, 498–610n). It is not unusual for some Aristophanic comedies (and, presumably, comedies of other contemporary comic poets) to have two parabases (see, e.g., *Eq.* 1264–1315; *Ach.* 971–99; *Nu.* 1115–30). Second parabases generally are concerned less with the persona of the poet than with satirizing various politicians or prominent individuals (cf. Hubbard 1991, 16–40). By the end of Aristophanes' career, the parabasis seems to have become obsolete, at least in his work.

parados. Marks the entrance of the chorus into the orchestra (or dancing area) and, with the parabasis and agon, is one of three major structural elements of Old Comedy. In *Knights*, the parados begins at line 242.

paradosis. Technical term for the reading transmitted in the authoritative text.

paraprosdokeion. Surprise substitution of a word or phrase in a passage for comic effect.

pnigos (pl. pnigoi). "Choker"; a brief lively unit in which a series of lines are uttered apparently without taking a breath (Hephaestion 135 G; Pollux 4.14). Some pnigoi may seem impossibly long to recite in a single breath, but a trained actor, whose voice was necessarily strong, may have been perfectly able to recite a lengthy pnigos.

proagon. The "precontest" in which the chorus and/or the characters announce the subject of the play or dispute the issues at hand; it usually precedes the agon.

prologue. Explains the situation of the play, through a monologue or dialogue, and sets the plot in motion. A prologue is usually in iambic trimeter, but other meters, particularly hexameters, can also be used. The prologue of *Knights* comprises lines 1–241.

scholion (pl. scholia). Ancient scholarly comments (often abridged) or notes, whether written in the margins of a text or interlineally (on their development, see Dickey 2007, 11–16). The scribe who made the notes is called the scholiast.

skene. A building with a low stage on which the actors performed and with a central door representing the entrance to the primary building in the play.

strophe. A stanza of a choral song, to which the antistrophe corresponds.

Suda. A massive tenth-century Byzantine encyclopedia of the ancient Mediterranean world.

testimonium (pl. testimonia). The ancient or medieval sources that quote or paraphrase parts of an ancient text. This term is also used to denote statements about an author or works beyond that found in the author's texts or fragments (Sommerstein 2019, s.v.).

Bibliography

Abel, Lionel. 1963. *Metatheatre: A New View of Dramatic Form*. New York: Hill and Wang.

Ademollo. F. 1994. "Aristofane, *Cavalieri* 336, 480, 545, 602." *Atene e Roma*, 173–81.

Anderson, C. A. 1989. "Themistocles and Cleon in Aristophanes' *Knights*, 763ff." *AJP* 110:10–18.

Anderson, C. A. 1991. "The Dream Oracles of Athena, *Knights* 1090–95." *TAPA* 121:149–55.

Anderson, C. A. 1995. *Athena's Epithets: Their Structural Significance in Plays of Aristophanes*. Leipzig: Teubner.

Anderson, C. A. 1998. "An Unnoticed Gecko Joke in Aristophanes' *Clouds* 169–74." *CP* 93:49–50.

Anderson, C. A. 2003. "The Gossiping Triremes in Aristophanes' *Knights*, 1300–1315." *CJ* 99:1–9.

Anderson, C. A. 2008a. "Archilochus, His Lost Shield, And the Heroic Ideal." *Phoenix* 62:255–60.

Anderson, C. A. 2008b. "Athena's Big Finger: An Unnoticed Sexual Joke in Aristophanes' *Knights*." *CP* 103:175–81.

Anderson, C. A. 2011/12. "Athena and Sparta at the Ending of *Lysistrata*." *CJ* 107:143–47.

Anderson, C. A., and T. K. Dix. 1997. "Politics and State Religion in the Delian League: Athena and Apollo in the Eteocarpathian Decree." *ZPE* 117:129–32.

Anderson, C. A., and T. K. Dix. 2004. "Small States in the Athenian Empire: the Case of the Eteokarpathioi." *Syllecta Classica* 15:1–31.

Anderson, C. A., and T. K. Dix. 2014. "Λάβε τὸ βυβλίον." In *Between Orality and Literacy: Communication and Adaptation in Antiquity*, edited by R. Scodel, 77–86. Leiden: Brill.

Arnott, W. G. 1996. *Alexis: The Fragments; A Commentary*. Cambridge: Cambridge University Press.

Arnott, W. G. 2007. *Birds in the Ancient World from A to Z*. London: Routledge.

Arnott, W. G. 2010. "Middle Comedy." In *Brill's Companion to the Study of Greek Comedy*, edited by G. W. Dobrov, 279–331. Leiden: Brill.

Austin, C., and S. D. Olson. 2004. *Aristophanes: Thesmophoriazusae*. Oxford: Oxford University Press.

Bagordo, A. 2016. *Fragmenta Comica. Vol. 10.9, Aristophanes Frr. 590–674: Ubersetzung und Kommentar*. Heidelberg: Verlag Antike.

Bakola, E. 2010. *Cratinus and the Art of Comedy*. Oxford: Oxford University Press.

Barber, E. J. W. 1992. "The Peplos of Athena." In *Goddess and Polis: The Panathenaic Festival in Ancient Athens*, edited by J. Neils, 103–17. Princeton: Princeton University Press.

Barkan, I. 1936. "Capital Punishment in Ancient Athens." PhD diss., University of Chicago.

Barletta, B., W. B. Dinsmoor, and H. A. Thompson. 2017. *The Sanctuary of Athena at Sounion*. Princeton: American School of Classical Studies at Athens.

Barrett, W. S. 1964. *Euripides: Hippolytus*. Oxford: Clarendon.

Bennet, L., and W. B. Tyrrell. 1990. "Making Sense of Aristophanes' *Knights*." *Arethusa* 23:235–54.

Bicknell, P. J. 1986. "Agasias the Donkey." *ZPE* 62:183–84.

Biles, Z. P. 2001. "Aristophanes' Victory Dance: Old Poets in the Parabasis of *Knights*." *ZPE* 136:195–200.

Biles, Z. P. 2002. "Intertextual Biography in the Rivalry of Aristophanes and Cratinus." *AJP* 123:169–204.

Biles, Z. P. 2011. *Aristophanes and the Poetics of Competition*. Cambridge: Cambridge University Press.

Biles, Z. P., and S. D. Olson. 2015. *Aristophanes: Wasps*. Oxford: Oxford University Press.

Blaszczak, W. 1932. "Götteranrufung und Beteuerung: Untersuchungen zu volkstümlichen ausdrucksformen in der griechischen literatur." Pt. 1. PhD diss., University of Breslau.

Blaydes, F. H. M. 1892. *Aristophanis Equites*. Halle: In Orphantrophei Libraria.

Boardman, J., et al. 1981–99. *Lexicon Iconographicum Mythologiae Classicae, vols. 1-8*. Zurich: Artemis.

Boedeker, D. 1984. *Descent from Heaven: Images of Dew in Greek Poetry and Religion*. American Classical Studies 13. Chico, CA: Scholars Press.

Boegehold, A. L. 1982. "A Dissent at Athens ca 424–421 B.C." *GRBS* 23:147–56.

Boegehold, A. L. 1999. *When a Gesture Was Expected: A Selection of Examples from Archaic and Classical Greek Literature*. Princeton: Princeton University Press.

Bosher, K. G. 2012. *Theater Outside Athens: Drama in Greek Sicily and South Italy*. Cambridge: Cambridge University Press.

Bowie, A. M. 1993. *Aristophanes: Myth, Ritual and Comedy*. Cambridge: Cambridge University Press.

Bowie, A. M. 2010. "Myth and Ritual in Comedy." In *Brill's Companion to the Study of Greek Comedy*, edited by G. W. Dobrov, 143–76. Leiden: Brill.

Bowie, E. L. 1986. "Early Greek Elegy, Symposium and Public Festival." *JHS* 106:13–35.

Bremer, J. M. 1993. "Aristophanes on His Own Poetry." In *Aristophane: Sept exposés suivis de discussions*, edited by E. Degani, J. M. Bremer, and E. W. Handley, 125–72. Geneva: Fondation Hardt.

Broneer, O. 1938. "Excavations on the North Slope of the Acropolis." *Hesperia* 7:228–43.

Bugh, G. R. 1988. *The Horsemen of Athens*. Princeton: Princeton University Press.

Burkert, W. 1985. *Greek Religion: Archaic and Classical*. Cambridge, MA: Harvard University Press.

Burnyeat, M. F. 1997. "Postscript on Silent Reading." *CQ* 47:74–76.

Buxton, R. 1994. *Imaginary Greece: The Contexts of Mythology*. Cambridge: Cambridge University Press.

Cairns, D. 1993. *Aidos: The Psychology and Ethics of Honour and Shame in Ancient Greek Literature*. Oxford: Clarendon.

Calhoun, G. M. 1913. *Athenian Clubs in Politics and Litigation. Bulletin of the University of Texas. Humanistic series*, 262. Austin, TX: University of Texas.

Camp, J. M. 2001. *The Archaeology of Athens*. New Haven: Yale University Press.

Camp, J. M. 2010. *The Athenian Agora: Site Guide*. 5th ed. Princeton: American School of Classical Studies at Athens.

Campbell, D. A. 1988. *Greek Lyric*. Vol. 2. Cambridge, MA: Harvard University Press.

Carawan, E. 1990. "The Five Talents Cleon Coughed Up (Scol. Ar. *Ach.* 6)." *CQ* 40:137–47.

Carter, L. B. 1986. *The Quiet Athenian*. Oxford: Clarendon.

Casabona, J. 1966. *Recherches sur le vocabulaire des sacrifices en grec de origines à la fin de l'époque classique*. Aix-en-Provence: Ophrys.

Casson, Lionel. 1996. *Ships and Seafaring in Ancient Times*. Austin: University of Texas Press.

Charitonides, C. 1935. *Aporrheta*. Thessaloniki: Triantaphyllou.

Christiansen, K. A. 1984. "The Theseion: A Slave Refuge at Athens." *AJAH* 9:23–32.

Cohen, D. 1983. *Theft in Athenian Law*. Munich: Beck.

Collard, C. 2018. *Colloquial Expressions in Greek Tragedy: Revised and Enlarged Edition of P. T. Stevens's "Colloquial Expressions in Euripides."* Stuttgart: Franz Steiner Verlag.

Colvin, S. 1999. *Dialect in Aristophanes: The Politics of Language in Ancient Greek Literature*. Oxford: Clarendon.

Compton-Engle, G. 2015. *Costume in the Comedies of Aristophanes*. Cambridge: Cambridge University Press.

Connor, W. R. 1963. "Two Notes of Diopeithes the Seer." *CP* 58:115–18.

Connor, W. R. 1971. *The New Politicians of Fifth-Century Athens*. Princeton: Princeton University Press.

Coulon, V., and H. van Daele. 1972. *Aristophane*. Vol 1. Paris: Sociéte d'édition Les Belles Lettres.

Cribiore, R. 2001. *Gymnastics of the Mind: Greek Education in Hellenistic and Roman Egypt*. Princeton: Princeton University Press.

Crosby, M. 1950. "The Leases of the Laureion Mines." *Hesperia* 19:189–312.

Cullard, E. 2016. *Eustathios of Thessalonike: Commentary on Homer's "Odyssey."* Vol. 1, *On Rhapsodies A–B*. Uppsala: Uppsala Universitet.

Dalby, A. 2000. "'Topicos Oinos': The Named Wines of Old Comedy." In *The Rivals of Aristophanes: Studies in Athenian Old Comedy*, edited by D. Harvey and J. Wilkins, 397–405. London: Duckworth; Classical Press of Wales.

Davidson, J. 1993. "Fish, Sex and Revolution in Athens." *CQ* 43:53–66.

Davidson, J. 1997. *Courtesans and Fishcakes: The Consuming Passions of Classical Athens*. London: HarperCollins.

Denniston, J. D. 1927. "Technical Terms in Aristophanes." *CQ* 21:113–21.

Denniston, J. D. 2005. *The Greek Particles*. 2nd ed., revised by K. J. Dover. Oxford: Bristol Classical.

Deubner, L. 1932. *Attische Feste*. Berlin: H. Keller.

Dickey, E. 1996. *Greek Forms of Address: from Herodotus to Lucian*. Oxford: Clarendon.

Dickey, E. 2007. *Ancient Greek Scholarship: A Guide to Finding, Reading, and Understanding Scholia, Commentaries, Lexica, and Grammatical Treatises, from Their Beginnings to the Byzantine Period*. Oxford: Oxford University Press.

Diels, H. 1951–52. *Die Fragmente der Vorsokratiker*. 6th ed., revised with additions and index by W. Kranz. 3 vols. Berlin: Weidmannsche Verlagsbuchhandlung.

Dodds, E. R. 1951. *The Greeks and the Irrational*. Berkeley: University of California Press.

Dover, K. J. 1959. "Aristophanes, *Knights* 11–20." *CR* 9:196–99.

Dover, K. J. 1968. *Aristophanes: Clouds*. Oxford: Clarendon.

Dover, K. J. 1972a. *Aristophanic Comedy*. London: Batsford.

Dover, K. J. 1972b. "The Scholia on the *Knights*." *CR* 22:21–24.

Dover, K. J. 1975. "Portrait-Masks in Aristophanes." In *Aristophanes und die alte Komödie*, edited by H. J. Newiger, 155–69. Darmstadt: Wissenschaftliche Buchgesellschaft Abt. Verl.

Dover, K. J. 1976. "The Freedom of the Intellectual in Greek Society." Τάλαντα 7:24–54.

Dover, K. J. 1978. *Greek Homosexuality*. Cambridge, MA: Harvard University Press.

Dover, K. J. 1987. *Greek and the Greeks: Collected Papers. Vol., 1, Language, Poetry, Drama*. Oxford: Blackwell.

Dover, K. J. 1989. *Greek Homosexuality*. 2nd ed. Cambridge, MA: Harvard University Press.

Dover, K. J. 1993. *Aristophanes: Frogs*. Oxford: Clarendon.

Dover, K. J. 1994. *Greek Popular Morality in the Time of Plato and Aristotle*. Rev. ed. Indianapolis: Hackett.

Dover, K. J. 1997. *The Evolution of Greek Prose Style*. Oxford: Clarendon.

Dover, K. J. 2002. "Some Evaluative Terms in Aristophanes." In *The Language of Greek Comedy*, edited by A. Willi, 85–97. Oxford: Oxford University Press.

Dover, K. J. 2004. "The Limits of Allegory and Allusion in Aristophanes." In *Law, Rhetoric, and Comedy in Classical Athens: Essays in Honour of Douglas M. MacDowell*, edited by D. L. Cairns, R. A. Knox, and I. Arnaoutoglou, 239–49. Swansea: Classical Press of Wales.

Dunbar, N. 1995. *Aristophanes: Birds.* Oxford: Clarendon.

Edmunds, L. 1987a. "Aristophanic Cleon's 'Disturbance' of Athens." *AJP* 108:233–63.

Edmunds, L. 1987b. *Cleon, Knights, and Aristophanes' Politics.* Lanham: University Press of America.

Farmer, M. 2017. *Tragedy on the Comic Stage.* Oxford: Oxford University Press.

Ferguson, W. S. 1948. "Demetrius Poliorcetes and the Hellenic League." *Hesperia* 17:112–36.

Fisher, N. R. E. 1992. Hybris: *A Study in the Values of Honour and Shame in Ancient Greece.* Warminster: Aris and Phillips.

Fletcher, J., and A. Sommerstein. 2008. Horkos: *The Oath in Greek Society.* Liverpool: Liverpool University Press.

Fornara, C. 1973. "Cleon's Attack against the Cavalry." *CQ* 23:24.

Forsdyke, S. 2005. *Exile, Ostracism, and Democracy: The Politics of Expulsion in Ancient Greece.* Princeton: Princeton University Press.

Fowler, R. L. 1987. "The Rhetoric of Desperation." *HSCP* 91:5–38.

Fraenkel, E. 1950. *Aeschylus: Agamemnon.* Vols. 1–2. Oxford: Clarendon.

Fraenkel, E. 1962. *Beobachtungen zu Aristophanes.* Rome: Edizioni di storia e letteratura.

Frederiksen, R., E. Gebhard, and A. Sokolicek, eds. 2015. *The Architecture of the Ancient Greek Theatre: Acts of an International Conference at the Danish Institute at Athens, 27–30 January 2012.* Århus: Århus University Press.

Frisk, J. I. H. 1960–72. *Griechishes Etymologisches Wörterbuch, vols. 1–2.* Heidelberg: n.p.

Gildersleeve, B. L. 1900. *Syntax of Classical Greek from Homer to Demosthenes.* New York: American Book.

Ginouvès, R. 1962. *Balaneutikè: Recherches sur le bain dans l'antiquité grecque.* Paris: Éditions de Boccard.

Goldhill, S. 1990. "The Great Dionysia and Civic Ideology." In *Nothing to Do with Dionysos? Athenian Drama in Its Social Context*, edited by J. Winkler and F. Zeitlin, 97–129. Princeton: Princeton University Press.

Goldhill, S. 1994. "Representing Democracy: Women at the City Dionysia." In *Ritual, Finance, Politics: Athenian Democratic Accounts Presented to David Lewis*, edited by R. Osborne and S. Hornblower, 347–69. Oxford: Clarendon.

Gomme, A. W. 1958. "Notes on Greek Comedy." *CR* 8:1–2.

Goodwin, W. W. 1897. *Syntax of the Moods and Tenses of the Greek Verb.* Rev. ed. London: Macmillan.

Gould, J. 1973. "Hiketeia." *JHS* 93:74–103.

Green, J. R. 1996. *Theatre in Ancient Greek Society.* London: Routledge.

Grenell, B. P., and A. S. Hunt, eds.1899. *Oxyrhynchus Papyri, 2.* London: Egypt Exploration Fund.

Grossmann, G. 1950. *Politische Schalgwörter aus der Zeit des Peloponnesischen Krieges.* New York: Arno.

Habash, M. 1995. "Two Complementary Festivals in Aristophanes' *Acharnians.*" *AJP* 116:559–77.

Habicht, C. 1970. *Gottmenschentum und griechische Städte.* Munich: Beck.

Halliwell, S. 1980. "Aristophanes' Apprenticeship." *CQ* 30:33–45.

Halliwell, S. 1982. "Notes on Some Aristophanic Jokes (*Ach.* 854–9; *Kn.* 608–10; *Peace* 695–9; *Thesm.* 605; *Frogs* 1039)." *LCM* 7:153–54.

Halperin, D. M. 1990. "The Democratic Body: Prostitution and Citizenship in Classical Athens." In *One Hundred Years of Homosexuality, and Other Essays on Greek Love,* edited by D. M. Halperin, 88–112. New York: Routledge.

Hamdorf, F. W. 1964. *Griechische Kultpersonifikationen der vorhellenistichen Zeit.* Mainz: Von Zabern.

Handley, E. 1989. "Comedy." In *The Cambridge History of Classical Literature, vol. 1, Greek Literature, pt. 1, Early Greek Poetry,* edited by P. Easterling and B. M. Knox, 355–425. Cambridge: Cambridge University Press.

Hansen, P. A., ed. 1983–89. *Carmina Epigraphica Graeca.* Vols. 1–2. Berlin: Walter de Gruyter.

Harris, D. 1995. *The Treasures of the Parthenon and Erechtheion.* Oxford: Clarendon.

Harris, E. 2013. *The Rule of Law in Action in Democratic Athens.* New York: Oxford University Press.

Harris, W. V. 1989. *Ancient Literacy.* Cambridge, MA: Harvard University Press.

Harrison, A. R. W. 1968. *The Law of Athens: The Family and Property.* Vol. 1. Oxford: Clarendon.

Harrison, A. R. W. 1971. *The Law of Athens: Procedure.* Vol. 2. Oxford: Clarendon.

Heath, M. 1987. *Political Comedy in Aristophanes.* Göttingen: Vandenhoeck und Ruprecht.

Henderson, J. J. 1987. *Aristophanes: Lysistrata.* Oxford: Clarendon.

Henderson, J. J. 1990. "The Demos and the Comic Competition." In *Nothing to Do with Dionysos? Athenian Drama in Its Social Context,* edited by J. J. Winkler and F. I. Zeitlin, 271–313. Princeton: Princeton University Press.

Henderson, J. J. 1991a. *The Maculate Muse: Obscene Language in Attic Comedy.* New Haven: Yale University Press.

Henderson, J. J. 1991b. "Women and the Athenian Dramatic Festival." *TAPA* 121:133–47.

Henderson, J. J. 1998. *Aristophanes: Acharnians; Knights.* Cambridge, MA: Harvard University Press.

Henderson, J. J. 2003a. "Demos, Demagogue, Tyrant in Attic Old Comedy." In *Popular Tyranny: Sovereignty and Its Discontents in Ancient Greece,* edited by K. A. Morgan, 155–80. Austin: University of Texas Press.

Henderson, J. J. 2003b. "When an Identity Was Expected: The Slaves in Aristophanes' *Knights*." In *Gestures: Essays in Ancient History, Literature, and Philosophy Presented to Alan Boegehold*, edited by G. W. Bakewell and J. P. Sickinger, 63–73. Oxford: Oxbow Books.

Henderson, J. J. 2013. "The Comic Chorus and the Demagogue." In *Choral Meditations in Greek Tragedy*, edited by R. Gagné and M. G. Hopman, 278–96. Cambridge: Cambridge University Press.

Henderson, J. J. 2017. "Thucydides and Attic Comedy." In *The Oxford Handbook of Thucydides*, edited by R. Balot, S. Forsdyke, and E. Foster, 604–20. Oxford: Oxford University Press.

Henrichs, A. 1976. "Despoina Kybele: Ein Beitrag zur religiösen Namenkunde." *HSPh* 80:253–86.

Hermann, K. F. 1835. *Disputatio de Persona Niciae apud Aristophanem*. Marburg: n.p.

Herwerden, H. van 1862. *Exercitationes criticae in poeticis et prosaicis quibusdam Atticorum monumentis*. The Hague: M. Nijhoff.

Horn, W. 1970. *Gebet und Gebetsparodie in den Komödien des Aristophanes*. Nuremberg: Hans Carl Nürnberg.

Hornblower, S. 1991. *A Commentary on Thucydides, Books 1–3*. Vol. 1. Oxford: Clarendon.

Hornblower, S. 1996. *A Commentary on Thucydides, Books 4–5.25*. Vol. 2. Oxford: Clarendon.

Hornblower, S. 2008. *A Commentary on Thucydides, Books 5.25–8.109*. Vol. 3. Oxford: Oxford University Press.

Hubbard, T. K. 1991. *The Mask of Comedy: Aristophanes and the Intertextual Parabasis*. Ithaca, NY: Cornell University Press.

Hughes, A. 2012. *Performing Greek Comedy*. Cambridge: Cambridge University Press.

Hunter, V. J. 1990. "Gossip and the Politics of Reputation in Classical Athens." *Phoenix* 44:299–325.

Hunter, V. J. 1994. *Policing Athens: Social Control in the Attic Lawsuits, 420–320 B.C.* Princeton: Princeton University Press.

Hurwit, J. 1999. *The Athenian Acropolis: History, Mythology, and Archaeology from the Neolithic Era to the Present*. Cambridge: Cambridge University Press.

Imperio, O. 2004. *Parabasi di Aristofane: Acarnesi, Cavalieri, Vespe, Uccelli*. Bari: Adriatica Editrice.

Jocelyn, H. D. 1980. "A Greek Indecency and Its Students: ΛΑΙΚΑΖΕΙΝ." *PCPS*, n.s., 26:12–66.

Johnson, W. 2000. "Towards a Sociology of Reading in Classical Antiquity." *AJP* 121:593–627.

Jones, N. F. 2004. *Rural Athens under the Democracy*. Philadelphia: University of Pennsylvania Press.

Judeich, W. 1931. *Topographie von Athen*. Munich: Beck.

Kanavou, N. 2011. *Aristophanes' Comedy of Names: A Study of Speaking Names in Aristophanes*. Berlin: Walter de Gruyter.

Kassel R., and C. Austin, eds. 1983–. *Poetae Comici Graeci*. Vols. i, ii, iii/2, iv, v, vi/1, vii, viii to date. Berlin and New York. De Gruyter.

Katz, J. 1999. "*Homeric Hymn to Hermes* 296: τλήμονα γαστρὸς ἔριθον." *CQ* 49:315–19.

Keller, O. 1909–13. *Die antike Tierwelt*. 2 vols. Leipzig: Verlag von Wilhelm Engelmann.

Kiehl, E. J. 1852. "Bladvulling." *Mnem.* 1:49.

Kirchner, J. E., ed. 1981. *Prosopographia Attica*. 2 vols. Chicago: Ares.

Kleinknecht, H. 1937. *Die Gebetsparodie in der Antike*. Stuttgart: W. Kohlhammer.

Kleinknecht, H. 1939. "Die Epiphanie des Demos in den *Rittern*." *Hermes* 77:58–65.

Knox, B. 1968. "Silent Reading in Antiquity." *GRBS* 9:421–35.

Koenen, L. 1959. "Tereus in den Vögelen des Aristophanes." In *Studien zur Textgeschichte und Textkritik,* edited by H. Dahlmann, R. Merkelbach, et al., 83–87. Cologne: Westdeutscher Verlag.

Koenen, L., and R. Merkelbach. 1976. "Apollodorus (περὶ θεῶν), Epicharm und die Meropis." In *Collectanea Papyrologica: Texts Published in Honor of H. C. Youtie,* edited by A. E. Hanson, 16–17. Bonn: Rudolf Habelt.

Konstantinidou, K. 2014. "Oath and Curse." In *Oaths and Swearing in Ancient Greece,* edited by A. Sommerstein and I. C. Torrance, 6–47. Berlin: Walter de Gruyter.

Körte, A. 1905. "Inschriftliches zur Geschichte der attischen Komödie." *RhM* 60:425–47.

Koster, W. J., et al. 1969. *Scholia in Aristophanem*. Pt. 1, no. 2, *Prolegomena de comoedia*. Groningen: J. B. Wolters.

Kraus, W. 1985. *Aristophanes' politische Komödien: Die Acharner, die Ritter*. Vienna: Verlag der Österreichischen Akademie der Wissenschaften.

Kugelmeier, C. 1996. *Reflexe früher und zeitgenössischer Lyrik in den alten attischen Komödie*. Stuttgart: Teubner.

Kühner, R., and F. Blass. 1978. *Ausführliche Grammatik der griechischen Sprach. Vol. 1, Elementar- und Formenlehre*. Reprint, Hannover: Hahn.

Kühner, R., and B. Gerth. 1978. *Ausführliche Grammatik der griechischen Sprach. Vol. 2, Satzlehre*. Reprint, Hannover: Hahn.

Kyriakaki, N. 2007. *Aristophanes und Eupolis: Zur Geschichte einer dichterischen Rivalität*. Berlin: Walter de Gruyter.

Labiano Ilundain, J. M. 2000. *Estudio de las Interjecciones en las Comedias de Aristófanes*. Amsterdam: A. M. Hakkert.

Lambert, S. D. 1993. *The Phratries of Attica*. Ann Arbor: University of Michigan Press.

Landfester, M. 1967. *Die Ritter des Aristophanes: Beobachtungen zur dramatischen Handlung und zum komischen Stil des Aristophanes*. Amsterdam: B. R. Grüner.

Lapatin, K. 2001. *Chryselephantine Statuary in the Ancient Mediterranean World.* Oxford: Oxford University Press.

Lawler, L. B. 1944. "The Dance of the Ancient Mariners." *TAPA* 75:20–33.

Lawler, L. B. 1964. *The Dance in Ancient Greece.* Middleton, CT: Wesleyan University Press.

Lech, M. L. 2009. "The Knights' Eleven Oars: In Praise of Phormio? Aristophanes' *Knights* 546–7." *CJ* 105:19–26.

Lech, M. L. 2017. "Aristophanes *Knights* 600: Spartan or Athenian Drinking Cup?" *GRBS* 57:599–606.

Lefkowitz, M. 1981. *The Lives of the Greek Poets.* London: Duckworth.

Lefkowitz, M. 1984. "Aristophanes and Other Historians of the Fifth-Century Theater." *Hermes* 112:143–53.

Lewis, D. M. 1977. *Sparta and Persia.* Leiden: Brill.

Lewis, D. M., E. Erxleben, and K. Hallof. 1998. *Inscriptiones graecae. Vol. 1, Inscriptiones Atticae Euclidis anno anteriores, no. 3, Indices.* Berlin: Walter de Gruyter.

Lewis, S. 1996. *News and Society in the Greek Polis.* London: Duckworth.

Lilja, B. 1972. *The Treatment of Odours in the Poetry of Antiquity.* Helsinki: Societas Scientiarum Fennica.

Lind, H. 1985. "Neues aus Kydathen: Beobachtungen zum Hintergrund des *Daitales* und der *Ritter* des Aristophanes." *MH* 42:249–61.

Lind, H. 1991. *Der Gerber Kleon in den "Rittern" des Aristophanes.* Frankfurt am Main: P. Lang.

Lippman, M., D. Scahill, and P. Schultz. 2006. "*Knights* 843–59, the Nike Temple Bastion, and Cleon's Shields from Pylos." *AJA* 110:551–63.

Littlefield, D. J. 1968. "Metaphor and Myth: The Unity of Aristophanes' *Knights.*" *Studies in Philology* 65:1–22.

Llewellyn-Jones, L., and J. Robson, trans. 2010. *Ctesias: "History of Persia"; Tales of the Orient.* London: Routledge.

López Eire, A. 1996. *La lengua coloquial de la comedia aristofánica.* Murcia: Universidad de Murcia.

Luppe, W. 2000. "The Rivalry between Aristophanes and Kratinos." In *The Rivals of Aristophanes: Studies in Athenian Old Comedy,* edited by D. Harvey and J. Wilkins, 15–20. London: Duckworth; Classical Press of Wales.

Lynch, K. 2011. *The Symposium in Context: Pottery from a Late Archaic House near the Athenian Agora.* Hesperia Supplement 46. Princeton: American School of Classical Studies at Athens.

Ma, J. 2009. "Empire, Statuses, and Realities: Looking at the Athenian Empire from Elsewhere." In *Interpreting the Athenian Empire,* edited by J. Ma, N. Papazarkadas, and R. Parker, 125–48. London: Duckworth.

MacDowell, D. M., ed. 1962. *Andocides: "On the Mysteries."* Oxford: Clarendon.

MacDowell, D. M. 1971. *Aristophanes: Wasps.* Oxford: Clarendon.

MacDowell, D. M. 1978. *The Law in Classical Athens*. Ithaca, NY: Cornell University Press.

MacDowell, D. M. 1990. "The Meaning of ἀλαζών." In *Owls to Athens: Essays on Classical Subjects Presented to Sir Kenneth Dover*, edited by E. M. Craik, 287–94. Oxford: Clarendon.

MacDowell, D. M. 1995. *Aristophanes and Athens: An Introduction to the Plays*. Oxford: Oxford University Press.

MacDowell, D. M. 2018. "The Athenian Procedure of *Phasis*." In *Studies on Greek Law, Oratory, and Comedy*, edited by I. Arnaoutoglou, K. Kapparis, and D. Spatharas, 159–70. London: Routledge.

MacQueen, B. D. 1984. "On the Correct Understanding of *Eu Diabas*." *AJP* 105:453–57.

Marr, J. 1995. "The Death of Themistocles." *G&R* 42:159–67.

Marr, J. 1996. "History as Lunch: Aristophanes, *Knights* 810–19." *CQ* 46:561–64.

Mastomarco, G. 1979. "L'escordio 'segreto' di Aristofane." *Quaderni di Storia* 10:153–96.

Mattingly, H. B. 1990. "Some Fifth-Century Attic Epigraphic Hands." *ZPE* 83:110–22.

Meineke, A. 1865. *Vindicarium Aristophanearum Liber*. Leipzig: Ex officina Bernhardi Tauchnitz.

Mikalson, J. 1972. "The Noumenia and Epimenia in Athens." *HTR* 65:291–96.

Mikalson, J. 1975. *The Sacred and Civic Calendar of the Athenian Year*. Princeton: Princeton University Press.

Mikalson, J. 1983. *Athenian Popular Religion*. Chapel Hill: University of North Carolina Press.

Millis, B. W. 1997. "Antiphanes Fr. 46 K-A and the Problem of Spartan Moustaches." *CQ* 47:574–78.

Millis, B. W., and S. D. Olson. 2012. *Inscriptional Records for the Dramatic Festivals in Athens: IG II² 2318–2325 and Related Texts*. Leiden: Brill.

Molitor, M. V. 1980. "Aristarchos' Note on ΈΜΠΟΔΙΖΩΝ ΊΣΧΑΔΑΣ: *Equites*, 755." *Hermes* 108:12–14.

Morgan, T. J. 1999. "Literate Education in Classical Athens." *CQ* 49:46–61.

Moritz, L. A. 1949. "ΆΛΦΙΤΑ–a Note." *CQ* 43:113–17.

Morrison, J., F. Coates, and N. B. Rankov. 2000. *The Athenian Trireme: The History and Reconstruction of an Ancient Greek Warship*. Cambridge: Cambridge University Press.

Most, G. W. 2006. *Hesiod: Theogony, Works and Days, Testimonia*. Cambridge, MA: Harvard University Press.

Muecke, F. 1998. "Oracles in Aristophanes." *Seminari Romani di Cultura Greca* 1:257–74.

Nagy, G. 1990. *Pindar's Homer: The Lyric Possession of the Epic Past*. Baltimore: Johns Hopkins University Press.

Neil, R. A., ed. 1901. *The Knights of Aristophanes*. Cambridge: Cambridge University Press.

Neils, J. 1992a. "The Panathenaia: An Introduction." In *Goddess and Polis: The Panathenaic Festival in Ancient Athens*, edited by J. Neils, 13–27. Princeton: Princeton University Press.

Neils, J. 1992b. "Panathenaic Amphoras: Their Meaning, Makers, and Markets." In *Goddess and Polis: The Panathenaic Festival in Ancient Athens*, edited by J. Neils, 29–52. Princeton: Princeton University Press.

Newiger, H.-J. 1957. *Metapher und Allegorie: Studien zu Aristophanes*. Munich: Beck.

Nordgren. L. 2015. *Greek Interjections: Syntax, Semantics, and Pragmatics*. Berlin: Walter de Gruyter.

Ober, J. 1989. *Mass and Elite in Democratic Athens: Rhetoric, Ideology, and the Power of the People*. Princeton: Princeton University Press.

Olson, S. D. 1990. "The New Demos of Aristophanes' *Knights*." *Eranos* 88:60–67.

Olson, S. D. 1998. *Aristophanes: Peace*. Oxford: Clarendon.

Olson, S. D. 1999. "Kleon's Eyebrows (Cratin. Fr. 228 K-A) and Late 5th-Century Comic Portrait-Masks." *CQ* 49:320–21.

Olson, S. D. 2002. *Aristophanes: Acharnians*. Oxford: Oxford University Press.

Olson, S. D. 2007. *Broken Laughter: Select Fragments of Greek Comedy*. Oxford: Oxford University Press.

Olson, S. D. 2016. "Scenes for an Ill-Spent Youth (Aristophanes, *Knights* 411–12)." *CQ* 66:774–75.

Olson, S. D. 2017. *Fragmenta Comica. Vol. 8.1, Eupolis Frr. 1–146: Introduction, Translation, and Commentary*. Heidelberg: Verlag Antike.

Olson, S. D., and R. Seaberg. 2018. *Fragmenta Comica. Vol. 3.6, Kratinos Frr. 299–514: Translation and Commentary*. Heidelberg: Vandenhoeck und Ruprecht.

Olson, S. D., and A. Sens. 1999. *Matro of Pitane and the Tradition of Epic Parody in the Fourth Century BCE: Text, Translation, and Commentary*. Atlanta, GA: Scholars Press.

Olson, S. D., and A. Sens. 2000. *Archestratos of Gela: Greek Culture and Cuisine in the Fourth Century BCE: Text, Translation, and Commentary*. Oxford: Oxford University Press.

Orth, C. 2017. *Fragmenta Comica. Vol. 10.3, Aristophanes Aiolosikon-Babylonioi Frr. 1–100: Übersetzung und Kommentar*. Heidelberg: Verlag Antike.

Osborne, M. J. 1981. "Entertainment in the Prytaneion at Athens." *ZPE* 41:153–70.

Osborne, R. 1987. *Classical Landscape with Figures: The Ancient Greek City and Its Countryside*. Dobbs Ferry, NY: Sheridan House.

Ostwald, M. 1986. *From Popular Sovereignty to the Sovereignty of Law: Law, Society, and Politics in Fifth-Century Athens*. Berkeley: University of California Press.

Owens, E. 1983. "The Koprologoi at Athens in the Fifth and Fourth Centuries B.C." *CQ* 33:44–50.

Paga, J., and M. M. Miles. 2016. "The Archaic Temple of Poseidon at Sounion." *Hesperia* 85:657–710.

Page, D. 1955. *Sappho and Alcaeus: An Introduction to the Study of Ancient Lesbian Poetry*. Oxford: Clarendon.

Papachrysostomou, A. 2016. *Fragmenta Comica. Vol. 20, Amphis: Translation and Commentary*. Heidelberg: Verlag Antike.

Parke, H. W. 1977. *Festivals of the Athenians*. Ithaca, NY: Cornell University Press.

Parker, L. P. E. 1997. *The Songs of Aristophanes*. Oxford: Clarendon.

Parker, L. P. E. 2007. *Euripides: Alcestis, with Introduction and Commentary*. Oxford: Oxford University Press.

Parker, R. 1983. *Miasma: Pollution and Purification in Early Greek Religion*. Oxford: Clarendon.

Parker, R. 1996. *Athenian Religion: A History*. Oxford: Clarendon.

Parker, R. 2005. *Polytheism and Society at Athens*. Oxford: Oxford University Press.

Parker, R. 2011. *On Greek Religion*. Ithaca, NY: Cornell University Press.

Patera, Maria. 2015. *Figures grecques de l'épouvante de l'antiquité au présent: Peurs enfantines et adultes*. Leiden: Brill.

Peppler C. W. 1910. "The Termination -κος, as Used by Aristophanes for Comic Effect." *AJP* 31:428–44.

Peppler C. W. 1921. "Comic Terminations in Aristophanes." Pt. 5. *AJP* 42:152–61.

Perry, B. E. 1936. *Studies in the Text History of the Life and Fables of Aesop*. Haverford, PA: American Philological Association.

Petersen, W. 1910. *Greek Diminutives in -ιον: A Study in Semantics*. Weimar: Wagner.

Phillips, D. D. 2013. *The Law of Ancient Athens*. Ann Arbor: University of Michigan Press.

Pickard-Cambridge, A. 1988. *The Dramatic Festivals of Athens*. 2nd ed., revised by J. Gould and D. M. Lewis. Oxford: Clarendon.

Poliakoff, M. B. 1987. *Combat Sports in the Ancient World*. New Haven: Yale University Press.

Poultney, J. 1936. *The Syntax of the Genitive Case in Aristophanes*. Baltimore: Johns Hopkins University Press.

Power, T. 2010. *The Culture of Kitharôidia*. Washington, DC: Center for Hellenic Studies.

Pritchett, W. H. 1971. *The Greek State at War*. Pt. 1, *Ancient Greek Military Practices*. Berkeley: University of California Press.

Pritchett, W. H. 1979. *The Greek State at War*. Pt. 3, *Religion*. Berkeley: University of California Press.

Probert, P. 2003. *A New Short Guide to the Accentuation of Ancient Greek*. Bristol: Bristol Classical.

Pulleyn, S. 1997. *Prayer in Greek Religion*. Oxford: Clarendon.

Pütz, B. 2003. *The Symposium and Komos in Aristophanes*. Stuttgart: J. B. Wetzler.

Rau, P. 1967. *Paratragödia: Untersuchung einer komischen Form des Aristophanes*. Munich: Beck.

Reckford, K. J. 1987. *Aristophanes and Old-New Comedy. Vol. 1, Six Essays in Perspective*. Chapel Hill: University of North Carolina Press.

Rehm, R. 1988. "The Staging of Suppliant Plays." *GRBS* 29:263–307.

Renehan, R. 1976. *Studies in Greek Texts: Critical Observations to Homer, Plato, Euripides, Aristophanes and Other Authors*. Göttingen: Vandenhoeck und Ruprecht.

Revermann, M. 2006. *Comic Business: Theatricality, Dramatic Technique, and Performance Contexts of Aristophanic Comedy*. Oxford: Oxford University Press.

Reynolds, L. D., and N. G. Wilson. 1991. *Scribes and Scholars: A Guide to the Transmission of Greek and Latin Literature*. 3rd ed. Oxford: Clarendon.

Rhodes, P. J. 1972. *The Athenian Boule*. Oxford: Clarendon.

Rhodes, P. J. 1994. "The Ostracism of Hyperbolus." In *Ritual, Finance, Politics: Athenian Democratic Accounts Presented to David Lewis*, edited by R. Osborne and S. Hornblower, 85–98. Oxford: Oxford University Press.

Rhodes, P. J. 2004. "Aristophanes and the Athenian Assembly." In *Law, Rhetoric, and Comedy in Classical Athens: Essays in Honour of Douglas M. MacDowell*, edited by D. L. Cairns and R. A. Knox, 223–37. Swansea: Classical Press of Wales.

Ridgway, B. S. 1992. "Images of Athena on the Akropolis." In *Goddess and Polis: The Panathenaic Festival in Ancient Athens*, edited by J. Neils, 119–42. Princeton: Princeton University Press.

Roisman, J. 2006. *The Rhetoric of Conspiracy in Ancient Athens*. Berkeley: University of California Press.

Rosen, R. 1988. *Old Comedy and the Iambographic Tradition*. Atlanta, GA: Scholars Press.

Rosen, R. 1989. "Trouble in the Early Career of Plato Comicus: Another Look at P. Oxy. 2737.44–51 (*PCG* III 2, 590)." *ZPE* 76:223–28.

Rosen, R. 2000. "Cratinus' *Pytine* and the Construction of the Comic Self." In *The Rivals of Aristophanes: Studies in Athenian Old Comedy*, edited by D. Harvey and J. Wilkins, 23–39. London: Duckworth; Classical Press of Wales.

Rosen, R. 2010. "Aristophanes." In *Brill's Companion to the Study of Greek Comedy*, edited by G. W. Dobrov, 227–78. Leiden: Brill.

Rosenbloom, D. 2004. "Ponêroi vs. Chrêstoi: The Ostracism of Hyperbolos and the Struggle for Hegemony in Athens after the Death of Perikles." *TAPA* 134:55–105, 302–58.

Rothwell, K. S., Jr. 1990. *Politics and Persuasion in Aristophanes' "Ecclesiazusae."* Mnemosyne Supplement 111. Leiden: Brill.

Rothwell, K. S., Jr. 2007. *Nature, Culture, and the Origins of Greek Comedy: A Study of Animal Choruses*. Cambridge: Cambridge University Press.

Ruffell, I. 2002. "A Total Write-Off: Aristophanes, Cratinus, and the Rhetoric of Comic Competition." *CQ* 52:138–63.

Rusten, J., ed. 2011. *The Birth of Comedy: Texts, Documents, and Art from Athenian*

Comic Competition, 486–280. Translated by J. Henderson, D. Konstan, R. Rosen, J. Rustin, and N. Slater. Baltimore: Johns Hopkins University Press.

Rutherford, W. G. 1881. *The New Phrynichus.* London: Macmillan.

Saldatti, V. 2014. *Cleone, un politico ateniese.* Bari: Edipuglia.

Seaford, R., ed. 1988. *Euripides: Cyclops.* Oxford: Clarendon.

Shapiro, H. A. 1990. "Oracle-Mongers in Peisistratid Athens." *Kernos* 3:335–45.

Shear, T. L. 1937. "The Campaign of 1936: The Captured Spartan Shield." *Hesperia* 6:347–48.

Shear, T. L., Jr. 1970. "The Monument of the Eponymous Heroes in the Athenian Agora." *Hesperia* 39:145–222.

Sidwell, K. 2009. *Aristophanes the Democrat: The Politics of Satirical Comedy during the Peloponnesian War.* Cambridge: Cambridge University Press.

Siewert, P. 1979. "Poseidon Hippios am Kolonus und die athenischen Hippeis." In *Arktouros: Hellenic Studies Presented to Bernard M. W. Knox,* edited by G. Bowersock, W. Burkert, and M. Putnam, 280–89. Berlin: Walter de Gruyter.

Sifakis, G. M. 1971. *Parabasis and Animal Choruses: A Contribution to the History of Attic Comedy.* London: Athlone.

Silk, M. S. 2000. *Aristophanes and the Definition of Comedy.* Oxford: Oxford University Press.

Simon, E. 1983. *Festivals of Attica: An Archaeological Commentary.* Madison: University of Wisconsin Press.

Slater, N. W. 1986. "The Lenaean Theatre." *ZPE* 66:255–64.

Slater, N. W. 1999. "Making the Aristophanic Audience." *AJP* 120:351–68.

Slater, W. J. 1976. "Symposium at Sea." *HSCP* 80:161–70.

Slings, S. R. 1992. "Written and Spoken Language: An Exercise in the Pragmatics of the Greek Sentence." *CP* 87:95–109.

Smith, C. F. 1928. *Thucydides: History of the Peloponnesian War.* Vols. 1–2. Cambridge, MA: Harvard University Press.

Smith, N. D. 1989. "Diviners and Divination in Aristophanic Comedy." *CA* 8:140–58.

Smyth, H. W. 1956. *Greek Grammar.* Revised by G. Messing. Cambridge, MA: Harvard University Press.

Snell, B., R. Kannicht, and S. Radt, eds. 1971–2004. *Tragicorum Graecorum Fragmenta, vols. 1–5.* Göttingen: Vandenhoeck und Ruprecht.

Snodgrass, A. 1967. *Arms and Armour of the Greeks.* London: Thames and Hudson.

Sommerstein, A. H. 1977. "Notes on Aristophanes' *Wasps.*" *CQ* 27:261–72.

Sommerstein, A. H. 1980. "Notes on Aristophanes' *Knights.*" *CQ* 30:46–56.

Sommerstein, A. H. 1981. *Aristophanes: Knights.* Warminster: Aris and Phillips Classical Texts.

Sommerstein, A. H. 1998. *Aristophanes: Ecclesiazusae.* Warminster: Aris and Phillips Classical Texts.

Sommerstein, A. H. 2000. "Platon, Eupolis and the 'Demagogue-Comedy.'" In *The*

Rivals of Aristophanes: Studies in Athenian Old Comedy, edited by D. Harvey and J. Wilkins, 439–51. London: Duckworth; Classical Press of Wales.

Sommerstein, A. H. 2001. *Aristophanes: Wealth*. Warminster: Aris and Phillips Classical Texts.

Sommerstein, A. H. 2005. "A Lover of His Art: The Art-Form as Wife and Mistress in Greek Poetic Imagery." In *Personification in the Greek World: From Antiquity to Byzantium*, edited by E. Stafford and J. Herrin, 161–71. Aldershot: Ashgate.

Sommerstein, A. H. 2009. *Talking about Laughter, and Other Studies in Greek Comedy*. Oxford: Oxford University Press.

Sommerstein, A. H. 2010. "The History of the Text of Aristophanes." In *Brill's Companion to Greek Comedy*, edited by G. W. Dobrov, 399–422. Leiden: Brill.

Sommerstein, A. H. 2014. "The Informal Oath." In *Oaths and Swearing in Ancient Greece*, edited by A. Sommerstein and I. C. Torrance, 315–47. Berlin: Walter de Gruyter.

Sommerstein, A. H., ed. 2019. *Encyclopedia of Greek Comedy*. Hoboken, NJ: Wiley-Blackwell.

Sommerstein, A. H., and I. C. Torrance. 2014. *Oaths and Swearing in Ancient Greece*. Berlin: Walter de Gruyter.

Sparkes, B. A. 1962. "The Greek Kitchen." *JHS* 82:121–37.

Sparkes, B. A. 1975. "Illustrating Aristophanes." *JHS* 95:122–35.

Spence, I. G. 1993. *The Cavalry of Classical Greece: A Social and Military History with Particular Reference to Athens*. Oxford: Clarendon.

Spiller, H. A., J. R. Hale, and J. De Boer. 2002. "The Delphic Oracle: A Multidisciplinary Defense of the Gaseous Vent Theory." *Journal of Toxicology: Clinical Toxicology* 40:189–96.

Spyropoulos, E. S. 1975. "Magnès le Comique et sa place dans l'histoire de l'Ancienne comodie attique." *Hellenika* 28:247–74.

Starkey, J. 2018. "The Origin and Purpose of the Three-Actor Rule." *TAPA 148*: 269–97.

Stengel, P. 1910. *Opfergebräuche der Griechen*. Leipzig: Teubner.

Stevens, P. T. 1976. *Colloquial Expressions in Euripides*. Wiesbaden: Franz Steiner Verlag.

Stone, L. M. 1981. *Costume in Aristophanic Comedy*. New York: Arno.

Storey, I. 1989. "The 'Blameless Shield' of Cleonymus." *RhM* 132:247–61.

Storey, I. 2003. *Eupolis: Poet of Old Comedy*. Oxford: Oxford University Press.

Storey, I. 2008. "'Bad' Language in Aristophanes." In *Kakos: Badness and Anti-Value in Classical Antiquity*, edited by I. Sluiter and R. M. Rosen, 119–42. Mnemosyne Supplement 307. Leiden: Brill.

Storey, I. 2010. "Origins and Fifth-Century Comedy." *In Brill's Companion to the Study of Greek Comedy*, edited by G. W. Dobrov, 179–225. Leiden: Brill.

Storey, I. 2011. *Fragments of Old Comedy*. Vols. 1–3. Cambridge, MA: Harvard University Press.

Stronk, J. P., trans. 2010. *Ctesias' Persian History: Introduction, Text, and Translation.* Düsseldorf: Wellem-Verlag.

Stroud, R. 1974. "An Athenian Law on Silver Coinage." *Hesperia* 43:157–88.

Struck, P. T. 2005. "Divination and Literary Criticism?" In *Mantikê: Studies in Ancient Divination*, edited by S. I. Johnston and P. T. Stuck, 147–65. Leiden: Brill.

Svenbro, J. 1990. "The 'Interior' Voice: On the Invention of Silent Reading." In *Nothing to Do with Dionysos? Athenian Drama in Its Social Context*, edited by J. J. Winkler and F. I. Zeitlin, 366–84. Princeton: Princeton University Press.

Taillardat, J. 1965. *Les Images d'Aristophane: Études de langue et de style.* Paris: Société d'édition Les Belles Lettres.

Talbert, R. J., and R. S. Bagnall. 2000. *Barrington Atlas of the Greek and Roman World.* Princeton: Princeton University Press.

Taplin, O. 1983. "Tragedy and Trugedy." *CQ* 33:331–33.

Taplin, O. 2012. "How Was Athenian Tragedy Played in the Greek West." In *The Theater Outside Athens: Drama in Greek Sicily and South Italy*, edited by K. Boscher, 226–50. Cambridge: Cambridge University Press.

Thiercy, P. 1997. *Aristophane: Théâtre complet.* Paris: Gallimard.

Thomas, R. 1989. *Oral Tradition and Written Record in Classical Athens.* Cambridge: Cambridge University Press.

Thomas, R. 2009. "Writing, Reading, Public and Private 'Literacies': Functional Literacy and Democratic Literacy in Greece." In *Ancient Literacies: The Culture of Reading in Greece and Rome*, edited by W. Johnson and H. Parker, 13–45. Oxford: Oxford University Press.

Thompson, D. W. 1936. *A Glossary of Greek Birds.* London: Oxford University Press.

Thompson, D. W. 1947. *A Glossary of Greek Fishes.* London: Oxford University Press.

Thompson, H. A. 1952. "Excavations in the Athenian Agora: 1951." *Hesperia* 21:83–113.

Thompson, H. A. 1959. "Activities in the Athenian Agora." *Hesperia* 28:91–108.

Thompson, H. A., and R. E. Wycherley. 1972. *The Agora of Athens: The History, Shape, and Uses of an Ancient City Center.* Princeton: American School of Classical Studies at Athens.

Thomson, G. 1939. "The Postponement of Interrogatives in Attic Drama." *CQ* 33:147–52.

Todd, S. C. 1993. *The Shape of Athenian Law.* Oxford: Clarendon.

Torrance, I. C. 2014. "'Of Cabbages and Kings': The *Eideshort* Phenomenon." In *Oaths and Swearing in Ancient Greece*, edited by A. Sommerstein and I. C. Torrance, 111–32. Berlin: Walter de Gruyter.

Traill, J. 1975. *The Political Organization of Attica: A Study of the Demes, Trittyes, and Phylai, and Their Representation in the Athenian Council.* Hesperia Supplement 14. Princeton: American School of Classical Studies at Athens.

Travlos, J. 1971. *Pictorial Dictionary of Ancient Athens*. New York: Hacker.

Vaio, J. 1973. "Manipulation of Theme and Action in Aristophanes' *Lysistrata.*" *GRBS* 14:369–80.

Vanderpool, E. 1953. "New Evidence for the Location of the Attic Deme Kopros." *Hesperia* 22:176–77.

Vanderpool, E. 1966. "A Monument to the Battle of Marathon." *Hesperia* 35:93–106.

van Leeuwen, J. 1900. *Aristophanes: "Equites."* Leiden: Sijhoff.

Vergados, A. 2012. *The "Homeric Hymn to Hermes": Introduction, Text and Commentary*. Berlin: Walter de Gruyter.

Wallace, R. W. 1997. "Poet, Public, and 'Theatrocracy': Audience Performance in Classical Athens." In *Poet, Public, and Performance in Ancient Greece*, edited by L. Edmunds and R. W. Wallace, 97–111. Baltimore: Johns Hopkins University Press.

Weinrich, O. 1929. "Die Seher Bakis und Glanis, ein Witz des Aristophanes." *Archiv für Religionswissenschaft* 27:57–60.

Welsh, D. 1979. "*Knights* 230–3 and Cleon's Eyebrows." *CQ* 29:214–15.

Werres, J. 1936. *Die Beteuerungsformeln in der attischen Kömodie*. Bonn: K. Triltsch.

West, M. L. 1971. *Iambi et Elegi Graeci*. 2nd ed. Oxford: Clarendon.

West, M. L. 1978. *Hesiod: Works and Days*. Oxford: Clarendon.

West, M. L. 1982. *Greek Metre*. Oxford: Clarendon.

West, M. L. 1989. "The Early Chronology of Attic Tragedy." *CQ* 39:251–54.

West, M. L. 1992. *Ancient Greek Music*. Oxford: Clarendon.

Westlake, H. D. 1980. "The *Lysistrata* and the War." *Phoenix* 34:38–54.

Whitehead, D. 1986. *The Attic Demes, 508/7—ca. 250 B.C: A Political and Social Study*. Princeton: Princeton University Press.

Wilamowitz-Moellendorff, U. von. 1964. *Lysistrate*. Berlin: Weidmannsche Verlagsbuchhandlung.

Wilkins, J. 2000. *The Boastful Chef: The Discourse of Food in Ancient Greek Comedy*. Oxford: Oxford University Press.

Willi, A. 2002. *The Language of Greek Comedy*. Oxford: Oxford University Press.

Willi, A. 2003. *The Language of Aristophanes: Aspects of Linguistic Variation in Classical Attic Greek*. Oxford: Oxford University Press.

Wilson, N. G., ed. 2007a. *Aristophanis Fabulae*. Vols. 1–2. Oxford: Oxford University Press.

Wilson, N. G. 2007b. *Aristophanea: Studies on the Text of Aristophanes*. Oxford: Oxford University Press.

Winkler, J. J. 1990. "*Tragoidia* and Polis." In *Nothing to Do with Dionysos? Athenian Drama in Its Social Context*, edited by J. J. Winkler and F. I. Zeitlin, 20–62. Princeton: Princeton University Press.

Wohl, V. 2002. *Love among the Ruins: The Erotics of Democracy in Classical Athens*. Princeton University Press. Princeton.

Wycherley R. E. 1978. *The Stones of Athens*. Princeton: Princeton University Press.

Yalouris, N. 1950. "Athena als Herrin der Pferde." *MH* 5:19–101.

Young, S. 1939. "An Athenian Clepsydra." *Hesperia* 8:274–84.

Zimmermann, B. 1984–87. *Untersuchungen zur Form und dramatischen Technik der Aristophanischen Komödien*. Vols. 1–3. Königstein: Anton Hain.

Zweig, B. 1992. "The Mute Nude Female Characters in Aristophanes' Plays." In *Pornography and Representation in Greece and Rome*, edited by A. Richlin, 73–89. Oxford: Oxford University Press.

Index of Personal Names

References are to line numbers in the play and/or the commentary; references to page numbers are in italics.

Index of Gods

References are to line numbers in the play and/or the commentary; references to page numbers are in italics.

Agathos Daimon, 85, 106–8

Apollo, 229, 1015, 1024, 1047, 1072, 1081, 1233, 1240, 1248, 1270–73 (oaths to Apollo: 14, 870, 941, 1041)

Artemis, 660

Athena, 446, 581–94, 656, 763, 903, 1090–95, 1168–89, 1203; *19*

Demeter: (oaths to Demeter 435, 461, 698, 812, 833, 1021)

Hermes, 639 (oath to Hermes: 297)

Nike, 589

Poseidon, 551–64, 609 (oaths to Poseidon: 144, 338, 366, 409, 609, 843, 899, 1035, 1201); *18*

Zeus, 410, 500, 1253, 1390 (oaths, passim)

Index of Places and Peoples

References are to line numbers in the play and/or the commentary; references to page numbers are in italics.

Printed and bound by CPI Group (UK) Ltd, Croydon, CR0 4YY

09/06/2025

14685647-0002